ISLAM WITHOUT ALLAH?

**The Rise of Religious
Externalism in Safavid Iran**

ISLAM WITHOUT ALLAH?

The Rise of Religious Externalism in Safavid Iran

Colin Turner

CURZON

First Published in 2000
by Curzon Press
Richmond, Surrey
http://www.curzonpress.co.uk

© 2000 Colin Turner

Printed and bound in Great Britain by
TJ International, Padstow, Cornwall

British Library Cataloguing in Publication Data
A catalogue record of this book is available from the British Library

Library of Congress in Publication Data
A catalogue record for this book has been requested

ISBN 0–7007–1447–2

Contents

Introduction   vii

1. Belief and Submission Reconsidered   1
   Introduction   1
   The Koran on *īmān* and *islām*   4
   The Koran and *islām*   6
   The difference between *īmān* and *islām*: the Sunni view   8
   Koranic exegesis and *islām*   9
   The concepts of *īmān* and *islām* in Twelver Shi'ite Traditions   14
   The concepts of *īmān* and *islām* in Shi'ite exegesis   16
   Knowledge in Islam: what is *'ilm* and who are the *'ulamā*?   20
   Knowledge in the Traditions   23
   Evolution of the terms *'ilm* and *fiqh*   25
   Popular perception of the terms *'ilm* and *'ulamā*   30
   Contemporary Muslim scholars and *'ilm*   31
   The Koran on *'ilm* and *'ulamā*   34

2. Religion in medieval Iran and the rise of the Safavids   43
   Introduction: internalism and externalism defined   43
   Twelver Shi'ism in the pre-Safavid era   49
   Sufism and pro-Shi'ite extremism (*ghuluww*)   53
   Sufism   53
   Extremism or *'ghuluww'*   57
   The rise of the Safavids   58

3. The consolidation of Safavid power and the rise of
   Twelver Shi'ite externalism   72
   Introduction   72
   The Twelver Shi'ite *fuqahā*: guardians of externalism   75
   The evolution of the role of the Twelver Shi'ite jurist   77

v

Enter the externalists: from Jabal 'Amil to Isfahan 79
Of Shah and Shaykh: Isma'il and Karaki 82
The reign of Shah Tahmasp: the *fuqahā* take root 87
Indigenous opposition to Twelver Shi'ite
Externalism: the Persian 'aristocracy' 90
Shah Isma'il II to Shah 'Abbas I 97
The externalists: their milieu and teachings 104
In search of Twelver Shi'ite internalism 116
The non-externalists: their milieu and teachings 125
The reigns of Shah Safi and Shah 'Abbas II 135

4. **'Allama Majlisi: externalist** *extraordinaire* 148
Introduction 148
The Majlisi family 151
The forefathers of Muhammad Baqir Majlisi 151
Muhammad Baqir's formative years 154
The public career of 'Allama Majlisi 162
Majlisi and the post of *mullā-bāshī* 165
Majlisi's written works 166
Oceans of light? Majlisi's *Bihār al-anwār* 170
Majlisi vis-à-vis Sufism and other 'innovations' 172
Majlisi's interpretation of the terms *'ilm* and *'ulamā* 177
The descendants of 'Allama Majlisi 179

5. **Externalism in focus: the Twelver Shi'ite doctrines of**
intizār **and** *raj'a* 187
Introduction 187
Messianism in Islam 187
The term *al-mahdi* and its early use 189
The Mahdi in the Traditions 191
Sunni Traditions on the Mahdi 192
The Mahdi in Shi'ite Traditions: Volume XIII of Majlisi's *Bihār* 193
The concept of *intizār* 194
The occultation of the Imam: a test for the Twelver Shi'ites 195
The Traditions on *intizār* 198
The politico-religious implications of *intizār* 202
The return of the Twelve Imams: the doctrine of *raj'a* 215
The historical development of the doctrine of *raj'a* 216
The doctrine of *raj'a* in the *Bihār al-anwār* 218
The general Traditions on *raj'a* 218
The curious Tradition of Mufaddal b. Umar 223

The *raj'a*: a major factor in Twelver Shi'ite externalism   230
Safavid Shi'ism and Alid Shi'ism: a contemporary critique   232

6. **Conclusions**   244

Select Bibliography   253

Index   263

Introduction

The present work was conceived over a decade ago as a study of the life and works of 'Allama Muhammad Baqir Majlisi, compiler of the encyclopaedic *Bihār al-anwār* and a figure whose career is linked inextricably with the crystallization of Twelver Shi'ite orthodoxy in late Safavid Iran. So far-reaching has been the impact of Majlisi's vast literary output, and so revered is his name among Twelver scholarly circles, that a Sunni contemporary, 'Abd al-'aziz Dihlawi, was moved to opine that Twelver Shi'ism could alternatively be called *dīn al-Majlisi*, or the 'Majlisite religion'.

Given Majlisi's stature and legacy, the paucity of primary source material on his life and achievements came as both a surprise and a cause for dismay, and it soon became clear that an extended article or short monograph was as much as I could expect from such meagre pickings. Yet the man continued to fascinate me, not least because contemporary opinions of him are so strikingly polarized: while some believe that he was the 'renewer' (*mujaddid*) for his own time, others excoriate him as a bigot and a falsifier of Traditions. Other scholars have described the period in which Majlisi lived, and, by extension, the whole of the Safavid era, as a time of constant conflict between 'Sufi and jurist', and it eventually became clear that the diametrically opposed opinions held about Majlisi to some extent reflect this.

Majlisi is seen as embodying the victory of the exoteric over the esoteric; of the *zāhir* over the *bātin*; of the letter of the law over its spirit; and of external submission to God's laws over internal submission to God himself – and it was these polarities which now held my attention. Accordingly, my writing plans changed in a manner and at a pace commensurate with my apprehension of the tension between *zāhir* and *bātin*, between the exoteric and the esoteric, which, it is claimed, bubbled beneath the surface of scholarly life and discourse in Safavid Iran.

My general assumption, gained from research into the dynamics of the 'faith and works' issues broached by Muslim scholars past and present, was that *zāhir* and *bātin*, the 'external' and the 'internal', were complementary facets of the same approach to the Islamic revelation. Yet while in theory this is supported by the Koranic text, historically the two aspects have been artificially separated, with two distinct groups of scholars - or, more precisely, two modalities of scholarly approach - emerging to represent them, each championing its own discursive formation and plotting its own path but with little or no reference to the other, apart, that is, from claims and counter-claims to exclusivity of truth.

Another variable - one which, at first glance, appears quite unconnected - is the distinction between *īmān* (belief) and *islām* (submission, either in the personal sense, i.e. to God, or in the external sense, i.e. adherence to the communal religion known as Islam). The catalyst for my enquiries in this regard came in the form of a contemporary Shi'ite critique of the Islamic Revolution of 1979. Shortly after the creation of the first Islamic Republic in Iran, the late Shaykh Mahmud Elbisani was moved to comment that "what is needed is not a revolution of Islam but a revolution of *īmān*. For without *īmān*, all we are left with is 'Islam without Allah'..."

Implicit in this view is the idea that Islam often exists without *īmān* as its foundation, and that the majority of Muslims may actually be adherents of the communal religion of Islam without having any strong foundations of belief. Such ideas are not peculiar to Shi'ite thought: one Sunni scholar, Said Nursi, also asserts that "there are many adherents of Islam (*muslim*) who are not believers (*mu'min*), just as there are many believers who do not adhere to Islam."

I then began to explore the possibility that the Sufi-jurist 'rift' referred to in the context of Safavid Iran might in some way be connected to the *īmān/islām* dichotomy. In time it became clear that there was indeed a connection, and that the overwhelming dominance over the Islamic world of learning enjoyed by the *mulla* and the *mufti* was linked inextricably with the question of which particular facet of the Islamic revelation - the internal or the external, the exoteric or the esoteric - was accorded primacy.

More importantly, it became clear that the subject had received little or no attention from Western scholars. While the terms *īmān* and *islām* have been covered extensively, this has been done primarily from the point of view of semantics. The nature of knowledge (*'ilm*) in Islam has also received much scholarly attention in Western academic circles, but the crucial link between *'ilm* and *īmān/islām* has hardly, if ever, been explored. The terms *'ilm* and *'ulamā*, and their relationship with the predominance of the external over the internal, of Islam over *īmān*, must be grasped fully if one is to understand why it has been possible for two theoretically interdependent but historically antagonistic approaches – the externalist and the internalist – to come into existence.

Thus I decided not to abandon Majlisi completely but rather to use him as a point of reference in a deeper study of the rise of religious externalism in Safavid Iran.

Methodology

The theoretical - and theological - basis of the study hinges on the Koran and the Traditions. The Koranic concepts of *īmān* and *islām*/Islam have been discussed and commentaries on them, both Sunni and Shi'ite, have been reviewed and analysed. One of the major factors underlying the tendency to ignore, or the inability to distinguish between, the different aspects of the term *islām* is the fact that the early commentaries and *hadīth* collections present the subject with a certain amount of ambiguity. These commentaries and collections are discussed and their significance for the spread of externalism clarified. More ambiguous still is the interpretation of the terms *'ilm* and *'ulamā* by various Muslim scholars through the ages. I have attempted to show the lack of harmony between the Koranic concept of *'ilm* and *'ulamā* and those interpretations proffered by both Shi'ite and Sunni scholars, classical and modern. More importantly, the 'semantic shift' undergone over time by the terms *'ilm* and *'ulamā* has been discussed at length; perception of this 'shift' is crucial to our understanding of why the externalist or exoteric aspect of Islam has been able to prevail over the internalist approach to the Islamic revelation.

Safavid Iran provides a perfect backdrop against which the internalist/externalist dichotomy and the rise of the *faqīh* (jurist) may be contextualised historically. That Twelver Shi'ism is a natural breeding ground for esotericism has hitherto been axiomatic for many Western scholars. Yet the advent of the Safavid dynasty was the first in a long series of blows to internalist thought and teaching in Iran. I have attempted to show that although the religious orientation of the majority of the Iranian people prior to the Safavid era was markedly pro-Alid, it was in fact at odds with the doctrines of the Twelver Shi'ite jurists (*fuqahā*) who were imported to act as guardians of the new Safavid state religion. In this respect I have called into question the idea that the establishment of Twelver Shi'ism was a natural extension of pre-existing Shi'ite sympathies, but rather that the new religion was a political tool used to impose doctrinal unity on a populace that was definitely non-externalist in its religious proclivities.

A study of the development of Twelver Shi'ism in Safavid Iran comprises the middle section of the work. Here the respective outlooks of the externalist and non-externalist/internalist scholars come into focus. The academic output of both groups is reviewed extensively, as is their interaction with the Safavid regime and its rulers. The contention forwarded by scholars such as Said Amir Arjomand and Muhammad Taqi Danishpazhuh that Safavid Iran was the scene of a prolonged and bitter struggle between internalism and externalism is reappraised. Crucial, though, to this section is the question of non-externalism *per se*: in what sense, if any, can orthodox Twelver Shi'ism, given its antagonism towards any kind of religious orientation other than its own, be said to possess an internalist face?

Following on from this is a study of 'Allama Muhammad Baqir Majlisi and his works. Of all the Safavid Twelver Shi'ite scholars, none is more famous: the works which bear his name are, historically, the most widely read of all popular Twelver Shi'ite religious writings of the period. Yet he contributed virtually nothing to the development of Twelver jurisprudence (*fiqh*) or *hadīth* as scholarly disciplines. To what, then, are his popularity and importance in the eyes of his peers and the masses attributable? An attempt has been made to answer this question by reviewing some of his key writings, particularly those relating to the 'heresy' of Sufism and to the question of the legitimacy of Safavid rule, which Majlisi supported unreservedly.

Finally, Majlisi's presentation of the twin doctrines of *intizār* and *raj'a* have been appraised and analysed in depth. The Twelver Traditions supporting these doctrines are particularly representative of the spirit of 'imamocentric' externalism championed so staunchly by Majlisi. The concept of the 'return' to earth of the Mahdi and the other eleven Shi'ite Imams has been discussed in terms of the externalisation of one of the major principles of Islamic belief, namely the Resurrection. Also tentatively explored is the link between Twelver Shi'ite externalism in the Safavid era and the revolutionary Shi'ism of the Islamic Republic. To what extent do the *fuqahā* of today resemble their Safavid counterparts, and is it possible to describe the Twelver Shi'ism prevalent today as a natural extension of the orthodoxy championed by Majlisi?

A note on the sources

In Chapter 1, the theoretical basis of the work, it is the Koran and the Traditions which constitute the major source material. A selection of both Shi'ite and Sunni *hadīth* collections and works of Koranic exegesis, classical and modern, has been consulted. This material concentrates not only on the question of *imān* and *islām* but also on that of *'ilm* and *'ulamā*; in the context of the latter, secondary sources such as the works of Muslim modernists (Shari'ati, Mutahhari *et al*) have been used.

The pre-Safavid era in Iran, the subject of Chapter 2, has been covered extensively in Western circles by a wealth of eminent scholars such as Hinz, Glassen, Mazzaoui, Schimmel and Savory, and it is upon the works of these and other erudite writers and thinkers that I draw for the historical perspective. However, the chapter is not simply a re-hash of existing material but rather a fresh juxtaposition of facts and ideas which yields a new view of a well-explored area of research.

The consolidation of Twelver Shi'ite externalism in the Safavid era constitutes Chapter 3. Again I have availed myself of the standard secondary source works on the period, narratives by European travellers to Iran during the 16th and 17th centuries, and a number of important primary works by Safavid jurists, philosophers and historians. In this context, several hitherto neglected works have been used extensively. Danishpazhuh's *Fihrist*, for example, is a mine of information on Safavid writers and their works. Afandi's *Riyād al-'ulamā*, a comprehensive biographical dictionary of mainly Safavid scholars, was of inestimable value in unearthing information about the externalist Twelver *fuqahā* and their output. Mulla Sadra's *Sih Asl*, the most important anti-externalist document of the Safavid era, also features prominently in the chapter – as far as I know, for the first time in any Western work on the politico-religious history of Safavid Iran.

For the biography of Majlisi in Chapter 4, I have relied heavily on Tabarsi's *Fayd al-qudsī*, the only comprehensive account of the man's life and works that we have. *Fayd al-qudsī* appears to be an almost verbatim reworking of parts of Aqa Muhammad Kirmanshahi's *Mir'āt al-ahwāl*, which I have also consulted for information on the descendants of Muhammad Baqir Majlisi. Other primary source material has been used, but virtually none of it contains material that cannot be found in these two key works. Standard biographical dictionaries such as *Qisas al-'ulamā*, *Lu'lu'at al-Bahreyn* and *Rawdāt al-jannāt* have also been used. And, understandably, Majlisi's own works have been studied at some depth, as have those who wrote about or against him. Again, Danishpazhuh's Fihrist proved invaluable in this respect.

Chapter 5, on the doctrines of *intizār* and *raj'a*, depends almost entirely on Majlisi's *Bihār al-anwār*, in particular Volume XII (vols. 51, 52 and 53 of the new printed edition).

Chapter 1

Belief and submission reconsidered

Introduction

One of the earliest foci of theological speculation among Muslim scholars was the relationship between belief (*īmān*) and submission (*islām*), and whether there is a meaningful distinction between them. The question was prompted initially by disagreement over whether certain sins committed by Muslims would result in their loss of belief (*īmān*) or their expulsion from the fold of Islam. The Murji'ites were particularly vocal in the debates which centred upon this issue.[1]

That there exists a substantive conceptual difference between *īmān* and *islām* is something which, in the first half of this chapter, we shall attempt to clarify with the aid of evidence from the Koran, the Traditions (*ahādīth*) – both Sunni and Shi'ite – and various works of Koranic exegesis or *tafsīr*. What we must bear in mind, however, is that the issue at hand transcends the purely theological, and that in no way are we endeavouring to seek a solution to the kind of problem raised by the Murji'ites and their contemporaries. Rather, our aim is to attempt to show how confusion surrounding the terms *īmān* and *islām*, and the collapse of the distinction between them, has facilitated the rise to predominance of the jurist in the Islamic world of learning; the gradual limitation of the concept of knowledge (*'ilm*) in Islam to the domain of jurisprudence; and the consolidation of nomocentric legalism as the dominant discourse of resurgent Islam and the Muslim scholarly community. Furthermore we aim to show how the failure to recognize that there are in fact at least two modalities of *islam* adumbrated by the Koran has, wittingly or otherwise, diverted attention away from those Koranic precepts which emphasize the acquisition of self-knowledge, divine gnosis, submission and belief over the regulations, rites and rituals of Islamic orthopraxy.

1

As far as the Koran is concerned, the process whereby a man comes to believe in a Creator can be said to start with the act of *tafakkur* (thought or deliberation). The Koran declares in no uncertain terms that the whole of the cosmos is, as it were, a vast open book which is to be pondered, understood and interpreted. It also points out that those among mankind who possess intelligence, insight, understanding, discernment and knowledge will ultimately be able to know the meaning of the 'Book of Creation', for the cosmos is replete with 'signs' (*āyāt*) which point to its Creator: the cosmos 'speaks' to man as a revelation of God.[2] The cosmos is held to possess a meaning over and above itself: knowledge about the cosmos is deemed to be of use only if it leads man to the realisation that there is a Creator. At this point – or rather at every point of realisation – man may submit to the knowledge he has obtained or he may choose to ignore or cover (*kafara*) it and deny the divine origin of the cosmos.[3] If he submits to the knowledge he has acquired concerning the Creator of the cosmos, he will have entered the initial stages of *islām* (submission).

In theory, the logical outcome of this initial stage of submission is acceptance of, and adherence to, the commands of the Creator, which manifest themselves in the code of social, economic and political regulations known as the Islamic *sharī'a*. Personal acts of obedience such as prayer, fasting, almsgiving and pilgrimage are an integral part of this code: one who adheres to these regulations is known as a Muslim, and is accepted as a member of the Islamic community (*umma*). There are, thus, two basic forms of submission: one which is internal and concerns *īmān*; and one which is external and concerns the outward display of obedience.

As we shall see, the Koran declares that, more often than not, man submits externally without submitting internally, which means that whoever is born into a Muslim community cannot assume that he is automatically a believer simply because his parents and culture are Muslim. Naturally, it is not our concern to prove either quantitatively or qualitatively that most Muslims are not true believers in their own revelation: such an undertaking would be as presumptuous as it would methodologically implausible. The point we wish to make here is that the Koran itself posits a very clear difference between, firstly, *īmān* and *islām*, and secondly between submission to God (*islām*) and submission to God's laws (Islam). That there exists a huge majority for whom Islam in its external manifestation is practically synonymous with the internal act of belief and submission referred to as *islām* is admitted by Muslim and non-Muslim scholars alike.[4] What is generally overlooked, however, is the fact that this tendency to ignore, or inability to recognise, the difference between *īmān* and the two

2

types of *islām* has served to divert scholarly attention from the fundamentals of the faith (*usūl al-dīn*) to the secondary principles (*furu' al-dīn*): since *īmān* is internal and cannot be gauged by others it has gradually been overshadowed by Islam, which is external and governed by a code of rules and regulations, the derivation, interpretation and implementation of which constitute the domain of highly specialised knowledge occupied by the *faqīh* or jurist. In actual fact, the Koran affirms that belief is susceptible to increase and decrease; however, when belief is equated with Islam, the fact that a believer's *īmān* is either on the increase or the decrease tends to be ignored: since Islam is a static concept, *īmān* is also understood to be static. As a result, the commands in the Koran which call on the believers to examine themselves and their belief constantly are either overlooked or misinterpreted. Consequently, the concept of *da'wa* or 'inviting to belief' is focused erroneously on non-believers outside the Islamic community; within the Islamic community itself, the lion's share of Islamic teaching is taken by the *faqīh*, who instructs the people in Islam but not in *īmān*. According to the Malaysian scholar Naquib al-Attas, confusion and error among Muslims concerning the concept of knowledge has led to the rise of false leaders in all spheres of life, particularly in those fields of knowledge which are not obligatory (*fard al-'ayn*). Al-Attas says:

> The rise of false leaders in all spheres of life which follows from loss of *adab* and confusion and error in knowledge respectively means in this particular case the rise of false *'ulama* who restrict knowledge (*al-'ilm*) to the domain of jurisprudence (*fiqh*). They are not worthy followers of the *mujtahidun*..... they are not men of keen intelligence and profound insight, nor are they men of integrity in keeping the trust of right spiritual leadership. Notwithstanding the fact that the Holy Koran repeatedly condemns it, they delight in endless controversy, disputations and polemics which succeed only in making mountains out of jurisprudential molehills in whose blind paths the generality of Muslims are left guideless and bewildered.[5]

Confusion in belief, says al-Attas, stems from ignorance of *tawhīd* and the fundamental articles of faith and other related essentials of belief. As a result, inordinate attention is directed to the category of knowledge known as *fard al-kifāya*[6] – those secondary principles which on the individual level relate to matters of personal conduct and on the social level to questions of state and society. Ignorance of *tawhīd*, facilitated by the false assumption that *īmān* and *islām* are synonymous, and over-emphasis on the secondary branches of knowledge (*furū'*) pave the way for the ascendance of the *faqīh*; the fact that the word *'ilm* as used in the Koran is open to interpretation further enables the *faqīh* to consolidate his position by conveniently 'limiting' knowledge to the domain of jurisprudence.

Thus it is that the question of differentiation between *īmān* and *islām* (submission) and Islam, plus the relationship between this differentiation and the concept of knowledge in Islam, must be understood if we are to discover why, from among all categories of Muslim scholars, it is the *faqīh* who has been able to achieve such prominence and influence in the Islamic world of learning, especially in the context of Twelver Shi'ism and Twelver Shi'ite Iran.

The Koran on *īmān* and *islām*

The term *īman* is the verbal noun of the fourth form of the root *āmana*, which connotes trust, loyalty and security. The fourth form has the double meaning of to believe and to protect or place in safety.

There are over five hundred and seventy references in the Koran to words which are derived from the root *āmana*. Of these, almost half describe 'those who believe'. A cursory study of the Koran reveals that the derivatives of the root *āmana* preponderate to an overwhelming degree over the derivatives of the root *aslama*, to submit. That belief and submission are different is clear; the constant use of the word 'belief' or 'believers' would suggest quite conclusively that *īmān* is the most crucial element in a believer's make-up. Hundreds of verses in the Koran contain counsels of wisdom, commands or admonitions beginning with the phrase "O ye who believe!" And the definition of a believer – one who has *īmān* – can be found in numerous verses in the Koran.

The principal requirement of belief in the Koranic sense of the word is that the individual should attain to a state of perception and reflection in which he sees all the world not as 'natural' phenomena but as signs or *āyāt* of God. All of the 'natural' world is claimed by the Koran to point to Him.[7] The word *āyāt* denotes not only the verses of the Koran but also the material constituents of the cosmos. Intellect is the prerequisite of belief: the use of reason has to be applied to the signs in order for belief to obtain. Verse 29:35, for instance, describes the destruction of those who defied the prophet Lot as a sign for those who have understanding.[8] According to Sayyid Ali Husayni Khamini'i, *īmān* is something 'without which all actions and efforts are fruitless and ultimately futile.'[9] As for the role of the intellect and reason

4

in belief, he says that:

> Belief must be the result of a conscious choice and the use of personal awareness and understanding, not the result of blind acceptance and imitation (*taqlīd*). It is thus that true believers can be differentiated from the masses, whose belief is generally worthless and without substance.[10]

Belief must be held primarily in five – or, according to some, six – things: God, prophethood, angels, the revealed Books, the Last Day, and Divine Decree and Determining (*qadā wa qadar*).[11] Believers are those who, when God is mentioned, 'feel a tremor in their hearts, and when they hear His signs rehearsed, find their faith strengthened and put all their trust in their Lord.'[12]

The word *zāda*, translated in the above verse as 'strengthened', connotes the idea of increase; from this verse one understands that belief may increase or decrease, and that fluctuations in belief depend on the individual's reaction to the aforementioned 'rehearsal of signs' (*tilāwat al-āyāt*). Indeed, verse 8:4 confirms that there are degrees of belief.[13] In verse 9:124, the constant revelation of new aspects of God's truth is posited as a reason for the increase in faith of the believers. Since belief is connected to deliberation and intellectual contemplation of the 'signs', and since the revelation of signs is held to be constant,[14] it appears that the only way a believer can retain and increase his belief is through constant awareness, deliberation and remembrance.[15] In verse 4:136, the believers are exhorted to believe in God, a command that would be meaningless were belief not open to increase and decrease.[16]

Thus the prerequisites of belief – namely deliberation upon the *āyāt*, the selective use of '*aql* or reason, and remembrance of the Creator – must be pursued constantly if belief is to be increased. Belief cannot, on these terms, be static: the Hanafite stance which allows for no increase or decrease in belief should therefore be understood not in terms of quality of belief but in terms of the number of 'articles of faith' that are to be believed in. Even though some schools include 'acts of righteousness' within belief, it is clear that the concept of *īmān* is fundamentally different from the acts which it engenders: *īmān*, according to the Koran, can increase or decrease; the obligatory number of prayers, or days of fasting, or amount of *zakāt* cannot. Thus the overriding emphasis of the Koran rests upon the inner state of belief and not upon the external acts of obedience. The Koran does, quite understandably, stress the importance of 'acts of righteousness', but even the most superficial study of its verses shows that the Koran's pre-occupation with topics related to *īmān* far outweighs its commands to pray, fast and pay *zakāt*.[17] A famous Prophetic Tradition asserts that an hour's contemplation (*tafakkur*) is better than a year's worship - with the word 'worship' (*'ibāda*) understood as denoting external acts of devotion such as prayer and fasting. This is not to imply that such devotional acts are worthless; on the contrary, in verses such as 9:71, acts such as prayers, the giving of alms, and enjoining that which is good and forbidding that which is bad are included within the definition of true belief. The verse in question acknowledges the value of acts but puts emphasis on the *īmān* which must underpin them; the Koran quite clearly affirms the fact that it is belief which enjoys primacy, and that actions are meaningful only if they are based on, and motivated by, a foundation of belief.[18] From the numerous counsels of wisdom and admonition that begin with the Phrase "O ye who believe!", it is clear that the Islamic revelation as a source of guidance and education approaches its followers principally in terms of belief.

The Koran and *islām*

The term *islām* is the verbal noun of the fourth form Arabic verb *aslama*, which means literally to commit or resign oneself, to submit to the will of God.[19] The first form verb *salima*, from which *aslama* is derived, connotes security and peace; consequently, one who submits his will to the will of God is supposed to enter a state of peace and security. Another derivation from this root is the word *salām*, used as a ritual greeting between Muslims. The word *salām* was possibly one of the first signs of reference to the communal faith of Islam – a badge, as it were, denoting the status of the individual as a Muslim. The Koran itself alludes to this: in verse 4:94, Muhammad and his companions are instructed not to accuse those who offer the customary salutation - *salām 'alaykum* - of being unbelievers, but rather to investigate the matter carefully. The salutation, therefore, is a sign that the individual has made at least a verbal proclamation of submission.[20]

The Koran points repeatedly to a prefiguration of *islām* in the faith of the prophets who preceded Muhammad. The words *muslim* and *hanīf* in this context are synonomous.[21] Verse 2:136 declares that there is no difference between the various prophets, and that the most salient common factor is their submission.[22] What Muslims and the 'people of the Book' (*ahl al-kitāb*) hold in common is the fact that they are all *muslim*;[23] the children of Abraham prayed to God to make them *muslim*,[24] and the children of Jacob tell their father on his deathbed that they will be *muslim* to the one God.[25] Joseph beseeches God to let him die as a *muslim* so that he may join the ranks of the blessed.[26] The disciples of Jesus declare their belief and submission, asking to 'bear witness that we are *muslim*.'[27] In these and other verses the word *muslim* is used in a sense which precedes its current meaning as one who believes in the particular religion of Muhammad or one who is part of the Islamic community. It clearly means individual submission to God, the kind of submission that follows on from and complements *īmān*.

The word *islām* as a noun of action has, then, a double meaning: primarily – and originally – that of submission; and secondly, adherence to the religion of Muhammad. In Medina, Islam attained self-consciousness when it became a separate religion with its own laws and codes of personal and societal behaviour. The word 'Muslim' was used to distinguish the members of the new community: it acquired a new meaning, distinct from the old one, which meant one who resigns himself to God. Although it is difficult to differentiate between the technical and ordinary usages of the word *islām* in the Koran, it is obvious that two distinct connotations are intended. Verse 2:112, for example, describes a state in which the whole self is submitted. Yusuf Ali interprets this as the whole inner self and, since the notion of *ihsān* is also mentioned, concludes that this *islām* must contain *imān* as well.[28] Given that the prophets and their followers before Muhammad adhered to *islām*, it is clear that the word when used in this sense does not signify the particular codified religion of Islam. To contrast with this, verse 5:4 has Muhammad declaring that he has 'chosen Islam for you as your religion';[29] this obviously refers to the outward profession of belief enshrined in the laws and codes of behaviour peculiar to him and his followers, namely Islam the communal code rather than *islām* the individual submission of the whole inner self.

Yet this is not to say that *islām* and Islam are two wholly separate concepts. According to Sayyid Hasan Askari,

> Islam is the only religion which consciously chose a name for itself.
> It did not call itself the name of its founder, or community or country.
> Its self-naming was descriptive and normative of the essential nature
> of man, namely, that he has the potentiality to remember and realise
> his original destiny; that he can live in an active state of *islam*, of
> surrender to God[30]

Thus according to the Koran, *islām* or personal surrender and submission to

7

God should lead logically to Islam, or adherence to the laws and codes of conduct revealed by God through the medium of Muhammad. One who has *īmān* should also have *islām*, and, as a corollary, Islam.

While the term 'Islam' denotes the adherence of a *muslim* to the Muslim community, the Koran mentions instances in which individuals claim to have submitted but, in actuality, have no real *īmān*. Their claim may be solely a verbal profession of faith, or it may be backed with the performance of certain acts of devotion such as prayer and fasting. The verse which demonstrates this situation most effectively is 49:14:

> The desert Arabs say: "We believe." Say: "Ye do not believe: only say that 'We have submitted,' for not yet has faith entered your hearts."

This verse is said to refer to the tribe of Banu Asad, who contrived to profess Islam in the presence of Muhammad in order to receive charity during a famine. The term 'submission' in this verse can thus mean only a verbal profession of adherence to Islam, and not the inner submission of the whole self that is understood from the majority of verses concerning *islām*.

The difference between *īmān* and *islām* will be delineated in full further on in this chapter; that the Koran accepts such a difference is clear from numerous verses, one of the most unambiguous being 2:208, in which the believers are instructed to enter wholeheartedly into *islām*. [31]

The difference between *īmān* and *islām*: the Sunni view

According to the *Musnad* of Ibn Hanbal, 'Islam is external; faith belongs to the heart'.[32] The act of 'surrender to God' is, therefore, in this sense expressed by holding fast to the ritual observances prescribed by religious law. God alone judges men's hearts and with them the reality of belief: man's judgement of his fellow men may concern itself only with externals, which constitute the domain of Islam. Thus the 'science of *fiqh*' has been called '*maqām al-Islām*' by the Sufis.[33]

Many Hanafites and Maturidites consider *islām* and *īmān* to be synonymous, yet define each of them separately as a verbal confession (*iqrār*), sometimes linking this with intimate adherence or with knowledge of the heart, or both. The second century (A.H.) work of Hanafite theology, *Fiqh al-akbar* and the third century *Wasiyyat Abī Hanīfa* ignore the question altogether. The *Fiqh-i Akbar II* draws a distinction: *islām* is equated with total surrender (*taslīm*) and total obedience (*inqīyād*) to the divine laws. According to this text, 'there is no faith without Islam and Islam without faith cannot be found'.[34] The Ash'arites and the Shafi'ites make a distinction between *īmān* and *islām*. Al-Ash'ari, for example, identifies *islām* with the two constituent parts of the *shahāda*, the verbal testimony which grants one admission to the community of the prophet,[35] and concludes that *islām* is different from *īmān*. In the *Ibāna*, it is stated that *islām* is wider than belief; accordingly, 'all *islām* is not faith.'[36] The later Ash'arites were able to claim that Islam, the observance of the prescriptions ordained by law, and above all the explicit profession of the *shahāda*, can all be practised without belief, and that belief (*tasdīq*) may exist without Islam. But Islam without belief is the way of the hypocrites (*munāfiqūn*); belief without Islam need not be culpable, in the event of some external obstacle, although it would be if the testimony to Islam were given through half-heartedness or weakness. It would then be a question of *fisq* (prevarication resulting from sin) rather than unbelief. The Shafi'ite scholar Al-Jurjani says that 'Islam is the verbal profession of faith without the agreement of the heart, while faith is the agreement of the heart and the tongue.'[37]

For Ibn Taymiyya, Islam is the 'external and, so to speak, social application of the law,' while '*īmān* is the interiorization of Islam.'[38] Since it is the external and social application of the law which is the binding force of the ideal Islamic society, it is with this Islam that the jurists are concerned. Wherever the Koranic prescriptions are observed communally, there Islam will be. The first point of reference for the jurist who is studying and formulating the statutes and laws of the *bilād al-Islām* is not so much *īmān* but rather the communal observance of those prescriptions which make up Islam. Thus a synonym of *dār al-Islām* was to be *dār al-'adl* ('domain of justice'), where the rights of men as ordained by the Koran are observed and protected. Anyone who describes himself as a Muslim means to affirm thereby his commitment not so much to the practices and personal observances of Islam as to the community of those who acknowledge the Koran and Muhammad.[39]

Koranic exegesis and *islām*

Whereas *īmān* is used generally as an expression of the internal response to, and affirmation of, God's revelation to man, the term *islām* possesses an inherent flexibility that allows it to encompass diversity and often extremes of understanding within the expressions of a single writer. That there exists a clear distinction between the communal and personal aspects of the term *islām* is obvious from the verses of the Koran. The much cited 'Banu Asad verse' (49:14) shows that *īmān* is to be distinguished from *islām*; another important point which emerges from this verse is that *islām* itself may be understood on two different levels: the wholehearted, personal submission of the individual, which is an integral part of belief; and the communal expression of submission known universally as the religion of Islam. According to Kenneth Cragg,

> There is the general and the specific; the idea and its definitive expression; the thing itself and the thing in its 'institution'. Islam organises *islam*, enshrines it and defines it.[40]

Theoretically, then, the Islamic community consists of individuals who have come to believe in God and submitted themselves to Him. For the average Muslim, these two aspects – the personal and the communal – have traditionally been indistinguishable, even though the distinction is clear when one compares the Banu Asad verse, in which the submission referred to is both communal and, more importantly, strictly nominal, with verses such as 2:112, in which the notion of submission is that of the whole self.[41] Likewise, verse 4:94 concerns the possibility of nominal submission, represented in this case by the symbolic salutation (*salām*) offered by one Muslim to another, whereas verse 31:22, for instance, refers to the submission of the whole inner self, plus *ihsān* or the selfless worship of God.[42]

An individual who submits his inner self totally to the will of God is, by definition, a *muslim*: the logical corollary of his act of submission is an external display of faith that will enter him automatically into the community of Islam. If *islām* is personal and Islam communal, then he will be both *muslim* and Muslim.[43] This position is similar to statements in formal logic such as "All Frenchmen are Europeans but not all Europeans are Frenchmen." All *muslims* are Muslims, but not all Muslims are *muslims*. The conflation of the two aspects of the term in the minds of the majority of the Muslim masses may be a reflection of the fact that in the very early days of Islam it might indeed have been possible to assert that all Muslims were also *muslims*, for the simple reason that it was only through the union of *muslims* that the first Muslim community was able to exist. Furthermore, the era of Muhammad and his companions is idealized by Muslims in general as the 'ideal age' or 'age of felicity' (*'asr al-sa'āda*), in which Muhammad 'perfected the religion.'[44] It is possible, then, that the desire to preserve the concept of an ideal age and an exemplary Islamic community actually prevented the earlier exegetes not only from drawing a clear distinction between the personal and communal aspects of the term *islām*, but also from admitting openly the possibility that an individual may be Muslim but not *muslim*.

However, changes in understanding of the term *islām* do appear to have taken place; this much can be understood from a comparative study of works of Koranic exegesis.

For Fakhr al-din al-Razi, *islām* must always constitute a matter for the heart; if not, it cannot be called *islām*. As such, *islām* becomes coterminous with *īmān*. Al-Razi agrees that while *īmān* and *islām* are different in generality, they are one in existence.[45] Rashid Rida offers a similar interpretation when he says that both *īmān* and *islām* are considered to constitute 'specialized belief' (*iman khass*), the only religion (*dīn*) acceptable to God, and the only means of human salvation.[46] For other exegetes, both Shi'ite and Sunni, *islām* is part of *īmān* and constitutes one element in the acceptance and confirmation (*tasdīq*) of Divine Unity (*tawhīd*), whereby man proclaims his sincere belief in the unity (*ahadīyya*) and unicity (*wāhidīyya*) of God and incorporates into his own existence and worldview the integrity that is based on *tawhīd*. Here, *īmān* precedes submission (*islām*), forming together the two initial steps of a process of belief that is mentioned repeatedly in the Koran: *īmān* always precedes *islām*, good deeds (*a'māl sāliha*), emigration (*hijra*) and so on.[47] Many other exegetes do apprehend a basic difference between *īmān* and *islām*, admitting that *islām* can have a purely external meaning while *īmān* refers to the internal belief in, and confirmation of, the Divine Unity and all of the sacred truths that recognition of the Divine Unity brings into focus. When the term *islām* is isolated, it can be seen as both the expression of individual submission to the will of God and as the name of the group of those who have submitted. The American scholar Jane Smith describes the aspect of individual submission as a 'vertical relationship' between the Creator and the created, and the aspect of communal submission as a 'horizontal relationship' between the individual and the Muslim community.[48] This interpretation overlooks one important point, however, namely the fact that there are two definitions of *islām*: the true state of inner submission (*islām*), and the adherence – be it as a logical corollary of *islām* or purely in name only – to the external rites and rituals that comprise the religion of the community, Islam.

Traditionally, writers have used the form 'Islam' when referring to the

11

historical Muslim community with its objectification and systematisation of beliefs and ritual practices. This usage generally masks the fact that the term also denotes personal submission, with which Western writers are generally more concerned when attempting to analyse and define *islām*.

In the early exegetical literature, the apparent intention is the 'unified' meaning of *islām* as both individual submission and plural condition. Ibn 'Abbas, one of the earliest recorded exegetes who is accepted by Sunnis and Shi'ites alike, states unequivocally that *islām* signifies *tawhīd* (Divine Unity, or rather the acceptance thereof), yet also declares that one can be born into *islām*/Islam. In his interpretation of verse 3:83 he claims that the word *taw $^{\prime an}$* ('willingly') denotes those who are born into *islām*/Islam and *karh^{an}* those who 'enter *al-islām* by the sword.'[49] Thus there seems to have been no conscious conceptual distinction made by the earlier exegetes between the individual responsibility to carry out the specific commandments of God and the fact that these regulations are incumbent on all of the members of the community and thus characterize that group itself.

In the exegesis of al-Tabari, another stage in the understanding of *islām* can be discerned: the purely verbal – and thus necessarily external – submission through which the individual becomes a member of the community (*milla*) of Islam. This lacks the depth of *iman*, which involves knowledge (*'ilm*) and affirmation within the heart of the individual (*tasdīq bi'l qalb*). However, this *iman* is consonant with the deeper *islām*, which in turn is nothing but the perfection of belief (*takmīl al-īmān*); as such it constitutes the total surrender of the heart, mind and body. In other words, it is the emotional response which leads to the external acts of obedience. Al-Tabari cites the much-quoted Banu Asad verse (49:14) as an example of how one enters *millat al-islām*, thus becoming Muslim but not necessarily *muslim* or *mu'min*.[50]

Other exegetes did not seem to feel the need to make such a clear distinction, leaving it open as to whether the *dīn* to which they refer is the personal *islām* of the individual or the communal state of the followers of Muhammad. Early discussions tended to centre upon the circumstances of Muhammad's time and thus it is not surprising that their interpretation of the term *islām* reflected this 'unified' understanding of its individual and communal aspects. The focal point of their discussions is the Muslim community at the time of the Prophet. Al-Tusi, for instance, talks about the entry of all Arabs into *islām* at the time of the Prophet, but fails to throw any light on the condition of the Muslim community of his own era. Such *tafsīr* works deal almost exclusively with the 'occasions of revelation' (*asbāb al-nuzūl*) and interpret verses for the most part with reference to the events that occurred during the twenty-three years of Koranic revelation. Although the earlier exegetes do not allow themselves room for speculation (which is more germane to the particular type of Koranic interpretation known as *ta'wīl*), modern Koranic commentators do discuss their own times and circumstances. Rashid Rida, for instance, attacks what he sees as the ethnocentricity (*jinsiyya*) of modern Muslims:

> For *al-din*, if it is not the true *islam* (i.e. submission) is nothing but codified formalities (*rasm*) and uncritical acceptance (*taqlid*) which people adopt as a bond for ethnic identity (*jinsiyya*), an instrument of partisanship, and a means for worldly gain. This kind of *islam* increases the soul in evil and the hearts in corruption.[51]

As for the word *al-dīn* and its plural *adyān*, these became standard from the fifth century in the interpretation of verses such as 61:7-9, where *al-islām* is to be proclaimed over all religions. The interpretations of *dīn* and Islam are closely intertwined. It appears most likely that the Koranic exegetes intended a contrast between the religion of Islam and other faith communities when they used the term *adyān*, even though the word used in 61:9 is singular and could easily mean the personal response of individuals rather than a plurality of religious systems.[52] The Koranic promise that *dīn al-islām* would be victorious over all other religions can easily be understood in terms of social and political dominance at a time when the Islamic state was clearly in a position of burgeoning power.

Therefore, several developments in the understanding of *islām* on the 'horizontal plane' of the relationship between individual and community can be discerned. It would appear that during the formative years of Koranic exegesis, the perception of *islām* as both personal submission and communal adherence – with no distinction made between the two – was tantamount to a simple expression of unity. There then follows the stage in which it appears that a form of self-conscious definition took the place of the earlier unconscious or automatic amalgamation of the two elements in one term: *islām* came to be defined clearly in terms of personal response and individual submission to the will and dictates of God. Gradually, indications of a more reified understanding of *islām* as a *dīn* or religion (Islam) emerged.

In modern works of Koranic exegesis, things are on the whole quite different: we now begin to find specific references to *islām* as something distinct from personal submission. Rashid Rida, for example, constrasts what he calls 'real *islām*' (*al-islām al-haqīqī*) with 'habitual' or 'conventional' (*'urfī*) Islam, indicating that it is the association by ethnic identity with the religion of one's nationality or culture than may actually militate against, and prevent true submission to, the will of God.[53] Interpretations such as this represent a shift from the unity of individual submission and group identity to a firm distinction between the two. As stated previously, this distinction is highlighted in several verses of the Koran; for reasons already indicated, the exact connotations of this distinction were masked by what was most likely a desire on the part of the exegetes to preserve unity. Ibn 'Abbas talked about being born into *islām*/Islam yet failed to indicate in what sense this differs from the *islām* of personal submission. Rashid Rida on the other hand contrasts *al-islām al-jinsī* with *al-islām al-haqīqī*. There is one sense in which Rida does intend the unity of two meanings in one term: this is in his vision of an ideal society in which all members are freed from purely communal affiliations to the point where they are able to experience true personal *islām*. While the unity expressed by earlier generations was of the individual and the actual, here it is of the individual and the ideal, or what was, as opposed to what could be.

Thus for the traditional Koranic exegetes, the term *islām* is used both as the individual act of submission and as the generic name for the community of those who have (in theory) submitted, with greater emphasis – as in the Koran – on the first element. There is no reference in the early literature to the 'ideal', only to the 'actual. For the modern exegetes, true *islām* is the sincere submission of the individual and, ideally, the community, but it is *islām* in its real (*haqīqī*) rather than its conventional (*'urfī*) sense that is required.

The concepts of *īmān* and *islām* in Twelver Shi'ite Traditions

According to the sixth Shi'ite Imam, Ja'far al-Sadiq, *islām* is the verbal proclamation of the *shahādatayn*. In a Tradition narrated by al-Mufaddal, the Imam states that it is this proclamation which qualifies a man to be a member of the Muslim community: his blood (that is to say, his life) becomes respected and protected; things maybe entrusted unto him; he may enter into marriage with a Muslim woman, and so on. However, the rewards to be had in the hereafter stem from *īmān* (*al-thawāb 'alā al-īmān*). In a similar Tradition, al-Sadiq states that *īmān* is 'proclamation' (*iqrār*) along with actions (*a'māl*), whereas *islām* is proclamation without actions.[54] On the difference between *īmān* and *islām*, al-Sadiq states that *islām* is the 'external condition' (*al-wajh al-zāhirī*) by which Muslims are identified: this consists of the proclamation of the *shahādatayn* plus the performance of prayers, the giving of religious taxes (*zakāt*), fasting, pilgrimage and the like. *īmān* on the other hand, is all of the above plus recognition of the concept of *wilāya*.[55] One who believes in the importance of prayer and fasting but does not recognise *wilāya* is a misguided Muslim. *īmān* is that which involves the heart and thus leads man to God; *islām* consists of external words and actions. The word *wilāya* is used here in its Shi'ite sense; whether the narration is genuine or not is another question. As far as the Koran is concerned, the kind of *wilāya* understood by the Twelver Shi'ites does not constitute a principle of belief; indeed there are even certain Twelver scholars who oppose the customary inclusion of *imāma* in the fundamentals of faith and declare it instead to be a 'principle of *madhhab* rather than a principle of belief'.[56]

The important point which emerges from this Tradition is that *īmān* and *islām* are perceived to be conceptually different, with *īmān* concerning the heart and thus forming the basis for Islam, which consists of all matters external and practical such as prayers and fasting and the like. The fifth Shi'ite Imam, Muhammad al-Baqir, reiterates the above in a Tradition which has it that it is *īmān* alone which can lead man to God: actions, obedience and submission to God are but confirmations of belief.[57] Islam comprises those external words and deeds which identify a man as one of a community of Muslims. Islam does not require *īmān*, but *īmān* requires Islam. In this context, Islam and *iman* may be likened to the *masjid al-harām* and the *ka'ba*: the *ka'ba* is in the *masjid al-harām*, but not all of the latter is in the former. With the *ka'ba* here representing *īmān*, the Tradition is confirming that whoever has *īmān* will also have Islam, but not everyone who has Islam will have *īmān*. Al-Baqir at this point quotes verse 49:14, which deals with the opportunistically superficial submission of the Banu Asad tribe. The *mu'min* and the Muslim are on par as far as their special rights are concerned, but the *mu'min* is more exalted in the sight of God by virtue of the fact that his actions are based on true belief and not on blind imitation (*taqlīd*) or by force of geographical or cultural circumstance.[58]

In reply to a letter from one of his followers, al-Sadiq clarifies further the difference between *īmān* and *islām*: belief, he states is the conviction ('*aqīda*) of the heart, coupled with a confession (*iqrār*) of this belief by the tongue, and also the implementation of the 'pillars of Islam' such as prayers and fasting.[59] Islam is an 'external matter'; it may be that a person becomes Muslim before he becomes a true believer, but no-one can become a true believer unless he also becomes Muslim. Al-Sadiq is confirming here that the crucial component is belief (*īmān*), and that it is possible to be a Muslim

15

without actually being a believer. He then appears to confuse the issue by declaring that a person will not be a believer unless or until he becomes a Muslim.

The ambiguity here stems from the fact that 'real' and 'nominal' *islām* cannot be differentiated in Arabic by giving the latter a capital I, as can be done in English. As shown, it is possible to adhere nominally to the religion of Islam and partake of all the benefits that membership of the Muslim community brings, but without any true belief or firm conviction. Once again, the verse which deals with the superficial acceptance of Islam the religion by the Banu Asad is ample proof of this. However, al-Sadiq is correct when he asserts that a believer cannot actually be a believer unless he has made a total submission (*islām*; *taslīm*) to the truths in which he has come to believe. The Tradition makes sense only if al-Sadiq has in mind the category of submission described as *islām* (with a small i); this *islām* may be seen as a perfection of *iman* and, as such, part of the process of belief itself. It is the kind of submission which should logically lead to the performance of 'good deeds', the main elements of which are the 'pillars of Islam'. It is thus expected that a *muslim* also be a Muslim, but it is by no means a foregone conclusion that a Muslim will also be a *muslim*. (Here the word *muslim* accords with *islām* and is used to denote true submission, whilst Muslim denotes an adherent – nominal or actual – of the religion of Islam). Al-Sadiq concludes the Tradition by asserting that Islam precedes *īmān* and constitutes the preliminary to belief. If someone commits a sin – big or small – he abandons his *īman* but does not leave his Islam. If he repents and prays for forgiveness, he will re-enter a state of *īmān*. He will not be considered an unbeliever unless he regards that which is illicit to be licit, and vice-versa; in this case he will leave *īmān* and Islam altogether. This person, according to the Tradition, is like one who first enters the *haram* and the *ka'ba*, but then commits a crime and is thrown out of both and then executed.

The question of *īmān* and *islām* in Shi'ite exegesis

According to the contemporary Shi'ite scholar 'Allama Tabataba'i, *islām* can be seen to operate on several levels. The lowest level of *islām*, or submission, concerns the 'acceptance of the externals', or the commands and prohibitions of the religion (*dīn*) of Islam. These are affirmed by declaration of the *shahādatayn*, the act of witnessing which takes place when an individual accepts Islam as his religion. It is this spoken formula which admits one into the fold of Islam and secures membership of the community of Muslims, 'whether or not the heart confirms the tongue.'[60] To support his assertion that the act of witnessing which renders the individual a Muslim may take place with little or no inner conviction, the 'Allama cites the already mentioned verse which describes the nominal entrance into Islam of the Banu Asad tribe.

The first stage of *īmān* then follows: this comprises affirmation (*tasdīq*) by the heart, in what the 'Allama terms a general (*ijmālī*) manner, of the concepts enshrined in the *shahādatayn*. At this stage most of the subsidiary (*far'ī*) commands of the religion are translated into practice. This heralds the second stage of *islām*, wherein the heart 'submits to most of the truths in a deep and comprehensive (*tafsīlī*) manner.'[61] This stage of submission also engenders acts of righteousness (*a'māl sāliha*), although there may still be faults in the believer and instances in which he strays from the path and commits sins. In order to confirm the existence of a stage of *islām* which comes after the initial stage of *īmān*, and which differs from the nominal submission represented in the Banu Asad verse, the 'Allama quotes two other verses, 43:69 and 2:208: the first is one of the verses in which belief in the signs (*āyāt*) of God is stated categorically as preceding submission to God's will;[62] the second is a command from God to the believers to enter into *islām* wholeheartedly.[63]

After the second stage of *islām* comes the second stage of *īmān*. This consists of strong and comprehensive belief (*al-īmān al-tafsīlī*) in all of the truths of Islam. For the 'Allama, this state is expressed in such verses as 49:15, in which the believers are described as those who have believed in God and His messenger and have never since doubted.[64] Also cited is verse 61:11, in which the believers are told to strengthen their belief in God and His prophet and to strive in His cause.[65]

The third stage of *islām* then follows. Having progressed this far, the individual is now able to submit all of his animal appetites, all of those facets of his make-up which are inclined to ephemeral pleasures and worldly allurements, to the will of the Creator. Influenced by his belief, he will begin to worship God as though he were seeing Him.[66] In both his internal and external senses, he will see nothing that is not submitted to its Creator and to the dictates of 'divine decree and determining' (*qadā wa qadar*). The 'Allama refers to verse 4:65, in which it is stated that real belief can obtain only when there is the fullest conviction on the part of the believer, and when no resistance is offered against the decrees of God.[67] Thereupon follows the third stage of *īmān*, crystallized – according to the 'Allama – in verses 1-11 of the *sura al-Mu'minūn* (The Believers). The second and third stages of *islām* are virtually identical since both are characterized by their insistence on submission to the commands of God, which is in turn facilitated by *ridā* (contentment in the face of whatever God decrees), *sabr* (patience), and sincerely motivated acts of righteousness. When a man reaches the third stage of *islām* he will have been transformed into a totally obedient slave of God, yet it is clear that the dominion of God over His creation is far more meaningful than can be understood from the conventional master-slave relationships obtaining in the human realm. God's ownership, asserts the 'Allama, is absolute: man is totally dependent upon the Creator for all things and can exercise no independent power or authority over his own essence, attributes or actions. Thus God's power and dominicality cannot be compared with the authority of a human master over his human slave.

As man's submission increases, God gradually reveals to him the reality of the Creator-creature relationship. This 'revelation' is purely a 'gift of grace' from God: man has no power over it and cannot work consciously towards obtaining it. The 'Allama quotes verses concerning the prophet Abraham, who, although having accepted God's legislative (*tashrī'ī*) command to submit, asked at the end of his life for 'submission' for himself and his family.[68] Since submission is something which, logically speaking, is initiated by the believer, Abraham's plea points to something which was clearly out of his hands. This is what the 'Allama refers to as the fourth stage of *islām*; yet it appears more likely that Abraham's petition was not for a vision in which God's absolute ownership would be revealed, but rather for the safeguarding of the submission he had already made. The 'Allama's claim that this stage of submission is a gift from God does not fit in with the understanding of submission as a state which is initiated consciously by the believer. Furthermore, Abraham could have had no clear insight into the level of his family's belief or their eligibility for the kind of vision described in the narrative.

The fourth stage of *īmān* entails the total application of all of the above to all of the situations in which the believer finds himself. Verses 10:62-4 are cited as a demonstration of this stage of *īmān*, in which the believers are aware of their total dependence upon God and realise that no cause can have an effect without the permission of the Creator. This is the stage of *wilāya*, at which point the believer is raised to the exalted status of 'friend of God' (*walī Allāh*).

From this cursory study of Traditions and Koranic exegesis, several facts emerge. Firstly, that *īmān* and *islām* are conceptually different is, in the Shi'ite as in the Sunni view, evident from several Koranic verses. Secondly, the fact that *īmān* is the basis for *islām*/Islam and thus totally fundamental is also a matter for agreement between various Shi'ite and Sunni scholars, past and present.

There is considerable confusion, however, surrounding the different interpretations of the word *islām*, and the inability – or unwillingness – on the part of certain earlier exegetes to make, as the Koran does, a distinction between personal submission (*islām*) and membership of the communal religion (Islam). As we have seen, initially this might have been the result of a desire to preserve unity, or a reflection of the belief that in the very earliest Islamic community, all Muslims were also *muslims*. As the community expanded, the possibility that people would profess adherence to the faith purely for the social and material benefits that membership of the community might bestow upon them increased. The case of the Banu Asad is but one example.[69] In addition, ambiguity in the use of the word *islām*, which in Arabic cannot be differentiated from the word Islam by the use of capitals as it can in English, tended to blur the distinction between the internal, personal submission of the individual (*islām*) and the formal profession of adherence to the religious community (Islam). Equivocal statements such as those made by Ibn 'Abbas give the impression that *islām* is a question more of birthright than of personal and individual submission.[70] Equally misleading is the Tradition attributed to Ja'far al-Sadiq in which belief is considered possible only through *islām*. While this may be the case if, by the word *islām*, the personal submission of the individual is intended, it is not true as far as Islam is concerned. In this light, it is not difficult to understand why an individual born into an Islamic environment may consider himself to be a believer merely by virtue of affiliation to the Muslim community, and thus, by equating Islam with *īmān*, shift the emphasis that should, according to the Koran, be on the latter to the former. Thus by the 6th/12th century, al-Ghazali was able to castigate the Muslim community on the grounds that 'the science of the path of the hereafter, which our forefathers trod and which includes what God calls in His Book law, wisdom, knowledge, enlightenment, light, guidance, and righteousness, has vanished from among men and been completely forgotten.'[71] And by the 20th century, exegetes such as Rashid Rida were able to discount the beliefs of countless fellow Muslims as 'an instrument of partisanship and a means of worldly gain.'[72]

Given that both *īmān* and *islām*/Islam are supposed to involve a conscious choice[73] – and, by implication, knowledge and reason – on the part of the individual, to what extent has the preponderance of Islam over *īmān* affected the way in which the Islamic revelation has been, and is still being, communicated to the masses by Muslim scholars? It is to the question of knowledge or *'ilm* that we now turn.

Knowledge in Islam: what is *'ilm* and who are the *'ulamā*?

There have been countless expositions on the nature and function of knowledge (*'ilm*) in Islam – more so, arguably, than in any other religion – and this is no doubt because of the pre-eminent position and crucial role accorded to knowledge in the Koran.[74] These expositions encompass the nature of knowledge in its entirety. Distinctions have been made between the knowledge of God (*'ilm Allāh*) and the knowledge of man about God (*'ilm bi'llāh*), and religion, and the world, and things sensible and intelligible; and about spiritual knowledge and wisdom. Thus *'ilm* has been understood to mean various things: the received revelation or Koran; the revealed law (*sharī'a*); the *sunna*; Islam; *īmān*; spiritual knowledge (*'ilm al-ladunnī*); wisdom (*hikma*); gnosis (*'irfān*); thought (*tafakkur*); science (to which the plural *'ulūm* is applied); and education. Works have been produced on these themes from the very beginning of Islam up until the present day, although most emerged before the tenth century AH. Such works include: exegeses on the Koran; commentaries on the Traditions of the Prophet by compilers of the various *hadīth* collections; works on law and jurisprudence, and those of other foremost jurists concerned specifically with the elucidation of knowledge and discernment; books on knowledge written by various scholars, savants, sages and imams among both the Sunnis and Shi'ites; treatises by the Mu'tazilites, the theologians, the philosophers and the Sufis; lexicons and dictionaries of technical terminologies in *tasawwuf* and philosophy and the arts and sciences (*al-funūn*) by various grammarians, philologists, scholars and men of letters; and anthologies and other works connected with education and *belles-lettres*. Obviously a comprehensive survey of the literature dealing with the Islamic understanding of the concept of *'ilm* is a monumental task, far beyond the scope of this study. Furthermore the present work is not concerned with the philosophical or epistemological definition of knowledge;[75] rather, our aim here is to show, via a cursory overview of how *'ilm* is presented in the Koran and Traditions, that the term has for the most part been stripped of its original meaning. The multiplicity of meanings that the word *'ilm* inspires has had far-reaching consequences for the Muslim masses, not only in the way in which they are guided 'religiously' but also as far as political authority is concerned.

The development of disciplines such as the interpretation of the Koran and the Traditions, and the method of application of social, economic and political laws derived from these two sources, was inevitable given the nature of the Islamic revelation and the practical demands of the Islamic community founded in Medina under the leadership of Muhammad. Interpretation of the Koran was one of the earliest branches of learning to come into existence. The Iranian scholar and cleric 'Abd al-Rida Hijazi is of the opinion that during the life time of Muhammad, there was no need for books or writings dealing with the 'Koranic sciences', since anyone who had any questions concerning the Koran and its interpretation had only to ask the Prophet himself.[76]

The Koranic 'sciences' (*'ulūm al-Qur'ān*) developed rapidly after the death of Muhammad, with many disciplines coming into existence. The importance attached by the Koran to the acquisition of knowledge, together with the apparent ambiguity of the term *'ilm* itself, gave rise to a wide range of 'sciences', each one of which, it is claimed, can be traced back directly to the Koran itself. Each of the intellectually-oriented members of the community would, according to his personal ability or preference, busy himself with a certain aspect of the revelation. The Prophet's son-in-law, Ali b. Abi Talib – the first Shi'ite Imam – is said to have been the first person to teach the correct pronunciation and method of recitation of the Koran; this he did by clarifying the rules of Arabic grammar and teaching them to one Abu al-Aswad al-Du'uli.[77] It is also claimed that the famous exegete Ibn 'Abbas was instructed in the science of exegesis by Ali when the latter was Caliph.[78]

The Iranian cleric, 'Allama Burqa'i, also traces all branches of what he calls 'Islamic science' back to the Koran, and outlines briefly the various aspects of the Koran which were emphasized and the disciplines which such emphasis engendered. Interest in the letters and sounds of the revealed words, he says, brought into existence the 'science' of recitation (*'ilm al-tajwīd*), or the reading of the Koran in accordance with established rules of pronunciation and intonation; some individuals focused on the usage and positioning of words, thus creating the 'science' of grammar and syntax (*'ilm-i sarf wa nahw*); contemplation upon the various styles of writing and copying of the Koran led to the flourishing of calligraphy (*'ilm-i rasm al-khatt*); those who pondered the possible meanings of words and phrases paved the way for the 'science' of exegesis (*'ilm al-tafsīr*); those who focused their attention on rational proofs and examples of Divine Unity heralded the foundation of the 'science' of theology (*'ilm al-kalām*); investigation into how rules and regulations necessary for the functioning of social life can be extracted or deduced from the verses of the Koran led to the birth of the 'science of principles' (*'ilm al-usūl*), or the principles of

21

Islamic jurisprudence; contemplation on the lives and achievements of the prophets foreshadowed the 'science' of history (*'ilm al-tārīkh*); the study of those verses in which the Koran discusses the kinds of behaviour that lead to either reward or punishment in the hereafter brought into being the 'science' of ethics and morality (*'ilm al-akhlāq*); those who deliberated upon the numerous Koranic verses which deal with cosmic phenomena founded the 'natural' sciences and became pioneers in the fields of physics, mathematics, astronomy, medicine, alchemy, geography, and so on.[79] Burqa'i's list of what he terms 'Koranic sciences' is extensive; he points out that all of the progress made by Muslim scholars in their various fields during the first centuries of Islam happened as a result of the Islamic revelation and the emphasis therein on the acquisition of *'ilm*.[80]

The development of the these branches of knowledge did not of course take place all at once: the formation of each discipline happened gradually, each in accordance with the practical needs of the burgeoning Islamic community. For example, the earliest activity – and most highly developed expression – of the Islamic community in its foetal stages was in law rather than in theology; the practical demands of the community necessitated the stabilization and standardization of the processes of law long before the need was felt for a formal discipline of theological speculation such as *kalām*.[81] This is not to say that metaphysical matters were not discussed in the early days of Islam; indeed, most of the Meccan verses are replete with matters metaphysical, and it is inconceivable that such questions would have been overlooked by Muhammad and the early converts to the new faith. The appearance of formally structured branches of Islamic knowledge or science took place much later than this. Initially, anyone proficient in any of the aforementioned fields would, as 'one who knows', be entitled to be called an *'ālim* (possessor of knowledge) in his own discipline. Yet it appears that in the first few decades after Muhammad's death, each scholar was titled according to his own particular field; Ali b. Abi Talib, for instance, was, by virtue of his pioneering work in Koranic exegesis, called *ra'is al-mufassirīn* (lit. chief of the exegetes).[82] It was not until later, when the various branches of knowledge had been structured into more formal disciplines of learning and instruction, that the nebulous term *'ulamā* came to be used as a blanket expression to cover any group of Muslim scholars, regardless of their specialization.

The apparent ambiguity of the term *'ilm* as used in the Koran left the way open for each group of scholars to insist on the necessity of acquiring the particular branch of knowledge which happened to be its speciality. According to Muhammad, the acquisition of knowledge is incumbent upon every Muslim man and woman; this assertion forms one of the most celebrated Prophetic Traditions concerning the question of knowledge, and is accepted by both Sunnis and Shi'ites.[83] The fact that the Tradition does not specify the type of knowledge to be acquired suggests that in the early days of Islam there was a consensus as to the meaning and connotations of the term '*ilm*. However, as Ghazali points out in *Ihyā 'ulūm al-dīn*, Muslim scholars disagreed as to exactly which branch of knowledge a Muslim was to acquire. As a result, he says, they split into approximately twenty different groups.[84] The scholastic theologians (*mutakallimūn*) insisted that *kalām* was obligatory since it is through this discipline above all that the unity of God, His essence and attributes, can be demonstrated logically. The jurists (*fuqahā*) insisted on *fiqh* because the lawful, unlawful, forbidden and permissible things of everyday life and worship are determined through it. The exegetes (*mufassirūn*) and traditionists (*muhaddithūn*) stood for *tafsīr* and *hadīth*, claiming that it is only through these two endeavours that all other sciences can be reached. The Sufis, Ghazali says, pointed to Sufism as the obligatory branch of knowledge, and so on. Each group was able to elevate its own particular specialization to the status of the obligatory knowledge intended in the Prophetic Tradition quoted above.[85]

Knowledge in the Traditions

In the corpus of sayings attributed to Muhammad – and, for the Shi'ites, the Imams – there can be found hundreds of Traditions concerning the question of knowledge and the excellence of those who acquire and disseminate it. Some of these sayings are so well known in the Muslim world that they have entered everyday language as proverbs and maxims. Sayings such as, 'Seek knowledge, even though it be in China,'[86] and 'I (Muhammad) am the city of knowledge, and Ali is its gateway'[87] have been incorporated into many works of literature and poetry; the Tradition, 'The acquisition of knowledge is incumbent on every Muslim man and woman'[88] was one of the slogans used even by Iran's Reza Shah in his educational reform programme of the 1930s. According to the Traditions, whoever treads the path towards the acquisition of '*ilm* will be placed on the road to Heaven by God;[89] those with knowledge ('*ulamā*) are the custodians (*umanā*) of religion;[90] the '*ulamā* are the inheritors of the prophets;[91] one with knowledge ('*ālim*) who benefits from that knowledge is better in the sight of God than 70,000 devotees ('*ābid*);[92] to behold the face of one with knowledge ('*ālim*) is an act of worship;[93] he who acquires knowledge, acts upon it and imparts it to others only to please God is proclaimed as victorious and magnificent by all existing beings throughout the realms of the heavens;[94] knowledge is man's hope of immortal life, and so on.

Most of the Traditions in both Shi'ite and Sunni compilations do not state whether the term '*ilm* is to be understood as a specific branch of knowledge or not. However in two major woks of *hadīth* – Kulayni's *al-Kāfī* for the Shi'ites and Bukhari's *Sahīh* for the Sunnis – there are sections which deal specifically with the transmission of Traditions. The seventeenth chapter of *al-Kāfī* deals solely with the transmission of Traditions, without the term '*ilm* being used once.[95] Yet the fact that this and a further five chapters at the end of Kulayni's *Kitāb-i fadl al-'ilm* deal almost exclusively with the transmission, learning and teaching of Traditions and are included under the title of '*ilm* points to the fact that the Traditionists saw themselves as '*ulamā* and were thus predisposed to interpreting '*ilm* as '*ilm al-hadīth* (science of Traditions). In *Sahīh al Bukhārī*, the implication is more explicit: the term *ahl al-'ilm* is interpreted by the compiler as denoting the *mujtahidūn*, or those who exert themselves in the field of independent judgement, which at the time of Bukhari meant the *muhaddithūn*, the narrators and interpreters of Traditions.[96]

There are certain Traditions in which the actual meaning of the word '*ilm* is expounded by either the Prophet or the Imams. One such example is a Tradition known as the *hadith al-tathlith* (lit. the 'trinity' tradition). Muhammad was once asked to define the term '*ilm*. He answered by saying that it consists of three things: *āya mukhama*; *farīda 'ādila*; and *sunna qā'ima*. The problem here is one of interpretation. Knowledge of *āya mukhama* (lit. "sound 'signs' or verses") can be understood to be the knowledge of those verses in the Koran the meanings of which are precise and unequivocal; knowledge of *farīda 'ādila* (lit. "just obligation") can be taken to imply the knowledge of obligatory acts to be performed by Muslims in everyday life; knowledge of *sunna qā'ima* (lit. "upright code") can be understood as the knowledge of the Muhammadan *sunna* or code of legal imperatives and prohibitions. As such, all three sub-divisions would fall into the domain of 'scriptural' sciences such as *hadīth* and *fiqh*. Sayyid Muhammad Rizvi, a contemporary translator of *al-Kāfī* into English, has interpreted the Tradition in this way.[97] Muhammad Fayd al-Kashani, a prominent Shi'ite scholar of the middle Safavid period, approaches the Tradition differently. Kashani interprets *āya muhkama* as referring to the principles of belief (*usūl al-'aqā'id*); *farīda 'ādila* as referring to ethics and morals ('*ilm al-akhlāq*); and *sunna qā'ima* as referring to *fiqh*.[98] Mir Damad, another Safavid scholar, interprets *āya muhkama* as 'major jurisprudence'

24

(*fiqh al-akbar*); *farīda 'ādila* as 'minor jurisprudence' (*fiqh al-asghar*); and *sunna qā'ima* as the knowledge of ethics and morals.[99] The basic problem with Traditions is one of interpretation, which is compounded by the fact that there can often be found several different versions of the same narrative in different sources. In this sense, the interpretation of Traditions is far more problematic than the exegesis of the Koran. As far as the Traditions concerning *'ilm* are concerned, the vast majority do not specify the actual meaning of the word *'ilm* and thus it becomes open to each group of scholars to interpret them as it wishes. Kashani, for example, who was inclined towards the 'esoteric', sees the Tradition in question as focusing on the fundamentals of belief, whereas it would be equally as feasible for an expert in the exoteric, 'scriptural' sciences - *fiqh* and *hadīth* - to interpret the Tradition according to his own criteria and in favour of his own branch of knowledge. In the context of our enquiry, the most notable example in which an expert in a particular branch of the Islamic sciences has limited the term *'ilm* to his own specialization is that of Muhammad Baqir Majlisi, whose life and works will be evaluated in Chapter Four. Primarily a *muhaddith* or narrator of Traditions, Majlisi interprets *'ilm* unequivocally as *'ilm al-hadīth*.[100]

Evolution of the terms *'ilm* and *fiqh*

The verbal noun *'ilm* is the broadest word in the Arabic language denoting knowledge. It is often equated with *ma'rifa* or *shu'ūr*, but there are marked variations in its usage.[101] The verb *'alima* (to know) covers one or two accusatives as it indicates knowledge of a thing or a proposition (as in the German *kennen* or *wissen*). In its early usage *'ilm* was the knowledge of definite things such as the Koran, *hadīth*, *sharī'a* and so on, as we have seen in the preceding section on the *hadīth* collections. *fiqh*, however, was used originally to mean the independent use of the intellect as a means of acquiring knowledge, but the word *faqīh* (one who is intelligent or knowing) has come to indicate a minor canon lawyer or jurist: the *faqīh* is one who is able, through the independent use of his powers of reason, to decide points of law by his own judgment in the absence or ignorance of a Tradition bearing on the case in question. In the older theological language, *fiqh* was used in contrast with *'ilm*, which, besides knowledge of definite things such as the Koran and *tafsīr*, had come to denote the accurate knowledge of legal decisions handed down by the Prophet and his companions. *'ilm* and *fiqh* were considered distinct qualities of the theologian; al-Mujahid defines the

25

sum total of all wisdom as being composed of '*al-Qur'ān, al-'ilm wa al-fiqh.*'[102] Al-Mujahid's definition limits the application of the terms to two well-defined areas of scriptural knowledge, thus showing clearly that by his time, considerable changes in meaning had occurred. The fact that the word '*ālim* may also be applied – in its broadest sense – to denote one who is proficient in *fiqh* means that a *faqīh* could easily be referred to as an '*ālim*, thus conflating the two terms. The gradual broadening of the word '*ilm* – as was demonstrated earlier – to any of the so-called Koranic sciences meant that the word '*ālim* was often used to denote a scholar in the broadest sense, especially one using intellectual processes.

Against these gradual changes in meaning there have been vigorous protests by many Muslim thinkers, the most notable of them being Ghazali, who did not believe that the praise given in the Koran to the '*ulamā* can apply to mere canon lawyers and jurists (*fuqahā*).

Ghazali enumerates five terms denoting branches of knowledge – all of which he classifies as praiseworthy (*mamdūh*) – which had undergone a semantic shift by his lifetime. These are: *fiqh; 'ilm; tawhīd; hikma* and *tadhkīr*. The word *fiqh*, which by Ghazali's time had come to signify jurisprudence, was claimed by him to have been changed by 'limitation' (*tahdīd*). Whereas *fiqh* originally meant 'discernment of the Truth', it was subsequently limited to 'the knowledge of unusual legal cases, the mastery of the minute details of their origins, excessive disputation on them, and the retention of the different opinions which relate to them.'[103] Ghazali states that as far as the Koran is concerned, the term *fiqh* denoted the 'science of the hereafter and the knowledge of the subtle defects of the soul, the influences which render works corrupt, the thorough realization of the inferiority of this earthly life, the urgent expectation of bliss in the hereafter, and the domination of fear (of God) over the heart.'[104]

Ghazali cites a verse in the Koran in which the believers are told that whenever they embark upon a fighting expedition, they should leave behind a contingent of individuals who will busy themselves with *tafaqquh* so that they may admonish the fighters when they return. According to Ghazali, it is *fiqh* which brings about such a warning and such a fear, and not the 'details of ordinary divorce or divorce through *li'an* or manumission ('*ataq*), *salām* contracts and hire, rental and lease (*ijāra*) conditions, which are the domain of jurisprudence and produce neither warning nor fear.'[105] Ghazali contends that devotion given exclusively to the affairs of jurisprudence actually serves to harden the heart and remove from it the kind of fear which should be a result of *fiqh* in its original sense. In verse 7:179, the Koran states that those who are destined for hell have hearts which do not understand (*lahum qulūb lā yafqahūn)*; in Ghazali's opinion, the word 'understand' here is connected with belief and not with legal opinions. 'Allama Tabataba'i confirms Ghazali's statements on the corruption of the term *fiqh*: in his interpretation of verse 9:122 he says that the true meaning of *tafaqquh* is the understanding *(fahm)* of 'all religious knowledge *(ma'ārif-i-dīnī)*, both fundamental *(usūl)* and secondary *(furū')*.' He adds that the term *fiqh* cannot be limited to the knowledge of the 'practical rules' *(ahkām-i 'amalī)* of religion - namely, *fiqh* - as it has been by the Muslim *'ulamā*.[106]

Ghazali does not go so far as to say that the term *fiqh* cannot be applied to the independently reached decisions of jurists on points of Islamic law, but rather emphasizes that the term was originally applied to the 'science of the hereafter'; the restriction that took place in the term created ambiguity which, he argues, caused some men to devote themselves solely to jurisprudence, thus neglecting the science of the hereafter and the nature of the soul and heart. The type of 'esoteric' knowledge facilitated by *fiqh* (in its original sense) is abstruse and difficult to live by; furthermore, to attain through it candidacy for office or a position of power, prestige and wealth, is simply not possible. For this reason, Ghazali says, Satan used the change in the term *fiqh* to 'make the neglect of the science of the hereafter, and the change in the connotation of the term, attractive to the human heart.'[107]

Clearly, Ghazali condemns the misuse of the term *fiqh* but does not deny that jurisprudence has its place in Islamic society. However, he states that it is a branch of knowledge that is *fard al-kifāya*: its acquisition is of merit but not obligatory. As long as at least one person in the community is versed in the science of jurisprudence, the obligation to acquire that knowledge ceases to be binding on the rest of the community, who are then supposed to practise *taqlīd* or emulation of the chief jurist in their midst.[108]

According to Ghazali, jurisprudence is connected with religion only indirectly: since this world is the preparation for the hereafter, it is the fundamentals of belief which are its foundation. The regulation of social life and form of government are secondary – albeit indispensable – adjuncts to the fundamentals of belief, and it is the regulation of social life and government, with its myriad rules and laws, that forms the domain of the jurist. The heart is removed from this domain, since attention is focused only on the outward confession (Islam) and not the inward intention.[109] Concerning prayer, for example, the jurist is entitled to give his opinion as to whether or not it has been performed in accordance with the prescribed regulations, but is unable to pass judgement regarding the hidden intentions of the worshipper. The jurist, claims Ghazali, is proficient in a branch of knowledge which relates to the welfare of the believer in *this* world. Were one to enquire from a jurist about divorce, or inheritance, or gambling, he would probably be able to recite volumes of minute details concerning these matters, most of which would never be used or needed; however, were one to enquire of him about sincerity (*ikhlās*) or the nature of hypocrisy (*riyā* or *nifāq*), he would hesitate to express an opinion, even though the knowledge of these is an obligatory ordinance, the neglect of which brings about damnation in the hereafter.[110] A study of Ghazali's *Ihyā* shows that by his time, the proliferation of jurists was such that 'the town is crowded with those who are employed in giving legal opinions and defending cases.'[111]

Ghazali expresses shock at the fact that some *fard al-kifāya* activities – most notably jurisprudence – are preferred to other fields of *fard al-kifāya* science such as medicine. He says that the reason could be that disciplines such as medicine 'do not lead to the management of religious endowments (*awqāf*), execution of wills, possession of the money of orphans, and appointment to judicial and governmental positions through which one exalts himself above his fellow men and fastens his yoke upon his enemies.'[112] Ghazali's vitriol is reserved, clearly, not for the science of jurisprudence *per se*; indeed he goes to great lengths to extol early jurists and scholars of the scriptural sciences such as al-Shafi'i and Ahmad b. Hanbal, who were not only pious but were also quick to recognise the excellence of those versed in the esoteric sciences.[113] Ghazali's attack is aimed at those individuals who contrived to exploit the discipline of jurisprudence for their own ends.

Confusion over the term *islām*/Islam, which, as we have already seen, results in inordinate emphasis on externals, facilitates further the popularity of the *faqīh*; as al-Attas says, the preoccupation with the Islamic state and the *umma* in modern times is another indication of the exaggerated kudos accorded to the acquisition of *fard al-kifāya* knowledge such as jurisprudence. The gradual domination of the Islamic sciences by the jurists – so berated by Ghazali – cannot be seen solely as the machinations of 'learned men who have espoused evil,' as Ghazali puts it; rather, we should try to understand it in terms of supply and demand. The majority of Muslims inclined towards Islam rather than *islām*, thus creating a demand for scholars who deal with externals rather than questions of belief. Traditionally, this demand had been met by the experts in *fiqh* (in the sense of jurisprudence), the *fuqahā*.

As far as the term '*ilm* is concerned, Ghazali bemoans the change in meaning that it too has undergone. Originally, '*ilm* was applied to man's knowledge of God, His miracles, and His works among His servants and creatures. However, the true meaning of the term came to be altered – as in the case of the word *fiqh* – by limitation, until it became more commonly applied to those who debate cases of jurisprudence. Ghazali argues that most of what is said in the Koran and traditions concerning *'ilm* relates to those who have knowledge of God, His ordinances, His works, and His attributes. The semantic shift, together with the fact that *'ilm* and *fiqh* became virtually coterminous, resulted in the term *'ulamā* being applied to many who were ignorant of the true Koranic sciences of *tafsīr* and *hadīth*, but who were well versed in casuistry and were thus in a position to parade before the masses as 'versatile, learned men.'[114]

From Ghazali's comments it is clear that for him, *'ilm* can be perceived on two different yet complementary levels. First and foremost, *'ilm* signifies man's knowledge of God and His attributes. Secondly, the term can be applied to any one of the disciplines which sprang up as a result of the Islamic revelation, such as exegesis and the transmission of Traditions. What Ghazali objects to most vehemently is the limitation of the word *'ilm* to any one particular branch of knowledge and learning. Not only is limitation detrimental to the offending scholars and their followers – the Muslim masses – but it also reveals neglect on their part of the most fundamental knowledge, namely man's knowledge of God, without which all other disciplines are ultimately worthless.

'Allama Tabataba'i holds similar views. In his interpretation of Koranic verses in which the terms *'ilm* and *īmān* occur side by side, he says:

> It is clear that the meaning of *'ilm* and *imān* in these verses denotes conviction (*yaqīn*) and adherence to those things which conviction necessitates. The word *'ilm* when used in the Koran means certainty of knowledge regarding God and His signs, while *īmān* signifies belief in the incumbency of those things which such knowledge necessitates.[115]

Both Shi'ite and Sunni schools in theory hold that *'ilm* is a prerequisite of *īmān*. Thus it can be understood that what is intended fundamentally by the term *'ilm* cannot be limited to any one branch of knowledge; rather, it must refer to man's knowledge of God. In his commentary on a Tradition attributed to Ja'far al-Sadiq, the Iranian scholar Ali Tihrani points out that belief in the realities of *tawhīd* cannot be attained without deliberation (*tafakkur*) and proofs based on knowledge (*barāhin-1 'ilmī*): whilst there may exist knowledge without belief, there can never be belief without knowledge. Belief has different levels and can be strengthened only in accordance with the amount of effort spent on thought, deliberation and the acquisition of knowledge. Tihrani also explains that the intellectual perception of the existence of God, the validity of the prophethood of Muhammad and other fundamentals of belief do not necessarily culminate in belief.:

> Knowledge and perception are the product of the intellect (*'aql*), whereas belief is the produce of the heart (*qalb*)... Satan was well-versed in all of the fundamentals of belief but was still branded an infidel by God. A philosopher too may explain at great length all the rational proofs for the existence of God yet still not believe, since his knowledge does not rise above his intellect... intellectual knowledge of the unity of God (*tawhīd-i 'ilmī*) must be translated into acceptance of the heart (*tawhīd-i qalbī*).[116]

Popular perception of the terms *'ilm* and *'ulamā*

Ghazali's objection that the term *'ilm* had, by his time, undergone a transformation in meaning and had come to denote any kind of Muslim scholar – the jurist in particular – is still valid today. Throughout the Islamic world it is the *mujtahid*, the *mullā* and the *muftī* – all renowned chiefly for their prowess in the scriptural sciences – who are revered by the majority of Muslims as *'ulamā*. Naturally there are individuals – mostly scholars themselves such as Tabataba'i, Tihrani and al-Attas – who draw careful distinctions between the various kinds of knowledge and emphasize that the fundamental category of *'ilm* is that which involves the recognition of, and belief in, God.

In the context of Shi'ite Iran in particular it was not until the turn of the present century that the meaning of the terms *'ilm* and *'ulamā* were reconsidered in intellectual circles. Until then, the terms were used unequivocally to denote 'religious' knowledge – knowledge of the scriptural disciplines - and those proficient in it. However, with the success of the industrial revolution and the rapid progress of all branches of natural science and technology in the West, plus the overwhelming influence that these developments had on the world of Islam, which had hitherto limited its perception of the concept of *'ilm* mainly to the scriptural disciplines, the term *'ilm* was broadened once more to denote 'natural science' and *al-'ulūm* to mean 'the sciences'. Reformist movements throughout the Muslim world took great pains to prove that scientific progress was not only reconcilable with the precepts of Islam but also predated by them. Whether the sole

intention of the major reformers was to make the acceptance of science –
and, in particular, science as spearheaded by the West – palatable to the taste
of the Muslim masses is a matter for speculation. If the desired effect was to
free the concept of '*ilm* from the monopoly of the jurists, the reformists
were, to an extent, successful. Muslim thinkers did indeed begin to re-
appraise the term '*ilm*, but instead of reuniting it with its original meaning as
understood by the likes of Ghazali and Tabataba'i, for the most part all that
they did was exchange one limited interpretation for another. A distinction
between 'religious' and 'secular' sciences – where 'religious' denotes the
scriptural sciences (*fiqh* and *hadīth*), and 'secular' the natural sciences – was
highlighted, even though the Koran admits of no such differentiation. If '*ilm*
had previously been limited – albeit erroneously – to the study of
jurisprudence, it was now limited to the study of science in the Western
sense of the term. Many books have since been written by Muslims extolling
the virtues of modern science and endeavouring to prove, as the early
reformers did, that 'science' and 'religion' ('*ilm wa dīn*) are compatible.

Contemporary Muslim scholars and '*ilm*

The general trend among contemporary Muslim writers is to show that the
term '*ilm* as used in the Koran and Traditions is not confined to 'religious'
knowledge but rather that it denotes the concept of knowledge in its broadest
sense. More particularly, their emphasis is upon the compatibility of modern
science with the teachings of the Koran; numerous works on this theme have
been authored by Muslim thinkers throughout the Muslim world.[117]

In *The Rights of Women in Islam*, Shaykh Yahya Nuri mentions the
Koranic emphasis upon the acquisition of scientific knowledge as 'one of
the greatest virtues of Islam.' The Koran encourages all men to learn and
teach, thus raising the acquisition of knowledge to the status of obligation.[118]
Nuri does not specify the type of knowledge adumbrated by the Koran, but
since his tract is an apologetic one in defence of the Islamic view of women
it may be understood that it is the acquisition of science that he is inferring
rather than that of *fiqh* or *hadīth* or, even, of divine gnosis. In other similar
works on the gender issue in Islam, objections raised by critics of Islam's
stance vis-à-vis women are countered with reference to the Koranic
emphasis on learning, education and the acquisition of knowledge.[119]

The late Iranian sociologist Ali Shari'ati gives several different opinions
on the question of '*ilm*. In his seminal work *Islāmshināsī*, he states that the
meaning of the term '*ilm* is general and cannot be limited to what he calls

31

the 'religious sciences':

> Some Muslims have endeavoured to limit the word '*ilm* as used in
> the Koran to the domain of religious knowledge or jurisprudence. In
> actual fact, the word '*ilm* is used in a general sense. This is clear from
> Prophetic traditions such as 'Seek knowledge, even though it may be
> as far as China'.[120]

In another, earlier work, *Fātima Fātima ast*, Sharia'ti had painted a different
picture of the terms '*ilm* and '*ulamā*, adopting a stance akin to that of
Ghazali:

> In Islam, the '*ālim* is not an uncommitted individual who happens to
> have lots of knowledge and knows lots of things. '*ilm*, in the mind of
> the true '*ālim* is not merely a mishmash of facts and information: in
> his heart it is like a ray of light...the light of God.[121]

Shari'ati goes on to say that the '*ilm* of the true '*ālim* is not something secret
or mysterious or supernatural; nor can it be confined to specific fields such
as history, geography, chemistry, jurisprudence and the like. These,
according to Shari'ati, are 'scientific facts' and not light. The '*ilm* which
brings guidance is the '*ilm* of faith ('*aqīda*) which is called *fiqh* in the Koran,
although *fiqh* today means knowledge of Islamic social laws and
contracts.[122]

In a later work, however, Shari'ati denounces the view he espoused in
Islāmshināsī as an erroneous one, one that is more in keeping with the views
of the modernists (*mutajaddidūn*). Quoting the Tradition of Muhammad
which extols the ink of those with knowledge over the blood of the martyrs,
Shari'ati asserts that the term '*ilm* should not be understood in a general
sense. Nor, he declares, is it to be understood as the 'founding fathers'
(*qudamā*) understood it, namely as being restricted to one particular field.
For Shari'ati, the trust (*amāna*) that was given to man by God was one of
responsibility: the greatest responsibility rests on the shoulders of the '*ālim*.
The kind of '*ilm* envisaged by the Koran, he says, is the knowledge which
lies in the possession of the 'enlightened intellectual' (*rawshanfikr*) and
should be understood in the framework of modern, popular and
revolutionary ideology.[123]

Murtada Mutahhari in his book *Insān wa īmān* points out the
contradiction between '*ilm* and belief in the Old Testament, and divides the
history of Western civilization into two main periods: the age of belief and

the age of *'ilm*:

> Islamic civilization can also be divided into two eras: the age of
> 'blossoming glory', namely the age of *īmān* and *'ilm*; and the age of
> decline, or the death of *īmān* and *'ilm*.[124]

Defining the term *'ilm*, he concludes that it is:

> Man's comprehensive and all-embracing view of the world; the result
> of mankind's collective efforts which have developed over the
> centuries. This view, which has been tempered by rules, conditions,
> laws and a language and logic peculiar to itself, is what is known al
> *'ilm* (i.e. science).[125]

Furthermore, he concludes that 'history, the natural sciences, and the study
of the human psyche' are the branches of science deemed most useful for
man by the Koran.[126]

In the view of Mihdi Bazargan, *'ilm* cannot be restricted to any one
subject and must be understood in the widest sense possible. According to
him, *'ilm* must be like a just judge – free, impartial and with the sole aim of
seeking the truth. Bazargan mirrors Ghazali's objection that each group of
scholars has limited the term *'ilm* to its own particular field. However, he
says:

> God gave to man the 'knowledge of the names': the Koran does not
> say 'The knowledge of God, or of things celestial (*malakūtī*)....':
> rather, the knowledge was of things which are named...it is the type
> of knowledge which takes the suffix '-ology' (e.g. biology, geology,
> sociology), and cannot be restricted to any one field.[127]

The Iraqi Shi'ite scholar, Muhammad Baqir Sadr, also equates *'ilm* with
modern science, pointing out that the Koran discusses many phenomena
which have only recently been understood in Western scientific *milieux*.[128]
Similar views are offered by the Sunni 'Allama Mahmud Shaltut, who states
that *'ilm* cannot be limited to 'religious knowledge' and should be
understood only in terms of knowledge of the physical creation.[129]

The Koran on *'ilm* and *'ulamā*

According to the Koran, the acquisition of knowledge begins with the act of contemplation (*tafakkur*) upon the signs (*āyāt*) of God. The cosmos is perceived to be a vast showcase in which these signs are revealed to man by the Creator; with the wise use of reason (*ta'aqqul*), man gains knowledge of these signs and thus in turn attains knowledge of God, the revealer of the signs. Both *tafakkur* and *ta'aqqul* are prescribed emphatically in numerous Koranic verses, with the Koran asserting that unbelief and blasphemy are the result of man's non-use of his innate ability to read the 'signs' in the cosmos. The creation of the heavens and earth; the alternation of night and day; the sailing of ships upon the oceans; rain, winds, and clouds; animals, vegetation and fruits; the celestial bodies; the existence of different colours; the creation of men and women and the inherent differences between them; the existence of different languages and races; old age and weakness; the growth of a foetus in its mother's womb; the prophets and their histories; the fate of bygone civilizations; the life of Muhammad and the circumstances surrounding his prophethood – all of these are portrayed by the Koran as 'signs' for men to ponder and approach with the correct use of their ability to reason. Man is enjoined to travel through the land in order that he may learn wisdom; upon those who wish not to understand, God shall place doubt, and neither signs nor warnings shall benefit them if they do not believe as a result of their unwillingness to understand. Whoever ignores the 'signs' is an oppressor of his own soul; he who 'hears' the signs but then rejects them will be punished.

The verses on *tafakkur* and *ta'aquul* show that the act of contemplation is enjoined on man in order that he may gain knowledge (*'ilm*) of the signs, and by so doing come to realise that they are created and must be attributed to an omnipotent Creator. Contemplation, then, precedes knowledge and belief. Yet believers are also ordered to make continuous *tafakkur* and *ta'aqqul*, which serve to maintain and increase belief. Indeed, numerous verses address those who already believe and encourage them to continue to contemplate the signs.

The knowledge gained through contemplation of the cosmos is considered worthless unless it leads to true and constantly renewed belief in the Creator. One may have knowledge of the signs but may not wish to attribute them to God. Knowledge which is not supplemented and perfected by belief, such as that in the possession of Pharaoh or Satan, is of no use and will be punished by hellfire. In the hands of evil men, knowledge can be dangerous, for knowledge of the 'signs' can be of profit only if it is used as a means with which to know God. That the Koran does use the term '*ilm* to connote knowledge of things and facts is borne out by verses such as 10:5, in which it is written that God created the sun and the moon and their various stages so that man might 'know the number of years and the count of time.' Yet the emphasis remains always on the assertion that knowledge about created things is of value only on the condition that it leads to, or strengthens, belief in God.

The evolution of the Islamic sciences highlighted earlier was sanctioned by the Koranic emphasis on contemplation and the acquisition of '*ilm*, but nowhere in the Koran can a verse be found which restricts knowledge to any one field or discipline. In fact, the Koran sees all knowledge of things as a means to an end, and not something that is to be pursued for its own sake. Indeed, the Koran declares quite categorically that the only men who fear God are 'those who know' ('*ulamā*), which obviously excludes those who pursue the knowledge of a thing for its own sake, namely without contemplating it consciously in order to gain knowledge about, and belief in, its Creator.

"Those truly fear God, among His servants, who have knowledge:
for go is Exalted in Might, Oft-Forgiving."

The use of the word '*ulamā* in this verse can, according to Ghazali, denote only those who are convinced of the existence of God and all His attributes; he adds that the 'goal of the science of practical religion is revelation, and the goal of revelation is to know God.' 'Allama Tabataba'i interprets the above verse in a similar fashion, concluding that the '*ulamā* are those who know God by His names and attributes and acts; theirs is a complete knowledge which bestows tranquility upon their hearts and wipes all doubt from their souls.

Thus the appropriation of the terms '*ilm* and '*ulamā* by Muslim scholars, past and present, to describe one particular branch of learning to the exclusion of others, has no Koranic justification. True '*ilm* is, in the Koranic sense, not the knowledge of *fiqh* and *hadīth* as the 'founding fathers' insisted; nor is it, as the modernists would have it, 20th century science and the study of nature. Following the argument of the Koran to its logical conclusion, we may say that while, for example, an '*ālim* (in the Koranic sense) may also be, say, a *faqīh* (in the post-Koranic sense), the reverse may not always be the case. Consequently, a *faqīh* may possess no real knowledge ('*ilm*) about God whatsoever.

Notes

1. For a concise historical study of the development of Islamic theological speculation, see: W. Montgomery Watt, *Islamic Philosophy and Theology* (Edinburgh, UEP, 1979). Pages 32-5 deal specifically with the Murji'ite sect.

2. Numerous Koranic verses present the universe and all that it contains as 'signs' or pointers to the existence of God; many of these verses end with one or more of the 'beautiful names' (*asmā al-husnā*) of God, thus inferring that contemplation of the cosmos has, or should have, as its direct corollary the attribution of the cosmos, as an act of creativity, to the possessor of those names.

3. *kafara* means to cover or hide something, and therefore by association alludes to the state of one who does not attribute the existence of the cosmos to God. For a more comprehensive study of the concept of *kufr*, see the article in *EI*, 2nd edition.

4. See: Ali Shari'ati, *Pidar, mādar, mā muttahamīm* (Tehran, 1976). Shari'ati's highly polemical tract inveighs against the blind imitation of Islam by what he believes to be the majority of Muslims, for whom rite and ritual are equated automatically with belief. See also: Rashid Rida, *Tafsīr al-manār* (Cairo, 1367-75) for a Sunni view of the same question; and: W. Cantwell Smith, 'The Special Case of Islam' in *The Meaning and End of Religion* (New York, 1964), pp. 75-108.

5. Syed Muhammad Naquib Al-Attas, *Islam, Secularism and the Philosophy of the Future* (London, Mansell Publishing, 1985), p. 112.

6. *fard al-kifāya* describes an act or practice that is obligatory for some Muslims only, in contrast with *fard al-'ayn*, which is obligatory for all Muslims.

7. Verses 30:20-27; 16:65-70, among others. There are approximately 400 references to 'signs' in the Koran, most of which deal with belief or unbelief in God's *āyāt*.

8. Verse 29:35 – "And We have left thereof an evident Sign, for any people who (care to) understand."

9. Sayyid Ali Khamini'i, *Tarh-i kullī-i andīsha-i islāmī dar Qur'ān* (Tehran, 1354 Sh./1975-76), p.11.

10. *ibid.*, p. 15.

11. Verse 2:285 mentions four: Allah, angels, books and prophets. Verse 4:136 mentions all of the above plus the day of judgement.

12. Verse 8:2 – "For, Believers are those who, when God is mentioned, feel a tremor in their hearts, and when they hear His Signs rehearsed, find their faith strengthened, and put (all) their trust in their Lord."

13. Verse 8:4 – "Such in truth are the Believers: they have grades of dignity with their Lord, and forgiveness, and generous sustenance."

14. Islam holds that God's creative act is beyond time and space, that the cosmos is being renewed constantly at each instant, and that the signs (*āyāt*) of God are being revealed incessantly in new forms and modes. It is claimed that the Koranic basis for this belief can be seen in verse 50:29 – "Every day in (new) splendour doth He (shine)." See also: Sadr al-din al-Shirazi, *al-Asfār al-*

arba'a, ed. by Muhammad Rida al-Muzaffar. (Tehran, 1378/1958/59), vol. 1, part 1, p.116 and vol. 1, part 2, p. 314.

15. Verse 3:191 – "Men who celebrate (*dhikr*) the praises of God, standing, sitting, and lying down on their sides, and contemplate the (wonders of) creation in the heavens and the earth, (with the thought): 'Our Lord! Not for naught hast Thou created (all) this! Glory to Thee! Give us salvation from the fire.'"

16. Verse 4:136 – "O ye who believe! Believe in God and His Apostle, and the scripture which He hath sent to His Apostle and the scripture which He sent to those before (him). Any who denieth God, His angels, His books, His Apostles, and the Day of Judgement, hath gone far astray."

17. There are 67 verses in which *salāt* (prayer) is mentioned, with 32 verses for *zakāt* (religious taxes), 9 for *hajj* (pilgrimage), and 7 for *sawm* (fasting).

18. Verse 9:71 – "The Believers, men and women, are protectors, one of another: they enjoin what is just, and forbid what is evil: they observe regular prayers, practice regular charity, and obey God and His Apostle. On them will God pour His mercy: for God is exalted in power, Wise."

19. *aslama* also embraces such meanings as: to forsake, leave, desert, give up, betray; to let sink, drop; to hand over, turn over; to leave, abandon, deliver up, surrender; to commit oneself; to declare oneself committed to the will of God; to become Muslim, embrace Islam. See: Hans Wehr, *Arabic-English Dictionary* (New York: SLS, 1976), pp. 424-5.

20. Verse 4:94 – "O ye who believe! When ye go abroad in the cause of God, investigate carefully, and say not to anyone who offers you a salutation: 'Thou art none of a Believer.'"

21. Verse 3:67 – "Abraham was not a Jew nor yet a Christian; but he was true in faith (*hanīf*) and bowed his will to God's (*muslim*), and he joined not gods with God."

22. Verse 2:136 – "Say ye: 'We believe in God, and the revelation given to us and to Abraham, Ismail, Isaac, Jacob, and the Tribes, and that given to Moses and Jesus, and that given to (all) Prophets from their Lord: we make no difference between one and another of them: and we bow to God (*muslimūn*)'"

23. In verse 10:72 the prophet Noah tells his people that the reward for his preaching to them is from God, for "I have been commanded to be of those who submit to God's Will (*muslim*)."

24. Verse 2:128 – "'Our Lord! Make of us *muslims*, bowing to Thy (Will), and of our progeny a people *muslim*, bowing to Thy (Will) '"

25. Verse 2:133 – "Were ye witnesses when Death appeared before Jacob? Behold, he said to his sons: 'What will ye worship after me?' They said: 'We shall worship thy God and the God of they fathers, of Abraham, Ismail and Isaac, the One God: to Him we bow (*muslimūn*).'"

26. Verse 12:101 – "Take Thou my soul (at death) as one submitting to Thy Will (*muslim*), and unite me with the righteous."

27. Verse 3:52 – "Said the disciples: 'We are God's helpers: we believe in God, and do thou bear witness that we are *muslims*.'"

28. Verse 2:112 – "Nay, - whoever submits his whole self to God and is a doer of good, - he will get his reward with his Lord, on such shall be no fear, nor shall they grieve."

29. Verse 5:4 – "This day I have perfected your religion for you, completed my favour upon you, and have chosen for you Islam as your religion."

30. Seyyed Hasan 'Askari. 'Religion and Development' in *The Islamic Quarterly*, vol. 30, no. 2 (1986), p. 79.

31. Verse 2:208 – "O ye who believe! Enter into Islam wholeheartedly..." The word *islām* here very likely connotes the personal submission of the self that goes to perfect *īmān*. For a concise explanation of the meaning of submission as the perfection of belief, see: Sayyid Muhammad Husayn Tabataba'i, *Tafsīr al-Mīzān* (Tehran, 1364 Sh./1985-86), vol. 1, p. 418. [This work will henceforth be referred to as *al-Mīzān*]. See also: Murtada Mutahhari, *'Adl-i ilāhī* (Tehran: Intisharat-i Islami, 1397/1976-77), pp. 350-53.

32. Ahmad b. Hanbal, *al-Musnad* (Cairo, 1313/1895-6), vol. 3, p. 184.

33. See the article entitled *islam* in EI, 2nd edition.

34. A.J. Wensinck, *The Muslim Creed* (Cambridge: CUP, 1932), p. 194.

35. Abu al-Hasan Ali al-Ash'ari, *Maqālāt al-islamīyyīn* ed. by 'Abd al-Hamid (Cairo, n.d.), vol. 1, p. 32

36. L. Gardet, 'ISLAM' in *EI*, new edition, vol. 4, p. 172.

37. *ibid.*, vol. 4, p. 173.

38. *ibid.*

39. *ibid.*

40. Kenneth Cragg, *The House of Islam* (Belmont: Dickenson, 1969), p. 5.

41. See footnote 28.

42. Verse 31:22 – "Whoever submits his whole self to God, and is a doer of good, has grasped indeed the most trustworthy hand-hold: and with God rests the End and Decision of (all) affairs."

43. Throughout this chapter, the personal and individual submission of a believer is referred to as *islām*, and the communal religion of which he is part as Islam. The words *muslim* and Muslim are used accordingly. It is hoped that the reader will not be unduly confused by this schema, but will appreciate the subtle difference between the two concepts and also the need for a way of differentiating between them.

44. See footnote 29 for a translation of this verse.

45. Fakhr al-din al Razi, *Mafātīh al-ghayb* (Istanbul, 1307/1891), vol. 7, pp. 608-09.

46. Rashid Rida, *Tafsīr al-Qur'ān al-karīm, tafsīr al-manār* (Cairo: Matba'at al-Kubra al-Amiriyya, 1367-1375/1948-1956), vol. 3, pp. 359-60.

47. The word *al-sālihāt* (righteous acts) occurs 62 times in the Koran: on each occasion it is preceded by the phrase 'those who believe', e.g. in verse 2:25 – "But give glad tidings to those who believe and work acts of righteousness that their portion is Gardens, beneath which rivers flow..." For a complete list, see: Muhammad Fu'ad 'Abd al-Baqi, *al-Mu'jam al-mufahris lī alfāz al-Qur'ān al-karīm* (Beirut, 1363/1943-44), pp. 411-2.

48. Jane I. Smith, 'Continuity and Change in the Understanding of *islam*' in *Islamic Quarterly*, vol. 16, no 3 (1972), pp. 129-30.

49. Ibn 'Abbas, *Tanwīr al-miqbās* (Tehran: al-Maktabat al-Islamiyya, 1377/1957-8), vol. 1, p. 189.

50. Abu Ja'far Muhammad b. Jarir al-Tabari, *Jāmi' al-bayān fī tafsīr al-Qur'ān* (Cairo, 1323-29/1900-11), vol. 26, p. 90.

51. Rashid Rida, *Tafsīr al-manār*, vol. 3. p. 358.

52. Verse 61:9 – "It is He Who has sent His Apostle with guidance and the Religion of Truth, that he may proclaim over it all religion, even though the Pagans may detest (it)."

53. Rashid Rida, *Tafsīr al-manār*, vol. 3, p. 361.

54. Muhammad b. Ya'qub al-Kulayni, *Usūl al-kāfī*, transl. and ed. by A.A. Khusrawi Shabistari (Tehran: Kitabfurushi-i Amiri, 1351 Sh./1972-73), p. 15.

55. *ibid.*, p. 16. For a clarification of the term *wilāya* which is used by Shi'ites and Sufis alike, but with radically different connotations, see: J. Spencer Trimingham, *The Sufi Orders in Islam* (Oxford: Clarendon Press, 1971), pp. 133-7.

56. Ali Shari'ati, *Tashayyu'-i alawī wa tashayyu'-i safawī* (Tehran, 1352 Sh/1973-74), p. 62.

57. Kulayni, *Usūl al-kāfī*, p. 16.

58. *ibid.*, p. 17.

59. *ibid.*, p. 18.

60. Tabataba'i, *al-Mīzān*, vol. 1. p. 418.

61. *ibid.*, p. 418.

62. Verse 43:69 – "(Being) those who have believed in Our Signs and bowed (their wills to Ours) in Islam."

63. Verse 2:208 – "O ye who believe! Enter into Islam wholeheartedly, and follow not the footsteps of the Evil One, for he is to you an avowed enemy."

64. Verse 49:15 – "Only those are Believers who have believed in God and His apostle, and have never since doubted, but have striven with their belongings and their persons in the cause of God: such are the sincere ones."

65. Verse 61:11 – "That ye believe in God and His apostle, and that ye strive (your utmost) in the cause of God, with your property and your persons: that will be best for you, if ye but knew."

66. Tabataba'i, *al-Mīzān*, vol. 1. p. 419.

67. Verse 4:65 – "But no, by thy Lord, they can have no (real) faith, until they make thee judge in all disputes between them, and find in their souls no resistance against thy decisions, but accept them with the fullest conviction."

68. Tabataba'i, *al-Mīzān*, vol. 1. p. 420.

69. Verse 49:14.

70. Ibn Abbas justifies his belief in the possibility of being 'born into Islam' by referring to verse 3:83

71. Abu Hamid Muhammad al-Ghazali, *Kitāb al-'ilm*, transl. by N.A. Faris (Lahore: Ashraf Press, 1962), p.2.

72. See footnote 51.

73. For example, verse 76:3 – "We showed him the Way: whether he be grateful or ungrateful (rests on his will)."

74. For an excellent study of the Islamic concept of *'ilm* see: Franz Rosenthal, *Knowledge Triumphant* (Leiden: Brill, 1970). Rosenthal says that the concept of knowledge has always dominated all aspects of Muslim intellectual, spiritual and social life, and believes that in Islam, knowledge has enjoyed a status unparalleled in other civilizations.

75. See: Fazlur Rahman, *The Philosophy of Mulla Sadra* (Albany: State University of New York Press, 1975). Pages 200-244 are given over to an appraisal of several Islamic theories of knowledge; the opinions of scholars such as Sadra, Ibn Sina, Fakhr al-din Razi, Farabi, and Suhrawardi are compared and analysed.

76. 'Abd al-Rida Hijazi, *Qur'ān dar 'asr-i fadā* (Tehran: Kanun-i Intisharat, 1354 Sh./1975-76), p. 170.

77. Zalim b. 'Amr Abu al-Aswad al-Du'uli, died 67/686-7.

78. Cited in Hijazi, *Qur'ān dar 'asr-i fadā*, p. 170.

79. Although the Koran itself admits of no difference between 'religious' and 'secular' knowledge, the aforementioned disciplines may be divided into the 'scriptural' and 'non-scriptural': the former denoting fields of study involving the Koran, the Traditions and the derivation of laws therefrom; the latter denoting what in secular terms would be called 'natural' or social sciences.

80. Sayyid Abu al-fadl 'Allama Burqa'i, *Muqaddima bar tābishī az Qur'ān* (Tehran, 1985), pp. 60-1.

81. See: H.A.R. Gibb, *Islam* (Oxford: OUP, 1975) for a lucid and comprehensive overview of the development of various branches of Islamic learning. Chapters 5 and 6 are particularly useful.

82. Hijazi, *Qur'ān dar 'asr-i fadā*, p. 170.

83. Muhammad b. Yazid Ibn Maja, *al-Sunan* (Cairo: Dar Ihya al-Kutub al-'Arabiyya, 1372/1952-53), intro., 16:9; Muhammad b. Ya'qub al-Kulayni, *Kitāb fadl al-'ilm*, transl. by Sayyid Muhammad Rizvi (Tehran: WOFIS, 1398/1977-8), p. 73.

84. Ghazali, *Kitāb al-'ilm*, p. 30.

85. *ibid.*, pp. 30-1.

86. *ibid.*, p. 18. See also Hasan Hasanzada Amuli, *Ma'rifat al-nafs* (Tehran: Markaz-i Intisharat-i 'Ilmi wa Farhangi, 1362 Sh./1983-84), vol. 3, p. 435.

87. Rosenthal, *Knowledge Triumphant*, p. 144.

88. See footnote 83.

89. Kulayni, *Kitāb fadl al-'ilm*, p. 85.

90. *ibid.*, p. 80.

91. *ibid.*, pp 78-79.

92. *ibid.*, p. 81.

93. Muhammad Baqir Majlisi, *Bihār al-anwār* 2ⁿᵈ edition (Beirut, 1403/1982-83), vol. 1, p. 195. This will henceforth be referred to as *Bihar II*.

94. Kulayni, *Kitāb fadl al-'ilm*, p. 88.

95. *ibid.*, pp. 131-7.

96. Abu 'Abdullah Muhammad b. Isma'il al-Bukhari, *Sahīh al-Bukhārī* (Istanbul: Hilal Yayinlari, 1298/1977-8), vol. 9, p. 309.

97. Kulayni, *Kitāb fadl al-'ilm*, p. 78.

98. Sayyid Muhammad Kazim 'Asar, *'Ilm al-hadīth* (Tehran, 1354 Sh./1975-76), p. 41.

99. *ibid.*, p. 41.

100. Majlisi's life and works will be appraised in Chapters Four and Five.

101. *ma'rifa* is 'coming to know by experience or reflection' and implies prior ignorance; thus it cannot be predicated of God's knowledge. *Shu'ūr* is perception, especially of details; the *shā'ir* is the perceiver, and also the poet. See the entry on *'ilm* in EI, second edition.

102. Tabari, *Jāmi' al-bayān*, vol. 3, p. 56.

103. Ghazali, *Kitāb al-'ilm*, p. 80.

104. *ibid.*, p. 80.

105. Verse 9:122 – "Nor should the believers all go forth together: if a contingent from every expedition remained behind, they could devote themselves to studies in religion (*tafaqquh*), and admonish the people when they return to them, - that thus they (may learn) to guard themselves (against evil)."

106. Tabataba'i, *al-Mīzān*, vol. 9, p. 640.

107. Ghazali, *Kitāb al-'ilm*, p. 83.

108. Ruhullah Khumayni, *Tawdīh al-masā'il* (Tehran, 1970), p. 2.

109. Ghazali, *Kitāb al-'ilm*, p. 83.

110. *ibid.*, p. 50.

111. *ibid.*, p. 51.

112. *ibid.*

113. *ibid.*, pp. 59-72.

114. *ibid.*, p. 84.

115. Tabataba'i, *al-Mīzān*, vol. 16. p. 325.

116. Ali Tihrani, *Akhlāq-i islāmī* (Mashhad, 1977), vol. 1, p. 68.

117. See for example: Hijazi, *Qur'ān dar 'asr-i fadā*; Maurice Bucaille, *La Bible, le Coran et le Science* (Paris: Seghers, 1976); and Dr. Yahya Naziri, *Qur'ān wa padīdahā-i tabī'at az dīd-i dānish-i imrūz* (Tehran, 1358 Sh./1979-80).

118. Shaykh Yahya Nuri, *Huqūq wa hudūd-i zan dar islām* (Tehran, 1340 Sh./1961-62), p. 121.

119. See: Murtada Mutahhari, *Huqūq-i zan dar islām* (Tehran, 1357 Sh./1978-79).

120. Ali Shari'ati, *Islāmshināsī* (Mashhad, 1347 Sh./1968-69), pp. 42-3.

121. Ali Shari'ati, *Fātima Fātima ast* (Tehran, 1336 Sh./1957-58), pp. 40-1.

122. *ibid.*, p. 12.

123. Ali Shari'ati, *Mas'ūliyyat-i shī'i būdan* (Tehran, 1352 Sh./1973-74), pp. 25-27.

124. Murtada Mutahhari, *Insān wa islām* (Tehran, 1357 Sh.1978-79), p. 28

125. *ibid.*, p. 12.

126. *ibid.*, pp. 92-94.

127. Mihdi Bazargan, *Gumrāhān* (Tehran, 1362 Sh./1983/84), pp. 92-3.

128. Sayyid Muhammad Baqir Sadr, *Inqilāb-i Mahdī wa pindārhā*, transl. by S.A. 'Alam al-Huda (Tehran, 1363 Sh./1984-85), p. 19.

129. 'Allama Mahmud Shaltut, *Sayrī dar ta'ālīm-i islām*, transl. by S.K. Khaliliyan (Tehran, 1344 Sh./1965-66), p. 146.

Chapter 2

Religion in medieval Iran and the rise of the Safavids

Introduction: internalism and externalism defined

In the preceding chapter it was concluded that according to the Koran, the ultimate goal of all human knowledge ('*ilm*) is the gnosis of God and His attributes: those who attain such knowledge, confirm it through belief (*īmān*) and then submit themselves (*islām*) are the true '*ulamā* in the Koranic sense of the word. Adherence to the *sharī'a* (Islam) is posited as logical concomitant of internal submission, but not an inevitable one: individuals may perceive themselves to be Muslims yet remain wanting in terms of both *īmān* and *islām*.

The Koran embraces both *īmān* – of which *islām* is a crucial component – and Islam, and Muhammad, as the pivotal channel through which revelation is expressed and objectified, is presented as the embodiment of both aspects. *īmān*, as the cornerstone and *raison d'être* of the revelation, focuses on the *haqīqa* or sacred truth of the Koranic *Weltanschauung*, whilst Islam, the body of rules and laws designed to regulate all aspects of the lives of those who have 'submitted', centres on the *sharī'a*. A high proportion of the Koranic verses revealed in Mecca concern the fundamentals of belief and divine gnosis: it is chiefly to these verses that the roots of later metaphysical and theosophical speculation can be traced. The verses revealed in Medina, where Muhammad finally succeeded in creating an environment of 'communal submission' - *islām* institutionalised as Islam - contain the bulk of the Koranic commands germane to the social, political and economic aspects of the Muslim's daily life. It is an oversimplification to suggest that the Meccan verses represent *īmān* and the Medinan verses Islam, for among the predominantly legalistic verses revealed in Medina one still encounters passages with a markedly Meccan tenor, replete with expositions of the Divine Names and Attributes, examples of God's workings in the cosmos, and divine imperatives to deliberate, acquire knowledge and believe. Indeed, the fact that the Medinan verses are not geared exclusively towards the externals of religion is an indication, perhaps, that while *īmān* is the cornerstone of Islam, it is not merely a stage which is passed on the way to Islam; rather, the reiteration in the Medinan verses of man's need for *īmān* shows that *īmān* is something which must be renewed and strengthened continuously. It is, in a sense, dynamic, whereas Islam is static. Muhammad, hailed by his followers as the *muballigh* (communicator) *par excellence* of the revelation, transmitted both his knowledge of God (*ma'rifa*) and his knowledge of the commands of God (*sharī'a*) to his people. Neither *iman* nor Islam was sacrificed for the sake of the other; rather, while their difference was recognised, their symbiosis was preserved.

While it does not sanction a formal, institutionalised 'clergy', the Koran does adumbrate the existence of a body of '*ulamā*: those who 'know' God and communicate their knowledge of Him and His commands to others. Given the theoretical interdependence of *īmān* and Islam, the ideal '*ālim* in the Koranic sense of the word would possess, and be able to transmit, knowledge pertaining to both aspects. In reality, however, relatively few Muslim scholars have succeeded in combining these two aspects – with *īmān* functioning as the *raison d'être* of Islam – as a basis for either learning or teaching. In practical terms, the pull towards Islam has always been far stronger than that towards *īmān*, and this has been reflected in the academic orientations of Muslim scholars throughout the ages.

An examination of the obstacles to belief and the psycho-spiritual dynamics underpinning man's tendency to gravitate towards Islam rather than *īmān* would entail a study of considerable depth on the nature and psyche of man as perceived and portrayed by the Islamic revelation, a task far beyond the scope of the present work. Suffice it here to say, then, that the domination of Islam over *īmān* is suggested by the Koran itself. The Koran holds that most human beings do not ponder the *āyāt* and, *ipso facto*, do not truly believe in a Creator; of those that do believe, moreover, most do so only deficiently, preferring to associate other idols with God rather than worship Him alone.[1] It also states, as we saw earlier, that what is perceived as *īmān* often turns out to be Islam in the guise of belief.[2] Thus, one of the deficiencies of belief may be the misplaced emphasis on Islam to the detriment of *īmān*: as Annemarie Schimmel observes, the great mass of Muslims have followed, and continue to follow, the exoteric facet of the Islamic revelation, while only a minority have had as their goal 'the salvific love and knowledge of God.'[3]

This divide between what Schimmel – among others – terms the esoteric and the exoteric is evident from the scholarly inclinations of the *'ulamā* and serves, thus, to split the vast historical body of Muslim scholars into two camps: one having knowledge of God (*ma'rifat Allāh*) as its goal; and the other, knowledge of God's commands (*awāmir Allāh*). Some writers use the terms *ahl al-bātin* and *ahl al-zāhir*; [4] the Safavid philosopher Mulla Sadra refers to the *ahl al-kashf* and the *ahl al-naql*, the former denoting those who use reason, contemplation and theosophical introspection to know God, the latter those whose lifework is the study and promulgation of the scriptural sciences (*al-'ulūm al-naqlīyya*).[5] One scholar, in the context of this dichotomy as it existed in Safavid Iran, talks of the perennial clash 'between Sufi and *faqīh*.'[6]

To avoid the pitfalls of ambiguity and misidentification, however, we should perhaps eschew here use of the terms 'esoteric' and exoteric', simply because the former tends to signify doctrines that are open only to the elect. And while it is true that, according to the Koran, real belief in, and knowledge of, God are attained only by a minority, the divine guidance upon which belief is predicated is, in theory at least, open to all.[7] Instead of 'esoteric' and 'exoteric' I suggest the terms 'internalist' and 'externalist'.[8] The designation 'internalist' is intended to denote any Muslim writer or thinker whose scholarly attention was focused primarily on the fundamentals of belief (*usūl al-īmān*) - Divine Unity (*tawhīd*), Prophethood (*nabuwwa*) and the Resurrection (*ma'ād*) - but more particularly on the acquisition and dissemination of knowledge of God and His attributes (*ma'rifa*). In this sense, internalism has often been articulated best by those attached in some way or other to Sufism and Sufi orders, although there are individuals included in this category who are not affiliated formally to any particular Sufi group: Ghazali and Mulla Sadra are two notable examples. By contrast, the term 'externalist' is used to signify those Muslim scholars who focused their academic efforts on the scriptural sciences (*al-'ulūm al-naqlīyya*), and whose primary consideration was the acquisition and promulgation of the 'secondary sciences' (*al-furū'*), particularly *fiqh* and *hadīth*. The internalist-externalist polarity has existed for almost as long as Islam itself, and should be seen as a reflection of the the skewed approach to belief (*īmān*) and action (Islam) of the vast majority of the Muslim commonalty. However, the aim is not to call into question either the level of belief of the 'externalists' or the level of Islam of the 'internalists': the issue here is simply one of emphasis and orientation. It would be an oversimplification to suggest that Muslim scholars are either wholly internalist or wholly externalist in approach and academic output. For true to the spirit of the Koran, there have always been scholars who have attempted to combine *īmān* with Islam, *usūl* with *furū'*, and *'aql* with *naql*, and who have reflected the synergy of the internal and the external aspects of the Islamic message in their writings: again, Ghazali from among the Sunnis and Mulla Sadra from among the Shi'ites are prominent examples. The concept of an internalist-externalist dichotomy exists in both Sunni and Shi'ite contexts, and the relevance of the issue for the modern Islamic community has also been recognized by representatives of both groups. In the view of the Sunni scholar, Muhammad Naquib al-Attas, as we have already seen, the rise of false *'ulamā* has led to the equally false identification of *'ilm* with the science of jurisprudence:

> Notwithstanding the fact that the Holy Koran repeatedly condemns it, they (the *'ulamā*) delight in endless controversy, disputations and polemics... in whose blind paths the generality of Muslims are left guideless and bewildered. This misguidance leads to emphasis on differences between the various *madhāhib* and to obstinate adherence to trivialities within them ... their incessant elaboration of trivialities leads to the neglect of the real problem of education. They are content at leaving the Muslim's basic education in *fardu 'ayn* knowledge at the infantile level while they allow the development of *fardu kifāyah* knowledge to increase tremendously. In this way the amount of secular knowledge increases and develops in the Muslim's life out of proportion to the religious so that the Muslim spends most of his adult life knowing more about the world and less about religion. Thus we have weak Muslims and weak and dangerous leaders whose comprehension and knowledge of Islam is stunted at the level of immaturity; and because of this Islam itself is erroneously made to appear 'underdeveloped', 'malformed' or left to 'stagnate.'[9]

While al-Attas defines the problem in terms of the erroneous elevation of *fard al-kifāya* knowledge – namely knowledge of the secondary sciences or *furū'* – to the point where it overshadows the more important *fard al-'ayn* knowledge, which he describes elsewhere as the knowledge of God,[10] the Shi'ite writer Mohammad Yusufi reaches a similar conclusion by focusing on the tension between *īmān* and Islam:

> Most Muslims are Muslims by name, custom and geographical situation alone: they neither ponder nor contemplate, and their belief – which is the lowest form of belief – they take for granted and never

question. For the common Muslim (*musalman-i 'āmi*) a believer is one who prays and fasts and pays alms, and the more he does these things, the better believer he is seen to be. For the common Muslim, belief is static (*thābit*) whereas action ('*amal*) is dynamic (*qābil-i kam wa ziyād shudan*). In reality, of course, the reverse is true. The fact that the majority of '*ulamā* are jurists (*fuqahā*) reflects the ignorance of the majority of the Muslim masses and their obsession with the external acts (*a'mal-i zāhirī*) which they believe constitute faith. The *faqīh* is like a doctor who thinks he can cure his patients by advocating cleaner clothes, while disregarding the fact that beneath those clothes the body is crippled by a thousand and one chronic diseases. The *faqīh* reinforces the lay Muslim's false assumption that the latter is a believer and that it is now the time for action, since action is a true indicator of belief ... this leads him further into the clutches of the *faqīh*, whose speciality is action over and above belief, and so the circle completes itself...[11]

Yusufi goes on to state that the *faqīh*'s aversion to matters that concern solely 'the knowledge of the soul (*nafs*) and the real place of the created being (*khalq*) vis-à-vis the Creator (*khāliq*) stems from his fear of the reality of belief, in which man is answerable not to the *mullā* or to the imam but to God himself.'[12] In an ideal Islamic community, he asserts, 'the domain of the *faqīh* would shrink, since it would become clear to all that his true importance - namely as a *faqīh* - is much less than that which he has historically come to expect and demand.'[13]

Yet unless we place these issues in some form of concrete historical context, they will stay at the level of the purely abstract, and their importance for our perception of contemporary developments in the Muslim world will remain obscured. Pre-Safavid and Safavid Iran provides a perfect backdrop against which the internalist/externalist dichotomy and the rise of the faqih may be contextualised historically.

In the summer of the year 907/1501-02, the thirteen-year old Safavid leader Isma'il, entered the town of Tabriz and proclaimed himself Shah; his first royal order was that the Muslim call to prayer (*adhān*) should henceforth be: 'I profess that there is no god but Allah, that Muhammad is the messenger of Allah, and that Ali is the *walī* of Allah.'[14] Thus was the Twelver Shi'ism established as the state religion of Iran. Or was it?

This momentous event, which was to change the socio-political and religious face of Iran beyond recognition, prompts us to pose several important questions. Why was Twelver Shi'ism in particular chosen as the

47

new state religion, and to what extent was political expediency a factor in the new dynasty's choice? In the light of the internalist/externalist dichotomy, which particular 'face' of Twelver Shi'ism would be shown to the people and why? How widespread was Twelver Shi'ism in Iran before the advent of Isma'il, and to what extent, if any, did its presence in pre-Safavid Iran serve to facilitate its introduction as the new state religion? The last of these questions, tackled first, provides a suitable starting point. According to Seyyed Hossein Nasr, the ground had been well prepared for what he calls the 'sudden establishment of Shi'ism' and for the 'rapid change' that came about as a result. He cites several centuries of growth of Shi'ite theology and jurisprudence, the development of Sufi orders with Shi'ite tendencies, and the establishment of Shi'ite political regimes before the Safavid period as the main factors in the transformation of the country into a predominantly Shi'ite state.[15]

Although Nasr's contentions are in one sense not wholly unjustifiable, it would be misleading to see them as explanations of what he implies was a relatively smooth change in religious orientation. The statement 'Shi'ism became the state religion' – considered axiomatic by modern historians covering the Safavid era – is extremely vague, since it implies that Shi'ism is an easily definable, monolithic entity. Yet Shi'ism, like Islam itself, can be all things to all men, and it is difficult to discuss the politico-religious history of the Safavid era without qualifying the terms Shi'ism, Sufism and Islam. If by the term Shi'ism Nasr and other writers have in mind the kind of belief system institutionalised by the Twelver Shi'ite *fuqahā* at the end of the Safavid period – namely what may be termed 'orthodox, externalist Twelver Shi'ism' - then Nasr's argument concerning pre-Safavid Iran becomes even less tenable. Although orthodox Twelver Shi'ism did not enter a cultural vacuum when it was invited into Iran, it did, nevertheless, enter as something of an unknown entity. As Mazzaoui remarks, Shi'ism was so novel that even the celebrated historian Rumlu had to do some calculations with various dates in order to determine when he had last heard or read about it.[16]

Given this, the unintentionally misleading assertions of Hossein Nasr may be modified as follows. Firstly, whilst it is true that (orthodox) Twelver Shi'ite theology and jurisprudence enjoyed several centuries of growth prior to the Safavid era, their development was down primarily to the endeavours of Arab scholars operating well outside the Iranian sphere. Secondly, Sufism of all hues and varieties did flourish in pre-Safavid Iran, and much of it with pro-Alid tendencies; however, this should not be construed as a sign that it was pro-Shi'ite in the orthodox sense of the term. Thirdly, the 'Shi'ite political regimes' that Nasr mentions were for the most part transient phenomena, and their Shi'ism was either nominal or heterodox.

What, then, was the state of religion in general, and Shi'ism in particular, in pre-Safavid Iran? It is to this question that we now turn.

Twelver Shi'ism in the pre-Safavid era

By the middle of the $5^{th}/11^{th}$ century, the foundations of Twelver Shi'ite theology and jurisprudence had been laid, and it is from this juncture that we are able to speak of an 'orthodoxy': the 'four books' of Twelver Traditions – the cornerstone of Shi'ite *fiqh* and *hadīth* – had long since been compiled;[17] Shi'ite scholastic theology or *kalām* had been purged of the extremism (*ghuluww*) it had exhibited in its foetal stages and had moved nearer to the quasi-Mu'tazilite doctrines with which it has generally been associated ever since; and important steps had been taken to define the principles of Shi'ite jurisprudence (*usūl al-fiqh*) and to establish the theoretical basis for the status and functions of the *fuqahā*. These developments took place in various traditional centres of Twelver Shi'ism such as Qum, Baghdad and Najaf, and were carried out by Arab and Persian scholars alike. An illustrious quintet of men, three of whom hailed from Iran, was chiefly responsible for assembling together the bare bones of orthodox Twelver externalism which were to be fleshed out and elaborated upon by later generations: Muhammad al-Kulayni (d. 329/940-01); Muhammad al-Qummi, also known as Ibn Babuya (d. 381/991-02); Muhammad al-Tusi, known as Shaykh al-Ta'ifa (d. 460/1067-68); Shaykh Mufid (d. 413/1022-23); and 'Alam al-Huda (d. 436/1044-45). Kulayni, Ibn Babuya and Shaykh al-Ta'ifa are commonly referred to as the 'first three Muhammads' and are widely recognised in Twelver circles as the 'founding fathers' of orthodox Twelver Shi'ism.

From the beginning of the $4^{th}/10^{th}$ century until the middle of the $6^{th}/12^{th}$ century, the most important scholars of the Twelver Shi'ite world had been Persian, but towards the end of the Saljuq era a shift occurred and for the next four centuries or so until the end of the Safavid era, the most important scholars were to be Arabs, and the most important Twelver centres were to flourish outside Iran. A relatively reliable snapshot of the geographical spread of Twelver Shi'ism emerges from the results of a statistical analysis of the geographical origins of the Twelver scholars living and working during the period in question. From tables compiled to show the origins of Twelver scholars who died from the $4^{th}/10^{th}$ to the $12^{th}/18^{th}$ centuries it becomes apparent that the peak period for Persian scholars was the $6^{th}/12^{th}$ century.[18] From the $7^{th}/13^{th}$ century onwards, Arab scholars led the field and Twelver Shi'ism was centred mainly outside of Iran proper. Al-Ahsa, Jabal 'Amil, Bahrein and Hilla became - and remained - the most important centres of Twelver scholarship until towards the end of the Safavid period.

Hamdullah Mustawfi Qazwini's geographical work *Nuzhat al-qulūb*, written in 740/1339-40, gives a similar picture of the incidence of Twelver Shi'ism in Iran and Iraq. Out of 63 place-name entries in which the religious orientation of the inhabitants is mentioned, only 14 are predominantly Twelver Shi'ite.[19] The traditional Twelver centres in Iran such as Rayy, Sabziwar, Kashan, Qum and the northern crescent of Mazandaran and Gilan are the major enclaves of Twelver Shi'ism in the immediate pre-Safavid period. According to Mustawfi, most towns and villages across Iran adhered to either the Shafi'ite or Hanafite rites, although no school of jurisprudence had a monopoly on any one location. Interestingly enough, Mustawfi describes the Twelver Shi'ites in most of the towns where they constituted a majority as 'bigoted'.[20] Interaction between the Twelvers and the adherents of the Sunni schools seems to have centred largely on the question of the superiority of Ali over the first three Caliphs. In *Majālis al-mu'minīn*, Qadi Nurullah al-Shushtari, a staunch Twelver, mentions several incidents in which the adherents of Twelver Shi'ism are seen as endeavouring to score cheap points over their Sunni compatriots through mockery and name-calling.[21] At the same time, Shushtari goes to great lengths to prove that pre-Safavid Iran was predominantly Twelver Shi'ite, and that many celebrated scholars renowned as Sunnis were, in actual fact, Twelvers operating under the cloak of *taqīyya* or dissimulation. For Shushtari, even one line of verse in Rumi's *Mathnawī* praising the family of Muhammad is enough to convince him that the poet was a Twelver Shi'ite.[22]

However, the fact that when Isma'il entered Tabriz he was unable to find anything that had been written on the principal tenets of Twelver Shi'ism save for a single manuscript on Twelver jurisprudence in an obscure private library, supports the theory that pre-Safavid Iran was, from the point of view of *madhhab* at least, predominantly Sunni.[23] Not even in Kashan, known on account of its staunch Shi'ism as *dār al-mu'minīn* ('the abode of the believers'), could a competent Twelver *faqīh* be found for more than a decade.[24]

During the Mongol and Ilkhanid periods, when the leading Twelver scholars were well established outside Iran, orthodox Twelver Shi'ism did make inroads into Iran, although it ought to be pointed out that attempts made by Twelver scholars to spread their doctrines were aimed at individual rulers rather than at the masses. Despite the barbarity of the Mongol invasions and the havoc that descended upon the Muslim community as a result, the period of Mongol/Ilkhanid rule was marked by a surprising atmosphere of religious tolerance. The liberal-mindedness of the Ilkhanid rulers on matters of religion paved the way for vigorous public debates between adherents of different groups and schools of jurisprudence, more often than not in the presence of the rulers themselves. The scholar largely responsible for the attempt to spread Twelver Shi'ism during the Mongol period was Ibn al-Mutahhar (d. 726/1325-26), known as 'Allama Hilli, who converted the Mongol sultan Uljaytu Khudabanda (reigned 1304-16 AD). After a contest at the Sultan's court between the representatives of the various schools of jurisprudence, in which 'Allama Hilli reportedly gave a convincing account of Twelver doctrines, Uljaytu accepted Twelver Shi'ism and decreed that it be proclaimed the religion of the land.[25] Yet Hilli's success turned out to be short-lived, for the Sultan soon 'renounced the *rāfidī* views and wrote to his provinces demanding allegiance of the people to the views of the Sunna and the Community.'[26]

Now 'Allama Hilli was first and foremost an externalist, ranking as by far the most outstanding Twelver scholar of his day, and thus it is not surprising that for him, the *da'wa* or 'call to faith' that every believer is expected to undertake took place primarily on the level of Islam rather than on that of *īmān*. Rarely, if ever, do the historical sources show externalists conducting long debates with each other – or with potential converts – on the necessity of self-knowledge or divine gnosis.[27] Worth noting here is that for the Twelver Shi'ite, the conversion of non-Shi'ite Muslims to Shi'ism is of greater import than the conversion of non-Muslims to Islam. If the fundamentals of *īmān* matter at all to Twelver externalists, it is not the fundamentals which they share with the Sunnis that concern them but, rather, the fundamentals of Twelver Shi'ite belief. For Hilli, the most important religious issue was that of *imāma*, and it was this concern that informed his missionary activities. Hilli was chastised on this account by the Hanbali jurist Ibn Taymiyya (d. 728/1327-28), who declared that Hilli's statement to the effect that *imāma* is the most important element in religion 'is a lie by the unanimous agreement (*ijmā'*) of all Muslims, since belief (*īmān*) is the most important.'[28]

During the post-Ilkhanid period – the era of the 'successor states' – the relationship between orthodox Twelver Shi'ism and the ruling dynasties becomes more nebulous. Shi'ite sources claim that many of these dynasties – in particular the Chubanids, Jalayirids and the Qara-Qoyunlu – espoused Shi'ite views, although it is unclear to what extent they were using Shi'ism as leverage to force obedience from their subjects. What *is* clear, however, is that the brand of Shi'ism they professed was far from orthodox: the poetry of Jahan Shah Qara Qoyunlu, for example, exhibits the kind of pro-Shi'ite extremism or *ghuluww* that was prevalent in the area at that time.[29]

Orthodox Twelver scholars, however, continued Hilli's campaign to reintroduce Twelver Shi'ism into Iran via the ruling elites. Ahmad b. Fahd al-Hilli (d. 841/1437-38) notched up the same kind of success as his predecessor Ibn al-Mutahhar by winning over Ispand, brother of Jahan Shah and governor of Iraq from 836/1432-33 to 848/1444-45. Ispand's conversion was also the result of an inter-*madhhab* contest at his court in Baghdad, and Twelver Shi'ism was adopted as the provincial state religion. It is not clear how long this state of affairs continued, but it is doubtful that it extended much beyond Ispand's tenure of office.[30] Ibn Fahd was the teacher of Muhammad b. Falāh (d. 866/1461-2), known as Musha'sha', the founder of the Musha'sha'iyya movement in south-east Iran. The movement's religious views were of the *ghulāt* variety and were eventually denounced by Ibn Fahd, who himself is said to have inclined towards extremism.

Another heterodox Shi'ite movement that had connections with certain mainstream Twelver scholars was that of the Sarbidarids, a pro-Shi'ite Sufi order that existed in Khurasan from 738/1337-8.[31] The Sarbidarids were a series of rulers who established a 'state' in expectation of the reappearance of the Hidden Imam, al-Mahdi. The Sarbidarid episode is interesting because it concerns what was basically a Sufi order that turned into a pro-Shi'ite military movement in order to gain power and, as Mazzaoui puts it, 'impose justice through tyranny.'[32] The same combination of Sufism, Shi'ism and military muscle was later to be found in the Safavid order, which, two centuries later, was to sweep to power in Iran. The last Sarbidarid ruler, Ali Mu'ayyad (766-787/1364-86) wrote a letter to the renowned Twelver scholar Muhammad b. Makki al-'Amili, asking him to come from Damascus to Khurasan to assist in the establishment of Twelver Shi'ism. Ibn Makki was unable to make the journey since he was in prison awaiting the outcome of his trial – he had been accused of heresy – but wrote instead *al-Lum'at al-Dimashqiyya*, an important work on Twelver *fiqh*, and dispatched it to Ali Mu'ayyad with the latter's messenger.[33] The Sarbidarid ruler's desire to establish Twelver Shi'ite orthodoxy has been seen as an attempt to create stability by establishing an organized religious legal code rather than keep his state under the influence of the extremists who had initially brought the dynasty to power, but who were, towards the end of Mu'ayyad's reign, proving to be something of a political liability.[34] The Sarbidarid dynasty collapsed before the plan could be implemented.

When the Safavids came to power over a hundred years later they used a strategy identical to that of the Sarbidarids, and one wonders exactly to what extent they were influenced by the earlier experiment.

Ibn Makkī was the leading scholar of his day; that he had connections with a heterodox movement does not detract from the fact that he was externalist in outlook and an astute defender of the Twelver Shi'ite orthodoxy.[35] His opposition to extremism is beyond doubt, as is that of Ibn Fahd, who went on to denounce the Musha'sha'iyya movement. The fact that these scholars latched onto extremists may be seen as a desire on their part to disseminate orthodox Twelver Shi'ite teachings at any cost. After all, they must have realised that the imposition of their highly legalistic, externalist doctrines would have acted as a natural neutralizer of extremist tendencies. Ibn Fahd and Ibn Makki, together with 'Allama Hilli, constitute what Mazzaoui calls the 'missing link' between the 'three early Muhammads' and the 'three later Muhammads' at the end of the Safavid era.[36]

Sufism and pro-Shi'ite extremism (*ghuluww*)

The main obstacle to the introduction and establishment of orthodox Twelver Shi'ism in Iran during the Mongol and Ilkhanid periods was the existence there of two potent forces that had already captured the intellectual and emotional allegiance of the vast majority of people, namely pro-Shi'ite extremism or *ghuluww*, and Sufism. The *laissez-faire* approach of the Mongol rulers to religion created an atmosphere in which all kinds of religious orientation were able to flourish, and from the end of the $6^{th}/12^{th}$ century there was a veritable explosion of Sufi and quasi-Sufi orders and movements, some orthodox and some extremist but nearly all of them with characteristics that have led them to be labelled pro-Shi'ite.

Sufism

To define the terms Sufi and Sufism, to chart the historical development of the phenomenon, and to describe the doctrines of the myriad Sufi groups, orders and individuals is clearly beyond the scope of the present work; on questions of doctrine, the reader is best served by any of a number of standard works on Sufi beliefs and practices.[37]

Trimingham aptly describes early Sufism as a 'natural interiorization of

Islam.'[38] It was:

> ... An assertion of a person's rights to pursue a life of contemplation, seeking contact with the source of being and reality, over against institutionalised religion based on authority, a one way Master-slave relationship, with its emphasis upon ritual observance and legal morality.[39]

According to Trimingham, we should see the early Sufi as one who recognises that true knowledge (*'ilm*) is knowledge of God (*ma'rifa*), which in turn can be reached only through the acquisition of self-knowledge (*ma'rifat al-nafs*);[40] furthermore, the emphasis for the Sufi is on *īmān* rather than on external religion (Islam). As such, it was in the early Sufi that internalism found its particular embodiment and expression. External religion was not eschewed, however: one of the most salient features of early Sufi teaching was its emphasis on adherence to the *sharī'a*, the channel through which Islam becomes manifest.[41] Early Sufism, then, preserved the harmony which is held to exist between the internalist and externalist aspects of the faith.

The designation 'early Sufism' is an important one, for with the passing of time the phenomenon underwent many changes: from being a term used simply to describe an individual's sincere and private internalism, Sufism became a blanket expression which covered many different forms of organised 'ways' and 'paths' to the truth. The gradual institutionalization of Sufism is described by Trimingham as having taken place in three stages: from the stage of the individual's personal submission to God, through the stage of communal surrender to the dictates of an Order (*tarīqa*), and finally to the stage of surrender to a person, or what Trimingham calls the *tā'ifa* stage.[42] In institutionalization lay the seeds of decay. As Trimingham puts it:

> Through the cult-mysticism of the orders the individual creative freedom of the mystic was fettered and subjected to conformity and collective experience. Guidance under the earliest masters had not compromised the spiritual liberty of the seeker, but the final phase involving subjection to the arbitrary will of the shaykh turned him into a spiritual slave, and not to God, but to a human being, even though one of God's elect.[43]

The spread of the Sufi orders across the Muslim world, especially during the Mongol and Ilkhanid eras, and the interaction of diverse cultural and religious traditions meant that innovative practices crept in, working at variance with the original aim of Sufism and creating sects and orders that were totally removed from the purely internalist spirit of the early adepts. It is for this reason that we are able to identify two kinds of Sufism: mainstream or 'high' Sufism, which remained more or less faithful to the ideals of the early Sufis and was typified by highly orthodox Sunni Orders such as the Mawlawiyya, centred in Anatolia, and the Naqshbandiyya, centred in Transoxania; and corrupted or 'folk' Sufism, present in Orders such as the Bektashiyya and the Hurufiyya, whose practices were highly questionable not only in the eyes of the externalists but also in the view of the 'high' Sufi adepts themselves. More will be said about these presently.

Sufism had existed in Iran from the earliest times; al-Maqdisi, writing in 365/975-76, says that in Shiraz, 'Sufis were numerous, performing the *dhikr* in their mosques after the Friday prayer and reciting blessings on the Prophet from the pulpit.'[44] During the Mongol and Ilkhanid eras, Sufis were still numerous, only now they had become institutionalized into Orders and were spread out over the whole country. Orders such as the Kubrawiyya, the Naqshbandiyya, the Nurbakhshiyya and the Safawiyya – not to mention a whole host of offshoot groupings and sub-sects – flourished openly and commanded the spiritual allegiance of vast numbers of people, educated and uneducated alike.[45] Indeed, to see Sufism as some kind of exotic mysticism confined to a few ecstatic Sufis who found themselves at cross-purposes with their fellow Muslims and who uttered strange sayings from time to time is, in fact, to ignore just how commonplace Sufism was in traditional Muslim society. Very often, tens of thousands of individuals were affiliated in some way or other to an Order in any one of the great cities. When Shah Ni'matullah, the founder of the Sufi order of the same name, visited Shiraz, over 30,000 people are reputed to have paid allegiance to him.[46] Describing the northern provinces of Iran as they were in the post-Mongol period, the Iranian scholar 'Abbas Iqbal writes:

At the end of the reign of Sultan Sa'id, the number of gnostics, Sufis and dervishes in Azarbaijan, Gilan and Mazanderan increased greatly: it reached the point where every district had a *shaykh* with his own group of disciples. Since Sultan Abu Sa'id did not allow anyone to harm these groups, they were left alone and no-one objected to them. Day by day the number of disciples increased. The majority of these belonged to the *ahl-i futuwwa* or the *ahl-i ukhuwwa*: these were a group of ordinary Sufis who endeavoured to spread the exalted principles of Sufism and gnosis (*'irfān*) among the masses, and by refining their own moral characters and strengthening the foundations of spiritual purity and brotherly love that existed between them, reap the benefits of their endeavours. These groups had established numerous *khāngāh, zawāyā* and Sufi hospices throughout the whole Islamic world thanks to the Caliph Nasir al-din, who had supported them. The commander of the Faithful, Ali b. Abi Talib was their spiritual patron, considered by them to be the supreme example of *futuwwa* and *ukhuwwa*. From the point of view of *madhhab*, they were without prejudice or fanaticism, they refrained from harming, killing and stealing from each other but strove to preserve manly morals and characteristics.[47]

The fact that Ali is held in particular esteem by the groups mentioned above does not suggest necessarily that they were in any sense of the term 'orthodox Twelvers.' Ali and the family of the Prophet have been revered by Sunnis and Shi'ites alike since the early days of Islam. The fact that most of the famous Sufi orders trace their line of spiritual descent back to Ali - often via other Imams - yet were Sunni as far as *madhhab* is concerned shows that devotion to the family of the Prophet and the 'house of Ali' is by no means a sure indicator of Shi'ism or proto-Shi'ism. For the Naqshbandiyya, a purely Sunni order, all twelve Imams are deserving of reverence and are even capable of functioning posthumously as spiritual guides.[48] Among the Sunnis, the Hanafites and the Shafi'ites have always been renowned for their devotion to the '*ahl al-bayt*' of the prophet, and since it was these two schools of jurisprudence which formed the majority in Iran during the period in question, the widespread nature of pro-Alid - but not pro-Shi'ite *per se* - tendencies is hardly surprising.[49] Similar expressions of devotion to the *ahl al-bayt* of Muhammad can be found among the Kubrawiyya, whose Sunnism is not open to doubt: Najm al-din Razi Daya, one of the leaders of the Order, chose Saljuq Anatolia partly on account of the supremacy there of Sunnism.[50] The Sunnism of the Ni'matullahiyya was also beyond question, as was that of the early Safawiyya, the Order which was to evolve into the Safavid dynasty. In this light, Hossein Nasr's assertion that the introduction of orthodox Twelver Shi'ism was facilitated by Sufi groups with Shi'ite leanings is dubious; even those Orders which did become openly pro-Shi'ite at the end of the period in question, such as the Nurbakhshiyya, did not become orthodox Twelver Shi'ites – at least not in the sense understood by those Twelver externalists operating in centres outside Iran who were later to bring their doctrines into the country and work actively for the suppression of Sufi brotherhoods, the Nurbakhshiyya being no exception.

Extremism or 'ghuluww'

The *ghulāt* (sing. *ghālī*) may be defined as those who were nominally Muslim but who ascribed to doctrines heretical enough to place them outside the pale of Islam. Beliefs such as *tashbīh* (anthropomorphism with respect to God), *tanāsukh* (transmigration of souls) and *hulūl* (Divine incarnation in man) formed the core of early *ghuluww*, which has existed since the initial spread of Islam itself. It is with Shi'ism in particular that *ghuluww* has traditionally been associated, its most salient feature in this respect being the extreme veneration of the Imams – Ali in particular – which has often manifested itself in the attribution of divine powers to both him and his progeny. Such doctrines were current during the lifetimes of the Imams themselves, and it is not until the establishment of the Twelver Shi'ite orthodoxy in the 4th/10th century that Shi'ite *ghuluww*, at least in its most extreme forms, was disowned by the majority of Twelver Shi'ite *'ulamā.*[51]

The Mongol and Ilkhanid periods, and particularly the latter half of the 9th/15th century, saw the flourishing of *ghuluww*-inspired popular movements in the Muslim world. The *ghulāt* were especially widespread in north-western Iran and Anatolia, which had experienced a massive influx of Turcoman nomadic tribes as a result of the Mongol invasions and earlier Saljuq tribal policy. The conversion of these tribes to Islam was for the most part nominal, and old shamanistic beliefs continued to dominate their religion. Like the early Shi'ite *ghulāt*, extremist groups of the immediate pre-Safavid period centred around Ali and the Mahdi (the Hidden Imam) in particular. Where the later groups differed, however, was in their crystallization into quasi-Sufi, militant movements that spearheaded various popular, anti-establishment revolts, culminating in the rise to power of the Safavids at the end of the 9th/15th century. As Trimingham observes:

> Sufi organisations tended to absorb popular movements since this was the only way whereby the ideals for which such movements of the spirit stood could survive.[52]

The 'coming-out' of Sufism, which went hand-in-hand with the decline of orthodox religion (both Sunni and Shi'ite), and the corruption of much of it into what Nadvi calls 'pirism', may be seen as crucial factors in the formation and spread of the *ghulāt* during this period: certain Sufi orders – notably the Yasawiyya of Anatolia – were already treading the road to open heterodoxy as a result of over-institutionalization, and the absorption of certain features of *ghuluww* would not have been difficult to achieve. The

Bektashiyya are a good example of the kind of admixture of folk-Sufism and pro-Alid *ghuluww* that was current in the area during the 14th and 15th centuries.[53] Extremist movements such as the Musha'sha' have already been mentioned, and reference will be made to other important groups further on.

Despite its appearance, to talk of *ghuluww* in terms of internalism and externalism is not possible. As far as *īmān* is concerned, the *ghulāt* cannot be classed as believers in the internalist sense of the word since their preoccupation is with the created rather than the Creator: the cult figure of Ali and the Imams are substituted for – or joined in partnership with – God. As far as externalism is concerned, the *ghulāt* were nominally Muslim yet rarely – if ever – obeyed the dictates of the *sharī'a*.[54] Thus the devotion of the *ghulāt* to the Imams should not be interpreted as a manifestation of Shi'ism in the orthodox sense, namely the kind of Twelver Shi'ism that flourished in the hands of the externalist *fuqahā* outside the Iranian sphere. Nor should the mistake be made of associating all Sufi Orders with *ghulāt* extremism: the fact that a group such as the Mawlawiyya in Anatolia was accepted by the Sunni establishment and was particularly vociferous in its condemnation of the *ghuluww*-inspired revolt of the Baba'i sect in the mid-7th/13th century confirms the existence of two basic trends in Sufi activity: the orthodox – Sunni - mainstream or 'high' Sufism of groups such as the Mawlawiyya; and the *ghulāt*- or folk-Sufism typified by groups such as the Bektashiyya and, later on, the Qizilbash supporters of the Safavids. It may be misleading to describe the second group as Sufis in the strict sense of the word, since compliance with the tenets of the *sharī'a* is a prerequisite not only of being Muslim in general but also of being Sufi in particular. To understand further the interaction of Sufism and *ghulāt* extremism, we now turn to the hybrid *par excellence* of those two currents: the Safavid movement.

The rise of the Safavids

A major paradox in Iranian religious history is the fact that what has been the state religion of the country for the past five centuries, namely Shi'ism with a predominantly externalist flavour, was imposed upon the largely Sunni population by a leader who was neither Shi'ite by name nor externalist by outlook. Nor, strictly speaking, were the Safavids Persian, although the precise geographical origins of the dynasty have yet to be traced conclusively.[55]

What was eventually to become a monarchical dynasty with externalist

Twelver Shi'ism as its religious buttress began as a Sufi *tarīqa* in the town of Ardabil in Azarbaijan at the beginning of the 8th century AH. Its founder, Shaykh Safi (d. 735/1334-35) was initiated into Sufism at the hands of Shaykh Taj al-din Ibrahim Zahidi (d. 700/1300-01), a *murshid* of Gilan whose daughter Shaykh Safi married. After the death of his father-in-law and mentor, Shaykh Safi became the head of the *tarīqa*, which was renamed Safawiyya, or the Safavid Order.

The main source of information concerning Shakh Safi, namely the *Safwat al-safā* of Ibn al-Bazzaz, portrays Shakh Safi as a man of great learning, wisdom, piety and popularity.[56] The Safavid Order was highly respected by the political authorities of Shaykh Safi's day and also during the leadership of his three immediate successors, Sadr al-din (d. 795-96/1393), Khwaja Ali (d. 832-33/1429) and Shaykh Ibrahim (d. 851/1447-8). The Ilkhanids and their chief ministers paid homage to Shaykh Safi, as did the Jalayirids to Sadr al-din and the Taymurids to Khwaja Ali.[57]

The reverence shown to the Order by the rulers of the day serves to highlight the general atmosphere of religious tolerance prevalent in pre-Safavid Iran: internalism, so long as it remained apolitical, was allowed to flourish and was even actively encouraged. The absence of any political threat from the early Safavid leaders is a reflection of their orthodoxy, both as Sunnis and as adherents of mainstream Sufism. According to Mustawfi, during the time of Shaykh Safi most of the population of Ardabil belonged to the Shafi'ite school of jurisprudence and were followers of Shaykh Safi.[58] It is said that in his entire life, Shaykh Safi 'followed the *sharī'a* to such an extent that in both word and deed he did not deviate from it by as much as a hair's breadth.'[59] The early *tarīqa* prized itself on its abstention from any inter-*madhhab* squabbling, preferring to follow those Traditions with the strongest chains of authority from the four schools of Sunnism.[60] As far as externals are concerned, then, Shaykh Safi was staunchly orthodox: this explains partly why the *tarīqa* did not present any political threat, since any kind of open opposition to the ruling power is anathema to mainstream Sunnism. Shaykh Safi's internalist leanings were mainstream Sufi, his spiritual pedigree stretching back to Ali and Muhammad through a long chain of Sufi leaders which includes such luminaries as Abu Najib al-Suhrawardi and Hasan al-Basri;[61] he was also versed in the works of the Persian Sufi poets Rumi and 'Attar. Mainstream or 'high' Sufism, in contrast with folk-Sufism or *ghulāt* extremism, does not encourage or condone overt political or militant opposition to the ruling regime: this also helps to explain the fact that dynasty after dynasty was able to accommodate and even revere the Safavid order and its leaders.

Shaykh Safi was succeeded by his son, grandson and great-grandson, each of whom maintained the *tarīqa* in much the same orientation and enjoyed the respect of the Jalayirid and Taymurid rulers. By the end of the leadership of Shaykh Ibrahim, the popularity and influence of the Safavid order had increased to such an extent that its leaders were able to act as intermediaries between political rulers and their opponents.[62] Their Order gained countless more devotees on account of the role it played as a safe haven from the political turmoil of post-Mongol Iran. Under the first four leaders of the Order, all indications are that the Safavids were an important conduit for the spread of internalist, Sufi doctrines in Azarbaijan, Khurasan and Anatolia. Neither Twelver Shi'ism nor *ghuluww* seems to have played any part in the Order's doctrines, and as Minorsky asserts:

> The Lords of Ardabil are highly respected shaykhs, leading a contemplative life, spending their time in prayers and fasting, and credited with supernatural powers.[63]

With the succession of Shaykh Junayd (d. 864/1459-60) in 851/1447-48, the Order underwent a momentous transformation, one which is not easy to explain and on which the sources of the time offer little help. The change in religious orientation was dramatic: contemplative, internalist Sufism gave way to openly heterodox *ghuluww*. Ibn Ruzbihan Khunji, the Sunni writer at the court of Sultan Ya'qub, son of Uzun Hasan Aq-Qoyunlu, states that the followers of the Order 'openly called Shaykh Junayd God (*ilāh*), and his son "Son of God" (*ibn Allāh*) ... in his praise they said, "he is the Living One, there is no God but he." Their folly and ignorance were such that, if someone spoke of Shaykh Junayd as dead, he was no more to enjoy the sweet beverage of life.'[64] Junayd's son, Haydar, was also revered as divine; according to Khunji, people came from far and wide to prostrate themselves at Haydar's feet, worshipping him as their god and neglecting the duties of the *sharī'a*.[65]

The transformation of the Safavids from an orthodox Sunni/Sufi Order into a sect which espoused the open heresy of pro-Alid *ghuluww* cannot be explained adequately in terms of a simple reorientation of religious belief. The sudden and dramatic *volte-face* was accompanied by a radical change in the Order's political leanings, transforming it into a militant movement which, in less than half a century, grew in intensity and ambition to the point where it was able to put Junayd's grandson Isma'il on the throne at Tabriz. In short, the religious change must be seen in the light of the political change, the conclusion being that the religious change was no more than a pretext for the political ambitions of Shaykh Junayd. Although history is littered with examples of religion being used for political ends, the case of Shaykh Junayd stands out particularly since it represents the very first in a series of steps that led to the creation of the Safavid state and, by extension, the establishment of externalist Twelver Shi'ism as the state religion. It is perfectly conceivable that had Junayd not made his momentous career move, the Order would have remained orthodox – in both the Sufi and Sunni sense – and, as a result, Shi'ism might never have been reintroduced into the bloodstream of Iranian history.

Junayd became the leader of the Safavid Order just a few months after the death of the last great Taymurid ruler, Shahrukh (d.850/1446-7). With the latter's demise, the political *status quo* in Iran and Transoxania was disrupted and the stage left open for the rival Aq-Qoyunlu and Qara-Qoyunlu dynasties to vie for overall power. It appears that it was at this point in time that Junayd began to nurture serious political ambitions, for as Khunji writes:

> When the boon of succession reached Junayd, he altered the way of life of his ancestors: The bird of anxiety laid an egg of longing for power in the nest of his imagination. Every moment he strove to conquer a land or a region. When his father Kwaja Shaykh-Shah (Ibrahim) departed, Junayd for some reason or other had to leave the country.[66]

Junayd was in fact expelled from Ardabil on the orders of the Qara-Qoyunlu leader Jahan Shah. The Ottoman historian Ashıkpashazade writes that Junayd's aspirations centred on nothing less than royal succession in Azarbaijan (and, by extension, in Iran proper), thus presenting the Qara-Qoyunlu leadership with an open threat. It was at this juncture that Junayd began to claim descent from Ali, stating that his (Junayd's) descendants had more right to rule the Islamic community than even the companions of the Prophet.[67]

From Ardabil, Junayd travelled through Anatolia to Konya, where he began to publicize widely his claims to Alid lineage. It appears that he also engaged in the dissemination of extreme Shi'ite doctrines, a move which angered both the ruler and the 'ulamā of Konya, who promptly had Junayd expelled from the city.[68] Junayd moved on to the town of Jabal Musa in northern Syria, where extremist Hurufi doctrines enjoyed considerable influence and popularity. In 861/1456-57, Junayd led his followers, formed by this time into a band of raiders (*ghuzāt*), in a campaign against the

Christian enclave at Trabzon. Eventually he settled in Diyarbakir, where he was warmly received by the Aq-Qoyunlu ruler, Uzun Hasan.[69]

The religious background of Junayd's followers is of considerable significance if we are to understand why Junayd changed his own religious orientation after the death of his father. The confused and unstable political atmosphere in the Ottoman empire that obtained after the disintegration of the Rum Saljuq state, together with the huge influx of Turco-Mongolian tribes – with their dubious religious doctrines – who were pushed westwards by conquerors from the east, had turned Anatolia into a place where all kinds of religious heterodoxy could flourish. Pro-Alid extremism was widespread, and there was a history of anti-establishment rebellion led by charismatic individuals with marked Twelver sympathies. Two notable uprisings were those of Baba Rasulallah Ishaq against the Saljuqs around 639/1240-41, and that of Badr al-din Samawna in 819/1416-17: although separated by almost two centuries, both were expressions of discontent, fuelled by extreme pro-Shi'ite doctrines and directed against the Sunni rulers of the time.[70] The ideological and political incompatibility of *ghuluww* and internalism can be seen in the fact that the earlier Baba'i revolt was opposed by the followers of Jalal al-din Rumi and his Mawlawiyya (or Mevlevi) Order.[71] As for Badr al-din, although his revolt was crushed, his teachings lived on among the Turcomans of Anatolia, some of whom were later to take up the cause of sects such as the Bektashis and the Safavids. The Bektashis were another heterodox group which enjoyed great influence in the region; its enigmatic leader, Hajj Bektash, drew heavily on the teachings of Baba Ishaq. According to Tschudi, the Bektashis 'are Shi'is, acknowledging the Twelve Imams ... the centre of their worship is Ali; they unite Ali with Allah and Muhammad into a trinity.'[72]

It was to this hotbed of religious heterodoxy that Junayd turned to seek support for his embryonic political and military ambitions. The unsettled Turkish tribes of rural Anatolia, with their history of anti-state militancy and their quasi-egalitarian religious extremism, would be ideal *ghāzi* material for the ambitious Junayd. Naturally, to secure their allegiance he would have to forsake the quietistic internalism of his mainstream Sufi and Sunni background, espousing in its place the extremist cause: this explains his claims to Alid descent. As Minorsky observes:

> It is possible that having discovered Shi'ite leanings among the Anatolians, he felt that a wider scope for his enterprise would open, with his own move in the same direction.[73]

Furthermore, Junayd's aspiration to 'royal' succession was enhanced considerably by his marriage to Uzun Hasan's sister. The Safavid leaders thereafter became 'princes of the land', and Junayd's marriage 'became known even in the farthest corners of Rum and Syria.'[74] With this judicious move, Junayd combined what the Iranian scholar Falsafi calls 'spiritual sultanate' (*saltanat-i ma'nawī*) with 'external sultanate' *saltanat-i suwarī*.[75] It was on this basis that he was able to lead his followers on raids and *jihād*, and to exchange the epithet of *shaykh* for that of *sultān*.[76]

Under the leadership of Junayd's son, Haydar, the Safavid Order became crystallized as a political movement with an increasingly extremist religious colouring. Having inherited his father's title as a mere babe-in-arms,[77] Haydar's education and upbringing became the collective responsibility of the *khulafā*, men who were drawn from among the Order's tribal following and who acted as a powerful link between the Safavid leadership and those tribes and clans which owed it allegiance.[78] The *khulafā* constituted what amounts to an informal regency council, whose duty was to take care of the spiritual, military and political responsibilities of the new heir.[79] The rise of the *khulafā* led the Order even further away from its orthodox religious roots; as Khunji remarks, 'they foolishly announced the glad tidings of (Haydar's) divinity ... they considered him as their god and, neglecting the duties of *namāz* and public prayers, looked upon the Shaykh as their *qibla*.'[80] Haydar's followers became known as the Qizilbash ('red-heads'), so called because of the red twelve-pointed cap which Haydar instructed them to wear.

Haydar had been installed in Ardabil in 874/1469-70 by his maternal uncle, Uzun Hasan, who had defeated Jahan Shah and the Qara-Qoyunulu dynasty and established authority over its former domains. The return of the Safavid Order to Ardabil prompted an influx of the movement's followers from eastern Anatolia and northern Syria. Haydar's ties with the Aq-Qoyunlu dynasty were strengthened further by his marriage to Uzun Hasan's daughter.

The end of Uzun Hasan's long and relatively stable reign saw the political situation in Iran take a downward course: Iran gradually degenerated into an arena of rivalry between the many princes, tribal chiefs and military commanders which comprised the Aq-Qoyunlu federation. Haydar's Qizilbash followers exploited the situation inside Iran to their own advantage, and his leadership was marked by extensive *ghāzi* activity against the 'infidels' of the Caucusus.[81] Uzun Hasan's son, Sultan Ya'qub, maintained cordial relations with the Safavids for as long as he could, although the increasingly militant and religiously extremist nature of the

Qizilbash forced him to order Haydar to cease military activity. Ignoring the warnings, Haydar marched on Darband in 893/1487-8; on his way he encroached upon the territory of Sultan Ya'qub's ally, the Shirvanshah: a battle ensued and the forces of the Shirvanshah, backed with reinforcements sent on the orders of Sultan Ya'qub, inflicted a crushing defeat upon the Qizilbash. Haydar was slain and his three eldest sons, Ali, Isma'il and Ibrahim were banished to Fars.

After the death of Sultan Ya'qub in 896/1490-91, the political situation deteriorated even further as a result of the bloody rivalry of the Aq-Qoyunlu princes. Sultan Ya'qub's son, Baysunqur (896-98/1490-93) was challenged by his cousin, Rustam, and fled to Shirvan for support from his ally, the Shirvanshah. Thus it was that Haydar's three sons were released. The eldest, Ali, was established as *padishāh* at Ardabil. However, Rustam felt threatened by the Qizilbash presence and finally deemed it necessary to eliminate his new ally altogether. Ali was duly assassinated and the Safavid Order, now totally in the hands of the *khulafā*, sought refuge in Lahijan at the court of the Zaydi ruler of Gilan, Karkiya Mirza Ali (883-910/1478-1505). It was there that Isma'il, still only a child, was groomed for his future role as active leader of the Order.

In Muharram 905/August-September 1499, Isma'il left Lahijan for Ardabil, accompanied by seven of the most influential members of his entourage.[82] Ordered to leave Ardabil by its governor, Isma'il and his retinue retired to Arjuwan on the Caspian coast. Meanwhile, his *khulafā* sent orders to Isma'il's followers in Anatolia and Syria to converge upon Erzincan come the following spring. Sources relate that 7000 followers drawn from the Turcoman tribes that formed the core of the Qizilbash rallied to the young leader's side.[83] From Erzincan the Qizilbash marched to Shirvan, where Isma'il was able to avenge his father's death by defeating Farukh Yasar. Consequently, the Aq-Qoyunlu ruler of Azarbaijan, Prince Alwand, advanced to Nakhchivan and prepared to meet a potential Safavid attack. The confrontation which followed resulted in an overwhelming victory for the Qizilbash. With the road to Tabriz now open, the Qizilbash entered the Aq-Qoyunlu capital and Isma'il proclaimed himself *shāh*. By 914/1508-09, when Isma'il succeeded in taking Baghdad, the whole country was more or less under his sway.[84]

In short, the Safavid Order began as an orthodox Sunni-Sufi *tarīqa* and under its first four leaders commanded the respect and reverence of rulers and masses alike. Totally in keeping with its mainstream religious internalism, the Order was politically quietistic and harboured no aspirations to temporal power or kingship. With the advent of Junayd, however, the

Order was transformed into a military organisation with a markedly extremist, pro-Shi'ite religious orientation. Under Haydar, the Order increased its military activity until it was possible, with the support of the fanatical and ultra-heterodox Qizilbash, to install Isma'il on the throne at Tabriz. In less than half a century, the Safavid brotherhood underwent a politico-religious metamorphosis that was eventually to change the face of Iran completely.

Shah Isma'il came to power at a time when Iran was dominated by two main religious currents: mainstream or 'high' Sufism; and *ghuluww* or extremist folk-Sufism with a strong Shi'ite flavour. The spirit of internalism lived on during this period in the form of the orthodox Sunni Sufi orders, of which the Safavids were, in their earlier stages, a prime example. From Anatolia through Iran and into Transoxania, 'high' Sufi orders such as the Mawlawiyya, the Ni'matullihiyya and the Naqshbandiyya were the main channels of internalist expression. Devotion to the family of Ali was as evident in these Orders as it was elsewhere, but this cannot be construed as *tashayyu'-i hasan* or 'moderate Shi'ism' as some writers have claimed.[85]

Ghuluww came in the form of popular movements and quasi-Sufi orders with highly unorthodox and even heretical beliefs, concerning in particular the Shi'ite Imams. Unlike the 'high' Sufis, the *ghulāt* seem to have deemed the *sharī'a* in abeyance, and its laws and ordinances largely went unheeded. Undisciplined religiosity – neither internalist nor externalist – allowed political and military ambition to run riot, and it was largely thanks to *ghulāt* agitation that the popular anti-establishment revolts of the time took place.

In the externalist sense, the majority of the Iranian populace was Sunni, adhering to the Shafi'ite or Hanafite schools of jurisprudence. The rise of Sufism in general and *ghuluww* in particular had gone hand-in-hand with a decline in orthodox religious externalism, although the adherents of the 'high' Sufi orders and groups such as the *ahl-i futuwwa* and *ahl-i ukhuwwa* endeavoured to remain faithful to their (Sunni) doctrines and to observe both internalist and externalist aspects of their religion. Orthodox Twelver Shi'ism, as we have already seen, had developed throughout the period largely outside Iran. Occasionally it re-entered Iran in the form of missionary activity carried out by Twelver jurists to promote their doctrines at the courts of various rulers. Apart from this, the orthodox Twelver Shi'ism of the *fuqahā* had made little impression upon the Iranian people. However, it was to this orthodoxy that the young Isma'il and his advisors were to look in order to calm and stabilize their infant state. It is to the arrival of the new orthodoxy and its interaction with the religious currents already prevalent in Iran that we now turn.

Notes

1. Both man's indifference to the 'signs of God' and the fact that most do not have a knowledge-based belief in the Creator are referred to many times in the Koran. For example, the phrase "Verily in this is a sign: but most of them do not believe" is used no less than eight times in Sura 26 (verses 8, 68,103, 121, 139, 158, 174 and 190). One of the most striking Koranic references to deficiency in belief comes in verse 12:106 – "And most of them believe not in God without associating (others as partners with Him!)"

2. The most salient example is the earlier mentioned Banu Asad verse, 49:14.

3. Victor Danner (with W.M. Thackston), *Ibn 'Ata'illah: The Book of Wisdom – Khwaja Abdullah Ansari: Intimate Conversations* (London: SPCK, 1979), p. 6.

4. Nurullah Shushtari, *Majālis al-mu'minīn* (Tehran: Kitabfurushi-Islamiyya, 1375-6/1955-57), vol. 2, p. 52.

5. Mulla Sadra Shirazi, *Tafsīr sūrat al-wāqi'a* (Tehran: Intisharat-i Mawla, 1404/1983), p. 127.

6. Muhammad Taqi Danishpazhuh (ed.), *Fihrist-i kitābkhāna-i ihdā'ī-i Āqā-i Mishkāt bi kitābkhāna-i dānishgāh-i Tihrān* (Tehran: Intisharat-i Danishgah-i Tihran, 1330-1338 Sh.1951-60), vol. 2, p. 608. This work will henceforth be referred to as: Danishpazhuh, *Fihrist*.

7. For an illuminating exposition of the Koranic concept of *hidāya* or guidance, see: Daud Rahbar, *God of Justice: A study in the Ethical Doctrine of the Koran* (Leiden, 1960), pp. 91-6.

8. The difference in approach between externalist and internalist scholars may be exemplified by comparing two radically different interpretations of a single Koranic verse such as 56:79, in which it is stated that the Koran is a book 'which none shall touch but those who are clean.' In Islamic jurisprudence, the realm of the externalist, this verse provides the scriptural basis for the rule which decrees that anyone in a state of ritual impurity may neither touch nor recite the verses of the Koran. However, the internalist interpretation given by Mulla Sadra embraces the assertion that the 'cleanliness' (*tahāra*) mentioned in the verse refers to the purity of heart that is needed before anyone can attempt to acquire knowledge of self and of God. See Sadra's *Sih Asl* (Tehran: Intisharat-i Mawla, 1365 Sh./1986-87), p. 105. Since the two interpretations are not contradictory, there is nothing to suggest that they cannot be posited at the same time; indeed, Ghazali, who probably did more than any other scholar to harmonize the internalist and externalist approaches, warns of the danger of favouring one interpretation over the other when both are equally valid. Mulla Sadra is adamant, however, that his internalist interpretation mirrors directly the true meaning of the verse, and that it is not bodily uncleanliness which prevent man from approaching the Koran but rather the 'filth of unbelief.' (*Sih Asl*, p. 105.) Sadra's rejection of the externalist interpretation of this verse does not mean that he was in any way opposed to the derivation of legal principles from the text of the Koran; his argument should be understood in the overall context of *Sih Asl* (See Chapter 3), which is vehemently anti-externalist but not anti-*fiqh*. The general impression given by Sadra is that rules of jurisprudence

can be understood only inferentially from the Koran, thus leaving all verses open to numerous interpretations. Examples in which internalist exegesis blatantly contradicts externalist interpretation do occur, such as Ibn al-'Arabi's notorious passage on the prophet Noah in his *Fusūs al-hikam*. Generally speaking, however, there is usually room to accommodate both internalist and externalist readings.

9. Al-Attas, *Islam, Secularism and the Philosophy of the Future*, pp. 112-3.

10. *ibid.*, pp. 77-9.

11. M.K. Yusufi, *Surūr al-'ārifīn* (Tehran, n.d.), pp. 3-4.

12. *ibid.*, p. 4.

13. *ibid.*, p.5.

14. The date of Shah Isma'il's coronation at Tabriz is still a matter of some controversy. Khwandamir puts the date as 906/1500-01, while Rumlu reports the accession among the events of 907/1501-02. The latter is the date most commonly accepted by modern historians. See Ghiyath al-din Khwandamir, *Habīb al-siyyar fī akhbār afrād al-bashar* (Tehran, 1333 Sh./1954-55), vol. 4, p. 467; Hasan Rumlu, *Ahsan al-tawārīkh: A Chronicle of the early Safavids*, ed. and transl. by C.N. Seddon (Baroda, 1931-4), vol. 2, pp. 25-6 and for the later historians: Ghulam Sarwar, *History of Shah Isma'il Safavi* (Aligarh, 1939), pp. 38-9.

15. See Nasr's article entitled 'Religion in Safavid Persia' in *Iranian Studies*, vol. 7 (Winter/Spring 1974), pp. 271-86, especially pp. 271-73. For a detailed account of the historical events which attended the rise of the Safavids, in particular their relationship with the Aq-Qoyunlu and Qara-Qoyunlu leaders, see: Walther Hinz, *Irans Aufstieg zum Nationalstaat im fünfzehnten Jahrhundert* (Berlin/Leipzig, 1936).

16. Michael M. Mazzaoui, *The Origins of the Safavids* (Wiesbaden, 1972), p.2.

17. For a brief history of early Twelver Shi'ism and the role played by the 'founding fathers' in the development of its doctrines, see: Moojan Momen, *An Introduction to Shi'i Islam: The History and Doctrines of Twelver Shi'ism* (New Haven: Yale University Press, 1985), pp. 61-91.

18. *ibid.*, pp. 84,91,97,123.

19. Hamdullah Mustawfi, *Nuzhat al-qulūb*, transl. by G. Le Strange (London: Luzac and Co., 1919), *passim*.

20. Qum, Avah, Farahan and Hillali were singled out by Mustawfi as having very bigoted Shi'ite populations.

21. Shushtari, *Majālis*, vol. 1. pp. 78, 84,85, 87, 98.

22. *ibid.*, vol. 2, pp. 110-11.

23. The manuscript concerned was a copy of *Qawā'id al-islām* by Hasan b. Yusuf al-Mutahhar al-Hilli (d. 762/1325-26) found in the private library of one Qadi Nurullah Zaytuni. See Rumlu, *Ahsan al-tawārīkh*, vol. 1, p. 61.

24. *ibid.*

25. Accounts of the conversion of Uljaytu to Twelver Shi'ism appear in Shushtari's *Majālis*, vol. 2, pp. 355-63; in Tunukabuni's *Qisas al-'ulamā*, pp. 269-71; and in Khwandamir's *Habīb al-siyyar*, vol. 3, p. 195.

26. Muhmamad b. 'Abdullah Ibn Battuta, *Rihla* (Beirut, 1960), p. 206.

27. Tunukabuni's *Qisas al-'ulamā*, with its potted biographies of over 150 Shi'ite scholars, carries no mention of any debate on matters concerning *īmān* or *ma'rifa*, although it abounds in stories of discussions on matters of law and jurisprudence. Shushtari's *Majālis*, despite the author's apparent Sufi inclinations, is similarly devoid of any substantial discussion of fundamentals of belief and divine gnosis.
28. Muhammad b. 'Uthman al-Dhahabi, *al-Muntaqā min minhaj al-i'tidāl* (Cairo, 1374/1954-55), p. 25.
29. For examples of Jahan Shah's poetry, see: Vladimir Minorsky, 'Jihan Shah Qaraqoyunlu and his Poetry' in *BSOAS*, vol. 16 (1954), pp. 271-97.
30. For a very brief account of the circumstances surrounding his conversion see: Shushtari. *Majālis*, vol. 2, p. 370. The inter-*madhhab* debate was held in 840/1436-7. Mirza Ispand died eight years later.
31. For a lucid account of the historical role played by the Sarbidarids, see: Karim Kishawarz, 'Nahdat-i sarbidārān dar Khurāsān' in *Farhang-i Irān zamīn*, vol. 10 (1962), pp. 124-224. Compare this with Shushtari's account in *Majālis*, vol. 1, p. 579 and vol. 2, pp. 366-67.
32. Mazzaoui, *Origins*, p. 67.
33. Zayn al-din al-'Amili, *al-Lum'at al-Dimashqiyya* (Tabriz, 1275-76/1955-57), p. 5. See also: Shushtari, *Majālis*, vol. 1, p. 579.
34. See: Jean Aubin, 'Tamerlan à Bagdad' in *Arabica* 9 (1962), p. 306. Aubin contends that the Sarbidarid rulers, menaced by the extremism of the common people who had been so inspired by the movement, saw that the only way to peace and stability was through religious and social conservatism.
35. For biographical details on the two scholars, see: Tunukabuni, *Qisas al-'ulamā*, pp. 255-59 (Ibn Makki) and p. 329 (Ibn Fahd).
36. Mazzaoui, *Origins*, p. 71.
37. One of the most comprehensive, and objective, is Trimingham's *Sufi Orders*, referred to below. The work of Seyyed Hossein Nasr, *Sufi Essays* (London, 1972), is an important one in the field. See also: Titus Burckhardt, *Introduction to Sufi Doctrine* (London, 1975) and Frithjof Schuon, *Islam and the Perennial Philosophy* (London, 1976).
38. J. Spencer Trimingham, *The Sufi Orders in Islam* (Oxford, 1971), p. 150.
39. *ibid.*, p. 2.
40. See Chapter 5 of Trimingham's *Sufi Orders* for an exposition of Sufi doctrine concerning the soul (*al-nafs*).
41. Nadvi quotes Junayd as saying, 'The external path (*sharī'a*) and internal path (*haqīqa*) of Islam are essentially the two sides of the same thing ... far from being antagonistic (they) corroborate each other.' See: Muzaffar al-din Nadvi, 'Pirism – Corrupted Sufism' in *Islamic Culture*, vol. 9 (1935), pp. 475-84.
42. Trimingham, *Sufi Orders*, pp. 102-3.
43. *ibid.*, p. 103.
44. Shams al-din Abu 'Abdullah al-Maqdisi, *Ahsan al-taqāsim*, ed. by M.J. de Goeje, 2nd edition (Leiden, 1906), p. 439.
45. See Chapter 2 of Trimingham's *Sufi Orders*.

46. Jean Aubin (ed.), *Materiaux pour la Biographie de Shah Ni'matullah Wali Kermani: Jami'-i Mufidi* (Tehran, 1956), p. 181.

47. 'Abbas Iqbal, *Tārīkh-i mufassal-i Irān* (Tehran, 1312 Sh./1933-34), vol. 1, p. 466.

48. Shaykh Ahmad Sirhindi, the originator of the Mujaddidi branch of the Naqshbandi *tarīqa* wrote passionate polemical attacks against the Twelver Shi'ites yet described the 12 Imams as the leaders of all men who would approach God through *wilāya* or sainthood. See his *Maktūbāt* (Lucknow, 1306), vol. 3, pp. 246-8.

49. Followers of the Hanafi rite resident in Qum in the 4th/10th century are reported to have even taken part in the *ta'zīya* or ritual commemoration of the martyrdom of Husayn. See: Muhammad Ja'far Mahjub, 'Az fadā'il wa manāqib-khwānī tā rawda-khwānī' in *Irān Nāmeh*, vol. 3, no. 3 (Spring, 1984), p. 424.

50. Najm al-din Razi, *Mirsād al-'ibād min al-mabda' ilā al-ma'ād*, ed. by M. Riyahi (Tehran, 1352 Sh.1973-74), p.20.

51. The beliefs of the early Shi'ites are treated summarily by Marshall G. Hodgson in his article, 'How did the early Shi'a become sectarian?' in *JAOS*, vol. 75 (1955), pp. 1-13. See also: B. Lewis, 'Some observations on the significance of heresy in the history of Islam' in *Studia Islamica*, vol. 1 (1953), pp. 43-63. R. Strothmann's article entitled 'Ghālī' in the *Shorter Encyclopaedia of Islam* is also illuminating.

52. Trimingham, *Sufi Orders*, p. 69.

53. The role of the Yasawiyya in Turkish Sufi history is an important one. See: Mehmet Fuat Köprülüzade, 'Türk edebiyatında mutasavviflar', summarised by L. Bouvat as 'Les premiers mystiques dans la literature turque' in *Revue du Monde Musulman*, vol. 43 (1921), pp. 236-82.

54. Ibn Ruzbihan, *Tārīkh-i 'ālam-ārā-i Amīnī*, abridged transl. by Vladimir Minosky under the title *Persia in A.D. 1478-1490* (London: Royal Asiatic Society, 1957). See pages 67-8 for a brief account of the antinomian tendencies of the Qizilbash.

55. The Iranian historian Ahmad Kasrawi was of the opinion that the Safavids were indigenous inhabitants of Iran and of pure Aryan stock. However, they spoke Azari, the native language of Azarbaijan. The main point for Kasrawi was whether the Safavids had been residents of Azarbaijan for a long time or had migrated there from Kurdistan. See: A. Kasrawi, *Shaykh Safī wa tabārish* (Tehran, 1342 Sh./1963-64) and also his article 'Bāz ham Safawiyya' in *Āyanda*, vol. 2, 1927-8. The Turkish scholar Zeki Velidi Togan re-examined the evidence and suggested that the ancestors of the Safavids may have accompanied the Kurdish prince Mamlan b. Wahsudan when the latter conquered Ardabil and the surrounding regions in 1025. See: Zeki Velidi Togan, 'Sur l'origine des Safavides' in *Melanges Louis Massignon* (Damascus, 1957), vol. 3, pp. 347-57. The studies of Kasrawi and Togan led them to conclude that the Safavids were not *sayyids* and that the alteration of their genealogy to support their claim regarding their supposed descent from Ali occurred either during the leadership of Khwaja Ali or around the time of the

accession of Shah Isma'il himself. The findings of Aşıkpaşazada, however, point to the alteration having taken place during the leadership of Shaykh Junayd. See: Aşıkpaşazada, *Tevarih-i Al-i Osman* (Istanbul, 1914), p. 265.

56. Tawakkul b. Isma'il Ibn Bazzaz, *Safwat al-safā* (India Office Ms. 1842), p. 106.
57. Mazzaoui, *Origins*, p. 53.
58. Mustawfi, *Nuzhat al-qulūb*, p. 81 (Persian text); pp. 83-4 (English translation).
59. Ibn Bazzaz, *Safwat al-safā*, p. 250a.
60. *ibid.*, pp.250b-251a.
61. *ibid.*, pp. 35b-36b.
62. See: Hamdullah Mustawfi, *Tārīkh-i guzīda*, ed. by A.H. Nawa'i (Tehran, 1336-39 Sh./1957-61), p. 675.
63. V. Minorsky (ed.), *Tadhkirat al-mulūk* (Cambridge: CUP, 1980), p. 189.
64. Ibn Ruzbihan, *Persia in A.D. 1478-1490*, p. 63.
65. *ibid.*
66. *ibid.*, p. 63.
67. Aşıkpaşazade, *Tevarih-i Al-i Osman*, pp. 264-69.
68. *ibid.*, pp. 265-66.
69. Ibn Ruzbihan, *Persia in A.D. 1478-1490*, p. 63.
70. See: H.J. Kissling, 'Badr al-din b. Kadi Samawna' in *EI*, 2nd edition.
71. See: J.R. Walsh, 'Yunus Emre: a 14th century Turkish hymnodist' in *Numen*, vol. 7 (1960), p. 177. Walsh asserts that the Mevlevi order in the 14th and 15th centuries enjoyed the patronage and protection of the authorities and was used by those in power 'to combat the anarchical tendencies of the rural orders, the Bektashis, the Baba'is and the Alevis.'
72. R. Tschudi, 'Bektashiyya' in *EI*, 2nd edition.
73. Vladimir Minorsky, 'Shaykh Bali Efendi on the Safavids' in *BSOAS*, vol. 20 (1957), p. 439.
74. Ibn Ruzbihan, *Persia in A.D. 1478-1490*. p. 64.
75. Nasrullah Falsafi, *Zindigānī-i Shāh 'Abbās-i Awwal* (Tehran, 1332 Sh./1953-54), vol. 1, p. 180.
76. *ibid.*
77. The sources are silent on the date of Haydar's birth. Minorsky reckons that he was about nine years old when Uzun Hasan installed him at Ardabil. See: Vladimir Minorsky, *La Perse au XVe Siecle entre la Turquie et Venise* (Paris: E. Leroux, 1933), p. 324.
78. An extensive if only approximate list of the tribes which were the mainstay of the early Safavids can be found in *Takhkirat al-mulūk*, p. 193.
79. On the *khulafā*, see Minorsky, *ibid.*, pp. 189-95. Also see R.M. Savory, 'The office of Khalifat al-Khulafa under the Safavids' in *JAOS*, vol. 85 (1965), pp. 497-502.
80. Ibn Ruzbihan, *Persia in A.D. 1478-1490*, pp. 66-68. *Namāz* is Persian for canonical prayer; *qibla* is the direction of Mecca to which Muslims turn in prayer.

81. Haydar led a first raid into the area in 891/1486 and during the following year launched a full-scale raid which brought him over 6000 Christian captives. See: Ibn Ruzbihan, *Persia in A.D. 1478-1490*, p. 70.
82. See Sir Denison Ross, 'The Early Years of Shah Isma'il, Founder of the Safavi dynasty' in *JRAS* (April, 1896), p. 315.
83. See: 'Abbas al-Azzawi, *Tārīkh al-'irāq bayna ihtilālayn* (Baghdad, 1935-50), vol. 3, pp. 316-17.
84. See: Annemarie Schimmel, 'The Ornament of the Saints' in *Iranian Studies*, vol. 7, pp. 105-6. Schimmel sides with Nasr in the assertion that Sufism and Shi'ism had, in pre-Safavid Iran, blended into a hybrid that was able to facilitate the advent of the Safavid dynasty. The word 'Shi'ite' is used throughout the article almost always without any kind of qualifying adjective. For example, her statement that 'some of the greatest masters of the Imamiyyah built parts of their system upon the works of Ibn 'Arabi' (p. 106) is both nebulous and misleading. She also cites the inclusion of Ja'far al-Sadiq in the Naqshbandi *silsila* as evidence of the spiritual proximity of Shi'ism and Sunni Sufism in pre-Safavid Iran.

Chapter 3

The consolidation of Safavid power and the rise of Twelver Shi'ite externalism

Introduction

> The care that Chiek-Sephi [Safi al-din] took to establish a particular
> sect, which was so very different from the other Mahometans, was an
> admirable invention to prevent the people from revolting, through the
> solicitations of either the Turks, Tartars, or Indians, who are all their
> neighbours.[1]

Although Sanson is mistaken in attributing the establishment of Twelver
Shi'ism in Iran to Shaykh Safi, his observation that its introduction was an
overt political ploy is a shrewd one. As noted previously, when Shah Isma'il
declared Twelver Shi'ism to be the new state religion, he and his advisers
were ignorant of Twelver Shi'ite law. Isma'il himself adhered to the same
brand of extremism espoused by his grandfather, Junayd. Isma'il's poetry,
written under the pen-name Khata'i, reflects this orientation. For example:

> I am Very God, Very God, Very God! Come now, O blind man who
> has lost the path, behold the Truth! I am that *agens Absolutus* of
> whom they speak.[2]

A Venetian merchant residing in Iran at the time attests to the fact that
Isma'il was believed by his followers to be immortal; the name of God was
forgotten and only that of Isma'il remembered, and the new ruler was
appealed to as both deity and prophet.[3]
Given the Safavids' spiritual allegiance to the Twelve Imams, it seems

72

only logical that Isma'il and his advisers would adopt a form of Islamic externalism in keeping with their pro-Alid stand, although it is not clear whether they realised how far removed their extremism was from the orthodoxy of the Twelver doctrines they were bent on introducing. What could not have been lost on them, however, was this: whatever the exact nature of its tenets, orthodox Twelver Shi'ism possessed a recognised legal framework and a highly elaborate body of dogma that could be grafted with comparative ease onto the kind of governmental system which the Safavids intended to create. The adoption of Twelver Shi'ism by previous, non-orthodox pro-Shi'ite dynasties such as the Sarbidarids - and, to an extent, the Ilkhanids - was proof that the doctrines of the Twelver Shi'ite orthodoxy could quite easily be adopted by such a political system, albeit not so much as a natural corollary of the system's religious orientation as a means of stabilization and institutionalisation. For once the Safavid 'revolution' had succeeded, the very elements that had effected its success – namely the fanatical and undisciplined Qizilbash – would have to be brought into check, and a strong centralized government established if the Safavids were to retain and expand their power. Twelver Shi'ite orthodoxy would have the desired stabilizing effect, and its immediate propagation was vital if the doctrinal uniformity that was so crucial to the Safavid retention of power in Iran was to come about. Furthermore, the adoption of Twelver Shi'ite religious law would, as Sanson remarked, effectively isolate Iran from its Sunni neighbours – the Ottomans to the west and the Uzbeks to the east – and in so doing create a stronger awareness of national identity. Thus, just as Isma'il's forefathers had embraced *ghuluww* in order to attain power, Isma'il and his advisers would use orthodox Twelver Shi'ism in order to maintain it.

Isma'il's adoption of Twelver Shi'ism should be seen, then, as an overtly political act rather than a desire to promote the creed *per se*. The author of *Surūr al-'ārifīn* considers the establishment of the Safavid regime in the light of the 'Mecca-Medina' paradigm discussed earlier. Muhammad's establishment of an Islamic society in Medina, he argues, was a 'natural' corollary of the 13 years he had spent in Mecca developing the 'basis of belief' (*asās-i īmān*), without which the legal apparatus of Islam is meaningless. It is worth quoting Yusufi's words in full, since they enable us to view the Safavid phenomenon in terms of the internalist-externalist dichotomy:

The idea that there can be a Medina without a Mecca is a Satanic trick (*dasīsa-i shaytānī*); without true and deep-rooted belief (*īmān-i haqīqī wa risha-dār*), the imposition of Islamic laws of jurisprudence is inevitably just another means of harnessing the masses...The whole history of Islam after the death of Muhammad is one continuous story of the imposition of the hide-bound religion of jurists (*dīn-i qishrī-i fuqahā*) under the auspices of tyrants; true belief, the outward expression of which in Islam is natural and unforced, is pushed to the periphery, or even actively suppressed... As for the (Safavids), they based their sultanate on neither true belief nor Islam, and thus had no choice but to look outside Iran for support, to the *fuqahā* of Syria and Bahrain, who soon flooded the country with doctrines quite alien to the vast majority of the Iranian people...[4]

Given Isma'il's erstwhile religious extremism and political aspirations, it is highly improbable that he entertained sincerely any ideas of 'creating a Medina' in Iran. What Yusufi does succeed in highlighting is the fact that the introduction of Twelver Shi'ism was conceived as a means of imposing doctrinal unity for the sake of political ends; he also reinforces the notion that orthodox Twelver Shi'ism was, if not completely alien, at least relatively unknown in Iran. More interesting than this, however, are his strictures against the *fuqahā*, whose introduction of what he calls 'Islam without Allah'[5] he describes as 'an insult to the very Imams in whose name they peddled their doctrines.'[6] To describe the religion of the *fuqahā* as 'Islam without Allah' suggests that the newly imported creed was almost exclusively externalist in nature. To imply that Twelver Shi'ism was alien to the Iranian people further implies that non-externalism was popular there and was somehow pushed to the periphery after the Safavid rise to power.

Given the fact that Sunnism was the majority rite in Iran prior to the advent of Isma'il, and that the propagation of Sunni jurisprudence by Hanafite or Shafi'ite *fuqahā* was widespread, it is an oversimplification to suggest that externalism *per se* was alien to Iran. Nearer to reality, perhaps, is the contention that Shi'ite externalism in particular was alien to Iran; that the new doctrine had to be imposed, very often by brute force, reflects not so much the difference in nature between Shi'ite and Sunni externalism, which is minimal, as the basic difference in the belief systems of Sunni and Shi'ite Islam upon which their respective externalist structures are founded. Had the fundamentals of belief held by the immigrant *fuqahā* been in keeping with those of the majority of the Iranian people, the change to Twelver Shi'ism would simply have involved a change in *madhhab* – itself of no more consequence, say, than a change from the Hanafite to the Shafi'ite rite or vice-versa. What occurred in Iran, however, was an almost total reorientation of religious outlook, commandeered by the externalist Twelver Shi'ite *fuqahā*, whose status as religious scholars was of far greater social and cultural significance than that of their Sunni counterparts. It is to the evolution of the role of the Twelver *fuqahā* that we now turn.

The Twelver Shi'ite *fuqahā*: guardians of externalism

As noted earlier, the acquisition and promulgation of the scriptural sciences by Muslim scholars has always tended to overshadow the pursuit of internalism, thus creating a duality of *naqlī* (scriptural) and *'aqlī* (rational) fields of learning. The preoccupation of the majority of Muslim scholars with the externals of religion led in time to the unintentional downplaying of the fundamentals of belief, so that a rift developed between what we have termed the 'internalist' and 'externalist' facets of the Islamic revelation. Knowledge of the self (*ma'rifat al-nafs*) and divine gnosis (*ma'rifat Allāh*) became the concern of the Sufi brotherhoods and individual gnostics who, for the most part, operated outside the accepted 'orthodoxy' - the body of scholars, teachers and preachers who deemed themselves responsible for spreading the Islamic revelation as they understood it.

Externalism has always dominated the official Islamic teaching institutions (*madrasa*), and while no externalist scholar would deny the importance of belief, it has always been the practical commands (*awāmir*) of God which have received the lion's share of Muslim scholarly attention: so much so, in fact, that the term *'ilm*, originally denoting the knowledge of man about his Creator, came to be synonymous with the academic pursuit of the scriptural sciences. The rift between internalism and externalism – and, more importantly, the usurpation of the term *'ulamā* by the externalist *fuqahā* – was given attention among Sunni scholars primarily by Ghazali, whose chief endeavour was to redefine the word *'ilm* and also to bring about a *rapprochement* between *'aql* and *naql*, between internalism and externalism and, by extension, between *īmān* and Islam. Ghazali's efforts were instrumental in effecting what may be seen as a minor reintegration of internalism into Sunni orthodoxy: Sufism, the main channel of internalist teaching, became more acceptable to the Sunni *fuqahā*, and organised Sufi orders brought into existence a religious organization parallel with that of the externalist orthodoxy. Although this tended in the long run to accentuate the internalist-externalist rift, it did create a climate in which the two groups were able to co-exist relatively peacefully. No doubt the fact that the vast majority of Sufi brotherhoods prior to the 9th/15th century were Sunni contributed to the compromise.

In the case of Twelver Shi'ism, a markedly different picture emerges. The vast majority of Twelver Shi'ite scholars has tended towards the narrative sciences (*al-'ulūm al-naqliyya*) and of all the facets of Twelver Shi'ite religious expression it is the scholarly legalistic religion of the *fuqahā* that has enjoyed predominance in terms of the respect and influence it enjoys. In this sense it is easy to draw parallels between the Shi'ite *fuqahā* and their Sunni counterparts.

However, to see the dominance of the *fuqahā* in the Shi'ite world in terms of the internalist-externalist dichotomy obtaining in the Sunni sphere would be a gross oversimplification. The reason for this is that the fundamentals of belief (*usūl al-īmān*) in Twelver Shi'ism contain elements that are unacceptable to Sunnism. The most important of these is, of course, the leadership or *imāma* of the Twelver Imams, which is basically the *raison d'être* of Twelver Shi'ism. So central is the notion of *imāma* to the Twelver Shi'ites, and so pervasive is its presence in their works and teachings, that the relationship of most Twelvers with the spiritual life developed on different lines from that of the Sunnis: whereas the latter found a channel for internalist expression mainly in Sufi forms of devotion, the Twelver Shi'ites had their own form of compensation for the spiritual deficiencies of legalistic religion, namely the cult of the Imam. Despite the fact that Sunnis and Shi'ites have three fundamentals of belief in common, it is the overriding emphasis placed by the Twelvers on the importance of *imāma* which raises the question: is internalism in general the same for Sunnis and Shi'ites, and if not, why not? This question will be dealt with presently. The predominance of externalism in Twelver Shi'ite learned circles may well represent and reflect, as it does in the Islamic world as a whole, the overwhelming tendency of the common Muslim towards external acts rather than internal, introspective belief and self-knowledge – a fact, as we saw earlier, that is acknowledged by the Koran and numerous Muslim scholars. In the Twelver Shi'ite sphere, however, it is the actual status of the *fuqahā* in the eyes of the Twelver faithful that has given the pursuit of externalism extra impetus, for theirs is a role which far outweighs in importance the one played by their counterparts in the Sunni world.

The evolution of the role of the Twelver Shi'ite jurist

Generally speaking it may be said that in matters of jurisprudence, Twelver Shi'ism differs no more from the four schools of Sunni *fiqh* than they differ among themselves. The major difference is one not of content but of principle: although both hold in common the Koran and the Traditions as their main sources of ritual and legal practice, the Twelver Shi'ites differ in that their Traditions rely usually on the words or actions of one of the Twelve Imams.

Prior to the 'occultation'[7] of the 12th Imam, the Mahdi, in 329/940-41, the most important activity among the Twelver Shi'ites was the collection and dissemination of Imami Traditions, and thus the earliest learned figures, such as Kulayni and Ibn Babuya, were *muhaddithūn*, or narrators of Traditions. The occultation of the Mahdi, however, created a serious vacuum in the Twelver Shi'ite leadership. Unlike the Sunnis, for whom the Caliph was the symbolic head of the community even when he ceased to exercise any political power, the Twelver Shi'ites had no such earthly figurehead to look to. Their true leader, the 'hidden' Imam, was in concealment, and the longer his absence continued the more the community found themselves in need of a leader to prevent its possible disintegration. The *muhaddithūn* took on the task of leadership themselves, basing their position on Traditions – said to have been received from the Mahdi during his 'lesser occultation' – which determined the role that they were to play during his concealment. One such Tradition, in the form of a proclamation issued by the concealed Imam via one of his representatives (*sufarā*), urged the Twelver Shi'ite community to 'turn to the narrators of our Traditions, because they are my proof to you, while I am the proof (*hujja*) of God to them.'[8]

Traditions such as the one above are notoriously ambiguous when it comes to defining the exact circumstances in which the *muhaddithūn* were to be 'turned to.' However, as the occultation of the Mahdi continued, the role of the *muhaddithūn* changed accordingly and they were able to extend their activities to the point where, by the last decade of the 4th/10th century, lay Twelvers were accepting the statements of their leading scholars as the actual edicts of the 12th Imam.[9] The *muhaddithūn* had evolved into *fuqahā* merely by dint of the prolongation of the occultation of the Mahdi. Prior to his concealment, the Twelver scholars had always consulted the Imam – either directly or via his representatives – on matters of jurisprudence: their chief function was to narrate the Traditions of the Imams, and this they continued to do during the early years of his absence.[10] Arguments based on reason (*'aql*) to deduce legal rulings (*ahkām*) had been proscribed by the early *muhaddithūn*; however, the seemingly interminable concealment of the Mahdi forced the Twelver Shi'ite scholars to offer rational (*'aqlī*) proofs for their Imam's existence – which had become a matter for heated debate – and thus men who had been mere narrators of Traditions became scholastic theologians (*mutakallimūn*).

The change in the role of the Twelver Shi'ite scholar can be seen in the works of Shaykh Mufid: whereas early Twelver writing such as that of Kulayni was purely the collection of Traditions, Mufid's works were largely treatises written in defence of the *imāma*, in particular the occultation of the 12th Imam. Furthermore with the passing of time new situations arose in which the laws of the *sharī'a* had to be applied, and since direct communication with the 12th Imam had ceased, someone had to be found to issue rulings. Thus it was that the Twelver scholars further expanded their role by undertaking *ijtihād* to answer questions of law and by so doing fill the vacuum created by the occultation of the Imam. Shaykh Mufid was in effect the first Twelver *mujtahid*, although the office was given a definite shape by al-Tusi.

The main functions of the Imam were considered to be: leading the *jihād*; effecting legal decisions (*tanfīdh al-ahkām*); imposing legal penalties (*iqāmat al-hudūd*); dividing the war booty (*qismat al-fay*); leading the Friday prayer (*salāt al-jum'a*); and receiving the taxes known as *zakāt* and *khums*. As the role of the Twelver Shi'ite scholar evolved from that of *muhaddith* – narrator of Traditions and legal rulings – to that of *faqīh/mujtahid*, or giver of legal rulings, the judicial functions of the Imam also began to fall into the sphere of jurisdiction of the *fuqahā*. For instance, during the early years of the Imam's concealment, the Twelver Shi'ite scholars had refused to arrogate to themselves authority over the half of the *khums* traditionally earmarked for the Imam, preferring instead to have it set aside in safekeeping until his reappearance. The other half of the *khums*, known as the *sādāt* share, was to be distributed among the Prophet's descendants by each individual himself. From the time of Shaykh Mufid, however, the *fuqahā* began to grant themselves authority over the *sādāt* share; Muhaqqiq al-Hilli (d.676/1277-78) went a step further by giving himself the right, as a *faqīh*, to deal with the Imam's share of the *khums*, known as the *sahm al-imām*, as well as the *sādāt* share. Al-Hilli also extended the judicial role of the *fuqahā* to iqāmat al-hudūd (the imposition of penalties, by the *fuqahā* themselves rather than by the temporal authorities). As for the issue of the Friday prayer (*salāt al-jum'a*), the question of whether or not it should be performed in the absence of the Imam is an old and thorny one, with implications   as I shall point out later on – that extend to the question of temporal authority and the legitimacy of government. Suffice it here to say that the authority of the *fuqahā* became established with such rapidity among the Twelver Shi'ites that from as far back as the time of Shaykh al-Ta'ifa, the *fuqahā* had been allowed to organise the Friday prayers in the absence of the Imam or his special representative (*nā'ib al-khāss*).[11] Muhaqqiq al-Karaki (d. 940/1533-34) was the first to suggest that the *fuqahā* were the general representatives (*nā'ib al-'ām*) of the Mahdi, although he restricted his application of this argument to the assumption of the duty of leading Friday prayers.[12] The concept of *nā'ib al-'ām* was taken to its logical conclusion in the religious sphere by Shahid al-Thani (d. 966/1558-59), who applied it to all of the religious functions and prerogatives of the Hidden Imam.[13] Thus the judicial authority of the *fuqahā* became a direct reflection of the authority of the Imam himself. It became obligatory to pay the religious taxes directly to the *fuqahā* as trustees of the Imam for distribution, and the donor who distributed them himself was considered to obtain no reward from God for doing so. Furthermore, Shahid al-Thani extended the range of those eligible to receive money from the *zakāt* to include the religious students (*tullāb*) and the *fuqahā* themselves, who thus became the recipients of the money as trustees and who were also able to spend the money on themselves and their circle of students. Even in the role of defensive *jihād*, Shahid al-Thani identified a role for the *fuqahā* to play.[14]

Thus up until the time of Shahid al-Thani, the *fuqahā* gradually developed the theoretical basis of their authority, evolving from mere narrators of the Traditions of the Imams into general representatives of the Mahdi and executors of his judicial functions during his absence.

Enter the externalists: from Jabal 'Amil to Isfahan

As we have seen earlier, from the middle of the 6th/12th century the centre of orthodox Twelver Shi'ite learning shifted from Qum, Baghdad and Najaf to areas well outside Iran proper. Hilla had been an important Twelver centre since its foundation in 495/1101-02, rising to pre-eminence a century later and remaining the most important seat of Twelver scholarship until the end of the 8th/14th century. Twelver communities also existed during this period in Bahrain, al-Ahsa, and in the area known as

Jabal 'Amil, the hill country which lies inland from Sayda and Sur in southern Lebanon.

Little is known about the scholars of Jabal 'Amil before the $6^{th}/12^{th}$ century, but from that time onwards the picture becomes clearer. In some of the towns and villages there were enclaves of Twelver scholars who handed down Traditions from father to son, forming 'learned families' of specialists in *fiqh* and *hadīth*, and attracting seekers of formal learning from elsewhere. There do not appear to have been large schools with permanent endowments; rather, scholarly activities took place in what was almost a kind of 'cottage industry' of the scriptural sciences, with scholars forming close networks through intermarriage.[15] Some of the most important and influential of these families lived in small towns lying on the trade route from Damascus. Mashghara – the birthplace of one of the towering figures of late-Safavid Twelver Shi'ite learning, Muhammad Hurr al-'Amili – and Jazzin were on the main road from Damascus to Sayda, and Mashghara also lay near a road running southward to Galilee. Karak Nuh, the birthplace of the first major Twelver Shi'ite émigré scholar in Safavid Iran, Shaykh 'Ali Karaki, lay in the Biq'a valley on one of the two main roads between Damascus and Ba'labak. Other centres of learning, however, such as Juba and Mays al-Jabal, lay on smaller routes and were in fact little more than villages.[16]

The remoteness of the district from the main centres of power, the small scale of life there, and the poverty of its resources all militated against the area being eyed covetously by the rulers of the great cities. Free from the threat of occupation, the Twelver Shi'ite heritage was preserved and allowed to flourish, attracting learned Twelvers from other parts of Syria. Muhsin al-Amin al-'Amili suggests that Twelver Shi'ite scholars from as far afield as Damascus and Aleppo may have found a home there, and points out that the first scholar of any renown in the district, Shams al-din Muhammad b. Makki, better known as al-Shahid al-Awwal (d. 786/1384-85), did not receive his *ijāzāt* from local scholars but went to Iraq and elsewhere to study.[17] Another reason for the persistence of the Twelver Shi'ite tradition in the area may be found in the relative tolerance and understanding that existed at the time between the Twelver Shi'ite and the Sunni scholars in the area. The possibility of confrontation was ever present, yet the two groups were able to learn and benefit from each other. The 'first martyr', al-Shahid al-Awwal, a native of Jazzin, studied under not only Twelver scholars but also Sunni scholars in Mecca, Medina, Baghdad, Damascus and Hebron. His main work was to clarify the methods and rules of jurisprudence on the basis of what he had learned from both Sunni and Twelver interpretations of *usūl al-fiqh*, maintaining that competent scholars should give legal judgements and that the people should have recourse to them rather than to judges appointed by unjust rulers. This emphasis upon the scholar or *'ālim*[18] in the community was perhaps a reflection of the position of the Twelvers in the Syria of his time, alienated as they were from the holders of power. He visited Damascus regularly and taught there, but it is a sign of the limits to Twelver activity that he was able to teach Twelver Traditions only clandestinely, because of the need for dissimulation (*taqīyya*). Despite his prudence he was imprisoned by the governor of Damascus on account of accusations brought by his enemies, and finally executed.[19]

The 'second martyr', Zayn al-din b. Nur al-din al-'Amili (d. 966/1558-59) came from a learned family in Juba. His father, grandfathers, and great-grandfathers were all *muhaddithūn*. Zayn al-din studied with his father in Juba, then in Mays, then in Karak Nuh. He also went to Damascus and then on to Cairo, where he spent periods of study with a number of Sunni scholars. He was proficient in all four schools of Sunni jurisprudence and taught them alongside his own Twelver *fiqh*. It is claimed that he was the first of the later Twelver scholars to write systematically about the transmission of Traditions, using methods and terminology taken from Sunni as well as Twelver Shi'ite sources. To a certain extent, the Twelver scholars of the pre-Safavid period lived in harmony with their Sunni counterparts, and there was relatively little of the bitter sectarian strife that was to break out once the Twelvers found a foothold in Safavid Iran.[20]

A study of the works of both Ibn Makki and Zayn al-din reveals that their output was overwhelmingly externalist in nature, and this to a very great extent characterizes the academic bent of the Twelver Shi'ite learned community in Jabal 'Amil and the outlying areas as a whole. In fact the Twelver Shi'ite internalist was, at this point in time, an exception, and the source upon which the nascent Safavid regime would draw to establish its newly chosen state religion was almost exclusively externalist in outlook. As the biographical dictionary *Riyāḍ al-'ulamā* – which we shall survey later – reveals, externalism was to remain the predominant feature of Twelver Shi'ite academic output right through until the end of the Safavid era; indeed it is hard to escape the impression that orthodox Twelver Shi'ism had – and still has – a particular predilection for the secondary, 'scriptural' sciences rather than anything else.

Of Shah and Shaykh: Isma'il and Karaki

The most prominent and historically significant Twelver Shi'ite *faqīh* of the early Safavid period was Shaykh 'Ali al-Karaki al-'Amili (d. 940/1533-34), whom Shah Isma'il invited to Iran to propagate Twelver Shi'ism. Shaykh Karaki moved from Jabal 'Amil to Arab Iraq quite soon after the rise of Shah Isma'il and is said to have visited the new ruler in Isfahan as early as 910/1504-05.[21] Karaki, in the tradition of Ibn Makki and Zayn al-din, was an externalist in outlook and covered, in his writings, most of the subjects in the field of *furū'* or secondary principles of Islam. Treatises on ritual ablution (*tahāra*), pilgrimage (*hajj*), foster relationships (*ridā'*), burial (*jināza*), contracts (*'uqūd*), supererogatory prayers (*du'ā wa ta'qībāt*) and various other matters related to the external practices of Islam form the core of his output; the question of *īmān*, self-knowledge and knowledge of God has no place in his considerable corpus of writings.[22] Karaki may therefore be considered to be the founding father of Twelver Shi'ite externalism in Safavid Iran, and the first Twelver scholar to disseminate Twelver Shi'ite doctrines on such a grand scale. Karaki travelled the length and breadth of Iran, extolling the virtues of Twelver Shi'ism and appointing prayer-leaders (*pīshnamāz*) in each town and village to teach the people the new creed. Such was the height of Karaki's profile that a Sunni scholar actually believed that Karaki was the founder of Twelver Shi'ism itself.[23]

The suitability of orthodox Twelver Shi'ism for the objectives of the new ruler is easily discernible when one considers the religious orientation of scholars such as Karaki. The consolidation of Safavid power depended on the ability of the new ruler to eradicate all potential centres of opposition. The existence of one of the very elements that had effected the Safavid revolution, namely the Qizilbash, was one such obstacle, for once the conquest of Iran was completed the extremism of the Qizilbash lost its political utility and became more of a burden than a blessing. Equally dangerous for Isma'il were the twin obstacles of Sufism – in all of its various manifestations – and Sunnism, to which the majority of the populace adhered.

The logical antidote to all of this was Twelver Shi'ism, spearheaded by the *fuqahā*. The externalist Twelver Shi'ite scholars had not at this point forwarded any explicit claims to political authority and thus posed no threat to the new regime. Religious authority also lay ultimately in the hands of the Shah; it was not until the end of Isma'il's reign that Karaki formulated his theory of the Twelver Shi'ite *mujtahid* as 'deputy of the

Imam', a status which was to confer religious – but not political – authority upon its holder.[24] As A.K.S. Lambton remarks, 'no Shi'i thinkers arose to do for the Shi'i theory what Mawardi and Ghazali had done for the Sunni.'[25] In the absence of any clear, well-defined political ethos, the *fuqahā* tended to accept kingly authority – although there were exceptions[26] – and, in some cases, even became vehicles for the allegation that the Safavid monarchs were direct descendants of Muhammad through the 7th Imam, Musa al-Kazim. The Safavid claim to politico-religious authority was enhanced by – but did not rest solely upon – their self-proclaimed Alid descent. Descent from Muhammad and the Imams conferred no uncertain prestige on the claimant, a fact borne out by the elevated position of the *sayyid* class in the eyes of the masses, both Shi'ite and Sunni alike. Devotion to the family of Ali was a phenomenon not restricted to Twelver Shi'ism. The Safavid claim to Alid descent undoubtedly helped to sweeten the pill and win the dynasty wider acceptance among the masses than would otherwise have been possible. However, descent from the Prophet and the Imams did not confer any automatic rights upon an individual or a dynasty to temporal rule, a fact of which the incoming Twelver Shi'ite *fuqahā* were no doubt aware. That they overlooked this not only points to a lack of practical political theory on their part, but also suggests that the golden and totally unprecedented opportunity that they had been given to introduce their doctrines in the form of a new state religion outweighed all considerations of who should or should not have the right to politico-religious rule.

Although state and *fuqaha* were in a sense mutually dependent, it was the state which enjoyed the firm upper hand. Karaki was a staunch and loyal supporter of the new regime, so much so in fact that he penned a treatise condoning the ancient custom of prostration (*sajda*) before kings, a practice that is highly suspect given the Islamic view that such acts of humility are to be performed before God alone.[27] Karaki's unswerving support for the Safavid regime was well reciprocated by both Shah Isma'il and his successor, Shah Tahmasp (r. 1524-1576): from the former he received an annual stipend of 70,000 dinars to finance himself and his students, while from the latter he received extensive land grants or *suyurghalat* in the form of villages and arable land in Iraq to the value of some 700 *tumān*.[28] It was, in fact, in defence of his relationship with the Safavid court and in response to his detractors that Karaki penned his famous treatise on land tax (*kharāj*), in which, apart from endorsing the authority of the Safavid regime by legitimising the *kharāj*, he justified his own wealth and proximity to the Safavid court by referring to the precedent set by the likes of Sayyid Radi, Sharif al-Murtada and Khwaja Nasir al-din Tusi.[29]

The suppression of Sunnism was not something that could be taken lightly, given the fact that the vast majority of the populace was Sunni. The ritual vilification of the first three 'rightly guided' Caliphs (al-khulafā al-rāshidūn), Abu Bakr, Umar and Uthman, was rigidly enforced, with bands of zealous Twelver faithful formed in each town to ensure that people adhered to the new anti-Sunni instruction. Karaki is reported to have taken part personally in the antics of these vigilante squads, patrolling the streets with a gang of youths and cursing aloud the first three Caliphs.[30] Karaki attacked Sunnism blatantly from the pulpit of every mosque in which he preached. It is reported that his open attacks on the first three Caliphs had repercussions in Mecca and Medina, where punitive measures were taken in revenge against the Twelver scholars resident there, a group of whom promptly wrote a letter of protest to Karaki.[31]

Although all Twelver Shi'ite teaching is, by its very nature, implicitly anti-Sunni, the kind of explicit attacks made upon the leading figures of Sunnism by the externalist Twelve fuqahā in Iran at the beginning of the Safavid period were unprecedented. According to a treatise written by Karaki, the cursing of the Caliphs, known as la'n, became a religious duty (wājib); in another tract the Sunnis were declared impure (najis), a ruling which in effect reduced them in the eyes of the Twelver Shi'ites to the level of dogs, swine, infidels and other such Islamically-defined objects of impurity.[32]

The nominal conversion of the Iranian populace was rapid, since, as we have seen, it consisted in only a slight change in the wording of the call to prayer (adhān) and the innovation of la'n. It is clear that many who made a formal profession of Twelver Shi'ism continued to retain a Sunni outlook in private; this much is borne out by the considerable support that Shah Isma'il II (reigned 1576-1577) was able to call upon for his plans to re-establish Sunnism as the religious norm some seventy years later.[33] The practice of dissimulation (taqiyya), which consists in masking one's true religious orientation in the face of threats from a hostile majority, had, prior to the advent of the Safavids, been an almost wholly Shi'ite phenomenon. Now, ironically, it was used as a defence mechanism by many Sunnis, for whom the concept was, in theory at least, highly suspect.[34] The Ni'matullahiyya Order, which, save for its devotion to the House of Ali, had previously shown no leanings towards orthodox Twelver Shi'ism, suddenly declared itself Shi'ite and intered into what was to be a relatively lengthy alliance with the Safavids. However, the fact that its teachings remained totally anti-sectarian and basically internalist, in keeping with its Sufi orientation, calls into question the sincerity of its conversion and suggests that it was, in fact, a form of *taqiyya*, effected in order to secure the continuation of the Order under the changed circumstances.[35] The stratagem of *taqiyya* meant that it was often impossible at first glance to be sure of anyone's true orientation; only a close look at the words and deeds of the individual would reveal the truth. The famous Dashtaki family of Shiraz, for example, enjoyed prominence as scholars during the closing decades of Taymurid rule and at the beginning of the Safavid era, and swam with the tide in order to protect themselves when the state religion changed. Consequently it was difficult to tell exactly where the family's true religious affiliations lay, especially since, as Danishpazhuh points out:

> The family had combined their status as nobles with a tradition of classical learning and culture and this had made them exceedingly proud of themselves; yet when the official religion changed, their own religious proclivities weakened as a result.[36]

Mir Jamal al-din Dashtaki Shirazi, a leading member of the family, was thought to be a Shi'ite by some and a Sunni by others.[37] In his book *Rawdat al-Ahbāb*, dedicated to Shir Ali Nawa'i, he heaps praise upon Ali but does not fail to mention the other rightly-guided Caliphs, a feature interpreted by Danishpazhuh as indicative of the author's Sunnism *and* Shi'ism.[38] However, the fact that while in Herat he gave sermons not only in the Jami' mosque and the famous Sultaniyya *madrasa* but also in the Ikhlasiyya *khāngāh* suggests a decidedly internalist, orthodox Sunni and probably Sufi orientation.[39]

Many were unwilling to resort to *taqiyya* and were forced either to flee or to stay and face the consequences of their refusal to acquiesce. One man who chose to leave his home was the historian, Ibn Ruzbihan. He writes:

> A group of heterodox people occupied the land and disseminated *rāfidī* views and sectarianism among the people. This has forced me to leave my homeland and choose exile after bidding farewell to my friends and loved ones. So I left my town and reached Qashan where I settled... where the views of the people of the Sunna and Community were widespread, and where there was no sectarianism or atheism.[40]

According to Ibn Ruzbihan, the mainly Sunni populace of Isfahan did not accept the 'law of the Sufi'.[41] One European chronicler present in the city at that time describes in graphic detail the heaps of smouldering bones in the streets and squares – all that remained of the new Shah's opponents. Five thousand people were reported to have perished.[42] In Fars, members of the influential Sunni Kaziruni family were severely persecuted. Wholesale massacre of opposition groups was, generally speaking, the exception rather than the rule, and in most cases it should be seen in terms of desire for revenge rather than religious conversion; in Azarbaijan for example, the Qizilbash sought out and killed all those who had fought against Haydar, most of whom were Turcoman.

In his oppression of Sufism, Shah Isma'il found a staunch ally in Karaki and the immigrant Twelver Shi'ite externalist *fuqahā*, for whom the composition of anti-Sufi treatises was *de rigueur*. Karaki's own written refutation of Sufi beliefs and practices held that the Sufis were beyond the pale of Islam altogether - a paradoxical ruling when one considers the quasi-Sufi orientation of his paymasters.[43] The harshest treatment was reserved for the Sunni orders, such as the Naqshbandiyya, which was particularly strong in Khurasan and Azarbaijan.[44] The assertion made by the author of *Rawdat al-jinān* to the effect that Shah Isma'il crushed *all* of the Sufi Orders is pure hyperbole. The Ni'matullihiyya, as we have already noted, continued to prosper, and other self-confessed Shi'ite Orders such as the Nurbakhshiyya were tolerated. On the whole, however, there can be no doubting the hostility of Isma'il and his leading *fuqahā* towards the Sufi brotherhoods, and their policy of suppression was one that was to be continued by their successors.

It is Shaykh Karaki, however, who towers above all other scholars in the early years of the Safavid era, and it is the rigid, almost fanatical externalism inherent in his writings and approach that was to set the tone for the future of Islam in Safavid Iran. The author of *Riyād al-'ulamā* ranks Karaki alongside 'Allama Hilli and Mawla Hasan al-Kashi, and asserts that the Twelver Shi'ite faithful should feel beholden to these three figures more than anyone else since it was they who initiated the spread of Twelver Shi'ism in Iran.[45]

Karaki was the first Twelver Shi'ite scholar to suggest that the Twelver *fuqahā* are the general representatives of the 'hidden' Imam, the Mahdi. He also ruled that there must always be a capable *mujtahid* present in the community for the commonalty to emulate (*taqlīd*) in matters of jurisprudence beyond their ken; in this context he also contradicted the 'Second Martyr', Zayn al-din, by declaring it unlawful to emulate a dead *mujtahid.*[46] Karaki's ruling on this matter, which Zayn al-din appears to have been pressured into accepting later on, paved the way for the grasping of total religious authority over the masses by the Twelver Shi'ite *fuqahā* and, by extension, for the victory of externalism over its rival orientations.[47]

The reign of Shah Tahmasp: the *fuqahā* take root

Shah Isma'il's successor, Shah Tahmasp (r. 1524-1576), who enjoyed the longest reign of all the Safavid rulers, continued his father's policy of converting Iran to Twelver Shi'ism and eradicating all potential sources and centres of opposition. Unlike his father, Shah Tahmasp had no delusions of divine incarnation and took firm and often violent steps to suppress extremism, even though his Turcoman adherents still venerated him as either God or the Mahdi.[48] Sunni communities, which continued to flourish even in such politically sensitive areas as Qazvin, were also dealt with harshly by Tahmasp.[49] Ironically enough, however, one of his chief ministers, Qadi Jahan, who twice served under him, was almost certainly a Sunni who adopted *taqiyya* for obvious reasons. Sufi Orders, especially those such as the Naqshbandiyya which had not forsaken its allegiance to Sunnism, continued to come under pressure.[50]

Under Shah Tahmasp both the exodus of Twelver Shi'ite *fuqahā* from Jabal 'Amil and other regions outside Iran and the growth of externalism initiated by Shah Isma'il and his leading *faqīh*, Shaykh Karaki, continued unabated. The fact that Shah Tahmasp sported a thick veneer of religiosity gave added impetus to the establishment of the Twelver Shi'ite *fuqahā* as important players on the socio-religious stage in Safavid Iran. Under Tahmasp's orders, externalist Islam was boosted by the closure of opium dens, taverns, gambling houses and brothels; members of his retinue were made to repent collectively; the *fuqahā* were ordered to 'enjoin the good and prohibit the bad' (*amr bi'l ma'rūf wa nahy 'an al-munkar*) from the pulpits; vast sums of money were donated to the holy shrines; shaving was forbidden, and so on.[51]

While it is pointless to speculate on the real degree of *īmān* held by Shah Tahmasp – or, indeed, by the other Safavid rulers – for reasons outlined in Chapter One, it is a fact that all of the Safavid rulers did initiate actions that were, on the surface at least, Islamically-oriented in the externalist sense. The fact that the private lives of the Safavid rules were littered with open infringements of the *sharī'a* has not prevented some

87

commentators from describing them as having great piety, a confusion of terms which reveals a basic ignorance of the difference between Islam and *īmān*, and the tendency to accord the attributes of 'piety' and 'devotion' to anyone who affects an open display of his religious inclinations.[52] The externalism of the Twelver Shi'ite *fuqahā* in Safavid Iran may not have encouraged consciously the hypocrisy of 'private vice and public virtue' inherent in the behaviour of its patrons, the Safavid Shahs; however, the Islam of the *fuqahā* was almost totally externalist in nature, and they did not concern themselves unduly with communicating the subtleties of self-knowledge and belief to their leaders. Given this, it is not difficult to understand why rulers such as Tahmasp, whose standing in the eyes of the people relied in part upon an external show of religiosity, would favour externalism and its champions: most of the Safavid rulers gravitated more naturally towards the nomocentric legalism of the externalist *fuqahā*.

Shaykh Karaki's role as chief propagator of Twelver Shi'ite externalism, which began during the reign of Shah Isma'il, continued and reached higher levels of intensity during the early years of Shah Tahmasp's long reign. The 'Twelver Shi'itization' of the basically Sunni populace continued and was given fresh impetus by Shah Tahmasp's exhortation to the *fuqahā* to preach. The standard Twelver Shi'ite catechisms were tracts entitled *Dawāzdah Imām*, or 'The Twelve Imams', written in fulsome praise of the twelve Shi'ite Imams and ordered by both Shah Isma'il and Shah Tahmasp to be read in mosques and to form the basis of the Friday prayer sermons.[53]

A leading member of another famous family from Jabal 'Amil, 'Izz al-din Husayn b. 'Abd al-Samad al-Harith al-Hamdani (d. 984/1576-77), a student of the 'Second Martyr' and father of Baha' al-din Muhammad, also known as Shaykh Baha'i (d. 1031/1621-22), travelled extensively throughout Fars and Khurasan, and played an important role in spreading Twelver Shi'ism in the eastern parts of the Safavid empire. He served as *shaykh al-islām* of both Qazvin, Shah Tahmasp's capital, and Herat; he is considered to be one of the first scholars in Iran to encourage the study of Twelver Shi'ite Tradition collections there.[54] He also enjoyed a cordial relationship with Tahmasp and his court, and his overt support of the regime was clear since he deemed Friday prayer to be a religious obligation (*wājib*), and himself led the Friday prayer congregation while in Khurasan.[55] But it was undoubtedly Shaykh Karaki who enjoyed the greatest influence with Shah Tahmasp, and it was the Shaykh's teachings more than those of anyone else in his time that went in the direction of accepting the rule of the Safavids and conferring a kind of legitimacy upon it: in his treatise on land-tax he argued that Muslims could collect the tax for the ruler and accept their share of it from him, even in the absence of the Imam; they must also perform Friday prayers in congregation even if the Imam is not present to lead them.

Such decisions obviously were in harmony with the interests of the dynasty, for in return, Shah Tahmasp issued a *farmān* (decree), confirming Karaki's self-appointed rank of deputy *(nā'ib)* to the Hidden Imam and according him responsibility for maintaining the *shari'a* as the supreme religious authority of the realm.[56] Copies of the decree were despatched to all major towns and cities of the kingdom and people were enjoined to follow the rulings of Karaki or face punishment.[57] During the reign of Shah Isma'il, both political and religious authority had been vested in the personage of the Shah, who was both ruler and head of the Safavid order. With the advent of Tahmasp, however, and the necessity that was felt to play down the extremist origins of the dynasty in favour of the new orthodoxy, religious authority was for all intents and purposes stripped from the ruler and devolved upon the *mujtahid*; given the flight from quasi-Sufist extremism to Twelver Shi'ite externalism, the separation of the religious from the political was inevitable and laid the foundations of an hierarchy of *fuqahā* that would be able to work, teach, and issue religious decrees independently of the state.

Tahmasp's *farmān* is of immense historical significance, therefore, since it marks the beginning of what is loosely termed the Twelver Shi'ite *'ulamā* as an autonomous centre of power. Yet it cannot be stressed sufficiently that the *fuqahā* were in no way invested with anything that could remotely be construed as political power. As noted previously, a coherent Twelver Shi'ite political ethos was conspicuous by its absence, and thus the separation of religious from political authority – the reinforcement of the allegedly false distinction (in Islamic terms) between politics and religion – by Shah Tahmasp did not serve to create a separate power base as far as government and politics were concerned. It is only in the light of the developments of the past hundred years, and in particular the formulation of the concept of *wilāyat al-faqīh* by Ayatullah Khumayni, that we can look back on Shah Tahmasp's espousal of externalism and his separation of religion from state as the foetal stages of current developments in the Twelver Shi'ite socio-political and religious sphere.

Indigenous opposition to Twelver Shi'ite externalism: the Persian 'aristocracy'

Overt opposition of the kind noted by Ibn Ruzbihan and Sanson to the forced conversion of the population to Twelver Shi'ism was both limited and short-lived. Nominally, at the very least, the majority became Twelver Shi'ite in a relatively short time. Objection and opposition to the presence and ever-growing influence of the immigrant *fuqahā*, and to the kind of doctrines they were importing with them, continued in more covert forms, and usually from beneath the umbrella of *taqiyya*.

Relying heavily on the work of Jean Aubin, the Iranian scholar Said Amir Arjomand has highlighted the difference in outlook, background and academic output between what he calls the 'clerical estate' and the 'dogmatic party', the former term alluding to the indigenous clerical notables in pre-Safavid Iran and the latter denoting the Twelver Shi'ite *fuqahā* who came to the country during the Safavid era. Arjomand casts light on the polarization of the two groups with respect to the major positions in the religious establishment and talks of 'a struggle for domination' between them.[58] While it is clear that there was indeed much bad blood between the indigenous notables and the immigrant *fuqahā*, it is not clear whether we are justified in describing their inevitable polarization as a 'struggle.' Although the two bodies of scholars were not the most amiable of bedfellows, the fact is that they co-existed relatively peacefully throughout the Safavid era. If domination of the religious sphere was to be the lot of the *fuqahā* – as indeed it so transpired – then it came as a result not of an all-out struggle for supremacy but of the fact that upon the arrival of the *fuqahā* into Iran, the indigenous scholars were simply not qualified or collectively astute enough to fill the positions that really mattered.

The complex of religious institutions inherited by the Safavid administration consisted basically of mosques, religious seminaries (*madrasa*), religious endowments (*awqāf*), and the offices of *qādī* and *shaykh al-islām*. These were controlled by the state through the office of *sadr*, the most important 'religious' position in the realm and one which tended to be hereditary in nature. The main function of the *sadr* was to supervise and administer the *awqāf* and the distribution of their revenues to students and scholars and also to charity. The *sadr* was also supposed to supervise the administration of the *sharī'a* as the chief judicial authority of the state, although as Arjomand points out, the propagation of religious doctrine and the establishment of doctrinal conformity and uniformity were not the primary functions of the *sadr*, which were to remain administrative and largely judicial in nature. The Safavid *sadr* was thus in essence clearly an extension of the Taymurid *sadr* as the foremost clerical administrator of the realm. The offices of *sadr* – there were ten, for example, during the reign of Shah Tahmasp – were filled almost without exception from the rank of the indigenous, scholarly 'aristocrats', many of whom carried the title of *sayyid*. This group, which Arjomand calls the 'clerical estate', was Sunni prior to the Safavid revolution, and was engaged mostly in administrative duties and judicial and religious functions. With the advent of Shah Isma'il, this group professed Twelver Shi'ism – nominally or otherwise – and entered the service of the Safavid rulers.

The cultural outlook of the Persian religious administrators was, as Arjomand points out, a fairly catholic one, unlike that of the immigrant Twelver *fuqahā*, whose *forte* was, above everything else, the scriptural sciences. The Persian clerics did not limit themselves to the scriptural sciences; indeed, in many cases they had had precious little knowledge of *fiqh*, be it Sunni or Shi'ite. Instead they favoured philosophy, grammar and logic, mathematics, astronomy, literature and poetry; in general they can be said to have championed the rational (*'aqlī*) rather than the scriptural (*naqlī*) sciences.[59]

The Twelver Shi'ite *fuqahā* were different from the Persian clerics in numerous respects. Having spent centuries in isolated hamlets in Arab lands as the religious leaders of minority Twelver communities, advising them on matters of rite and ritual and keeping alive the Traditions of the Imams and, by extension, Twelver Shi'ism itself, they lacked the broad administrative, financial and cultural base enjoyed by the Persian clerical class. Arjomand's assertion that the outlook of the Twelver *fuqahā* (whom he erroneously refers to as '*ulamā*) was 'strictly religious' is totally misleading and stems from his failure – and in this he is not alone – to differentiate between internalism and externalism.[60] The outlook of the Twelver Shi'ite scholars who hailed from Arab Iraq, Syria and Bahrain was strictly externalist: they were versed first and foremost in the narrative (*naqlī*) sciences of *fiqh* and *hadīth*, and it was this particular facet of the Islamic revelation that they emphasized above all else in their writings and teaching. As Arjomand points out, the geographical factor is of crucial importance in understanding the cultural orientation of the Twelver *fuqahā*: years of relative isolation, plus the tremendous legacy of persecution as a minority sect, help us to understand why the scriptural sciences were so prized among those of Twelver Shi'ite persuasion. The sayings of the Imams form the life source of the Twelver Shi'ite belief system, and in times of oppression it was only through the preservation and promulgation of the Traditions that Twelver Shi'ism was able to survive: as we have already seen, the first Twelver Shi'ite scholars were *muhaddithūn*, and the collection, collation and transmission of Twelver Shi'ite Traditions has understandably been of greater emotional importance than holds true in the case of the Sunni Traditions. Yet this is not the only factor. What Arjomand and other scholars of Twelver Shi'ism have failed to do is to recognise the importance of the *īmān*/Islam dichotomy and to realise that the overwhelming preponderance of strictly externalist interests among Twelver Shi'ite scholars is a reflection of the nature of Twelver Shi'ism itself, and not merely a corollary of geographical or socio-political constraints.

Given the nature of the office of *sadr* and the background of its previous incumbents, it is clear that the Twelver Shi'ite *fuqahā* were not suited to the post; out of the ten men who served as *sadr* during the reign of Shah Tahmasp, only one was a Twelver *faqīh*. The post of *shaykh al-islām*, or chief religious dignitary, of each city appealed more to the interests and abilities of the immigrant *fuqahā*, however, and it was these positions that they began to occupy. Also, their knowledge of Twelver doctrine and ritual made them the obvious choices for the posts of *mudarris* (teacher) in the colleges and *pīshnamāz* (prayer leader) and *khatīb* (preacher) in the mosques.

In short, then, in the offices of *shaykh al-islām, mudarris, khatīb* and *pīshnamāz*, the Twelver *fuqahā* were accommodated in Safavid society and found themselves in a position to play an extremely important role in the spread of orthodox Twelver Shi'ism among the Iranian population. Those who attained the rank of *mujtahid*, and could thus command the obedience in matters of rite and ritual of the Twelver masses, were in an even better position to make their influence felt.

The polarity between the Persian clerical class and the Twelver Shi'ite immigrants may be seen as a clash of outlook between *sadr* and *faqīh* or, more topically, between *sadr* and *mujtahid*, for the first sign of mutual antipathy between the two groups came in the form of a *contretemps* between the eminent Persian noble Mir Ghiyath al-din Mansur al Dashtaki al-Shirazi (d. 949/1542-43) and the *khātim al-mujtahidīn*, Shaykh 'Ali Karaki. The controversy was emblematic of the fundamental unease with which the groups viewed each other.

Ghiyath al-din, one of whose titles was 'Seal of the Philosophers' (*khātim al-hukamā*), was an expert in the rational sciences and would later

92

exert through his writings a considerable influence on no less a scholar than Mulla Sadra. Ghiyath al-din held the office of *sadr* jointly with Mir Ni'matullah Hilli, a student and adversary of Karaki, from 935/1528-29 until 938/1531-32.[61] The difference in his outlook from that of Shaykh Karaki was compounded by his total lack of accomplishment in the field of *fiqh*, and it was against the elevation of the *fuqahā* to positions of power and influence that he fulminated. One case in question concerned the decision taken by Shaykh Karaki while in Shiraz to realign the *qibla*, which he claimed was out of true. Ghiyath al-din, who had not yet risen to the position of *sadr*, objected strongly, saying that the determination of the correct angle at which to stand in prayer in order to face Mecca was a task for a mathematician and not a *faqīh*. Smarting at this affront, Karaki sent a note to Ghiyath al-din in which he quoted from the Koran:

"The fools among the people will say: 'What hath turned them from the Qibla to which they were used?' Say: to God belong both East and West: He guideth whom He will to a Way that is straight."[62]

To which Ghiyath al-din, not wishing to be outwitted, replied, also from the Koran:

"Even if thou wert to bring to the people of the Book all the signs (together) they would not follow thy Qibla; nor art thou going to follow their Qibla; nor indeed will they follow each other's Qibla. If thou after the knowledge hath reached thee, wert to follow their (vain) desires – then wert thou indeed (clearly) in the wrong."[63]

The verbal jousting of Shaykh Karaki and Ghiyath al-din, ostensibly over the question of the *qibla*, highlights both the basic difference in outlook of the two factions and the resolve shown by each group to go its own way and not acquiesce to the opposition.

The hostility between Karaki and Ghiyath al-din came to a head during Shaykh Karaki's second long sojourn in Iran, at which time Ghiyath al-din had become *sadr*. This time a fierce dispute ensued between the two in the presence of Shah Tahmasp himself. The Shah saw fit to back Karaki, who eventually persuaded the ruler to dismiss Ghiyath al-din from the post of *sadr*.[64] As Tahmasp himself writes:

At this time a learned controversy arose between the Mujtahid of the Age, Shaykh 'Ali b. 'Abd al-'Ali (al-Karaki) and Mir Ghiyath al-din Mir Mu'izz al-Mansur, the *sadr*. Even though the Mujtahid of the Age was triumphant, they did not acknowledge his *ijtihad*, and were bent on hostility. We took note of the side of Truth, and affirmed him in *ijtihad*.[65]

Tahmasp's later dismissal of Ghiyath al-din from the post of *sadr* marked another of the seals of approval given to the Twelver Shi'ite *fuqahā* and the externalist cause. The office of *sadr* was, in keeping with the wishes of Shaykh Karaki, conferred upon one Mir Mu'izz al-din Muhammad al-Isfahani, whom the author of *Tarīkh-i 'ālamārā-i 'Abbāsi* describes as a 'paragon of scholarship and a practical man.'[66] Karaki's influence on Tahmasp continued after his death in 940/1533-34, for in 942/1535-36 a student earlier recommended by Karaki, Mir Asadullah Shushtari, was appointed *sadr* and held the office until his death some twenty years later. However admirable Karaki might have been as an individual to Shah Tahmasp, it was obviously the forceful – and, for the Safavid regime, politically expedient – nature of his doctrine and rulings that pleased the ruler. After Karaki's death, a Persian cleric, Amir Nizam al-din 'Abd al-Hayy al-Husayni al-Jurjani, who was versed in both the rational and narrative sciences and had served at the court of Sultan Husayn Bayqara in Herat, came to the court of Tahmasp and requested that the Shah confer upon him the status of chief *mujtahid*; Tahmasp refused, adding that he wanted a *mujtahid* from Jabal 'Amil only.[67] Both Karaki's son and grandson, externalists in their own right, rose to prominence during the reign of Shah Tahmasp, as did many of Karaki's students and protégés, and many of the offices of *shaykh al-islām* went to eminent *fuqahā* from Jabal 'Amil.[68]

It should be noted at this point that the rise to prominence of the *fuqahā* was not synonymous with a decline in popularity of the Persian clerical class in the eyes of Shah Tahmasp. True, there was a certain amount of dislocation as posts such as *shaykh al-islām*, *mudarris* and *pīshnamāz* – all crucial for the effective spread of Twelver Shi'ism – were 'won' for the Twelver *fuqahā* by Shaykh Karaki; however, the post of *sadr* was to remain primarily in the hands of the Persian aristocrat-scholars, and the reverence shown by Tahmasp to this class – many of whom held the title of *sayyid* – showed no signs of weakening.[69] Ghiyath al-din, for example, despite being dismissed from the office of *sadr* at the request of Shaykh Karaki, remained a favourite of the Shah, who wrote an affectionate letter

94

to him in Shiraz, showered him with gifts, and gave him an important administrative position with responsibility for appointing and dismissing judges in the province of Fars.[70] Tahmasp patronized both Persian cleric and Twelver Shi'ite *faqīh*, effecting a balance between them which enabled them to co-exist relatively peacefully. Arjomand's description of the relationship between the two groups as a struggle for domination thus smacks somewhat of overstatement.

In his otherwise penetrating study of Twelver Shi'ism in Safavid and Qajar Iran, *The Shadow of God and the Hidden Imam*, Arjomand makes a number of sweeping generalizations that serve to obscure several important points. His black-and-white portrayal of what he calls the 'clerical estate' versus the 'dogmatic party' - the Persian cleric/scholars versus the Twelver Shi'ite *fuqahā* - summons up an image of a clash between two tightly delineated ideological domains, with no scope for the overlapping of interests and ideas and the vacillations in orientation that undoubtedly occur among Muslim scholars as a result of the fluid nature of belief and adherence to Islam. Not only is it a gross misrepresentation to portray the Twelver Shi'ite *fuqahā* as being engaged in the pursuit of 'strictly religious' knowledge, while the 'clerical estate' were engaged in the 'rational sciences' – as though religion were synonymous with *fiqh* and *hadīth*, and the pursuit of philosophy and theosophy were somehow removed from the sphere of religion – it is also an oversimplification to suppose that the two groups were as clearly defined in religious orientation as Arjomand makes them out to be.

It is a fact that the Twelver Shi'ite *fuqahā* became the teachers of many of the Persian clerics at a very early stage; at the request of Tahmasp, students were sent abroad to Syria, eventually to join the ranks of the indigenous scholars studying in Iranian centres of learning under the immigrant *fuqahā*. Mir Mu'izz al-din Muhammad al-Isfahani, who succeeded Ghiyath al-din as *sadr*, was a member of the Persian clerical class yet was a student and protégé of Karaki. And Mir Abu al-Wali, a notable *sayyid* from Shiraz who administered the shrine at Ardabil under Shah Tahmasp and served as *sadr* under Shah 'Abbas I, was an expert in *fiqh* and, by all accounts, 'a fanatical Shi'ite.'[71] The Persian clerics also proved much less unbending than the Twelver Shi'ite *fuqahā* in that they were more open to the assimilation of alien ideas and changes in orientation, even though on occasions this might have been out of expedience rather than sincere personal desire. Shams al-din Muhammad b. Ahmad Khafri Shirazi (d. 935/1528-29 or 951/1544-45), an erstwhile Sunni and student of Sadr al-din Muhammad Dashtaki Shirazi (d.

903/1497-98) who wrote treatises on gnosis (*'irfān*) in the Illuminationist or *ishrāqī* vein, had no interest in either dissimulation (*taqīyya*) or exile; in reply to his concerned son-in-law, who was horrified at the thought of being forced to curse the first three Caliphs, he is reported to have said, 'Go ahead and curse them – after all they were no more than three wretched Arabs!' [72] When Shah Isma'il took Azarbaijan and Shirvan and, as a result, many Sunni *fuqahā* and men of the pen took to their heels, Kashan was said to be left without either *qādī* or *faqīh*. Khafri, who was resident in Kashan at that time, was besieged with people asking him questions on points of the new jurisprudence. Khafri, despite having no knowledge whatsoever of *fiqh* – and especially of the Twelver Shi'ite variety – began to answer as he thought fit using pure guesswork. When Shaykh Karaki came to Kashan, he saw that Khafri's rulings were consonant with Twelver Shi'ite *fiqh* and promptly conferred upon him the title of deputy (*nā'ib*), to act as prayer leader and *muftī* (giver of legal rulings) in Karaki's absence. [73]

As Arjomand rightly asserts, it was possible for a Persian cleric to become Twelver Shi'ite and retain his non-externalist outlook; however it was impossible – thanks to the very nature of the new religion – for a Persian cleric to 'capture', as Arjomand puts it, a post such as that of *shaykh al-islām* from the so-called 'dogmatic party' and remain a non-externalist as far as the dictates of the post were concerned. For this reason, the Twelver Shi'ite *fuqahā* and their externalist doctrines were able to make an impression on the crucial posts of *shaykh al-islām*, *pīshnamāz* and *mudarris*, all of which were eventually theirs for the taking.

Another impression given by Arjomand which must be dispelled here is that if the interests of the Twelver Shi'ite *fuqahā* were externalist - 'religious' in Arjomand's terminology - then those of the Persian clerical class were internalist. It is a fact that the truly overwhelming majority of Twelver Shi'ite scholars were externalists, with no academic interests other than *fiqh* and *hadīth*; this is borne out, as we shall shortly see, by all of the major biographical dictionaries covering the scholars of the Safavid period. Iskandar Munshi's brief but revealing account of early Safavid *sayyids*/*sadrs* and *shaykhs*/theologians is divided roughly on the Persian cleric/Arab Twelver Shi'ite *faqīh* basis and constitutes an important source for Arjomand's findings. In it we see that, indeed, the Persian cleric/*sadr* class, the majority of whom were *sayyids*, pursued for the most part the rational ('*aqlī*) rather than the narrative (*naqlī*) sciences, with philosophy and theosophy (*hikma*) being the major trends. However this does not mean necessarily that the Persian clerical class held any kind of monopoly on internalism; although major internalist scholars such as Ghazali and Mulla Sadra were versed in philosophy and *hikma*, philosophy and *hikma* do not automatically connote internalism.

Thus we can say that the Twelver Shi'ite *fuqahā* – externalists – entered an arena that was for the most part non-externalist in religious orientation and, as far as the Twelver Shi'ite brand of externalism is concerned, almost totally alien. Opposition centred initially not upon the internalist/externalist dichotomy directly but indeed upon one of its side-effects: the elevation of the *fuqahā* to a level that was deemed unwarranted by their actual status. The rise to prominence of the *fuqahā* under the protection and patronage of the ruler, and their appropriation of the terms *'ilm* and *'ulamā* to describe themselves and their work, had delivered a serious blow to the religious permissiveness that had prevailed prior to the advent of the Safavids. And although the non-externalism typified by the pursuits of the Persian clerics and other indigenous scholars continued to flourish, the attacks upon Sunnism and certain strains of extremism must have brought it home that religious liberty was in danger of gradually ebbing away. Even before the end of Shah Tahmasp's reign a leading historian and member of the Persian clerical class noted that the 'ignorant (*juhalā*) were being turned into the learned (*fudalā*) and the learned accorded the status of the ignorant,' and that:

> Most of his (Tahmasp's) domains became devoid of men of excellence and knowledge, and filled with men of ignorance: and only a few men of (true) learning are to be found in the entire realm of Iran.[74]

Shah Isma'il II to Shah 'Abbas I

The influx of Twelver Shi'ite *fuqahā* into Iran, the indoctrination of the indigenous students and scholars in the new creed, and the assimilation of members of the Persian clerical class into the ranks of the Twelver learned hierarchy all continued apace throughout the reigns of the quasi-Sunni Isma'il II (1576-77) and the ineffectual Shah Muhammad Khudabanda (1577-87). That these rulers were content to continue their forefathers' policy of supporting the externalist cause, and that the Twelver *fuqahā* still saw fit to endorse Safavid rule, is clear from the fact that Shaykh Karaki's son, Shaykh 'Ali, presided over the coronation ceremony of both Isma'il II and Shah Muhammad, laying before them the 'rug of kingship' (*qālīcha-i saltanat*) to mark their accession.[75] Shah Muhammad's approval of the externalist cause was reflected in a series of measures designed to reflect the ruler's personal piety and adherence to the letter of the law: like his father, Shah Tahmasp, he repented publicly and issued edicts forbidding the consumption of wine and the pursuits of pastimes prohibited by the *sharī'a*.[76] Nevertheless, Shah Muhammad revered the Persian clerical class as much as Tahmasp had done, thereby preserving a balance – be it purposeful or incidental – between the two groups. Shah Muhammad's apparent eagerness to please all of those around him also gave rise to a recrudescence of Qizilbash inter-tribal factionalism and an increase in their demands on the state. It was the resurgence of Qizilbash power, thanks to the laxity and largesse of Shah Muhammad, that later led Shah 'Abbas I to take action against both the Qizilbash and the more unruly of the Sufi elements, and in so doing further strengthen his support for the externalist *fuqahā*.

Shah Isma'il II is the great anomaly of the Safavid dynasty inasmuch as he openly showed an unveiled predilection for Sunnism and was antagonistic towards the Twelver Shi'ite *fuqahā*. Reluctant to speak ill either of the Prophet's wife, 'Aisha, who was reviled by the Twelvers because of her hostility towards Ali, or of the first three Caliphs, Shah Isma'il II gave his support to a number of scholars who were suspected of holding pro-Sunni sympathies. One such scholar was Mirza Makhdum Shirazi, a *sayyid* of the Sayfi line and a descendant of Shah Tahmasp's minister, Qadi Jahan, himself a closet Sunni. Mirza Makhdum gave sermons (*wa 'z*) at the Haydariyya mosque in the capital, Qazvin, and drew large crowds to listen to them. Under Shah Isma'il II, the office of *sadr* was divided, with half of the post going to Mirza Makhdum.[77] Eventually, since he later made no effort to conceal his Sunni tendencies, he was dismissed from office.[78] Mawlana Mirza Jan Shirazi, an expert in the rational sciences who enjoyed great influence in his native town of Shiraz, was another of Shah Isma'il II's favoured scholars. Relying on the support of the ruler he was able to flaunt his Sunnism with relative impunity; after the death of the Shah he was forced to leave Iran for the more liberal atmosphere of the Indian sub-continent.[79]

Shah Isma'il II was particularly opposed to the ritual cursing (*la 'n*) of the three Caliphs and other enemies of the Twelver Shi'ites, and decreed that the practice be abandoned. Orders were given to the effect that anyone who uttered the imprecations would be punished severely. Furthermore, the Shah also paid money to anyone who was able to claim with sincerity that he or she had never cursed the Caliphs. Several of the Twelver Shi'ite *fuqahā* were barred from entering the Shah's presence, while the works of the rabidly anti-Sunni *mujtahid*, Mir Sayyid Husayn, were impounded.[80] Eulogies of the House of Ali were forbidden to be recited in mosques, a measure which incensed, among others, the fanatical Qizilbash, who were given to plastering the doors and walls of the mosques with pro-Alid love poetry.[81] In the end, Isma'il II's attempt to re-establish Sunnism had to be abandoned in the face of strong Qizilbash opposition.

The Shah Isma'il II affair is interesting for it serves to buttress the assertion that a considerable number of people had had recourse to *taqiyya* in order to conceal their Sunni beliefs. Also worthy of note is the fact that those leading scholars who proclaimed their Sunni proclivities and supported Isma'il II were non-externalist in religious orientation and of Persian origin; the joint holders of the office of sadr during Shah Isma'il II's short reign - Mirza Makhdum Shirazi and Shah 'Inayatullah Isfahani – were both scions of well-known aristocratic families. On the other hand, Shah Isma'il II's failure to revive Sunnism serves as an indicator of the extent to which the Twelver Shi'ite *fuqahā* had made their creed acceptable in Iran, and also of the influence that the *fuqahā* as individuals were capable of exerting.[82]

The objectives set out by the first Safavid ruler, Isma'il I – namely the subduction of Qizilbash extremism, Sunnism and Sufism, and the establishment of Twelver Shi'ite externalism – were pursued with no uncertain success by his great-grandson, Shah 'Abbas I (1587-1629), arguable the most politically adept and strategically astute of all the Safavid rulers. Shah 'Abbas introduced centralizing reforms of a sweeping nature, one of which focused on the army: introducing a new corps of mostly Georgian slave-soldiers (*ghulām*), he altered the composition of the military forces of his empire and reorganised the Qizilbash in a way that detracted considerably from their former power and influence.[83] Shah 'Abbas's staunch determination to ensure that loyalty and obedience to the Shah rather than membership of the Qizilbash was the sole criterion for advancement also manifested itself in his massacre of a large contingent of seasoned adherents of the Safavid Order known as the 'old Sufis of Lahijan.' They were accused of treason and of failing to place submission to the will of the leader (*murshid*) of the Order, namely Shah 'Abbas himself, before all worldly interests.[84] That his attack on their loyalty was merely a pretext for a massacre becomes obvious when one considers how the Shah had exploited the blind loyalty of his Turcoman followers in order to use them in menial jobs around his household and court, and how he had in any case been moving away from the concept of loyalty on the basis of the *murshid-murid* relationship towards the ideal of 'love for the Shah' (*shāhsiwānī*).[85]

Shah 'Abbas's rejection of extremism was also reflected in his suppression of the Nuqtawiyya, a highly unorthodox school of thought akin to Hurufism.[86] Although he himself had once taken a personal interest in the heretical Nuqtawi doctrines, the potential dangers that it, like any extremist creed, held for the dynasty soon became apparent to him and so he proceeded to extirpate the Nuqtawi leaders and their adherents. He also brought a virtual end to the Ni'matullahiyya Order in Iran, although not so much by brute force as by disdain and the withholding of royal patronage. Prior to the reign of Shah 'Abbas, the Order had enjoyed cordial relations with the monarchy and had become a conspicuous element in the Persian aristocracy. Under Shah 'Abbas, however, it began to sink into oblivion. The Shah, ever wary of the existence of potential centres of power, appears to have fulminated against the Order on account of their being arguably the most highly organized of the Sufi brotherhoods rather than any inherent dislike for their obviously internalist orientation; this is clear when one considers his own alleged penchant for the unorthodox *a la* Nuqtawiyya and the support he gave to individual, non-Order affiliated Gnostics.[87]

'Abbas also continued the persecution of Sunnis, especially at the outset of his reign when Sunnism was still strong in certain areas of the country,[88] the contempt shown by the monarch for his co-religionists stands in stark contrast with the respect he accorded non-Muslims.[89] These basic contradictions – the public suppression and private espousal of unorthodox beliefs; the suppression of Sufi Orders and the patronization of individual gnostics; intolerance of fellow Muslims (Sunnis) and tolerance towards non-Muslims – show that Shah 'Abbas I cut his religious coat according to his political cloth. Capable at times of acts of devastating cruelty, Shah 'Abbas nevertheless demonstrated at other times an almost excessive zeal for personal displays of religiosity and humility. On one occasion he is said to have made one of his *fuqahā* ride ahead of him in public while he followed on foot, a demonstration designed to portray him as a humble follower and respecter of the faith. He twice visited the shrine of Imam Rida in Mashhad on foot, endowing it with land, property and his own personal belongings.[90] Similar attention was lavished on the shrines in Najaf and Karbala. To be generous to Shah 'Abbas, one may conclude that he, in true externalist manner, held the erroneous view that *iman* is best gauged by actions (*a'māl*), and that the more exuberant and expansive

100

the outward display, the greater one's status as a believer (*mu'min*) becomes. A more realistic view, perhaps, may be that his piety was for the most part utilitarian, and that he used the external display of religiosity as a means of enhancing his legitimacy.

As Shah 'Abbas distanced himself over the years from his initial flirtation with extremism and adopted a politically more pragmatic policy of religious externalism, his patronage of the Twelver Shi'ite *fuqahā* increased accordingly. In 1003/1594-95, a large number of *fuqahā* were invited to Qazvin and entertained there by the ruler. Shah 'Abbas paid special attention to Shaykh Baha al-din 'Amili, better known simply as Shaykh Baha'i, who was to become the most eminent of all the Twelver Shi'ite scholars during the Shah's reign. As Aubin has noted, there was a 'parallel development between the elimination of the characteristically Safavid element and the consolidation of Twelver Shi'ism in Iran.'[91] With the help of Shaykh Baha'i, Shah 'Abbas built up Isfahan – which he had made his capital in 1006/1597-98 – into a thriving metropolis and important centre of Twelver Shi'ite learning.[92]

Another point worth noting is that with the emergence of Isfahan as the new focal point of Twelver learning, for the first time in history the majority of Twelver Shi'ite *fuqahā* in Iran consisted of indigenous scholars. The process initiated by Shaykh Karaki whereby many of the Persian clerics – the majority of whom were non-externalist – were assimilated into the body of Twelver Shi'ite *fuqahā* was now nearing completion with the reign of Shah 'Abbas. Thus we find an increasing number of the descendants of the early cleric-scholars and non-externalists entrenched in the pursuit of purely externalist knowledge. The influence exerted by the immigrant Twelver Shi'ite *fuqahā* on the indigenous scholars was to a certain extent reciprocated, although not, generally speaking, to the extent of forfeiting an externalist for a non-externalist or internalist outlook. Whereas those indigenous scholars who had been steeped in non-externalist pursuits were easily able to find a niche as *fuqahā*, there is no record in the sources of any immigrant Twelver Shi'ite *fuqahā* consciously re-orienting their interests in the direction of non-externalism or internalism: the assimilation of the incoming *fuqahā* manifested itself primarily in their becoming 'gentrified', in the sense that they became part of the landed classes.[93]

Another by-product of this process of assimilation was the emergence of a syncretist element in Twelver Shi'ite circles of learning. Shaykh Baha'i, for instance, was an authority on *fiqh* and *hadīth* who also had leanings towards the rational, non-externalist sciences. Whether or not he can be said to have combined the elements of internalism and externalism in the way one might argue they were intended to be combined, and in the proportions adumbrated by the Koran, is difficult to ascertain, although from a study of the titles of his works it would appear that externalism had the upper hand. His poetry, however, points the other way and demonstrates that a synthesis was possible, although extremely rare.

Baha'i's contemporary and friend, Mir Muhammad Baqir b. Muhammad al-Husayni al-Astarabadi (dd. 1041/1631-32), better known as Mir Damad, also combined the rational and scriptural sciences in his output, leaning heavily towards the non-externalist sciences of philosophy and theosophy.[94] He is credited with having founded the so-called 'School of Isfahan', the school of gnostic philosophy or '*irfān* that was to be the principal – and final – bastion of internalism in the Safavid period.

Although syncretism was not strictly speaking a by-product of the religiously enlightened and relatively liberal atmosphere engendered by Shah 'Abbas, the fact that internalism and externalism were able to co-exist in relative peace most certainly was. Again this must be attributed to the character of the ruler himself, and to the absolute authority that was invested in him as Shah, and, therefore, as patron of the religious scholars in his midst – internalist and externalist alike. Although, as we have seen, Shah 'Abbas withdrew his support from the organised Sufi Orders and was ruthless in his extirpation of extremists, his patronage of individual non-externalists continued – often to the detriment of the externalists. Shaykh Jawad b. Sa'id b. Jawad al-Kazimi, a student of Shaykh Baha'i and a prominent *faqīh* in his own right, held the office of *shaykh al-islām* in the town of Astarabad until a *contretemps* with some of the inhabitants led to their expelling him from the town. Shaykh Jawad duly appealed to Shah 'Abbas for help. However, not only did the Shah refuse to help the *faqīh*, he in fact went one step further and proceeded to banish him from the country. This apparently drastic course of action becomes easier to understand when one realises that Shah 'Abbas was a follower in spiritual matters of Sayyid Amir Muhammad Astarabadi, a Sufi adept and elder of the town, and the most vociferous of those who had called for Shaykh Jawad's expulsion.[95]

Although Shah 'Abbas was ready to adopt such measures as were illustrated above in deference to individuals, as far as the 'religious' classes as a whole were concerned he kept a firm upper hand in all of his dealings with them. The way he managed his leading scholars is best exemplified by an anecdote cited by Sir John Malcolm in his *History of Persia*:

It is related that when he (Shah 'Abbas) was one day riding with the celebrated Meer Mahomed Bauker Damad (Mir Damad) on his right hand and the equally famed Shaikh Bahaudeen Aumilee (Shaykh Baha'i) on his left, the king desired to discover if there lurked any secret envy, or jealousy, in the breasts of these two learned priests. Turning to Meer Mahomed Bauker, whose horse was prancing and capering, he observed, "What a dull brute Shaikh Bahaudeen is riding! He cannot make his animal keep pace with us." "The wonder is, how the horse moves at all," said the Moolah, "when he considers what a load of learning and knowledge he has upon his back." Abbas, after some time, turned around to Shaikh Bahaudeen, and said to him, "Did you ever see such a prancing animal as that which Meer Mahomed Bauker rides? Surely that is not the style for a horse to go in who carried a grave Moolah." "Your Majesty will, I am assured," said the shaykh, "forgive the horse, when you reflect on the just right he has to be proud of his rider." The monarch bent his head forward on his saddle, and returned thanks to the Almighty for the singular blessing He had bestowed upon his reign, of two wise and pious men, who, though living at a court had minds untainted by envy and hatred.[96]

Apart from demonstrating the unrivalled authority of the ruler over his theologians and *fuqahā*, the above anecdote shows that in the reign of Shah 'Abbas I the relative lack of antagonism and absence of hostility between externalism and non-externalism was such that exponents of both approaches – if Shaykh Baha'i is taken here to be predominantly externalist – were able to co-exist in harmony and lend support, even, to each other when the occasion demanded.

Before surveying the reigns of Shah 'Abbas I's immediate successors, Shah Safi (1629-42) and Shah 'Abbas II (1642-66), under whom non-externalism was able to flourish, an important excursus must be made into the respective realms of externalism and non-externalism/internalism in order to gain a firmer grasp of the nature of both orientations and to realise why *rapprochement* between them occurred only rarely, and how, at least up until the advent of Shah Sulayman in 1077/1666, a relatively peaceful but distanced co-existence was the most that could be achieved.

The externalists: their milieu and teachings

For a review of the Twelver Shi'ite externalists and their academic output in the Safavid period it is useful to look at what might be considered the most comprehensive – although not necessarily the most detailed – of the biographical dictionaries which deal with the lives and works of Twelve Shi'ite scholars, the six-volume work entitled *Rīyād al-'ulamā wa hīyād al-fudalā* (The Gardens of the Knowledgeable and the Sacred Domains of the Learned) by Shaykh 'Abdullah Afandi al-Isfahani.

Less parochial than *Lu'lu'at al-Bahrayn*[97] and *Amal al-'Āmil*,[98] both of which concentrate on scholars from two particular geographical areas, and more expansive than *Qisas al-'ulamā*[99] and *Rawdāt al-jannāt*, Afandi's work paints a vast portrait of Twelver Shi'ite scholarship on a canvas of history that stretches from the era of the founding fathers of Twelver Shi'ism – Shaykh Mufid, Shaykh Tusi et al – to the momentous years preceding the Afghan conquest of Iran in the early 12th/18th century. Fortunately for us, the bulk of the work concerns itself with the Safavid scholars: an estimated 90 per cent of the biographies included are of scholars operating during the Safavid era. The work is clearly not an exhaustive one, and indeed does not purport to be so. Little-known scholars studying and teaching in private in obscure corners of the realm do not, for obvious reasons, appear in these volumes, although the existence of such figures is inferred and used on occasions to illustrate anecdotes about the more prominent lights in the Safavid academic firmament. The fact that it is the obviously more prominent scholars who are listed by the author leaves one to imagine the extent to which scholars of academic orientations other than those which feature most frequently in the work were operating throughout the length and breadth of the country.

However, it was public prominence, proximity to court circles, and royal patronage that would undoubtedly determine which trend would be set, all of this fuelled by the bias of the rulers towards one orientation rather than another. Up until and including the reign of Shah 'Abbas I, externalism had been allowed to flourish unchecked. Non-externalism, certain expressions of which, as we have seen, were suppressed by the state, continued to prosper, albeit with numerous setbacks and difficulties for its proponents. It would continue to play an important role in the lives of the Iranian people during the reigns of both Shah Safi and Shah 'Abbas II, particularly through the gnostic philosophy of the 'School of Isfahan', more about which we shall read later. The Safavid era cannot, then, be seen as a backdrop against which Sufi and *faqīh* fought for prominence.[100]

Rīyād al-'ulamā should not be dismissed as being biased towards externalism. Afandi, despite being an externalist himself, is relatively – and refreshingly – fair in his assessment of his subjects, and should be considered as having portrayed an historical fact, namely that in Safavid Iran it was the externalist who enjoyed greater prominence and recognition.

Statistically speaking, Afandi's figures are staggering: of approximately 2412 scholars mentioned, 2345 are wholly or predominantly externalist in outlook. Afandi uses the terms *'ālim* (scholar; lit: 'one who knows'), *faqīh* (jurist), and *fādil* (scholar; one who has attained excellence, or *fadl*, in learning) to denote the externalists; he often uses all three terms simultaneously to describe the same individual. The change in meaning of the words *'ālim* and *faqīh* had by this time become engraved upon the psyche of all but the most discerning of scholars, and thus Afandi's use of the three terms together does not mean that he was aware of their semantic differences or that he was using them in their original Koranic form. For the vast majority of scholars in Afandi's time, the words *faqīh*, *'ālim* and *fādil* could mean only one thing: a person who had acquired a certain recognised proficiency in the assimilation and promulgation of the scriptural sciences. This is borne out, as we shall see shortly, by the individual biographies, which very in length from as little as one line to as much as over 30 pages.

The 67 individuals who are predominantly non-externalist in outlook are characterized for the most part by the epithets *filsūf* (philosopher), *hakīm* (sage or theosopher) or Sufi. Occasionally the words *faqīh* and *hakīm* appear together to describe the same person, denoting the fact that the scholar in question had presumably been able to embrace both externalist and non-externalist approaches in his writings. The true syncretist remains, however, a rare and exotic species as far as the Safavid scholarly realm is concerned. Shaykh Baha'i and Mir Damad, mentioned earlier, both covered the externalist and non-externalist aspects of Islam in their teachings, although in Shaykh Baha'i's case the externalist element far outweighed the non-externalist one, whereas Mir Damad struck more of a balance, thus standing out as one of the few genuine syncretists of the Safavid era. Most of the 67 non-externalists mentioned in *Rīyād al-'ulamā* do not take a syncretistic approach, however, and lean heavily towards the non-externalist disciplines, with some of them possessing no knowledge of *fiqh* or of the Arabic language whatsoever.

The use of the term 'non-externalist' here is intended to indicate that one cannot be sure how many of these scholars who are described as philosophers, theosophers or Sufis were actually internalists in the true sense of the word – despite the fact that philosophy, theosophy and Sufism are generally conducive to, but not the absolute prerequisites of, an internalist outlook *per se*. And to reiterate earlier comments it must be stressed that the list of non-externalists is certainly not an exhaustive one. It is clear that non-externalism had popular appeal throughout the Safavid era and did not begin to wane until the appearance of Muhammad Baqir Majlisi. *Rīyād al-ʿulamā*, therefore, in showing a preponderance of externalists may not reflect the true grass-roots orientation of the Iranian populace during the Safavid era, but it does show the extent to which Twelver Shiʿite externalism had supplanted its rivals in the academic sphere - the very place where it mattered and in which decisions as to what the future religious orientation of the people should be were taken.

As his appellation suggests, the externalist focuses his scholarly attention most fundamentally on *fiqh* and *hadīth*, the former covering the dictates of the *sharīʿa*, and the latter concerning the transmission and promulgation of the Prophetic Traditions, the body of which acts as a vehicle for the *sunna*. For Twelver Shiʿites, as we have already seen, the *hadīth* also includes the sayings of the Imams; in fact, the sayings of the Prophet are held valid only if an Imam or trusted companion of an Imam appears in the chain of transmission. When talking in terms of Twelver Shiʿite externalism, one must bear in mind that the Twelver Shiʿite perception of the scriptural sciences is an 'imamocentric' one; the difference in matters of rite and ritual between the four Sunni and the Twelver schools may indeed be negligible, but it is the spirit behind this difference, this 'imamocentrism', which is of importance.

The *imāma* being all-important in Twelver Shiʿism, it is no surprise to find that the Twelver Traditions focus as much on personalities – the Imams – as they do on legal and ritual detail. Thus the scope for work in the field of *hadīth* would appear to be much greater for the Twelver Shiʿites than for the Sunnis: not only is it the body of narrations concerning legal practices that they have to transmit but also the body of Traditions which deals with the issues specifically related to the *imāma*, or the concept of the Imamate itself; the socio-political and historical roles of the Imams; martyrdom; Mahdism; dissimulation, and so on. Any sect which is as determined as Twelver Shiʿism to insist on the necessity of specific divinely-appointed men - the Imams - for the preservation of the faith and the redemption of the individual inevitably promotes the development of a vast literature given over to the saga of these men. One of the most important media through which their story is told is the corpus of Twelver Traditions which comprise the 'Four Books' (*al-kutub al-arba'a*) mentioned earlier, as well as numerous other compilations spanning many centuries. Twelver Shi'ite Traditions can thus be divided into two basic categories: those which deal with the principles of Twelver Shi'ism; and those which focus on its personalities.

Underpinning Twelver Shi'ite doctrines are the fundamentals of belief (*usūl al-īmān*), of which there are five: Divine Unity (*tawhīd*); prophethood (*nabuwwa*); the resurrection (*ma'ād*); justice (*'adāla*); and the Imamate (*imāma*). The first there of these are common to all Muslims. As in the Sunni corpus of Traditions, a considerable number of Twelver Traditions deals with these fundamentals of belief;[101] far greater attention, however, is focused on the question of *imāma*, which, although it ranks second in the Twelver Shi'ite hierarchy of fundamentals, would appear to outstrip all others in terms of the number of Traditions pertaining to it. Consequently, the number of Traditions in the Twelver Shi'ite collections which deals with personalities - the Imams - is far greater than the number of Traditions in the Sunni collections which describe the life, behaviour and everyday practices of Islam's pivotal personality, Muhammad himself.

What should in reality be a peripheral element of Twelver doctrine, but which is in fact elevated by the externalists to a position of importance far beyond its Koranic status, is the body of rites and rituals known as the *furū'* or 'secondary principles' of Islam: the rules which govern all of the external and practical aspects of the faith such as prayer, fasting, almsgiving, pilgrimage and the like. These secondary principles are so extensive and comprehensive that virtually every facet of day-to-day human life is covered by them.

As was noted earlier, the difference in jurisprudential practice between the Sunnis and Twelver Shi'ites is often minimal; indeed, in many instances there is more discrepancy between the four Sunni schools of jurisprudence than there is between the Sunni schools as a whole and the Twelver Shi'ite school, more commonly known as the *madhhab al-ja'farī*, after its founder Ja'far al-Sadiq. The most salient common point between Sunnism and Twelver Shi'ism is that their scholars have traditionally concentrated their efforts on the study of secondary principles, and on their transmission to succeeding generations of scholars via the twin sciences of *fiqh* and *hadīth*. In this sense, externalism – and its predominance over non-externalism and internalism – is by no means an exclusively Twelver Shi'ite phenomenon. Nevertheless, for historical reasons outlined earlier, the cultivation of the scriptural sciences enjoyed greater momentum in the Twelver Shi'ite world of learning.

The Twelver Shi'ite predilection for the scriptural sciences – the cornerstone of externalism – can be seen in the scholarly output of the Twelver Shi'ite scholars in the Safavid period. As Afandi shows, just as the number of externalists heavily outweighs that of the non-externalists, so too does the *fiqh/hadīth* element preponderate over the non-scriptural one in the academic output of the Safavid Twelver scholars.

The exposition of matters of ritual and sacred law is the focal point of externalist teaching, and thus in the Safavid period as a whole, and particularly after the transfer of the capital from Qazvin to Isfahan, a plethora of works on the secondary principles emerged. The following subjects are the most conspicuous among Afandi's list of Twelver works of jurisprudence: the ritual prayer (*salāt*); fasting (*sawm*); *khums* and *zakāt*; pilgrimage (*hajj* and *zīyāra*); the regulations governing Friday prayers; ritual purity and impurity (*tahāra* and *najāsa*); divorce (*talāq*); the rules concerning the correct way of reciting the Koran (*qarā'a*); supererogatory prayers (*du'ā*); acts of worship to be carried out at various times of the day (*a'māl al-yawmiyya*); and foster-relationships (*rida*). These matters of rite and ritual, passed down to the faithful from the Prophet and/or the Imams, were presented in he form of general *hadīth* collections or in short treatises devoted to one particular topic. Very often a scholar would simply collect together all of the Traditions he had heard from his different teachers or gleaned from various sources concerning one subject in particular – ritual prayer for instance – and then distribute it as a treatise under his own name, often without adding any comment on, or explanation of, the narrative text. These Traditions would then be transmitted to his disciples, who would then be able to quote, use and transmit them upon teacher's authority. Such collations for the most part added nothing new to the Traditions in question and should be seen purely as a vehicle for the preservation of the material produced in the formative years of Twelver *hadīth* literature, the era of the first 'three Muhammads' and the four canonical books of Twelver Traditions.

Evidence suggests that the entire corpus of Twelver Shi'ite Traditions had been produced by the beginning of the 'Greater Occultation', and that all Traditions known today only from later works – such as those which appeared in the Safavid period – are, with some notable exceptions, more or less faithful reproductions of ancient material going back to the era of the Imams themselves. The importance of the *hadīth* literature for the Twelver Shi'ites – especially during those periods when they existed as a minority – as a vehicle through which they articulated their attitude towards their environment, formulated their customs and beliefs, and asserted themselves as a clearly defined socio-political and religious entity, was manifest in the fact that some scholars spent the best part of their lives on the compilation of a volume or volumes of Traditions, often travelling far and wide and risking life and limb to collect narrations from other scholars and from written sources.[102]

Externalism, with its emphasis on the narrative (*naqlī*) rather than the rational (*'aqlī*) sciences, lends itself more to repetition than to innovation. Thus in *Rīyād al-'ulamā* one comes across numerous works of glossography (*ta'līq* or *hāshīya*) and commentary (*sharh*), most of which centres on the pioneering works of the founding fathers of Twelver Shi'ite *fiqh* and *hadīth*. Afandi lists the titles of over 200 glosses or *hawāshī*; the *al-Lum'at al-Dimashqiyya* of Shahid al-Awwal alone had a dozen commentaries written on it.[103] Afandi also gives the titles of approximately 300 *sharh* or commentaries, and it is not unusual to find glosses on commentaries, or commentaries on commentaries.[104] For the most part, the externalist commentary or gloss consists of nothing more than interlinear or marginal notes, confined usually to explanations of abstruse passages or problematic words in the text. Only in the commentaries written by non-externalists do we find material that adds substantially to the original and thus stands as innovative, pioneering work in its own right: Lahiji's commentary on Shabistari's *Gulshan-i rāz* is a perfect example.[105]

Yet this is not to say that the Twelver Shi'ite externalists of the Safavid period did not have their innovators: we have already noted the steps taken by Shaykh Karaki to make the Twelver *faqīh/mujtahid* the general representative of the Hidden Imam. The question of *ijtihād* itself was a thorny one, and the focal point of much controversy throughout the Safavid period, eventually giving rise to the Akhbari-Usuli rift which shall be discussed presently. Suffice it here to say that even by the end of the Safavid period, the use of *ijtihād*, or independent reasoning, to arrive at legal rulings on issues with no precedent in Islamic jurisprudence was by no means settled. Those who did use *ijtihād*, however, used it to great effect – as Karaki's edicts and the public reaction to them demonstrate – and in the treatises written by the *mujtahidūn* one gets a glimpse of the precise and orderly thinking of the legalist, nomocentric mind, with its love of investigation into the most trivial of legal minutiae and its overt penchant for hair-splitting. The power of expression which comes across in some of these treatises is quite striking, and one wonders what effect these scholars would have had on an attentive audience had they focused their academic talents on the fundamentals of *imān* rather than – or, at least, as well as – the secondary principles of Islam. Shaykh 'Ali al-

Farahani's treatise on the prohibition (*hurma*) of tobacco, written in 1048/1638-39 and quoted in full in *Rīyād al-'ulamā*, is a fitting example of the kind of work produced by the Twelver Shi'ite *fuqahā* and *mujtahidūn* in Safavid Iran; it is also but one of countless such treatises that flooded through the *madrasas* and from the mosque pulpits in the form of sermons throughout the period.[106]

Among the works of the Twelver externalists, those concerned with the virtues and prerogatives of the Imams occupy a special position, and many treatises and *hadīth* collections on the subject were compiled throughout the era. The earliest known Traditions on the doctrine of *imāma* appear in Kulayni's *al-Kafī*, Kulayni having taken them from earlier works such as *Basā'ir al-darajāt* by Muhammad b. Hasan al-Qummi. These Traditions deal with issues such as the necessity of the Imam's existence, belief in the Imam as a prerequisite of *imān*, knowledge of the Imam (*ma'rifat al-imām*), and so on. These and similar Traditions were preserved by the Safavid *fuqahā* in new collections designed to enhance the status of the Imams in the eyes of the newly converted populace even further. Extolling the virtues of the Imams – a genre known as *manqabat–khwānī* - is as old a phenomenon as Twelver Shi'ism itself, but its expression in the form of collections of Traditions that focused solely on the personality, virtues, miracles and sufferings of the Imams moved up several gears in the Safavid period, the first such works being disseminated through early Safavid Iran by the father of Shaykh Baha'i and by the great-grandfather of Muhammad Baqir Majlisi, Shaykh Kamal al-din Darwish.[107]

In addition to those narratives in which the position of the Imam is central, there are numerous Traditions which stress the rights of each individual Imam by referring to words and actions of the Prophet which interpreted as referring explicitly to the Imam in question. The earliest collections often went under the titles of *khasā'is*, *manāqib* or *fadā'il* of 'Ali, as they highlighted the virtues and championed the right to rule of the first Shi'ite Imam. During the late Safavid period, the imamocentric nature of Twelver Shi'ite externalism was such that most of the twelve Imams, plus the Prophet's daughter, Fatima, had individual collections of Traditions compiled about them. Husayn b. 'Ali, the third Shi'ite Imam who was slaughtered at Karbala, provided the inspiration for a whole genre of hadith literature known as *maqtal-niwīsī*: Afandi cites various works of this nature with the title *Maqtal al-Husayn*.[108] These were similar in content to the *rawda* literature, the first and most salient example of which was the earlier *Rawdat al-shuhadā* by Husayn Wa'iz al-Kashifi, who was neither Twelver Shi'ite nor, strictly speaking, an externalist, but rather a Hanafite member of the Naqshbandiyya.

These Traditions, and others like them, were also used in theoretical works on the *imama* – tracts and treatises which argued for the necessity of the *imāma* through both scriptural and rational proofs. Many of those scholars listed by Afandi as *fuqahā* are also credited with works of *kalām*, or theology.

Now *kalām* is traditionally a rational or '*aqlī* science, concerned with proving through deductive reasoning the existence of God and His names, attributes and acts, but although it is a fact that the majority of externalists would most likely have had a basic grounding in *kalām*, this should not be construed as pointing to a rational, non-externalist or internalist bent on their part, although in certain instances this might indeed have been the case. The study and teaching of *kalām* does not indicate necessarily a scholarly bias towards non-externalism. In the case of the Twelver Shi'ite *fuqahā*, the use of the term *kalām* to describe some of their works is doubly ambiguous, for the simple reason that it has often been applied to treatises which aim to prove not the existence of God, which is the traditional function of *kalām*, but the necessity of the *imāma* or the validity of the claims of the Imams. One of the earliest examples of a Twelver Shi'ite work which subverts *kalām* in this way is Ibn Babuya's *al-I'tiqādāt al-imāma*, the prototype for Safavid works such *Ithbāt al-imāma*,[109] *Ithbāt-i wujūd-i sāhib al-zamān*,[110] or any of the twenty or so works of *kalām* that Afandi mentions with the simple title *al-Imāma*.[111] A concomitant of the use of *kalām* to prove the necessity of the *imāma* and the validity of the claims of the Imams is the appropriation of the term *ma'rifa* to denote knowledge not about God, as in the conventional understanding of the term, but about the Imam. Works were given over to this 'knowledge', without which one's belief as a Muslim was deemed incomplete.[112]

The Twelver *fuqahā* also produced a considerable amount of Koranic exegesis (*tafsīr*), although there was not nearly as much of this as there was of straightforward *fiqh* and *hadīth* material. Exegesis made by the Twelver externalists of the Safavid period is similar in style and format to that of the early Shi'ite works of *tafsīr*, in which the emphasis lies primarily on those Traditions narrated from the Imams which describe the reasons for the revelation (*asbāb al-nuzūl*) of a particular verse. Early works such as the anonymously penned *Tafsīr al-'Askarī*, attributed to the eleventh Shi'ite Imam, and the *Tafsīr al Qummī*, serve as prototypes for the kind of commentaries produced by the Safavid externalists. Often fiercely anti-Sunni in spirit, these works pay little or no attention to linguistic problems and tend to ignore many difficult passages entirely. Legal, linguistic and doctrinal problems do receive attention in later works, yet the essence of these expositions is still heavily imamocentric: many works of Koranic exegesis were compiled with the sole aim of proving that the virtues, rights and sufferings of the Imams are all foreshadowed in the Koran. A treatise entitled *Āyāt al-wilāya* by the Safavid *faqīh* and exegete Abu al-Qasim Sharifi, also known as Mirza Baba Shirazi, deals with some 300 Koranic verses purported to have been revealed concerning the 'Fourteen Immaculate Ones' (*chahārdah maʿsūm*).[113] Sayyid Sharaf al-din ʿAli Husayni al-Astarabadi al-Najafi, a student of Shaykh Karaki, wrote an exegesis on the same theme but under the title of *Taʾwīl*, which means the practice of extracting the hidden meanings that lie beneath the surface of the Koranic verses.[114]

By focusing on the secondary principles - the very things which set them apart from their Sunni co-religionists – and, more importantly, on the question of *imāma*, the Twelver Shiʾite works of *fiqh* and *hadīth* are implicitly anti-Sunni, this in spite of the fact that the scholars of both groups enjoyed a long history of relatively peaceful co-existence, with a *modus vivendi* based on their mutual agreement to differ. Although prior to the advent of the Safavids there were occasions on which sectarian hostility would transcend the level of more polemics, it was not until the establishment of the Safavid dynasty that the anti-Sunni posturing of the Twelver Shiʾite *fuqahā* took on more vehement and often hysterically hostile tones. The wave of sectarian killings that swept through Iran during the early years of Safavid rule has already been noted, as have the formation of the Tabarraʾiyyun, the corps of Twelver zealots who enforced the ritual cursing of the first three Caliphs, and the staunchly anti-Sunni writings of Shaykh Karaki.

Whether fuelled by their newly found freedom of expression or by the intermittent conflicts with the Sunni Ottoman state during the formative years of the Safavid era,[115] the Twelver Shiʾite externalists kept up a constant barrage of anti-Sunni polemics, the most damning of which, as we have already seen in Karaki's writings, deems the Sunnis to be infidels (*kuffār*) and ritually unclean (*najis*).[116] Prayer manuals such as *Dhakr al-ʿĀlamīn*, compiled by Muhammad Mahdi al-Qazwini (d. 1129/1716-17) and dedicated to Shah Sultan Husayn (1694-1722), includes curses upon the first three Caliphs and all who follow them.[117] Afandi cites several cases in which the extremism of the Twelver Shiʾite externalists' anti-Sunni invective led to disaster. One Twelver *faqīh*, for example, saw fit to show his opposition to Sunnism by defecating in the place where the

Hanafites prayed in Mecca; he was murdered as a result.[118] This bizarre behaviour on the part of the *faqīh* was not an isolated case: a certain Shaykh 'Ali al-'Amili al-Shami defecated on the grave of Mu'awiya for a whole year and preached on the spiritual benefits of this practice to the people.[119]

The Twelver Shi'ite externalist polemics directed against non-externalist scholars was in many cases no less scabrous than their fulminations against the Sunnis. The graves of well-known Sufi adepts such as 'Abd al-Rahman al-Jami and Abu Nu'aym al-Isfahani were defiled and numerous refutations of Sufism were written.[120] Anti-Sufi treatises were by no means monopolized by the externalists: Mulla Sadra, a non-externalist *par excellence*, also wrote such a treatise, entitled *Kasr al-asnām al-jāhiliyya* (Breaking the Idols of Ignorance). However, Sadra's objection was not to Sufism *per se* but to the antinomian tendencies of the *mutasawwifūn*, or pseudo-Sufis. The externalists evidently saw all Sufis as antinomian and thus did not specify whom they were attacking in their works, many of which carried the prosaic title *al-Radd 'alā al-sūfiyya* (Refutation of Sufism).[121]

Some insight into the general attitude of the externalists towards the non-externalists can be gained by reading Afandi's comments. Describing Muhammad Qawam al-din Isfahani, a philosopher and student of the renowned Mawla Rajab 'Ali Tabrizi, Afandi says that 'he had corrupt ideas (*'aqā'id fāsida*), lived as a recluse, and lacked any religious (*dīnī*) or divine (*ilāhī*) knowledge.'[122] Furthermore he did not know Arabic and no-one attended his funeral. Afandi constantly berates the non-externalists for their lack of Arabic. His remarks also reveal once again how the scriptural sciences had come to be equated with 'religious knowledge', a term that by the very use of the word *dīnī* automatically dismisses all other branches of learning as either ideologically suspect or downright heretical. Rajab 'Ali Tabrizi, a former teacher of Isfahani and someone who was visited personally by Shah 'Abbas II, is also derided by Afandi for his lack of Arabic and for the fact that he was ignorant of the 'religious' sciences.[123] Hasan al-Daylamani al-Jilani, who was versed in *hikma* and taught in the 'Abbasi mosque in Isfahan, is dismissed by Afandi as being mentally unbalanced; Afandi adds, somewhat cryptically, that 'Jilani was loved by other *hakīms* and Sufis.'[124] Mulla Sadra is also the target of vitriolic attacks from the externalist camp. Despite his fame and academic stature, Sadra appears to warrant no more than a few lines of terse comment in Tunukabuni's *Qisas al-'ulamā*, and even then the author contrives to denigrate him by casting aspersions on Sadra's sexuality.[125] Afandi, who

Danishpazhuh claims is among the least zealous of the Safavid *fuqahā*, is also dismissive of Sadra, albeit not so blatantly. Commenting upon Sadra's son, Ibrahim, a *faqīh*, Afandi says that he is 'living proof of the Koranic verse, "He brings life out of death"', thus equating the externalism of Sadra's son with life and the non-externalism of Sadra himself with death.[126]

However united a whole the Twelver Shi'ite *fuqahā* might have been as far as their pursuit of externalism and the vilification of their non-externalist rivals are concerned, on the main issues of the day they were as divided internally as any interest group could have been. Apart from the obvious differences of opinion that arose as a matter of course among the *fuqahā* on minor points of sacred law and ritual practice, two highly controversial matters fractured the Twelver Shi'ite *fuqahā* into various different and often overlapping ideological factions. These matters concerned the Friday congregational prayer (*salāt al-jum'a*), and the dual practices of *taqlīd* and *ijtihād*.

The question of whether or not the Friday congregational prayer should be performed in the absence of the Imam was one that fuelled much debate throughout the Safavid period, with many treatises being written either for or against its permissibility. The issue was related directly to the question of the Twelver attitude towards the state: those *fuqahā* who deemed Friday prayer permissible in the absence of the Imam were in favour of taking a more positive stand towards the state and political life in general, while those who deemed the Friday prayer illegal during the occultation preferred not to have dealings with the state, which, in the absence of the Imam, they believed to be inherently unjust. More about the political attitudes of the Twelver *fuqahā* will be said in Chapter Five in the section on *intizār*; suffice it here to say that the question of involvement in, or withdrawal from, matters of state as reflected in the Friday prayer controversy was one which occupied the attention of many scholars, and divided them, throughout the period.

The question of whether *ijtihād* and *taqlīd* were permissible or not was one that was posed during the Usuli-Akhbari debate, a controversy which raged throughout the second half of the Safavid era and which was to be of great importance for the standing of the Twelver Shi'ite *fuqahā* in post-Safavid Iran and up until the present day. Akhbarism was a school of thought revived early in the 11th/17th century by Muhammad Amin Astarabadi (d. 1033/1623-24).[127] In his work entitled *Fawā'id al-madaniyya*, Astarabadi attacks the rational, analytical approach to jurisprudence favoured by early Twelver *fuqahā* such as Tusi, Mufid and

114

Sharif al-Murtada, and by their Safavid counterparts, who came to be known, in contrast, as the Usuliyyun. The main difference between the two groups concerned the validity of the use of reason in connection with matters of law, with the Akhbariyyun endeavouring to revive what they saw as proper traditionalism by relying exclusively on the sayings of the Imams. For instance, Muqaddas Ardabili (d. 993/1585), an Akhbari and avowed abstainer from all matters of state and politics, never hesitated to reject the opinion of all previous Shi'ite jurists wherever they excluded Traditions on the basis of a rational argument.[128]

A corollary of this was the rejection by the Akhbariyyun of *ijtihād* and *taqlīd*. According to the Akhbariyyun, every individual believer must follow the *akhbār* (Traditions) of the Imams, for whose proper understanding no more than a knowledge of Arabic and the specific terminology used by the Imams is needed; if a conflict between contradictory Traditions cannot be resolved, abstention from a ruling is necessary.[129] Consequently, recourse to a *mujtahid* is prohibited, since obedience is due to God, Muhammad, the Imams and no-one else, with the rules emanating from the sacred law being deducible directly from the Traditions themselves.[130] Akhbarism thus posed a direct and very serious threat to the position of the Twelver Shi'ite *mujtahid* as adumbrated by Shaykh Karaki and aspired to by countless *fuqahā* from the inception of Safavid rule. The Akhbari-Usuli controversy occupied the time and energy of many Twelver externalists – and some non-externalists – but here again, as in the case of the debate on the Friday congregational prayer, scholarly attention was focused on a secondary rather than a fundamental issue.

Although the issues mentioned above split the externalists into often hostile factions, adding further divisions to the basic externalist/non-externalist rift, the borders between these factions were often blurred, with much overlapping of interests and loyalties. The 'pigeonhole disease', as Clifford Geertz would call it, is one that students of Safavid history have found almost impossible to escape. Said Arjomand, for example, claims that Akhbarism reflected the outlook of what he calls the 'clerical estate', which 'tended to prefer philosophy and hermeneutics and devotional mysticism.'[131] However, renowned Akhbari scholars such as Mawla Muhammad al-Jilani, Shaykh Khalil al-Qazwini, Shaykh Muhammad Hurr al-'Amili and Muhammad Tahir al-Qummi all opposed the pursuit of theosophy and Sufism, Qummi most vehemently so.[132] With regard to the issue of the Friday prayer, Qummi and Shaykh Khalil al-Qazwini could not be reconciled by their common adherence to Akhbarism, with the former declaring Friday prayer a religious necessity (*wājib*) and the latter deeming it unlawful (*harām*).[133] Arjomand attempts to tie up the Akhbari-Usuli division with the 'clerical estate – dogmatic party' dichotomy, but is clearly unable to do so. However hard one tries to impose rigid classifications on the Twelver Shi'ite *fuqahā* of the Safavid era, one cannot escape the fact that what they were about was strictly peripheral to the question of belief, self-knowledge and knowledge of the Divine, and that their controversies, polemics and endless hair-splitting over sacred law and legal minutiae were but a smokescreen to hide what can only be interpreted as indifference to the fundamental message of the Islamic revelation.

In search of Twelver Shi'ite internalism

Evidence suggests most strongly, then, that the pursuit of the non-scriptural, so-called rational sciences such as *falsafa* and *hikma* have traditionally been disfavoured by the Twelver Shi'ite *fuqahā*, who in this respect display attitudes similar to those of their Sunni counterparts. However, the emphasis on externalism – and, obviously, on their own particular brand of externalism – seems to have been considerably more marked among the Twelver Shi'ite scholars than among the Sunnis. As noted previously, prior to the Safavid regime there were no Sufi groups claiming to adhere to orthodox Twelve Shi'ism: all Sufi adepts belonged to one of the four Sunni schools of jurisprudence, and even those brotherhoods which professed Shi'ism at the outset of the Safavid era must remain suspect as far as the sincerity of their alleged *volte-face* is concerned. Furthermore, the toleration by Sunni *fuqahā* of non-externalist approaches to the Islamic revelation such as philosophy, theosophy and Sufism would appear to have always been greater than that shown by their Twelver Shi'ite counterparts. The attitude of Ibn Taymiyya, one of Sunnism's most vociferous anti-Sufi polemicists, towards Sufi figures such as Junayd and Bayazid is a good example in this respect.[134] The Twelver Shi'ite externalist attitude to disciplines outside the orbit of *fiqh* and *hadīth* has already been noted; Afandi sums it up when, while commenting on the fact that a certain scholar has been described as both a *hakim* and a *faqīh*, he says that to combine *hikma* and *fiqh* 'is to combine two diametrically opposed things' (*jam' bayn al-azdād*) and is thus impossible.[135]

Noted also is the tendency of the *fuqahā* to equate only *fiqh* and *hadīth* with 'religious' knowledge, all other approaches being in their eyes ideologically suspect. Here one point must be clarified. The Muslim *fuqahā* do not ignore the fundamentals of *iman*; it is simply that their orientation is towards the propagation of the externals of religion, the secondary principles (*furū' al-dīn*). The difference between externalism and internalism is thus primarily one of emphasis. Indeed any *faqīh* of note would be expected to have studied both the scriptural and the rational sciences; the fact that he became a *faqīh* would be a reflection of his own personal preference for the scriptural sciences, which are the tools of externalism, over the rational disciplines.

As the sources show, scholars would study the scriptural sciences under one teacher or series of teachers. The rational sciences, although in theory more conducive to the pursuit of internalism than the scriptural sciences, were ineffective in practice, however, as a means of leading the student towards self- or God-knowledge, since disciplines such as *kalām* had long since been channelled towards knowledge concerning the Imams (*ma'rifat al-a'imma*) and proof of their *imāma*. Yet as Afandi shows, those scholars with an internalist bent are nearly always credited with the title *hakīm*, or theosopher, and thus the possibility that an individual engaged in the pursuit of the intellectual sciences would incline to the heavily non-externalistic interests such as Sufism or gnosis ('*irfān*) was one which made the *fuqahā* wary. Again this must not be construed as implying that the *fuqahā* were opposed to anyone's attempt to know God *per se*. According to the author of *Surūr al-'ārifīn*:

> The hide-bound scholars (*qishrīyyūn*) are not scared that people may know God, as long as it is in the limited sense that is allowed by their frame or reference. What they (the *fuqahā*) are scared of is that the enquirer (*tālib*) may come to know God as God intends him to, in which case he (the enquirer) will realise that the claims of the hide-bound scholars to true knowledge are based upon nothing (*bar bād-i hawā ast*, lit. are upon air, i.e. baseless).

Faced, then, with what would appear to be the immiscibility of Twelver Shi'ite externalism and internalism, how does one interpret the theories of those such as Henry Corbin, who calls Twelver Shi'ism 'the sanctuary of Islamic esoterism'?[137] Or Hamid Algar, who talks of reconciliation between Sunnism and Shi'ism at 'the level of the esoteric'?[138] Or Hamid Enayat, who associates *bātin*, *ta'wīl* and *haqīqa* with the teachings of Twelver Shi'ism, and *zāhir*, *tafsīr* and *sharī'a* with the teachings of Sunnism?[139] Enayat's question, in which he attributes the externalist elements - *zāhir*, *tafsīr* and *sharī'a* - of these dual notions to the Sunnis and the internalist components - *bātin*, *ta'wīl* and *haqīqa* - to the Twelve Shi'ites, is totally at odds not only with the facts already mentioned concerning Sufism and Sunnism, or with the overwhelming preponderance of *fuqahā* over *hukamā* or Sufis in *Riyād al-'ulamā*, but also, as we have noted, with how the Twelver Shi'ite *fuqahā* see themselves, namely as the true guardians of religious and divine knowledge.

If by the terms *bātin* and *ta'wīl* Enayat is referring to the Twelver Shi'ite practice of finding hidden references to the Imams in the verses of the Koran, then the contention that Twelver Shi'ism is characterized in its interpretation of the Koran by a certain esotericism is to a certain extent correct. However, the search for inner, hidden meanings through an allegorical interpretation of Koranic verses by the Twelver *fuqahā* should not be confused with the concepts of *ta'wīl* and *bātin* as understood traditionally by the orthodox Sufis and other non-externalists, an example of which, from the pen of Mulla Sadra, was provided earlier.[140] The explicitly imamocentric interpretation of the Koran, known technically as *jary*,[141] cannot be seen as internalistically oriented, for the simple reason that the object sought is not knowledge about God (*ma'rifat Allāh*) but knowledge about the Imam (*ma'rifat-e imām*).

Yet one still has to account for those individuals who have been identified as Twelver Shi'ites – and who, more importantly, have identified themselves as such[142] – but whose religious orientation and academic markings differ profoundly from those of the externalist majority. To what extent are we justified in calling them Twelver Shi'ite internalists? A brief description of the life and works of two of them, Sayyid Haydar Amuli and Ibn Abi Jumhur, may help to answer this question. Amuli, incidentally, is the figure upon whom Corbin has mainly based his assertion that Twelver Shi'ism is the cradle of esotericism.[143]

In his most famous work, *Jāmi' al-asrār*, Haydar b. 'Ali b Haydar b. 'Ali al-Amuli (b. 720/1320; still alive in 787/1385-86), better known simply as Sayyid Haydar Amuli, states that he had at one time been a fanatical Shi'ite *faqīh*, but had then become a Sufi, giving up fanaticism in favour of tolerance.[144] Amuli states that his aim was to reconcile the *sharī'a* with the *haqīqa* or Truth, and to this end he took as his spiritual mentors the Imams of the House of 'Ali, and the 'people of unity' (*ahl al-tawhīd*) from among the Sufis, employing what he found in Shi'ite doctrines to confirm the truth of Sufism and vice versa.[145] In order to establish the closest possible contact between the two outlooks he used Ibn Maytham's commentary on the *Nahj al-balāgha*, Ibn al-Mutahhar's

Minhaj al-maqāl and Shaykh Tusi's *Tajrīd*. These, if not openly in favour of Sufism, do not oppose it. He also made extensive use of the works of Ghazali and Ibn al-'Arabi.

In Amuli's view, 'from the beginning of time to eternity, Divine knowledge and Godly truths have been attributed to 'Ali alone';[146] in his schema, all twelve Imams were connected to the Sufi adepts of their own times. For Amuli, the Imam and the Sufi *qutb* or 'pole' are one and the same.[147] He also expresses the opinion that there are two kinds of Shi'ism: one which is dependent or based on externals (*zāhir*) and whose sciences are the *sharī'a* and Islam; and another, which is based upon the internal or hidden (*bātin*), and whose sciences are *al-tarīqa* (the Path), *al-haqīqa* (the Truth), and *al-īqān* (the Certainty).[148] In Amuli's opinion, the final goal of knowledge must be *hikma*, and the ultimate realisation that nothing exists in reality but God.[149] Aiming to bring together the diverse elements within Sufism and Twelver Shi'ism, he made a conscious attempt to establish a new way, with *al-hikmat al-ilāhiyya* as the goal, conveyed through Sufism with a Twelver Shi'ite flavour. Eventually, however, he realized that he was unable to reconcile Sufi doctrines such as those concerning the *qutb* with Twelver beliefs, and readily admitted defeat.[150]

Ibn Abi Jumhur al-Ahsa'i (d. 901/1495-96) was born in Bahrain but spent most of his life travelling around Iraq and Khurasan. He was a follower of Haydar Amuli, whom he called the *qutb al-aqtāb* or 'Pole of Poles'. Like his spiritual master, Ibn Jumhur also attempted the integration of Sufism and Shi'ism; however, he went much further than Amuli insofar as he advocated explicitly the formation of 'one sect with one belief.'[151] Whereas Amuli centred on the supposed identicality of Sufism and Shi'ism, Ibn Jumhur was much more eclectic in his approach, drawing freely upon sources such as Bayazid al Bistami, Mansur Hallaj, 'Abdullah al-Ansari, Ibn al-'Arabi, Plato, Aristotle, Fakhr al-din Razi, Nasir al-din Tusi, Ibn Sina and Farabi.[152] He also sought to make use of Ash'arite theology, claiming that the whole essence of *tawhīd* is to prove the existence of one Creator.[153]

In his most famous work, *al-Mujlī*, an encyclopaedic treatise which deals with divine unity (*tawhīd*) and the divine acts (*af'āl*), Ibn Jumhur ignores almost all of the traditional works of the Twelver Shi'ite orthodoxy. Shaykh Mufid, for example, is mentioned only once – a deplorable attitude in the eyes of the externalists. Ibn Jumhur's *Ghawālī al-li'ālī* was denounced on the grounds that it included Traditions from Sunni sources, and as a consequence Ibn Jumhur was declared unreliable.[154] He was also branded a Sufi; no standard Shi'ite *faqīh* is mentioned as having been his student, although he himself claimed to have many. Only in the Ni'matullahi work *Tarā'iq al-haqā'iq* is he mentioned as 'one of the great *fuqahā* and investigators, who supported and improved the way of the Sufi shaykhs and laid the foundations of the religious doctrines.'[155] It is doubtful that the author of *Tarā'iq* is using the term *faqīh* in the sense understood today, however. Yet Ibn Jumhur's association with Twelver Shi'ism is clear, for like Haydar Amuli he believed that Ali was a saint (*walī*) and the 'Perfect Man' (*al-insān al-kāmil*), and that the Twelve Imams formed a chain of successive Sufi masters.[156]

In what sense, then, can Haydar Amuli and Ibn Jumhur be called Twelver Shi'ites? Are the externalism of the likes of Shaykh Karaki and the internalism of the likes of Amuli and Ibn Jumhur simply two sides of the same Twelver Shi'ite coin, just as the externalism of Ibn Taymiyya and the internalism of Ghazali are two sides of the same coin in Sunnism? Or are we, when discussing the respective approaches of, say, Shaykh Karaki and Ibn Jumhur, discussing two almost totally different and, in many respects, mutually alien forms of Shi'ism? Haydar Amuli reaffirmed the existence of two distinct groups within Shi'ism, and Afandi, with his diatribes on the incompatibility of *fiqh* and *hikma*, corroborates this.

It would appear, therefore, that we cannot talk about the internalism of the likes of Ibn Jumhur being to the externalism of Shaykh Karaki in the Shi'ite context as the internalism of Ghazali is to the externalism of Ibn Taymiyya in the Sunni context. The externalism of the Sunni *fuqahā* and the internalism of the Sunni *hukamā* and orthodox Sufis were never ideal bedfellows but at least they were able to function side by side in a spirit of mutual acceptance. This was because the internalism of the orthodox Sufis was theocentric in nature; however much at odds the Sunni *fuqahā* might have been with the Sufi adepts over the question of which facet of the Islamic revelation should receive most emphasis, they were unable to find fault with the basic doctrine of belief held by the Sufis, who, so long as they remained free of any antinomian tendencies, were tolerated and, in some cases, highly respected by the Sunni orthodoxy. In Twelver Shi'ism, however, apart from the three fundamentals of belief which form the basis of internalism and which are shared with the Sunnis, namely *tawhīd*, *nabuwwa* and *ma'ād*, there are two extra elements: *imāma*, or the imamate of the Twelver Imams, and *'adl* or Divine justice.[157] We have already seen how the issue of *imāma* is so central to Twelver Shi'ism that its *fiqh*, *hadīth*, *tafsīr* and *kalām*, while ostensibly playing the same role as in the Sunni sphere, developed gradually into disciplines devoted to promoting

120

the personae of the Imams themselves. The politico-historic development of the *imāma*, the continued 'absence' of the Twelfth Imam, and the natural tendency of lay Muslims to gravitate in orientation towards secondary matters all ensured that the issue of *imāma* overshadowed all other considerations. It would not be unfair to say at this point, then, that from the study of pre-Safavid and Safavid Twelver Shi'ite scholars and their writings it becomes clear that Twelver Shi'ism has two kinds of internalism: a theocentric internalism, focusing on *tawhīd*, *nabuwwa* and *ma'ād*, which it has in common with the Sunnis; and an imamocentric internalism, centred on the *imāma* and the Imams. The following schema emerges:

Sunni externalism:
> The focal point is the *sharī'a* or Islam, and the study and promulgation of *fiqh* and *hadīth* through four schools of jurisprudence: Hanafi, Shafi'i, Maliki and Hanbali.

Twelver Shi'ite externalism:
> The focal point is the *sharī'a* or Islam, and the study and promulgation of *fiqh* and *hadīth* though a single school of jurisprudence, the Ja'fari rite. As far as the external acts of worship (*a'māl*) are concerned, there are few differences between the Twelver Shi'ite and the Sunni schools of jurisprudence.

Sunni internalism:
> The focal point is belief (*īmān*) in God, the prophethood of Muhammad, and the resurrection. According to the Koran, belief can be attained only through the acquisition of knowledge about God that is manifest in His signs (*āyāt*), which include the souls (*anfus*) of men, and the rest of the created cosmos (*āfāq*). Knowledge of self (*ma'rifat al-nafs*) together with contemplation of the signs in the cosmos should, according to internalist thinking, lead to belief. Belief itself is subject to increase and decrease, depending on the personal state of the individual. The main channel of internalist thought in the Sunni sphere has traditionally been Sufism, although not exclusively so.

Twelver Shi'ite theocentric internalism:
> This is for all intents and purposes identical to Sunni internalism. Strictly speaking, since internalism focuses on belief, self- and

God-knowledge and the three fundamentals of *tawhīd*, *nabuwwa* and *ma'ād*, there can be no place for designations of *madhhab*. Algar's statement to the effect that Sunnism and Twelver Shi'ism are reconciled on the level of the esoteric is correct only if, by esoteric, he is referring to the theocentric internalism that is latent within Twelver Shi'ism, prevalent in the writings of scholars such as Haydar Amuli, Ibn Jumhur and Mulla Sadra, but played down or totally ignored by the *fuqahā*. However, reconciliation is something of a misnomer, since there can be no bringing together of two outlooks which are more or less identical. As far as internalism is concerned, the only salient difference between the outlooks of, say, Ghazali and Mulla Sadra, or Jalal al-din Rumi and Haydar Amuli, lies in the fact that Sadra and Amuli would have relied more on the Twelver Shi'ite Imams as channels of inspiration, accepting them as leaders (*a'imma*) in the spiritual and religious sense. It is this acceptance of the Imams as spiritual guides that connects the likes of Amuli and Sadra to Twelver Shi'ism and identifies them in the eyes of others as Twelver Shi'ites.

Twelver Shi'ite imamocentric internalism:
  This centres on knowledge (*ma'rifa*) of, and belief in, the Twelve Imams of the family of the Prophet. Without this crucial element, second only to *tawhīd* in the Shi'ite fundamentals of belief (*usūl al-dīn*), one's status as a believer in God is suspect; indeed, in Traditions attributed to the Imams themselves, belief in the Imam is the key to belief in God.[158] Although the Twelver Shi'ite externalist would not deny the importance of *tawhīd*, *nabuwwa* and *ma'ād*, it is clear from his academic output that beneath the heavy external layers of *fiqh* and *hadīth* it is the issue of *imāma* that provides him with spiritual relief from the deficiencies of legalistic religion.

It was noted earlier that Haydar Amuli was forced to admit his failure to 'reconcile' Sufism with Twelver Shi'ism, primarily because of the incompatibility of the Sufi concept of guidance and the Shi'ite belief in the infallible Imam. So long as Sufism – albeit in its purest, more orthodox form – kept as its ideal the realization, through self- and God-knowledge, of the internal reality which made the external *sharī'a* valid, and so long as the Twelver Shi'ite *fuqahā* retained the need for a mediatory Imam, belief in and knowledge of whom constitute the key to true faith, then a fusion of the two outlooks was never a possibility. Furthermore, the fact that the

Twelver *fuqahā* had, at the outset of the Safavid era, set themselves up as representatives of the Hidden Imam made a rapprochement between Sufism and Twelver Shi'ism even more unlikely. For according to the Sufis and other internalists, direct communion with God has always been a possibility, whereas for the Twelver Shi'ites, one must channel one's belief through the Imam or, in his absence, through his representative. Although Sufism also had its guides – the 'poles' or *aqtāb* – these were many: they were ordinary men singled out by God as a result of their spiritual progression and not because of their lineage. In Sufism, anyone could become an *'ālim*, a knower of God and His attributes; in the eyes of the majority of Twelver Shi'ite scholars, an *'ālim* was one who was able to communicate *fiqh* and *hadīth* or practise *ijtihād* and inspire the emulation (*taqlīd*) of the Twelver faithful. For the Sufis and other internalists, the *faqīh* has a limited and strictly peripheral role to play in the everyday life of the Muslim; for the Twelver Shi'ite, the *faqīh*, by virtue of his status as representative of the Hidden Imam, is a pivotal figure in Islamic social and spiritual life.[159]

As we have seen, Haydar Amuli and Ibn Jumhur espoused a distinctly theocentric internalism, their aim being the *haqīqa* as channelled through the Imams, among others. The Twelver Shi'ite externalist objection to the internalism of Amuli and Ibn Jumhur stems not only from the disinclination of these two scholars to use only Shi'ite sources in their writings but also from their elevation of the Twelve Imams to the status of *qutb* – a promotion which would have been seen by the externalists as a relegation, given the fact that for Amuli and Ibn Jumhur the Imams were not the only 'poles' in the universe. Yet it is the attachment of scholars and thinkers such as Amuli and Ibn Jumhur to the Twelve Imams that identifies them as Twelvers; and it is the fact that these two scholars were passionately theocentric in their internalism that has led a considerable number of writers to identify esotericism and gnosticism with Twelver Shi'ism.

Given the flexibility of the term 'Twelver Shi'ite', however, it is difficult to gauge the extent to which Amuli and Ibn Jumhur were Twelver Shi'ite, if at all. As we have already seen, attachment to the family of the Prophet has always been widespread among Muslims of all jurisprudential persuasions; in pre-Safavid Iran the devotion nurtured by non-Twelvers for Ali and the Imams prompted some writers to talk in terms of *'tashayyu'-i hasan'* or 'moderate Shi'ism' held by non-Shi'ites. Several of the Imams figure in Sufi chains of transmission and many Sufi Orders trace their spiritual heritage back to Ali himself. Such was the regard held for the Imams by the Sunni Naqshbandi *shaykh*, Shah Wali Allah of Delhi (1703-1762) that he wrote:

I have come to recognise that the Twelve Imams are *qutbs* of one and the same genealogical tree, and that consequent on their becoming extinct, *tasawwuf* has spread about.[160]

Shah Ni'matullah (d. 834/1431) in his poetry expressed the belief that the lovers of Ali are perfect believers and, as such, should choose the Sunni way, which, he declared, was his own.[161] A contemporary example of such appropriation of the Shi'ite Imams by a Sunni is that of Said Nursi, the Shafi'ite founder of the Nurcu movement in Turkey, who writes:

The *ahl al-sunna* are those who possess the truth (*haqīqa*), and those at the forefront (of the *ahl al-sunna*) are the Four Imams (of Sunnism) and the Twelve Imams of the *ahl al-bayt*.[162]

Devotion to the Twelve Imams clearly does not preclude affiliation to the *ahl al-sunna*; by the same token, then, it should not be seen as an automatic pointer to any kind of formal doctrinal attachment to Twelver Shi'ism. Furthermore, the way in which scholars such as Amuli and Ibn Jumhur – and, indeed, the majority of the 67 non-externalists mentioned in *Riyād al-'ulamā* – write about the Imams clearly sets them apart from the externalist Twelver Shi'ites, who see the Imams first and foremost not as the *means* of theocentric internalism but as the *aim* of imamocentric internalism. It is the imamocentrism of the Twelver Shi'ite *fuqahā* that militates against any kind of *rapprochement* between their approach to Islam and that which embraces the theocentric internalism of scholars such as Amuli and Ibn Jumhur. *Rapprochement* would have been possible only if the *fuqahā* had reoriented the position of the Imams in their belief system and viewed them not as virtually superhuman figures who must be 'known' and 'believed in', and whose representatives - the *fuqahā* - must be obeyed, but as channels of theocentric internalism and individuals who have no genealogical claim to sainthood (*wilāya*). This, however, would be tantamount to the 'de-Shi'itization' of Twelver Shi'ism, leaving something along the lines of Ibn Jumhur's ideal of one sect with one belief, and with it a drastic demotion of the role of *faqīh* and *mujtahid* in the Twelver Shi'ite socio-political and religious sphere.

The non-externalists: their milieu and teachings

A study of Safavid sources in general and *Rīyād al-'ulamā* in particular reveals three basic types of non-externalist orientation among the Safavid scholars and literati: the antinomian 'wandering' dervish or *qalandar* types; those scholars connected officially to one of the Sufi Orders; and the *hukamā* and philosophers operating independently from any formal Sufi brotherhood.

The term *qalandar* covers in its historical usage a wide range of dervish types. It was loosely applied in the Persian sphere to any wandering *faqīr* or mendicant, but it was also adopted by certain groups and even distinctive Orders were formed, hence the problem of defining the term. Shihab al-din Suhrawardi describes the *qalandariyya* as those who are so possessed by the intoxication of 'tranquility of heart' that they respect no custom and reject the conventions of society and social relationships. Maqrizi records that the *qalandariyya* made their first appearance in Damascus around 610/1213-14, having been introduced by the Persian refugee, Muhammad Yunus al-Sawaji (d. 630/1232-33), and a *qalandarī* hostel or *zāwīya* was built by the Haydari group there in 655/1257-58.[163] A *qalandarī*/Haydari hostel in Tabriz is mentioned by the author of *Rawdat al-jinān*,[164] and our sources make frequent references to the presence of these shabbily-dressed, morally reprehensible wandering dervishes in Safavid society. They appear as story-tellers in coffee-houses; as *du'āgū* or those who beg for money and pray for those who donate; and as street-corner preachers who were generally held in low esteem by the people.[165]

The antinomianism of the *qalandarīyya* precludes their being categorized according to the internalist/externalist schema. The true internalist, despite his relative lack of regard for the academic pursuit of *fiqh* and *hadīth*, does not disregard the outward, external profession of belief that is reflected in practices such as prayer and fasting. Thus the *qalandariyya*, despite their rejection of worldly desires and pursuits, do not qualify as internalists in the pure sense of the word.

Organised Sufism, the politico-historical development of which has already been touched upon, remained the most important potential channel of internalist teaching throughout the Safavid era. State and *fuqahā* hostility towards the organised Sufi brotherhoods, plus the infusion into the Sufi tradition of practices that were contrary to the internalist spirit, militated against the ability of the Orders to communicate fully the ideals of Sufism to the people at large.[166] In theory, if not in practice, the Sufi

125

path was inspired by a basically internalist outlook. An examination of the prose essays of one of the leading Sufi masters, Shah Ni'matullah Wali, shows that the subjects which interested him and his disciples most were generally internalist in tenor; in this respect, the Ni'matullahiyya is no different from any of the other organised Sufi brotherhoods.

Taking Shah Ni'matullah's work as an example, one sees that the emphasis rests primarily on the Koran and the Traditions as the major sources of inspiration. Exegesis (*tafsīr*) of the Koran or of individual verses of the Koran such as the famed 'Light Verse',[167] plus interpretations of Prophetic Traditions, play a large part in Sufi teachings. Jalal al-din Rumi's *Mathnawī*, although obviously of a totally different style to the prose works of Shah Ni'matullah, is nevertheless an internalist work that relies heavily upon Koranic verses for its inspiration. Internalist exegesis is concerned fundamentally with the implications of a certain verse or word for the individual who is seeking the path to self-knowledge and divine gnosis, whereas externalist exegesis usually boils down to nothing more than a brief exposition of the historical event underlying the revelation of the particular verse in question. Interpretations of the works of other Sufi masters also feature prominently in the Sufi internalist repertoire: Shah Ni'matullah, for example, produced four works on Ibn al-'Arabi's *Fusūs al-hikam* alone.[168]

The concept of *īmān* and its concomitants form the backbone of internalist teachings such as those typified by the treatises of Shah Ni'matullah. Belief, unity (*tawhīd*) and trust (*tawakkul*) are explored extensively. Metaphysical explanations of problems such as free-will and divine determining (*qadar*), the divine Essence, and God's names and attributes are given. Expositions of ontological problems, the stages of being, the five planes of existence (*hadarāt al-khamsa*), the archetypes (*amthāl*), cosmology, creation (*khilqa*), manifestation (*tajallī*), the concept of man as the microcosm and the cosmos as the macrocosm, and the Perfect Man (*al-insān al-kāmil*) – all can be found in the work of a typical Sufi writer such as Shah Ni'matullah. Treatises on jurisprudence are conspicuous by their absence, and the only time the externals of Islam are discussed is when the symbolism of acts of worship such as prayer and fasting are explained.

Sufi terminology and concepts are also explained in full in the treatises of Shah Ni'matullah: he wrote separate essays on particular terms and ideas, such as the meaning and secret of true belief, unity, poverty and trust. In other works he discusses the inner meanings of words such as Sufi, Sufism, reveller (*rind*), pole (*qutb*), miracle (*mu'jiza*) and (*karāma*), annihilation (*fanā*), permanence (*baqā*), love ('*ishq*), inspiration (*ilhām*), and so on. In theory, then, once the exclusivist wrappings of each individual Sufi Order with its own particular methods of teaching and promulgation are peeled back, there is revealed in the Sufi tradition a basically theocentric internalism which transcends all designations of *madhhab* and sectarianism. However, as we have seen, the organized Sufi brotherhoods fared badly in Safavid Iran – not because of their internalism but rather because of the fact that they were organised and thus posed a possible political threat – and so their potential as the most influential channel of internalist teaching was severely hampered.

Individual gnostics with no formal Sufi affiliations fared much better, however, and the gradual demise of organised Sufism in the Safavid period did not mean the end of internalism. Nearly all of the internalists listed in *Rīyād al-'ulamā* are noted for their penchant for Sufism, although only in a handful of cases are formal affiliations mentioned. The main internalist channels were *falsafa* and *hikma*, although individual internalists also appear as simple preachers (*wā 'iz*) or poets.

One scholar who attempted to communicate internalist teachings to the masses was the preacher, 'Abd al-Wahid Wa'iz al-Jilani.[169] Although the dates of his birth and death are unknown, it is clear from references in his work that he studied under the ubiquitous Shaykh Baha'i, although it is not certain whether he studied the '*aqlī* or the *naqlī* sciences with him.[170] Wa'iz al-Jilani's writings were almost exclusively internalist in nature, with many treatises written about the reality of the soul (*nafs*) and the path to self-purification and the gnosis of God. What makes him stand out particularly is the fact that he wrote most of his works in Persian; moreover his was a simple, lucid style suited more to the pulpit than the *madrasa*. He wrote over 50 treatises, and was at home in verse as in pose.[171] Unlike the great gnostic philosophers such as Mulla Sadra, Jilani aimed his teachings directly at the ordinary people to whom he preached. He is probably the most prolific author of internalist works in Persian in the whole of the Safavid period, yet he has remained totally overlooked by Western and, to a large degree, Iranian scholars.

In his treatise *Mi'rāj al-samā*, an explanation of the terms '*ilm* and '*ulamā* is given which is influenced heavily by Ghazali's *Ihyā 'ulūm al-dīn*. Jilani says that there are three types of scholar:

> Among the believers there are the 'people of transaction' (*ahl-i mu'āmala*) who know the commands (*awāmir*) of God but do not know Him; there are the 'people of apparent knowledge' (*ahl-i*

'ilm-i sūrī) who know God through rational proofs (*barāhin-i 'aqlī*) but who do not care to know His commands; and there are the 'people of certainty' (*ahl al-yaqīn*), and they possess real knowledge (*'ilm-i haqīqī*) of both God and His commands.[172]

Jilani qualifies his classification by saying that the *ahl-i mu'āmala* form the majority of Muslim scholars. Their remembrance (*dhikr*) of God, he says, is on their tongues but not in their hearts; their fear is of the people (*khalq*) and not of their Lord; they are humble in public (*zāhir*) but not in private, in front of God. They are the *fuqahā* and the transmitters (*rāwīyūn*) of Traditions; one may have recourse to them only as much as is strictly necessary.

The (*ahl-i 'ilm-i sūrī*) form the second category of Muslim scholars, and are much fewer in number than the *ahl-i mu'āmala*. They are the theologians (*mutakallimūn*) and the philosophers (*falāsifa*); if they have belief, they keep it in their hearts but not on their tongues; they fear mistakes of judgement and intellect (*khatā'-i 'aql*) but not sins; and they are humble before God but not before the people. One may have recourse to them and mix with them in moderation (*ikhtilāt-i kam*).

The (*ahl-i'ilm-i haqīqī*) form by far the smallest group of scholars. They remember God in their hearts and on their tongues; they are scared of inner pride (*ghurūr-i qalb*) and of external sins. They are the prophets (*mursalīn*), the saints (*awlīyā*), the gnostics (*'urafā*), and the pure Sufis (*sūfīyān-i sāfī-zamīr*), and they are the true teachers (*mu'allim*) of Muslims.[173]

Jilani quotes what he claims is a Prophetic Tradition in which Muhammad is reported to have instructed the Muslims to 'ask questions from the *'ulamā*, associate with the *hukamā*, and keep close company with *kubarā*'.[174] According to Jilani, the word *'ulamā* in the Tradition denotes the *fuqahā*, from whom legal rulings on matters of sacred law are obtained; the word *hukamā* refers to the *ahl-i 'ilm-sūrī*, who may be mixed with in moderation; while the *kubarā* (lit. the exalted or great ones) are the saints, gnostics and pure Sufis, whose company should be kept as much as possible since it provides benefit in this world and in the next.

The wretchedness (*shaqāwa*) of our society, Jilani continues, stems from a dearth of scholars with real knowledge and an overabundance of ignoramuses (*juhalā*) who imagine that simply by knowing transactions (*mu'āmalāt*) they can give themselves the exalted title *'ulamā*. Ask any *faqīh* how many times the words *Allāh akbar* must be recited during the ritual prayer, asserts Jilani, and he will spend a whole day recounting the various Traditions concerning the question; ask him the inner (*bātinī*) meaning of the very same words and he will tell you that he has no time to spare.[175] The vast majority, however, are liars and thieves (*kadhdhāb wa shayyād*) whose only desire is for fame and material well-being.[176]

Jilani also offers an insight into the methods of internalist teaching. The main focal points for communication of non-externalist thought in the Isfahan of his day were the Shaykh Lutfullah mosque, which Shah 'Abbas I had constructed for Shaykh Lutfullah al-'Amili al-Maysi, and the *madrasa* of the same name. Jilani mentions that many 'real scholars' (*'ulamā-i haqīqī*) studied and taught at the Shaykh Lutfullah *madrasa*, including Aqa Husayn Khwansari and Rajab 'Ali Tabrizi. Jilani himself says that the 'grace of God' (*lutf Allāh*) allowed him on several occasions to preach in the Lutfullah mosque, although his main teaching was done in private, 'in the manner of the prophet Noah.'[177] Jilani mentions the existence of regular *majālis* or meetings which would be held in what were presumably the private houses of notables and other scholars: the *majālis-i ikhwān* were held specifically for instruction in Islamic morals (*akhlāq*) and etiquette (*adab*), while the *majālis-i mukhlisīn* were held for instruction in gnosis (*ma'rifa*), and were no doubt designed to cater for those who were more advanced on the spiritual path. Jilani mentions with fulsome praise the feelings of brotherhood (*ukhuwwa*) that were generated at these meetings and laments the fact that true knowledge - *ma'rifat Allāh* - must remain hidden, like a 'moon-faced beauty beneath a veil' (*chū māhrukh-i rū girifta*).[178]

Scholars such as Jilani appealed directly to the masses as well as to like-minded individuals of their own intellectual standing. The tradition of gnostic philosophy or *'irfān*, epitomised by the so-called 'school of Isfahan' founded by Mir Damad and best exemplified by the teachings of Mulla Sadra, was, on the other hand, channelled through writings that are primarily theoretical and which were directed at that time mainly towards the elite among the small highly literate class of Twelver internalist scholars. Mir Damad, the son-in-law of Shaykh Karaki, was, as we have already seen, a syncretist in the sense that he combined both theocentric internalist and externalist elements in his work. An authority on the scriptural sciences, he was above all else a *hakīm* who opened up new vistas for Islamic philosophy and who was responsible for the rapid spread of *hikma* through his numerous writings and the training of numerous students.[179] The *hakīm-i ilāhī*, or theosopher, who emerged from Mir Damad's 'school' in Isfahan was a direct ideological descendant of earlier Muslim *hukamā* and philosophers such as Farabi, Haydar Amuli, Rajab

Bursi, Ibn Turka, Nasir al-din Tusi, Suhrawardi, Ibn Sina, Ghazali, and Ibn al-'Arabi.

Mulla Sadra Shirazi, the most famous of Mir Damad's students, followed his teacher's attempts to blend the teachings of Ibn Sina and Suhrawardi within a Twelver Shi'ite theocentric internalist frame of reference, but went much further by creating a synthesis of all the major intellectual perspectives of nearly a thousand years of Islamic intellectual life before him: the peripatetic philosophers, the Illuminationist (*ishrāqī*) philosophers, the Prophet and the Imams, the Sufis – all of them were unified and harmonised in the 'transcendent theosophy' (*al-hikmat al-muta'āliyya*) of Mulla Sadra. More importantly, Mulla Sadra reiterated the need for direct internalist objectives in the pursuit of philosophy – hence the term 'gnostic' philosophy or *'irfān* – and advocated sincerity of purpose (*khulūs*), single-minded devotion (*tawajjuh*) and the light of belief (*nūr al-īmān*) in philosophic pursuits, which alone, he believed, will result in intuitive certainty and direct appropriation of the truth. This, for Sadra, is what is meant by *hikma* or wisdom. Sadra denounces those who use philosophy for other than purely internalist aims, to satisfy worldly desires and to gain power and fame, who end up with a sterile philosophy, full of doubts and uncertainties, and far from the intended goal, which is to know God and man's destiny.[180] Knowledge of God (*ma'rifa*) is the whole objective of philosophy, according to Sadra, and philosophy is the crown of all knowledge.

Above all of the designations given to Sadra, be he philosopher or theosopher, Sufi or theologian, he was before everything else a die-hard, self-confessed internalist who devoted himself almost exclusively to *'irfān* and who kept almost total silence on the question of the particular ritual or legal prescriptions and the accepted structure of legal interpretation of the Koran and the Traditions. His understanding of the Koran and Traditions is based largely on the interpretations summarized in the works of Ibn al-'Arabi, although Sadra gives no hint anywhere of any formal Sufi affiliation on his part. His selection of sayings of the Twelver Shi'ite Imams is restricted mainly to the more contemplative, internalist teachings of Imam 'Ali and Imam Ja'far al-Sadiq. Sadra's position *vis-à-vis* Twelver Shi'ism is similar to that of Amuli and Ibn Jumhur in the sense that he saw the Imams as channels of theocentric internalism rather than as the objects of imamocentric internalism. His understanding of the reality of the Imams and the questions of *imāma* and *wilāya* distances him from the popular understanding prevailing among the majority of Twelver Shi'ite scholars, namely the *fuqahā*; all of Sadra's works are directed towards a deeper questioning of the most basic popular assumptions as to what it means to 'know' the Imams, as his *Hikmat al-'arshīyya* (Wisdom of the Throne) demonstrates.[181] His belief in *'irfān* as the true goal of all knowledge, his scant regard for the scriptural sciences as an academic pursuit, and his choice of ideologically 'suspect' writers and thinkers for the inspiration behind the articulation of his belief in all his works – all of these set him at serious odds with the *fuqahā* of his time, so much so that part of his life was spent in exile.[182] A study of his life, works and philosophy is beyond the scope of our present enquiry, although a brief review of his only Persian work, *Sih Asl* (The Three Principles), would not be without direct relevance to the question of externalism and the definition of the term *'ilm*.

On one level, *Sih Asl* is a theosophical treatment of the 'science of the soul' (*'ilm al-nafs*), which Sadra maintains is the 'key to all sciences'. In fourteen chapters Sadra outlines the path that an individual must take in order to know the reality of his own soul and to refine it in order to reach the ultimate goal: knowledge of, and belief in, God, His angels, His revelation, His messengers and the Last Day. Sadra also describes the obstacles – the diseases of the soul – that the traveller (*sālik*) is likely to encounter on his journey. On another level, however, *Sih Asl* constitutes a severe and often vitriolic attack upon the externalists and their teachings; as such it is one of the most direct and coherent of its kind to have been written, second only perhaps to Ghazali's *Ihyā*, parts of which it resembles.

The fact that *Sih Asl* was written in Persian suggests that Sadra intended it to be read by as wide and academically varied an audience as possible; the work seems to have been directed primarily at the largest group of potential readers: the less sophisticated and relatively uneducated Twelver Shi'ite *fuqahā*, who already tended to perceive the tradition in which Sadra was working as being without inherent value and even heretical and anti-Islamic. The antagonism that the treatise created among the externalists may be reflected in the fact that it has gone unmentioned in all but one of the standard biographical dictionaries which cover the life and works of the Safavid scholars.[183] That Sadra took a great risk in producing so vituperative an attack on the externalist community, on the majority of scholars of his time, is beyond doubt: *Sih Asl* comes across as a passionate outpouring of personal feeling, and of concern for an outlook – the internalist outlook – which by the reign of Shah 'Abbas I was in grave danger of being swamped and suffocated by the forces of externalism. 'The time for patience is over,' writes Sadra in the introduction, 'and now I must speak out.'[184]

Sadra's anti-externalist strictures, woven as they are in and out of his description of the path the soul must take to self- and God-knowledge, focus on the twin concepts of *īmān/islām* and *'ilm*. There is a world of difference, he says, between the Islam which is professed by the tongue and the *īmān* which is held by the heart. To declare oneself to be a Muslim does not necessarily mean that one believes in the tenets of Islam, despite the fact that one may on the surface be performing the external actions that a Muslim is supposed to perform.[185] The real believer is one who is deeply cognizant (*'ārif*) of God, His angels, His messengers, His books, His prophets, and the Resurrection.[186] Sadra points out that the kind of Islam that is adhered to through custom and inheritance actually acts as a barrier between the individual and true belief.[187] True belief, which, Sadra says, in Sufi terminology is called *wilāya*, cannot enter a heart that has not reformed itself, has not cast out all the attachments it has formed to this world.[188] Superficial knowledge, nominal professions of Islam, prayers that are performed by way of custom, fasts and pilgrimages that are carried out through force of habit – all of these conceal a deep attachment to the world and are dysfunctional to belief and to salvation in the hereafter.[189] Belief in the hereafter, opines Sadra, is one of the greatest pillars of the religion. Yet few people are able to base their belief in the hereafter on cogent proofs; rather, most people accept the existence of the afterlife on hearsay, and thus prefer to 'imitate' (*taqlīd*) rather than use their God-given intellects to reason for themselves. Ibn Sina, he says, whom everyone calls the 'master of Islamic philosophy', is one such person whose belief in the hereafter was imitative.[190] True belief in God and the hereafter, unlike imitative belief, can be gained only through self-knowledge (*ma'rifat al-nafs*), which is the key to all sciences.[191] Sadra considers *ma'rifat al-nafs* to be part of the 'science of divine unity' (*'ilm al-tawhīd*), about which he writes:

> The people of this age know nothing of the 'science of Unity' or of God-knowledge (*'ilm-i ilāhī*); in my whole life I have met none that has such knowledge. And as for (self-knowledge), the scholars of today are totally devoid of it, not to mention the people. And most believe only in things which they can immediately experience (*mahsūsat*).[192]

Whoever fails to gain self-knowledge cannot know God, says Sadra.[193] Furthermore, without self-knowledge, all actions are baseless and without value.[194] True knowledge is that which is gained through the gradual

132

discovery and unveiling of the truth (*mukāshafāt*), not that which deals with transactions (*mu'āmalāt*) or other branches of knowledge;[195] the true knowledge postulated by the Koran, and which lay in the possession of the Prophet and his companions, was not *fiqh* or *kalām*, astronomy or philosophy. True knowledge – the knowledge of the self and of God – is derived from contemplation of the inner meanings (*butūn*) of the Koran and the Traditions, and not from the detailed, formal study of their outer husks (*zawāhir*).[196]

Continuing with the theme of superficial exegesis of the Koran, Sadra mentions the verse which is also used as the basis for the *fiqh* ruling that states that someone who is not ritually clean (*tāhir*) cannot touch the Koran. Sadra asserts that *tahāra* (purity) describes the state of the heart and not of the body; it is clear that those engaged in formal sciences (*'ulūm-i rasmī*) such as *fiqh* have no need of ritual purity to be able to study those sciences. Those sciences, he observes caustically, are more conducive to personal ambition and worldly desires than to purity of heart and intention.[197] He also cites the previously mentioned Koranic verse which states that only 'those with knowledge' (*'ulamā*) truly fear God; the knowledge which inspires fear of God, says Sadra, is most certainly not *fiqh*.[198]

Having outlined the meaning of *īmān* and the distinction which should be drawn between it and Islam, and having established that *'ilm* as adumbrated by the Koran is the knowledge of the self (*ma'rifat al-nafs*) which leads to the knowledge of God's unity (*'ilm-i tawhīd*), Sadra turns his attention to the exponents of externalism:

Some of those who appear to be learned but who are evil and corrupt, some of the theologians (*mutakallimūn*) who are devoid of correct logic and stand outside the circle of rectitude and salvation, those who follow the religious law (*mutasharri'*) yet know nothing of the law of servitude to God, and have strayed from the path of belief in the origin of man (*mabda'*) and his return to God (*ma'ād*), have tied the rope of blind imitation (*taqlīd*) around their necks and made the denigration of the dervishes their slogan.[199]

Many of those who attribute knowledge and learning to themselves, says Sadra, are unaware of the realities of the soul, of its states and its diseases. They profess by the tongue to believe in the hereafter but are constantly in the service of the *nafs*, this world and their own caprices.[200] Most of them consider the hereafter as they consider this world; consequently the acts of worship they perform are meaningless, and the endless jurisprudential investigations they make into these acts of worship is even more meaningless. As a result, their worship amounts to nothing more than self-worship.[201] They have made the abode of this world their *qibla* and the doors of kings and sultans the prayer-niche unto which they turn in supplication and in expectation of their daily bread.[202] They spend their time in conversation with those whose hearts are dead and whose natures are evil. Addressing the *muhaddithūn* in particular, Sadra says that the real science which enables one to understand the realities of *īmān* is 'the science of uncovering' ('*ilm-i mukāshafa*), and then asks them:

> Why do you deny this (i.e. *mukāshafa*)? Why do you say that it is easy or useless? And why do you accord so much importance to sciences that can be mastered in six months, and call the purveyors of those sciences 'scholars of religion' ('*ulamā-i dīn*)? If true knowledge is that which you possess, which can be learnt only through Traditions and from teachers, why does God, in many verses in the Koran, forbid the blind imitation of others in matters of belief and in the fundamentals of the faith?[203]

Most externalists, according to Sadra, suffer from the diseases of the soul. If only they would recognise these diseases and admit that their belief and actions are futile, they might be able to help themselves. However, it is difficult for them to admit their weaknesses, given the fact that 'having spent time studying and copying out the teachings and writings of the old masters, memorizing their words...they have become enamoured of the praise which is heaped upon them by the masses, by the flattery lavished upon them by idiots.'[204]

Knowledge of transactions (*mu'āmalāt*) should only be to the point of necessity, says Sadra, whereas to know too much – as the *fuqahā* do – when such knowledge is not required of one will be a burden in the hereafter. Not only is it a waste of time, it brings about incalculable pride: every kind of wretchedness that has befallen the people has been caused by the pride of the purveyors of '*ilm-i zāhir* (superficial or external knowledge) and action without belief. The holy Imams were killed, ultimately, not by daggers or by poison but by the aggravation caused to them by the pseudo-'*ulamā* ('*ulamā-i 'ālim-namā*).

Sadra further berates the externalists for pandering to the whims of the rich and powerful, and for cultivating the admiration of ignorant believers merely in order to attain fame, wealth and worldly glory.[205] One of the results of their devilish pride and the insidious whisperings of their concupiscent souls is that most externalists – especially the theologians – rely upon their deficient powers of reason and upon corrupted and falsified Traditions.[206] Basing their teachings on pure hearsay, the theologians wish to correct and perfect the laws of God without the basis of gnosis and purely by means of the senses, which are limited and deficient. Many are the theologians who debate and argue about the essence, attributes and names of God, yet describe Him in a way that would, were they to use the same words to describe a village headsman, put him to shame. Most externalists cannot be called human, let alone men of knowledge; since belief in the hereafter is contingent upon self-knowledge, and since most of these so-called scholars are bereft of such knowledge, it may be said that most of the self-styled *'ulamā* are little better than infidels (*kuffar*).[207]

Such was the invective of Mulla Sadra against a force that was perceived to be taking the commanding position in the socio-religious life of the Iranian people, literate and illiterate alike, during the mid-Safavid period. One wonders whether it was not his philosophical bent but rather his anti-externalist stance that set so many of the externalists against him in later years. Whatever the case may be, *Sih Asl* remains the most damning anti-externalist document ever written by a self-confessed Twelver Shi'ite against the majority of his co-religionists.

The reigns of Shah Safi and Shah 'Abbas II

In his treatise *Himam al-thawāqib*, Shaykh 'Ali al-Farahani, whose work on the prohibition of tobacco was mentioned earlier, notes with considerable distaste the fact that Shah Safi (1629-42) was less than enthusiastic about propagating Twelver Shi'ism, and that not only had he ceased to have close and cordial relations with the Twelver Shi'ite *fuqahā*, but he had also become lax towards Sunnism.[208] One particular manifestation of Shah Safi's tolerant attitude was his commissioning of a Persian translation of Ghazali's *Ihyā*; the *fuqahā* duly protested, demanding that repressive measures be taken against the Sunnis. Shah Safi refused.[209] All in all it is clear that with the advent of Shah Safi the tide was beginning to turn, and the trend was set in favour of non-externalism, which was to reach its zenith during the reign of Shah 'Abbas II (1642-66).

Shah 'Abbas II's patronage of the non-externalist scholars of his day stemmed more, it would seem, from his own indifference to the externals of Islam – according to a historian of his time he was constantly inebriated[210] - than from any inherent personal penchant for the non-externalist orientation *per se*. His desire to encourage the non-externalists was also manifest in his choice of Sayyid Husayn b. Rafi' al-din Muhammad Khalifa Sultan, also known as Sultan al-'ulama, as his vizier in 1055/1645-46.[211] Sayyid Husayn (d.1066/1655-56) was a syncretist who tried to emphasize the gnostic element in the Traditions of the Twelve Imams, and who had served as vizier under both Shah 'Abbas I and Shah Safi. His appointment to the office of vizier by Shah 'Abbas II was vehemently opposed by Mirza Qadi, the *shaykh al-islām* of Isfahan, whom the Shah promptly dismissed.[212] It is interesting to compare this incident, which was emblematic of a serious decline in the influence of the externalist *fuqahā*, with Shah Tahmasp's dismissal of Mir Ghiyath al-din Mansur Dashtaki Shirazi a century earlier, and to consider the extent to which the relative fortunes of externalist and non-externalist had been reversed.

The circle of independent non-externalists and loosely Order-affiliated Sufi adepts patronised by Sayyid Husayn and Shah 'Abbas II was an illustrious one which included Muhammad Taqi al-Majlisi, 'Abd al-Razzaq al-Lahiji, Muhammad Baqir Sabziwari, Rajab 'Ali Tabrizi, Aqa Husayn al-Khwansari and Mulla Muhsin Fayd al-Kashani – figures which span the whole spectrum of Twelver Shi'ite non-externalism. Muhammad Taqi al-Majlisi (d. 1070/1659-60), the father of Muhammad Baqir, was an adherent of the Dhahabi Order; Shah 'Abbis II is said to have had great respect for him and commissioned a commentary by him on Ibn Babuya's *Man lā yahduruhu al-faqīh*.[213] 'Abd al-Razzaq al-Lahiji (d. 1072/1661-62), a student and son-in-law of Mulla Sadra, expounded in his Persian work *Gawhar-i murād* the principles of the Twelver Shi'ite *imāma* within a framework of gnostic philosophy in which the knowledge of the soul and the knowledge of God feature strongly.[214] Muhammad Baqir Sabziwari (d. 1090/1679-80) wrote books on *fiqh* as well as commentaries on treatises of philosophy, and was something of a syncretist in the mould of Shaykh Baha'i.[215] Rajab 'Ali Tabrizi, the hermit philosopher and gnostic, was visited by Shah 'Abbas II on several occasions; the king was said to hold the recluse in great awe.[216] Aqa Husayn al-Khwansari (d. 1098/1686-87), another syncretist, wrote treatises on *fiqh* and philosophy, having studied the scriptural sciences under Muhammad Taqi al-Majlisi and the rational sciences under Mir Findiriski (d. 1050/1640-41), the renowned Sufi philosopher and recluse.[217]

Above all, however, it was Mulla Muhsin Fayd al-Kashani who received the lion's share of royal favours and attention, with Shah 'Abbas II ordering his personal physician, Hakim Kuchak – himself a philosopher of no uncertain worth – to build a Sufi hostel for Kashani in Isfahan. Kashani, also a student and son-in-law of Mulla Sadra, was as comfortable writing treatises on *fiqh* as he was writing on philosophy, although it was clear where his priorities lay.[218] In the treatise *Raf' al-fitna*, Kashani distinguishes clearly between two types of knowledge: *'ilm al-zāhir* and *'ilm al-bātin*, the former denoting knowledge of the sacred law (*sharī'a*) and the latter consisting of knowledge of the truth (*haqīqa*). The second, says Kashani, is the true science or *hikma*, from which the real knowledge of man's origin (*mabda'*) and 'return' (*ma'ād*) can be extracted. He also attacks the *fuqahā*, whom he accuses of working for fame and power and who are considered to be *'ulamā* by the masses but who are, in reality, ignoramuses (*juhalā*).[219] In true Akhbari fashion he inveighs against the orthodox *fuqahā* on account of their attempts to impose by force the concept of *nahy 'an al-munkar* (forbidding the forbidden) on a people that have no grasp of the concept of belief and submission.[220] The sacred law - the commandments of the Prophet and the Imams - should, he says, be understood directly with the aid of God and without the mediation of the *fuqahā*, whose practice of *ijtihād* and condonation of *taqlīd* amount to an adulteration of the *sharī'a*.[221]

Such was the relationship between Kashani and Shah 'Abbas II – whose patronage of non-externalists had led to his being given the soubriquet 'dervish-loving Shah' (*shāh-i darwīsh dūst*) – that Kashani was able to treat the Shah's orders and requests lightly, without feeling the least fear of royal displeasure or retribution. In 1065/1654-55, the Shah ordered Kashani by leter to go to Isfahan to perform the Friday prayer there. Kashani, who at the time was residing in Kashan, took several months to reply, saying that he preferred to stay and perform the Friday prayer in his own town with his own people, and that to come to Isfahan 'would be at odds with my desire for peace and isolation.'[222]

Shah 'Abbas II's disenchantment with the mainstream Twelver Shi'ite *fuqahā* was evident also from his patronage of the eminent Akhbari theologian and *faqīh*, Khalil b. Ghazi al-Qazwini (d. 1089/1678-79), also known as Burhan al-'ulama. A student of both Shaykh Baha'i and Mir Damad, Qazwini was initially a lecturer and administrator of the holy shrine in Rayy before moving to Mecca and finally settling in Qazvin. In 1064/1653-54, Shah 'Abbas II gave a lavish banquet for all of the eminent scholars of Qazvin, and singled out Qazwini to write a Persian commentary on Kulayni's *al-Kāfī*. Qazwini immediately reciprocated the royal attention by pointing out to the Shah that his reign had been foreshadowed in the Traditions as one of the auspicious events leading up to the reappearance of the Hidden Imam.[223] However, not only did Qazwini oppose Sufism and *hikma*, he also inveighed against the teachings of the astronomers and physicians, asserting that all knowledge must come directly from the Traditions of the Imams such as those collated in *al-Kāfī*, all of which are correct and must be acted upon without question.[224] Shah 'Abbas II's two most trusted personal physicians, the brothers Muhammad Husayn and Muhammad Sa'id al-Qummi, were also gnostic philosophers and Sufi adepts of the Akhbari school.

Shah 'Abbas II had thus surrounded himself with scholars whose religious orientations were anathema to the orthodox Twelver Shi'ite *fuqahā*, not only in the sense that philosophy and *hikma* were favoured above *fiqh* but also because of the Akhbari stance of many of them. This *melange* – non-externalism, Akhbari *fiqh* and royal patronage – threatened to undermine the whole edifice of othodox Twelver Shi'ite externalism and deal a *coup de grace* to the nascent concepts of *ijtihād* and *taqlīd*, thereby changing the face of Twelver Sh'ism in Iran forever. What the Twelver Shi'ite *fuqahā* were in need of was a charismatic spokesman – another Shaykh Karaki perhaps – and an externally religious-minded Shah who could be easily influenced. Little could they have known, during what for them must have been the dark days of Shah 'Abbas II's reign, that they would soon be provided with both.

Notes

1. Nicolas Sanson, *The Present State of Persia* (Paris, 1695), p. 128.
2. See: Vladimir Minorsky, 'The Poetry of Shah Isma'il I' in *BSOAS*, VOL. 10 (1942), p. 1047a. On the veneration of Isma'il, see: Erika Glassen, 'Schah Isma'il, ein Mahdi der Anatolischen Turkmenen?' in *ZDMG* 121 (1971), pp. 61-9.
3. The Hakluyt Society, *Travels of Venetians in Persia* (London, 1873), p. 206
4. Yusufi, *Surūr al-'ārifīn*, p. 6.
5. *ibid.*
6. *ibid.*, p. 7.
7. The question of the occultation of the 12ᵗʰ Shi'ite Imam will be discussed in Chapter Five. For a more detailed and comprehensive treatment see: Jassim M. Hussain, *The Occultation of the Twelfth Imam* (London: Muhammadi Trust, 1982) and Abdulaziz Abdulhussein Sachedina, *Islamic Messianism* (Albany: State University of New York Press, 1981).
8. Muhammad b. Hasan Hurr al-'Amili, *Wasā'il al-shī'a* (Beirut, 1391/1971-72), vol. 18, p. 101.
9. Muhammad b. 'Ali al-Saduq, *Kamāl al-dīn wa tamām al-ni'ma* (Tehran, 1395/1975-76), p. 81.
10. *ibid.*, p. 10. See also: Muhammad b. Hasan al-Tusi, *al-Fihrist* (Mashhad, 1972), pp. 268 and 363.
11. Norman Calder, *The Structure of Authority in Imami Shi'i Jurisprudence* (Unpublished Ph.D. thesis, SOAS, University of London, 1980), pp. 73-4.
12. *ibid.*, pp. 163-65.
13. *ibid.*, pp. 84-5, 112, 125-6 and 147-51.
14. Calder, *The Structure of Authority*, p. 157.
15. Muhsin al-Amin al-'Amili, *Khitat Jabal 'Āmil* (Beirut, 1983), p. 182.
16. M. Gaudefroy-Demombynes, *La Syrie a l'epoque des Mamelouks* (Paris, 1923), pp. 70,74 and 246; J. Sourdel Thomine, 'Inscriptions arabes de Karak Nuh' in *Bulletin d'Etudes Orientales* 13 (1941-51), pp. 71-84.
17. al-'Amili, *Khitat Jabal 'Āmil*, pp. 77-8.
18. *'ālim* here denotes 'scholar' in general, i.e. in the non-Koranic sense of the word.
19. For biographical details of Shahid al-Awwal, see: Mirza 'Abdullah Afandi al Isbahani, *Rīyād al-'ulamā wa hīyād al-fudalā* (Qum, 1401/1980-81), vol. 5, pp. 185-91.
20. *ibid.*, vol. 2, pp. 365-86.
21. See: *Anonomous History of Shah Isma'il* (British Library Ms. Or. 3248 [Ross Anonomous]), p. 113a.
22. For a list of Shaykh Karaki's works, see: Afandi, *Rīyād al-'ulamā*, vol. 3, pp. 441-60.
23. Danishpazhuh, *Fihrist*, vol. 3, p. 1098
24. Karaki made clear his stance in his controversial treatise on *kharāj*; see: Danishpazhuh, *Fihrist*, vol. 3, pp. 1964-5.

25. A.K.S. Lambton, 'Quis Custodiet Custodes' in *Studia Islamica*, vol. 6 (1956), p. 133.
26. Muqaddas Ardabili (d. 993/1585) and Shaykh Ibrahim Qatifi (still alive in 947/1540-01) were two leading Safavid scholars who actively dissociated themselves from the state. Those who deemed the performance of the Friday congregational prayer unlawful in the absence of the Imam were those who were most likely to regard kingly authority with suspicion. See the section on *intizār* in Chapter Five.
27. Mirza Makhdum Shirazi, *al-Nawāqid lī-bunyān al-rawāfid* (British Museum Ms. Or. 7001), p. 98b.
28. Afandi, *Rīyād al-'ulamā*, vol. 3, p. 450.
29. Danishpazhuh, *Fihrist*, vol. 3, p. 1964.
30. *ibid.*, vol. 3, p. 1965.
31. *ibid.*
32. Afandi, *Rīyād al-'ulamā*, vol.2, p. 67.
33. See: Iskandar Munshi, *Tārīkh-i 'ālamārā-i 'Abbāsi*, ed. by E. Yarshater, transl. by R. Savory (Boulder, Colorado, 1978), vol. 1, pp. 294-330 on the question of Isma'il II and Sunnism.
34. A classic example of Sunni learned criticism of Shi'ite practices such *taqīyya* can be seen in: Taqi al-din Ibn Taymiyya, *Minhaj al-sunnat al-nabawiyya fī naqd kalām al-shī'at al-qadariyya* (Cairo, 1962), vol. 1, p. 43).
35. See Nasrollah Pourjavady/Peter Lamborn Wilson, *Kings of Love: The Poetry and History of the Ni'matullahiyya Sufi Order* (Tehran, 1978), pp. 47-9 and *passim*.
36. Danishpazhuh, *Fihrist*, vol. 2, p. 581.
37. *ibid.*
38. *ibid.*, vol. 2, p. 581.
39. *ibid.*
40. Ibn Ruzbihan, quoted in: Nurullah Shushtari, *Ihqāq al-haqq*, ed. by Ghaffari (Tehran, 1376/1956-57), vol. 1, pp. 25-6.
41. Jean Aubin, 'Şah Isma'il et les notables de l'Iraq persan' in *Journal of the Economic and Social History of the Orient*, vol. 2 (1959), p. 59.
42. *ibid.*
43. For details of Karaki's anti-Sufi treatises, see: Afandi, *Rīyād al-'ulamā*, vol. 3, p. 444.
44. See: Roger Savory, 'A 15th Century Propagandist at Harat' in *American Oriental Society, Middle West Branch, Semi-centennial volume* (London, 1969), pp. 196-97; Tabrizi, *Rawdāt al-jinān*, vol. 1, pp. 98-104, 214-16 and 416-18.
45. Afandi, *Rīyād al-'ulamā*, vol. 1, p. 308.
46. Danishpazhuh, *Fihrist*, vol. 3, p. 1658.
47. *ibid.*, vol. 3, p. 1664 for details of Shahid al-thani's treatise on *ijtihād*.
48. See: Hakluyt Society, *A Narrative of Italian Travels in Persia in the Fifteenth and Sixteenth Centuries* (London, 1873), vol. 49, part 2, p. 223. See also: Jean Aubin, 'La politique religieuse des Safavides' in *Le Shi'isme Imamite* (Paris: Colloque de Strasbourg), p. 239.

140

49. Mirza Muhammad Tahir Nasrabadi, *Tadhkira-i Nasrābādī* (Tehran: Furughi, 1352 Sh./1973-74), pp. 207-8.
50. For a brief account of Naqshbandi fortunes in early Safavid Iran, see: Hamid Algar, 'The Naqshbandi Order: A Preliminary Survey of its History and Significance' in *Studia Islamica*, vol. 44 (1976), in particular p. 139.
51. Qadi Ahmad Ghaffari, *Tarīkh-i jahān-ārā* (Tehran, n.d.), p. 302; K. Röhrborn, *Provinzen und Zentralgewalt Persiens im 16 und 17 Jahrhundert* (Berlin, 1966), p. 70.
52. In this context, see: Said Amir Arjomand, *The Shadow of God and the Hidden Imam* (Chicago: The University of Chicago Press, 1984), pp. 188-91, 200.
53. Danishpazhuh, *Fihrist*, vol. 3, p. 1312; Tunukabani, *Qisas al-'ulamā*, p. 262.
54. See: Afandi, *Rīyād al-'ulamā*, vol. 3, pp. 108-21 for comprehensive biographical details on the father of Shaykh Baha'i.
55. *ibid.*, p. 115.
56. The *farmān* appears in *Rīyād al-'ulamā*, vol. 3, pp. 455-60.
57. Danishpazhuh, *Fihrist*, vol. 3, p. 1964.
58. Arjomand, *The Shadow of God*, p. 132.
59. See: Munshi, *Tārīkh-i 'ālamārā*, vol. 1, pp. 229-50 for potted biographies of the major scholars – Twelver Shi'ite and Sunni – of the early Safavid period.
60. Arjomand, *The Shadow of God*, p. 132.
61. Munshi, *Tārīkh-i 'alamārā*, vol. 1, pp. 230-1
62. Afandi, *Rīyād al-'ulamā*, vol. 3, p. 454. The Koranic verse quoted is 2:142.
63. *ibid.* The Koranic verse quoted is 2:145.
64. *ibid.*
65. Shah Tahmasp, *Tadhkira-i Shāh Tahmāsp* (Calcutta, 1912), p. 14.
66. Munshi, *Tārīkh-i 'ālamārā*, vol. 1, p. 231.
67. Afandi, *Rīyād al-'ulamā*, vol. 3, p. 88.
68. *ibid., passim.*
69. For details of Tahmasp's largesse, see: Munshi, *Tārīkh-i 'ālamārā*, vol. 1, pp. 229-244.
70. Afandi, *Rīyād al-'ulamā*, vol. 3, p. 454.
71. Munshi, *Tārīkh-i 'ālamārā*, vol. 1, p. 237.
72. Danishpazhuh, *Fihrist*, vol. 3, p. 125.
73. *ibid.*
74. Arjomand, *The Shadow of God*, p. 133.
75. Qadi Ahmad Qummi, *Khulāsāt al-tawārīkh* (Berlin: Deutsche Staatsbibliothek, MS Orient no. 2202), pp. 255a-256.
76. A.H. Nawa'i (ed.) *Asnād wa mukātabāt-i tārīkhī; Shāh 'Abbās-i Awwal* (Tehran, 1352 Sh./1973-74), vol. 1, pp. 118-19.
77. Afandi, *Rīyād al-'ulamā*, vol. 4, p. 32.
78. Munshi, *Tārīkh-i 'ālamārā*, vol. 1, p. 237.
79. *ibid.*, vol. 1, p. 246.
80. Afandi, *Rīyād al-'ulamā*, vol. 2, pp. 62-75.
81. Munshi, *Tārīkh-i 'ālamārā*, vol. 1, p. 321.
82. *ibid.*, vol. 1, p. 318.

83. For an account of 'Abbas I's reconstruction of his armed forces, see: Roger Savory, *Iran Under the Safavids* (Cambridge: CUP, 1980), pp. 78-83.
84. Nasrullah Falsafi, *Zindagānī-i Shāh 'Abbās-i Awwal* (Tehran, 1332 Sh./1953-54).
85. Savory, *Iran Under the Safavids*, p. 83.
86. On the Nuqtawiyya heresy, see Mahmud Natanzi, *Nuqāwat al-āthār fī dhikr al-akhyār*, ed. by I. Ishraqi (Tehran, 1350 Sh./1971-72), pp. 515-24.
87. Arjomand, *The Shadow of God*, p. 119.
88. See: Jean Aubin, 'Les Sunnis du Larestan et la chute des Safavides' in *Revue des etudes islamiques*, vol. 33 (1965), p. 152 for examples of anti-Sunni measures taken by Shah 'Abbas.
89. Representatives of foreign monastic orders such as the Carmelites, the Augustinians and the Capuchins were given permission to establish convents and to proselytise actively. See: Savory, *Iran Under the Safavids*, pp. 100-101.
90. Savory, *Iran Under the Safavids*, p. 101.
91. Quoted by Arjomand in *The Shadow of God*, p. 112.
92. The rise to prominence of Isfahan, particularly under the auspices of Shah 'Abbas, has been charted by Savory in *Iran Under the Safavids*, especially Chapter 7.
93. Shaykh Karaki's great-grandson, Mirza Habibullah, and the latter's son, Mirza Mahdi, were apparently assimilated into the 'aristocracy' as inheritors of vast landed estates in central Persia accumulated by their forefathers. Both acquired the title 'Mirza' whilst in the service of the Safavid rulers; Mirza Habibullah became *sadr* for Shah Safi in 1041/1631-32 and Mirza Mahdi succeeded him in 1064/1653-54. See: Iskandar Beg Turkuman/Muhammad b. Yūsuf, *Dhayl-i tārīkh-i 'ālamārā-i 'Abbāsī* (Tehran, 1317 Sh.), p. 91.
94. For biographical details of Mir Damad, see Sadr al-din Shirazi, *al-Shawāhid al-rubūbiyya*, ed. by J. Ashtiyani (Mashhad, 1346 Sh./1967-68), pp. 83-90).
95. Afandi, *Rīyād al-'ulamā*, vol. 1, p. 118.
96. Sir John Malcolm, *History of Persia* (London, 1815), vol. 1, pp. 371-2.
97. Yusuf al-Bahrani, *Lu'lu'at al-Bahrayn*, ed. by M.S. Bahr al-'Ulum (Najaf, 1386/1966-67).
98. Muhammad b. Hasan Hurr al-'Amili, *Amal al-Āmil*, ed. by A. Husayni (Najaf 1385/1965-66).
99. Muhammad Tunukabuni, *Qisas al-'ulamā* (Tehran, n.d. [c. 1880]). A printed edition (Tehran, n.d.) has also been used for this study: it will be referred to as *Qisas II*.
100. Danishpazhuh, *Fihrist*, vol. 2, p. 608.
101. See, for example, the collection of Twelver Shi'ite Traditions on *tawhīd* in: William C. Chittick (ed.), *A Shi'ite Anthology*, (London: Muhammadi Trust, 1980), pp. 23-65.
102. See: Tunukabuni, *Qisas al-'ulamā*, pp. 330-4 for an interesting account of the harrowing experiences undergone by one such aspiring *faqīh*, Shaykh Ni'matullah Jaza'iri, in his quest for externalist knowledge.
103. Afandī, *Riyād al-'ulamā*, vol. 6, pp. 147-8.

104. *ibid.*, p. 144.
105. Shaykh Muhammad Lahiji, *Sharh-i gulshan-i rāz*, ed. by K. Sami'i (Tehran, 1337 Sh./1958-59)
106. Isfahani's treatise appears in its entirety in *Rīyād al-'ulamā*, vol. 4, pp. 273-6.
107. For biographical details of Kamal al-din Darwish, see: Karl-Heinz Pampus, *Die Theologische Enzyklopädie Bihār al-Anwār* (Bonn, 1970), pp. 55-6.
108. Afandi, *Rīyād al-'ulamā*, vol.6, p. 238.
109. *ibid.*, vol. 6, p. 94; vol. 3, pp.252 and 429.
110. *ibid.*, vol. 5, p. 96; vol. 6, p. 95.
111. *ibid.*, vol. 6, p. 109.
112. *ibid.*, vol. 6, p. 66.
113. Danishpazhuh, *Fihrist*, vol. 1,p. 1.
114. *ibid.*, vol. 1, p. 23.
115. The relationship between Safavid Iran and the Ottoman Empire has been dealt with extensively in: Adel Allouche, *The Origins and Development of the Ottoman-Safavid Conflict* (Berlin: Klaus Schwarz Verlag, 1983). Chapters 3 and 4 are particularly relevant.
116. While Shi'ite jurisprudence no longer deems valid Karaki's ruling on Sunnis, unbelievers are still classed as *najis* or ritually impure.
117. Danishpazhuh, *Fihrist*, vol. 1, p. 112; Afandi, *Rīyad al-'ulamā*, vol. 5, p. 192.
118. Afandi, *Rīyād al-'ulamā*, vol. 5, p. 154.
119. *ibid.*, vol. 4, p. 192.
120. Mirza Makhdum Shirazi, *al-Nawāqid*, pp. 90b-91a.
121. Afandi, *Rīyād al-'ulamā*, vol.6, p. 167.
122. *ibid.*, vol. 2, pp. 315-16.
123. *ibid.*, vol. 2, p. 283.
124. *ibid.*, vol. 1, p. 185.
125. Tunukabuni, *Qisas al-'ulamā*, p. 251.
126. Afandi, *Rīyād al-'ulamā*, vol.1, p. 26.
127. See: *ibid.*, vol 5, pp. 35-6 for biographical details.
128. Ahmad b. Muhammad Ardabili, *Majma' al-fā'ida wa al-burhān* (Tehran, 1272/1855-56), *passim*.
129. E. Kohlberg, 'Akbārīya' in *Encyclopaedia Iranica*, vol. 1, p. 717.
130. Moojan Momen, *An Introduction to Shi'i Islam: The History and Doctrines of Twelver Shi'ism* (New Haven: Yale University Press, 1985), pp. 224-25.
131. Arjomand, *The Shadow of God*, p. 146.
132. For an account of Qummi's attacks on Muhammad Taqi Majlisi and Mulla Khalil Qazwini, both of whom were favoured by Shah 'Abbas, see: Ma'sum 'Ali Shah, *Tarā'iq al-haqā'iq* (Tehran, 1339 Sh./1960-61), vol. 1, pp. 177-8.
133. Afandi, *Rīyād al-'ulamā*, vol. 2, p. 261: Danishpazhuh, *Fihrist*, vol. 3, p. 1358.
134. Though an externalist through and through, Ibn Taymiyya is said to have found the ideals of Sufism in keeping with the core truths of the Koran; his anti-Sufi strictures came not as a reaction to Sufism per se, but to the antinomian excesses committed in its name.
136. Afandi, *Rīyād al-'ulamā*, vol. 2, pp. 264-5.
137. Henry Corbin, *En Islam Iranien* (Paris, 1971), vol. 3, p. 254.

138. Hamid Algar, 'Shi'ism and Iran in the eighteenth century' in: T. Naff and R. Owen (eds.), *Studies in Eighteenth Century Islamic History* (London, 1977), p. 288.
139. Hamid Enayat, *Modern Islamic Political Thought* (London: The Macmillan Press, 1980), p. 22. *bāṭin* is explained as the inner or secret meaning of the Koran while *zāhir* is the outer or apparent meaning: *ta'wīl* is the hermeneutic or allegorical interpretation of the Koran while *tafsīr* is the literal interpretation and straightforward clarification of its verses; *haqīqa* is the Truth of the revelation, and *sharī'a* is the Law.
140. See note no. 8 to Chapter Two.
141. See Tabataba'i, *al-Mizān*, vol. 1, pp. 50-1 for an explanation of the term *jary*.
142. Qadi Nurullah Shushtari (d. 1019/1610-11), the author of *Majālis al-mu'minīn* and *Ihqāq al-haqq*, while identifying himself as a Twelver, fits into the picture neither as an externalist nor an internalist; although he appears to champion the Sufi cause, his zeal for Twelver Shi'ism leads him to force every renowned scholar, poet and literateur of the past into the Shi'ite mould. Rumi, for example, is on the flimsiest of pretexts classed by him as a staunch Shi'ite. For details of Shushtari's life and works, and of his zeal for putting the Twelver tag on all and sundry, see: Afandi, *Rīyāḍ al-'ulamā*, vol. 5, pp. 265-75, especially p. 269.
143. See: Henry Corbin and Osman Yahya, *La Philosophie Shi'ite* (Tehran, 1969), pp. 6-15.
144. Haydar al-Amuli, *Jāmi' al-asrār wa manba' al-anwār* (India Office Library, MS Arberry 1349), p. 121b.
145. *ibid.*, p. 2a-b.
146. *ibid.*, pp. 108b-109a.
147. *ibid.*, p. 105a.
148. *ibid.*, p. 19a.
149. *ibid.*, p. 24b.
150. *ibid.*, p. 122a.
151. Ibn Abi Jumhur al-Ahsa'i, *al-Mujlī* (Tehran, 1329/1911), p. 165.
152. *ibid., passim.*
153. *ibid.*, p. 110.
154. A brief biographical sketch of Ibn Abi Jumhur can be found in: Danishpazhuh, *Fihrist*, vol. 3, pp. 625-27.
155. Ma'sum 'Ali Shah, *Tarā'iq al-haqā'iq*, vol. 1, p. 135.
156. al-Ahsa'i, *al-Mujlī*, pp. 371 and 376.
157. Although both Sunnis and Twelver Shi'ites agree that God is just (*'ādil*), the Sunni theologians for the most part believe that whatever God does is just, whereas the Twelver Shi'ites, along Mu'tazilite lines, believe that God does whatever is just. For a Twelver Shi'ite exposition of the concept of Divine justice, see: Murtada Mutahhari, *'Adl-i ilāhī* (Tehran: Intisharat-i Islami, 1398/1977-78).
158. While 'belief in the Imam' meant, for Safavid externalists, affirmation of the actual Twelve Imams as conduits through which man's approach to God must

be directed, in contemporary Shi'ite circles it is understood as affirmation of the principle of *imāma* in its political sense

159. In Sunni externalism the *faqīh* is pivotal as far as the purely religious orientation of the community is concerned; in Twelver Shi'ism, however, with the question of occultation and *ijtihād/taqlīd*, the *faqīh* is theoretically much more powerful than his Sunni counterpart.

160. See: J.M.S. Baljon, *Religion and Thought of Shah Wali allah Dihlawi 1703-1762* (Leiden: E. J. Brill, 1986), p. 72.

161. Shah Ni'matullah, *Kulliyyāt-i ash'ār-i Shāh Ni'matullāh Walī*, ed. by J. Nurbakhsh (Tehran, 1352 Sh./1973-74), pp. 684-5.

162. Mustafa Zaki al-'Ashur, *Badī' al-zamān Sa'īd Nūrsī* (Köln: Mihrab, n.d.), p. 165.

163. Taqi al-din Maqrizi, *al-Khitat* (Cairo, 1326/1908-09), vol. 2, p. 433.

164. Husayn Karbala'i Tabrizi, *Rawdāt al-jinān wa jannāt al-janān* (Tehran, 1344 Sh./1965-66), vol. 1, pp. 467-8.

165. Sanson, *The Present State of Persia*, pp. 153-4; Rafael du Mans, *Estat de la Perse en 1660*, ed. by C. Schefer (Paris, 1890), pp. 216-7.

166. 'Faction-fighting' between various Sufi groups during the reign of Shah 'Abbas, who actually encouraged the phenomenon, was one such practice. See: Falsafi, *Zindagānī-i Shāh 'Abbās-i Awwal*, vol. 2, p. 238.

167. Verse 24:35.

168. Pourjavady/Wilson, *Kings of Love*, p. 48.

169. See: Afandi, *Rīyād al-'ulamā*, vol. 3, pp. 384-6 for biographical details and list of works.

170. Muhammad 'Ali Mudarris, *Rayhānat al-adab* (Tehran, 1367/1947-48), vol. 4, p. 269.

171. S. Safari, *Armaghān al-awlīyā* (Mashhad, 1344 Sh./1965-66), vol. 1, p. 75.

172. *ibid.*, pp. 76-7.

173. *ibid.*, p. 78.

174. *ibid.*, p. 80.

175. *ibid.*, p. 82.

176. *ibid.*, p. 85.

177. *ibid.*, p. 88.

178. *ibid.*, p. 89.

179. On Mir Damad and the 'school of Isfahan', see: Henry Corbin, 'Confessions extatiques de Mir Damad' in *Mélange Louis Massignon* (Damascus, 1956), pp. 331-78.

180. For example, Sadra denounced Ibn Sina for pursuing medicine and a professional career despite his capacity for what Sadra considered to be the highest art – philosophy. See: Mulla Sadra-i Shirazi, *al-Asfār al-arba'a*, ed. by M.R. al-Muzaffar (Tehran, 1378/1958-59), vol. 4, p. 119.

181. See: James Winston Morris, *The Wisdom of the Throne: an Introduction to the Philosophy of Mulla Sadra* (Princeton University Press, 1981), especially part 2, section C.

182. For biographical details of Mulla Sadra, see: Seyyed Hossein Nasr, *Sadr al-din Shirazi and his Transcendent Theosophy* (Tehran, 1978), especially Chapter 2.

183. *Rawdāt al-jannāt, Rayhānat al-adab, Qisas al-'ulamā, Rīyād al-'ulamā, Amal al-āmil* and *Mustadrak al-wasā'il* all fail to mention *Sih Asl*; only in *Rawdat al-safā* is the treatise cited. See: Rida Quli Khan Hidayat, *Mulhaqāt-i rawdat al-safā* (Tehran, 1275/1858-59), vol. 8, p. 125.

184. Sadr al-din Muhammad b. Ibrahim Shirazi, *Risāla-i sih asl* (Tehran: Intisharat-i Mawla, 1360 Sh./1981), p. 42.

185. *ibid.*, p. 91.

186. *ibid.*, p. 91-2.

187. *ibid.*, p. 117.

188. *ibid.*, pp. 113-21.

189. *ibid.*, p. 132.

190. *ibid.*, p. 69.

191. *ibid.*, p. 40.

192. *ibid.*, p. 123.

193. *ibid.*, p. 46.

194. *ibid.*, p. 55.

195. *ibid.*, p. 96.

196. *ibid.*, p. 104.

197. *ibid.*, p. 105.

198. *ibid.*, p. 100.

199. *ibid.*, p. 39.

200. *ibid.*, p. 48.

201. *ibid.*

202. *ibid.*, p. 50.

203. *ibid.*, pp.102-103.

204. *ibid.*, p. 87.

205. *ibid.*, p. 88.

206. *ibid.*, p. 80.

207. *ibid.*, p. 51.

208. 'Ali Tugha'i al-Farahani, *Himam al-thawāqib*, (Tehran: Library of Madrasa-i Siphahsalar, MS. no. 1845).

209. *ibid.*, chapter 5.

210. Muhammad Tahir Wahid Qazwini, *'Abbāsnāma* (Arak, 1329 Sh./1950-51), p. 131.

211. Afandi, *Rīyād al-'ulamā*, vol. 3, p. 54.

212. Wali Quli Shamlu, *Qisas al-khāqānī* (British Library Add. MS. no. 7656), p. 52.

213. Muhammad Taqi's life and works are reviewed more comprehensively in Chapter Four.

214. Afandi, *Rīyād al-'ulamā*, vol. 3, pp. 114-5.

215. *ibid.*, vol. 5, pp. 44-5.

216. *ibid.*, vol. 2, pp. 283-5.

217. *ibid.*, vol. 2, pp. 57-60.

218. *ibid.*, vol. 5, pp. 180-2.

219. Muhsin Fayd al- Kashani, *Raf' al-fitna* (Tehran: Kitabkhana-i Markazi-i Danishgah-i Tehran, MS. No. 3303), pp. 1-7.

220. M.T. Danishpazhuh, 'Dāwarī mīyān-i pārsā wa dānishmand' in *Nashriyya-i Dānishkada-i Adabiyyāt-i Tabrīz*, vol. 9 (1336 Sh./1957-58), pp. 127-8.

221. Muhsin Fayd al-Kashani, *Ā'ina-i shāhī* (Shiraz, 1320 Sh./1941-42), p. 5.

222. Danishpazhuh, *Fihrist*, vol. 3, p. 2668.

223. *ibid.*, pp. 1357-8; Afandi, *Rīyād al-'ulamā*, vol. 2, pp. 261-66.

224. Danishpazhuh, *Fihrist*, vol. 3, p. 135.

Chapter 4

'Allama Majlisi: externalist extraordinaire

Introduction

The paucity of source material on his life and times means that no full, objective biography of 'Allama Muhammad Baqir Majlisi has ever been written. The most comprehensive account to date is given in *al-Fayd al-qudsī*, written in 1884 by Husayn b. Muhammad Taqi al-Nuri al-Tabarsi.[1] Although this contains much valuable information on Majlisi's forefathers, teachers, students and works, it contains very little on the man himself; the emphasis lies, as one might expect, on the importance of Majlisi's position in the history of Twelver Shi'ite learned scholarship. The same may be said of earlier accounts of Majlisi in *rijāl* collections such as *Lu'lu'at al-Bahrayn* and *Rawdat al-jannāt*.

Fayd al-qudsī itself appears to be an almost direct translation of an earlier work, *Mir'at al-ahwāl*, written in 1219/1804-05 by one Aqa Ahmad Kirmanshahi, a descendant of Majlisi, and thus it is clear that most contemporary accounts of Majlisi go back to the same source.[2] References to Majlisi and, occasionally, critical comments or illustrative anecdotes which do not appear in the aforementioned standard accounts of his life, can be found in other works, although usually with no mention of an original source. Such information is scattered and usually comes to light only incidentally. A reference work such as the *Fihrist* of Muhammad Taqi Danishpazhuh, for example, contains many such nuggets of information.[3]

There is scarcely any common ground between the supporters and critics of Majlisi in their appraisal of his life and achievements, although they are unanimous in acknowledging his fame, importance and, in the context of Twelver Shi'ism, his orthodoxy, not to mention his colossal output. To his supporters, Majlisi is 'unique in his own time';[4] he is the 'seal of the *mujtahids*' (*khātim al-mujtahidīn*);[5] he is the *mujaddid* (renewer of Islam)

148

divinely appointed for the 11th *hijra* century, and, as such, he is the inheritor of the Prophet Muhammad foretold by the latter himself when he informed his community that a 'renewer' or 'restorer' would follow him in each succeeding century.[6]

Criticisms of Majlisi are numerous and more often than not they are scathing. His detractors have labeled him a fanatic and a bigot; a ruthless oppressor of minorities; a charlatan, timeserver and impostor who forged Traditions in support of an oppressive regime; and the one who was ultimately responsible for the downfall of the Safavid regime and the havoc that ensued in the wake of the Afghan invasion.[7]

On the whole, Majlisi's detractors seem to be concerned not so much with what Majlisi actually said as with what he appears to have done. The word 'appears' is used deliberately for it seems that those who have lambasted Majlisi from the socio-political angle, citing his alleged persecution of religious minorities and also the fact that his propagation of outdated, superstitious and fanatical religious concepts undermined the Safavid state and expedited its downfall, have unwittingly based their criticisms of him on a misinterpretation of historical facts. The most striking example of this concerns the post of *mullā-bāshī* and the erroneous attribution of that title to Majlisi by Vladimir Minorsky, the translator and editor of the anonymously penned manual of Safavid administration, *Tadhkirat al-mulūk*, more about which shall be said presently.[8] Suffice it to say that no-one has studied Majlisi and his works solely from the point of view of religious ideology and orthopraxy, especially in the context of the internalist/externalist dichotomy. Even Said Arjomand, who has perhaps more than any other contemporary scholar shed some light on the religious impact of Majlisi's writings, seems to imply that Majlisi's Shi'ism is the definitive one, and thus misses the point.[9]

The little source material which is available reveals the fact that Majlisi's biographers focus their attention almost exclusively upon his vast literary output, concentrating chiefly on the enormous corpus of Twelver Shi'ite traditions known as *Bihār al-anwār*. For them, Majlisi's greatness is to be gauged primarily by the volume of his writings and the extent of the influence that his works had, and continue to have, on the Twelver Shi'ite community in Iran and further afield. This is not too difficult to understand once one has realised that Majlisi was the spokesman and representative *par excellence* of Twelver Shi'ite externalism and of those externalist scholars who attained prominence towards the end of the Safavid period. Concerned primarily with the exoteric trappings of Twelver Shi'ism, with Islam rather than *īmān*, this group succeeded in redefining Twelver Shi'ism in terms designed to conform with their own preoccupation with one particular branch of Islamic knowledge, namely *fiqh* and *hadīth*. It was under Majlisi that Twelver Shi'ite externalism became truly orthodox, while all other views were rejected and often forcibly repressed.

The exponents of the new orthodoxy, which one critic was moved to call the *dīn-i Majlisī*,[10] did not merely shift the emphasis from *īmān* to Islam; this did occur, but as already seen in previous chapters it is by no means a phenomenon confined to the *fuqahā* of 17th century Iran. What actually took place was a dramatic reformulation and reorientation of the Shi'ism of the founding fathers of the faith – a Shi'ism which, according to Mihdi Bazargan, represented at the outset a 'crystallization of the most exalted ideals that are Islam.'[11] Belief in the superiority of the family of the Prophet as interpreters of the Islamic revelation – a belief which, on a purely religious level, is by no means unacceptable to non-Shi'ites[12] – was manipulated by the new Twelver Shi'ite orthodoxy not only to preserve and deepen the rift between Twelver Shi'ism and its ideological rivals but also to further externalise Islam in a particularly overt Twelver Shi'ite externalist manner. The move from theocentrism to imamocentrism took its greatest strides during the Safavid period, and it was under the auspices of Majlisi, whose major achievement was to codify the disparate sayings of the Imams into a more or less coherent whole, that the externalisation of Islam in its Twelver Shi'ite form reached its zenith.

If, indeed, Majlisi's stature is to be gauged by his output, by the charisma accorded to him by the Twelver masses, and by the readership of the works bearing his name, then there is little doubt that he is *the* outstanding figure of the age. However, when one realises that hardly anything that Majlisi wrote can be called original in any sense of the word, and that he added nothing to the development of *fiqh* and *hadīth* in the way that his predecessors such as Shaykh Karaki had done, and when one considers the fact that even in his own limited field as collector and transmitter of Traditions he was far from scrupulous in his methodology, then one begins to wonder whether Majlisi can qualify to be called an *'ālim* – even in the Safavid sense of the word – at all. The over-estimation of Majlisi's value as a scholar in Twelver Shi'ite learned history is not an isolated case: similar misconceptions exist, for example, concerning Shaykh Baha'i.[13] This view of Majlisi as the greatest scholar of his age, with all its attendant eulogizing, can only be a product of the superficiality of externalist critique; equally short-sighted is the attitude of those who would, on the basis of Minorsky's misidentification of Majlisi as *mullā-bāshī*, demonise him.[14]

The Majlisi family

Muhammad Baqir was not the only member of his family to leave his mark on the socio-cultural and religious life of Safavid and post-Safavid Iran, although he is undeniably the most famous. Many of Muhammad Baqir's ancestors and descendants were writers, judges, preachers and *fuqahā*, and the overall impression one gets is of a classical 'learned family', one which bestowed continuity on the cultural life of Iran over several centuries. The emergence of the Majlisi family as a whole is linked inextricably with the renaissance of the Twelver Shi'ite *hadīth* sciences, and it is from this family in particular that a genuine Persian development of Twelver Shi'ism obtained its impetus. Furthermore, the transition from mainstream theocentrism to Twelver Shi'ite externalist imamocentrism, which found its deepest channel of expression in the works of Muhammad Baqir, was mirrored in the gradual change in the general religious orientation of the family, from the orthodox Sufism of pre-Safavid Iran to the heterodox externalism nurtured by Muhammad Baqir and his descendants.

The forefathers of Muhammad Baqir Majlisi

The earliest known ancestor of Muhammad Baqir to appear in the sources is Hafiz Abu Nu'aym Ahmad b. 'Abdullah b. Ishaq b. Musa b. Mihran Sipahani (d. 430/1038-39), the celebrated author of *Hilyat al-awlīyā*, *Tarīkh al-Isfahān* – also known as *Dhikr-i akhbār-i Isfahān* – and a compilation of forty traditions concerning the Hidden Imam entitled *al-Arba'īn fī Mahdī Āl-i Muhammad*. It has yet to be established whether Abu Nu'aym subscribed to the Twelver Shi'ite school or not; the fact that he collected traditions on the Hidden Imam does not imply necessarily that he had Twelver Shi'ite leanings, since there have been many Sunni authors who have produced similar compilations. In fact, Ibn-i Shahrashub in *Ma'ālim al-'ulamā* describes Abu Nu'aym as an *'āmī*, or Sunni; Muhammad Taqi al-Tustari in *Qāmūs al-rijāl* also calls him 'a simple-minded Sunni.' It is not surprising, therefore, to see that the leading scholars of the Safavid period went to great pains to reclaim Abu Nu'aym as a Twelver Shi'ite and thus spare Muhammad Baqir the embarrassment of having a Sunni Sufi as an ancestor.[15]

The more recent forefathers of Muhammad Baqir can be discussed with greater surety, beginning with Shaykh Hasan, Muhammad Baqir's great-great-grandfather. Shaykh Hasan lived in the second part of the 10th/16th century and was relatively well known as a *mujtahid* who helped to promulgate the new state religion of Twelver Shi'ism.[16] Shaykh Hasan's son, Kamal al-din Darwish Muhammad b.Hasan al-'Amili al-Natanzi al-Isfahani, studied under both Shaykh Karaki and the 'Second Martyr', Zayn al-din b. Ali al-'Amili al-Shami, and was reputedly the first scholar to make the Traditions of the Twelver Shi'ites accessible to the public at large in the city of Isfahan.[17] Several important scholars studied under him and narrated Traditions on his authority, the most notable being Muhammad Baqir's father, Muhammad Taqi Majlisi, and 'Abdullah b. Jabir al-'Amili.

Kamal al-din Darwish's daughter – unnamed in the sources as are most of those on the distaff side – was married to one Maqsud Ali al-Majlisi, the grandfather of Muhammad Baqir. Maqsud Ali was the first to carry the honorary epithet 'al-Majlisi', given to him reportedly on the grounds that his *majālis* (sermons or lectures) were of the most edifying and excellent kind. He is also known to have written poetry, and it is possible that he penned verses under the pen-name of Majlisi: an ode attributed to him is cited in *Tadhkirat al-qubūr*.[18] Another possible explanation for the name Majlisi is that Maqsud Ali might have hailed from a small village called Majlis on the outskirts of Isfahan.[19] It is certain, however, that he was the first in the family to carry the name and thus one must dismiss the later account of how Muhammad Baqir's swaddling clothes (*qundāq*) were blessed in a secret *majlis* by the Hidden Imam as a fabrication.

The union of Kamal al-din Darwish's daughter with Maqsud Ali al-Majlisi produced two sons, Muhammad Sadiq and Muhammad Taqi. Of the former, next to nothing is known. Muhammad Taqi, born in 1003/1594-95, was a contemporary of Mulla Sadra and studied under scholars such as Shaykh Baha'i and 'Abdullah b. Husayn al-Shushtari. Of his early life little is known, although he himself claims to have been versed in all of the religious sciences from an extremely early age. In his commentary on Shaykh Saduq's *Man lā yahduruhu al-faqīh*, he writes:

> Praise be to the Lord of all worlds! I knew everything at the age of four! That is to say, I knew all about God, prayers, and Heaven and Hell. I would pray the night prayers in the Safa mosque (in Isfahan) and I would perform the morning prayer there in congregation. I would advise the other children and instruct them in the verses of the Holy Koran and in the Traditions, as my father – God's mercy be with him – had instructed me.[20]

Muhammad Taqi's piety and steadfastness in prayer and meditation were such, writes Aqa Ahmad Kirmanshahi, that 'he was accused of being a Sufi.'[21] The extent and seriousness of Muhammad Taqi's alleged inclination towards Sufism cannot be known, although it is clear that he often frequented Sufi gatherings and enjoyed cordial relationships with various members of the Sufi brotherhoods. This much is admitted by Muhammad Baqir himself, who was later to deny his father's penchant for non-externalism by explaining it away as a form of *taqiyya*. To Muhammad Taqi is attributed a short treatise entitled *Tashwīq al-sālikīn* (Encouragement for Those on the Sufi Path), in which he professes allegiance to the Dhahabiyya Order.[22] The author also appears to be in agreement with Haydar Amuli, who had declared that Sufism and Twelver Shi'ism were fundamentally one and the same thing. Sufism and Divine gnosis, he says, must be defended against the 'formal sciences' (*'ulūm-i rasmī*) of the legalist *'ulamā*.[23]

Evidence of Muhammad Taqi's Sufi inclinations may be seen as being strengthened by the fact that he was patronized by Shah 'Abbas II, who favoured the non-externalist scholars and whose reign marks the zenith of 'high' Sufism and gnostic philosophy. 'Abbas II went to great lengths to show respect to the Sufi literati. He commissioned Muhammad Taqi to write a Persian commentary on Shaykh Saduq's *al-Faqīh* with the impressively royal title *Lawāmi'-i Sāhibqirānī* (The Augustean Lights). Although such evidence points to some kind of attachment to the non-externalist fraternity, it is not inconceivable that Muhammad Taqi might have adopted the Sufi cause temporarily in order to further his own aims. The issue is confused further by Danishpazhuh's assertion that a trip to Najaf in 1038/1628-29 brought about a radical change in Muhammad Taqi's outlook: subsequently he appears to have turned away from Sufism and inclined towards the *'qishrīgarī'* (superficial or 'hide-bound' legalism) of the *fuqahā*.[24] Another account relates how, during a visit to the shrine of Imam Ali, Muhammad Taqi had a dream in which the Imam instructed him to settle and teach in Isfahan, which was at that time gaining in importance as the main centre of Twelver externalism. In the light of conflicting evidence, then, the Sufism of Muhammad Taqi must remain a matter of conjecture.

Muhammad Taqi enjoys a prominent place in the gallery of learned Twelver Shi'ites primarily on account of the fact that he was the first to disseminate the Traditions and teachings of the Imams on a wide scale in Persian – although his output was nowhere near as extensive as that of his son. Apart from the aforementioned *Lawāmi'* he also wrote a commentary on the *Sahīfa-i Sajjādiyya*, the famous prayer manual of the 4th Imam, Zayn al-'Abidin, in both Arabic and Persian. Other Persian works include a commentary on the *Zīyārat al-jāmi'a* and various treatises on the Friday prayer, foster-relationships, *hajj* and so on. He also wrote a short tract on dreams and their interpretation, in which he recounts many of his own dream experiences, most of which involve the Imams.[25]

Muhammad Taqi incurred the wrath of several of the *fuqahā* of his day on account of the ambiguities surrounding his religious and ideological stand. His staunchest opponent was the vehemently anti-Sufi *faqīh*, Muhammad Tahir al-Qummi, who wrote a fiery polemical tract in refutation of Sufism, which was answered in kind in a treatise attributed to Muhammad Taqi.[26]

Mir Lawhi, more about whom will be said in Chapter Five, was another avowed enemy of Muhammad Taqi – as indeed he was of Muhammad Biqir – and it is reported that his dislike was so intense that he saw fit to desecrate the tomb of Hafiz Abu Nu'aym, the Majlisis' illustrious Sufi forefather.[27] Generally speaking, however, the few sketches of his life that do exist paint Muhammad Taqi in a favourable light: a man of extreme piety and asceticism whose paramount aim was to 'spread the Islamic *sharī'a*' – an overtly externalist ambition – and propagate the teachings of the Imams as handed down in their Traditions. In so doing he proved to be an able forerunner of his more famous son. Muhammad Taqi died in 1070/1659-60 and is buried in Isfahan.[28]

Muhammad Baqir's formative years

Muhammad Baqir Majlisi was born in 1037/1627-28 in the *dār al-'ilm* in Isfahan, one of seven children born to Muhammad Taqi and his wife, who was related to Shaykh 'Abdullah b. Jabir al-'Amili, a colleague of Muhammad Taqi and also, in later years, a teacher of Muhammad Baqir. Most sources agree on Muhammad Baqir's year of birth, encapsulated in the chronogram *jāmi' kitāb bihār al-anwār*.[29]

His hagiographers outline certain details concerning Muhammad Baqir's entrance into the world that are clearly designed to enhance his image as a charismatic religious leader. His swaddling clothes, it is related, were blessed by the Hidden Imam in a secret *majlis* which took place in a waking dream or vision experienced by Muhammad Taqi.[30] Another account tells how Muhammad Taqi, having spent a long night in tearful prayer and supplication, sensed that anything he might ask from God would almost certainly be granted. At a loss as to what to ask for, he suddenly heard the cries of the infant Muhammad Biqir and immediately asked God to make his son 'the propagator of the religion and *sharī'a* of the Prophet' and to grant him success in all his endeavours. The author concludes that Muhammad

Baqir's brilliant career was undoubtedly the result of his father's prayer.[31] Muhammad Taqi is also said to have forbade his wife to suckle the child whenever she was in a state of ritual impurity (*jināba*).[32] Such a prohibition has no Islamic basis whatsoever but would – in the minds of the simple Twelver Shi'ite believers – no doubt have added to the aura of purity that is seen naturally to surround a man of religion. Similar Traditions exist, of course, in the hagiographies of the Prophet and the Imams, and filter through inevitably to colour the life stories of the *fuqahā*.

Regrettably, little is known of Muhammad Baqir's formative years. Being the son of an already accomplished scholar, he would have received instruction in various aspects of Islam at a very early age in his father's home. The flexibility of the traditional Islamic *madrasa* system was such that the young Muhammad Baqir would have been able to pick and choose the teachers – even moving from one town to another if necessary – that he needed to instruct him in the basic yet comprehensive range of Islamic sciences in which a budding scholar was expected, but not obliged, to be versed. Muhammad Baqir undertook a full programme, studying most of the subjects on offer: *fiqh*, *hadīth*, biography of the learned Twelver Shi'ites (*rijāl*), principles of the transmission of Traditions (*dirāya*), Arabic language and literature, logic, theology and philosophy.[33]

A typical Twelver student at the time of Majlisi would most likely have opted for specialization in either the '*aqlī* sciences such as theology or philosophy, or the *naqlī* branches such as *fiqh* and *hadīth*, according to his own personal inclination. As already pointed out, the polarization of the '*aqli* and *naqli* sciences as far as learning and teaching biases are concerned is merely another manifestation of the artificial division between matters of *īmān* and matters of orthopraxy, between the *usūl* and the *furū'*. A scholar would, however, be expected to have ample theoretical knowledge of both fundamentals and secondary principles. Given the fact that a teacher's *forte* was either wholly in the '*aqlī* or wholly in the *naqīi* sciences – but rarely in both – a student would attend the lectures of one teacher or set of teachers for the former and another for the latter. Despite the fact that '*aql* and *naql* are designed in theory to complement and complete each other, it often happened that a student would attend the lectures of scholars who were at ideological loggerheads with each other. Muhammad Baqir, for example, studied under both his father and Muhammad Tahir al-Qummi, who were sworn enemies:

Majlisi the First (i.e. Muhammad Taqi) did not consider Muhammad Tahir an '*ālim*, and Muhammad Tahir was wont to inveigh publicly against (Muhammad Tahir) from the pulpit, yet Majlisi the Second (Muhammad Baqir) sat as a willing and grateful student at the feet of both. His thirst for knowledge and the belief that its acquisition was a religious duty tended to override any idea of divided loyalties.[34]

The leaders of the Twelver Shi'ite world of learning were first and foremost professors of *manqūl*, the scriptural sciences that form the basis of the externalist agenda. *Ma'qūl* was traditionally the preserve of the indigenous body of Persian scholars who had enjoyed supremacy before the influx of the immigrant *fuqahā*, although as we have seen there were individuals who were able to embrace the two branches without leaning too heavily towards either one. Since the fundamentals of *īmān* are connected more to the disciplines of *ma'qūl*, the latter was an essential component in a student's course of study. However, since *ma'qūl* covers a field in which a great number of non-externalists – gnostics, philosophers and Sufis, all bogeys of the Twelver *fuqahā* – were proficient, for most the study of its various disciplines was reduced to little more than a brief, theoretical survey of the fundamentals of belief. These were treated as concepts that are there to be known rather than fully understood, assimilated and then utilized as the indispensable basis and *raison d'être* of one's life as a believer, be one a scholar or a layman. An exposition of the fundamentals of belief boils down, then, to little more than the mechanical assimilation of facts and the clinical acquisition of a set of theological principles with which one is able to prove the truth and existence of the five *usūl al-dīn*, namely *tawhīd, nabuwwa, ma'ād, imāma* and *'adl*. For the externalist, these *usūl* are presented as ideas that are to be believed in summarily as the basis for the much more crucial task of complying with the external precepts of Islam, crystallized in the *sharī'a* and the laws of jurisprudence. For the externalist, the much safer course – and, considering its socio-political value, much the securer – was the total reliance on the sayings of the Imams, often to the exclusion of the use of reason (*'aql*) altogether. According to Majlisi:

> No human being can understand the excellent meanings of the Holy Koran and thus we must have recourse to the Pure Imams of the Holy Family (*tawassul bi a'imma-i 'itrat*). It is through them that we can understand the words of God; anyone who tries to think about God without having recourse to the Imams is doomed to perdition (*dalāla*), for surely theirs is the best guidance.[35]

Although the use of reason to fathom the complexities of belief was not proscribed by the Twelver Shi'ites, indiscriminate ratiocination was clearly deemed reprehensible, and the believer was encouraged to depend solely on the Traditions of the Imams, the best interpreters of which were, according to the externalists, the *fuqahā* and *muhaddithūn*. Theocentric *kalām* had also long since been overshadowed by an imamocentric theology which used reason to prove the legitimacy of the *imām*, so that when one reads about a scholar such as Majlisi having studied the '*aqlī* sciences, one may be sure that a large proportion of that scholar's theological schooling will have centred upon the discussion of rational proofs for the necessity of the *imāma*, the existence, occultation and longevity of the Hidden Imam, and so on.

Muhammad Bāqir was instructed in *ma'qūl* initially by his father. If Muhammad Taqi was a follower of the Dhahabiyya Order then it is also possible that he would have introduced his son to the teachings and practices of the Sufi adepts. However, there is nothing in the primary sources to suggest that Muhammad Bāqir had anything but a deep aversion to all understandings of Islam that deviated from the externalist norm. Claims such as those made by Said Arjomand that Muhammad Baqir was a Sufi who executed a sharp *volte-face* in mid career remain totally unsubstantiated.[36] What Muhammad Baqir did turn away from early on in his teaching career was the instruction of pupils in *ma'qūl*, more about which will be said later. Nevertheless, Muhammad Baqir studied under some of the most notable exponents of *ma'qūl* of his day. Among such teachers are Mulla Muhsin Fayd al-Kashani, an Akhbari in matters of *fiqh* and reportedly an adherent of the Naqshbandiyya. Along with Shaykh Muhammad Hurr al-'Amili, Kashani and Muhammad Baqir Majlisi make up the celebrated 'three later Muhammads' of the Safavid period, whose major works (*al-Wāfī, Wasā'il al-shī'a*, and *Bihār al-anwār*) are often compared in terms of impact with the canonical works of the 'first three Muhammads', namely Kulayni, Shaykh Saduq and Shaykh Tusi. The 'three later Muhammads' are seen as the driving force behind the revivification of *hadīth*-based sciences in the 10th/16th century.

The existence of an *ijāza*, issued by a scholar to a student to mark the latter's attainment of proficiency in a particular discipline, does not necessarily imply that the student actually attended his classes. Eligibility for an *ijāza* may have been based upon the student's performance in the *madrasa* setting, or upon a written piece of work submitted by the student for scrutiny by a particular scholar, or both. Sometimes an *ijāza* was procured through correspondence, as in the case of the *ijāza* issued to Muhammad Baqir by Nur al-din Ali b. Ali al-Husayni al-'Amili (d.

1068/1657-58), who lived in Mecca and who could have met Muhammad Baqir only during the latter's trips there, if at all.[37] Thus even though we have a list of Muhammad Baqir's teachers, it is uncertain exactly how much and for how long he studied under each one; consequently the extent of their influence upon his mindset cannot be readily ascertained.

Apart from his father, Muhammad Tahir al-Qummi, Hurr al-'Amili, Fayd al-Kashani and the aforementioned Husayni al-'Amili, the following are mentioned in *Fayd al-qudsī* as Muhammad Baqir's teachers:

i) Mulla Muhammad Salih al-Mazandarani (d. 1081/1670-71). He was Muhammad Baqir's brother-in-law. He wrote several treatises and commentaries on *hadīth* collections, the most important being a treatment of Kulayni's *al-Kāfī*.[38]

ii) Husayn Ali b. 'Abdullah al-Shushtari (d. 1069/1658-59). A *faqīh* of the Usuli school, he narrated Traditions on the authority of Shaykh Baha'i and also wrote several treatises on *fiqh*.[39]

iii) Rafi' al-din Muhammad al-Na'ini, also known as Mirza Rafi'a (d. 1080/1669-70 or 1099/1687-88). An eminent theologian and philosopher in the style of Fayd al-Kashani, he wrote treatises on the fundamentals of belief (*usūl al-'aqā'id*) and also wrote a philosophical work on the nature of existence.[40]

iv) Mir Sharaf al-din Ali al-Shulistani al-Najafi (d. 1065/1654-55). He lived in Mashhad, where he is buried. Also a teacher of Muhammad Taqi Majlisi, Najafi was an expert in *fiqh*, penning numerous tracts on legal issues such as the regulations covering the Friday prayer, the pilgrimage to Mecca, and so on.[41]

v) Ali b. Muhammad b. Hasan al-Shahidi al-Isfahani (d. 1104/1692-93). A descendant of Shahid al-thani, he wrote a commentary on *al-Kāfī* and penned, among other works, a short pamphlet denouncing those who allowed the performance of music and singing. He also wrote an anti-Sufi treatise. His *ijāza* for Muhammad Bāqir is dated 1068/1657-58.[42]

vi) Muhammad Mu'min al-Astarabadi (d. 1088/1677-78). Astarabadi was a resident of Mecca, where he was murdered by anti-Twelver elements. He was the son-in-law of the founder of the Akhbari school, Mulla Muhammad Amin (d. 1033/1623-24). His claim to fame is a a treatise on *raj'a*, a subject about which Majlisi also wrote extensively.[43]

vii) Muhammad b. Sharaf al-din Jaza'iri, known as Mirza Jaza'iri. He lived in Hyderabad. His *ijāza* for Muhammad Bāqir was given in 1064/1653-54.[44]

viii) Qadi Amir Husayn. He was a *muhaddith* upon whose authority Muhammad Baqir deemed the probably spurious *Fiqh al-Ridā* to be authentic.[45]

ix) Sadr al-din Ali al-Shirazi al-Hindi (d. 1120/1708-09). Like Hurr al-'Amili, al-Hindi was both Muhammad Baqir's student and teacher.[46]

x) Faydullah b. Ghiyath al-din Muhammad al-Quhba'i. He was a *muhaddith* who narrated Traditions on the authority of Sayyid Husayn al-Karaki.[47]

xi) Muhammad Muhsin b. Muhammad Mu'min al-Astarabadi (d. 1089/1678-79).[48]

xii) Abu al-Sharaf al-Isfahani.[49]

xiii) Mir Muhammad Qasim al-Tabataba'i al-Quhba'i.[50]

One is able to discern a wide range of orientations – some of them theoretically conflicting – among the teachers of Muhammad Baqir, from the Sufi inclinations of Fayd al-Kashani and the vehemently anti-Sufi stance of Muhammad Tahir al-Qummi, to the Akhbari jurisprudence of Hurr al-'Amili and the Usuli doctrines of al-Shushtari. Yet Muhammad Baqir was no syncretist, especially in the sense of combining *ma'qūl* with *manqūl* in the manner of his father or Shaykh Baha'i. Similarly, the idea that Muhammad Baqir held the middle ground between the Usuli and Akhbari extremes may on first reckoning be a sign that he was liberal enough in spirit to adopt freely from both doctrines, yet as 'Allama Burqa'i says:

> There is no way in which one can claim to hold both Akhbari and Usuli positions at the same time. If one is said to occupy a middle position, maybe it is because he wants to spread any kind of narration without feeling the need to call its authenticity (*sihha*) into question, while at the same time retaining the right of the *mujtahid* to use reason and be imitated as a *muqallad*: these two positions are logically inconsistent and therefore cannot be held by one person at the same time.[51]

In his introduction to *Bihār al-anwār*, Muhammad Bāqir confirms that as a youth he was eager to learn all of the Islamic sciences and that he was able to do so. He says that:

> I stepped into the rose-garden of knowledge, saw both flowers and thorns, filled my arms with its fruits, sipped a mouthful from each of its streams, and obtained as much benefit as I could.[52]

In trying to think how he might best encourage others to attain such

159

knowledge, Majlisi came gradually to realise that unless knowledge is taken from the 'leaders of religion (i.e. the Imams) who are the intellects of mankind',[53] it will remain bitter to the taste. 'The Koran,' he declares, 'does not deem the intellects of men sufficient to read that book,' and emphasizes his belief that no-one is able to understand it save for the Prophet and the Imams, who were chosen by God and to whose household the revelation was sent.[54] It was after becoming aware of this point, he says, that:

> I left that which I had wasted so much of my life trying to acquire and learn – even though those subjects are very popular nowadays – and went in pursuit of something that I knew would be useful for me in the life to come, although there is not much call for the study of *hadīth* these days.[55]

It is not clear at exactly which point in his career Majlisi decided to abandon the study of *ma'qūl*. It is certain from his own admission that he had been introduced to a wide range of rational sciences, and it is known from *Qisas al-'ulamā* that Majlisi even taught *ma'qūl* for a time. Tunukabuni relates how, one day, Majlisi was explaining the beliefs of the materialist Dahriyyun when one of his students began to enthuse over these beliefs, asserting that the 'religion of the materialists is the true one.' Majlisi tried to refute his student's claim but was unable to do so. Majlisi brought the class to an abrupt halt and vowed never again to teach philosophy or theology.[56] He also actively encouraged others from dabbling in the rational sciences. Mir Muhammad Husayn Khatunabadi, Majlisi's grandson and student, states that in his youth he was eager to study *ma'qūl* – philosophy in particular – but was persuaded by his grandfather during a trip to Mecca to forego his ambition and concentrate instead on the study of *fiqh* and *hadīth*.[57] Majlisi also ordered Ni'matullah al-Jaza'iri to abandon work on the highly gnostic, theosophical treatise he had embarked upon entitled *Maqāmāt al-nijāt*, which comprised an analysis of the 'most beautiful names of God' (*asmā Allāh al-husnā*) and their inner meanings.[58] Yusufi's remarks about the inherent dislike of the rational sciences on the part of the 'hide-bound' '*ulamā* are worth considering in the context of Majlisi's distaste for non-externalist academic pursuits:

> The hide-bound scholar recites a thousand and one Traditions that cover ablutions and prayers, but question him on the meaning of God's throne ('*arsh*) or the intricacies of the Divine Decree and Determining (*qadā' wa qadar*) and he can but remain silent. 'Know

the Imam,' he says, but how dare he suggest such a thing? How can someone who rejects the Prophet's command, 'Know thyself and thou shalt know God,' profess to know anyone else? And those from among the hide-bound *'ulamā* who do understand in theory the mysteries of God forbid their teaching because they know what will transpire in practice: one who truly knows God and serves only Him as his Master will have no need for 'Mr. Jurisprudent' (*āqā-i faqīh*) to act as intermediary between him and God, to consult the Koran (*istikhāra*) on his behalf, to collect his taxes (*khums wa zakāt*) and then squander them on the upkeep of yet more and more jurists who will carry on the same devilish process...[59]

Majlisi's rejection of *ma'qūl* meant that he would concentrate his efforts almost exclusively on the propagation of *fiqh* and *hadīth*, the two central pillars of *manqūl*. It is certain that he understood the dangers inherent in inordinate attention to non-externalist disciplines: the abundance of Sufi sects in which *manqūl* is almost totally ignored has always prompted attacks from jurist and theologian alike, and even many non-externalists have been quick to point out the folly of over-reliance on *'aql* as a basis for belief. The remedy, however, would seem not to lie in forsaking one for the other: in Koranic terms, the three components of *haqīqa*, *tarīqa* and *sharī'a* should all be present at the same time.[60] It is Majlisi's rejection of *ma'qūl*, his denunciation of all non-externalist forms of Islamic expression, and his total involvement with externalism that have led critics such as Yusufi, Arjomand and Shari'ati to claim that he was propelled by personal ambition rather than a sincere desire to purify the Islamic message by emphasizing *manqūl* to the exclusion of everything else. The rapid rise to power of the externalist *fuqahā* in the latter years of the Safavid era, especially during the reigns of weak and inefficient rulers such as Shah Sulayman (1666-93) and Sultan Husayn (1694-1722), and their occupation of the majority of religious posts such as that of *shaykh al-islām*, meant that in order to progress as a religious professional one had to concentrate on the field which happened to be the speciality of the majority. Both Shah Sulayman and Sultan Husayn favoured externalism and provided ample opportunity for the consolidation of the 'orthodoxy' by the Twelver *fuqahā*. Whatever Majlisi's real intentions, the advent of these two rulers was highly advantageous for his cause.

161

The public career of Muhammad Baqir Majlisi

Majlisi's first public appointment was to the office of *imām jum'a* or Friday prayer leader of Isfahan. None of the sources mention a date for his accession to the office, although Karl-Heinz Pampus suggests that it must have been during the 1660s.[61] The most probable time would have been shortly after Shah Sulayman's coronation in 1077/1666. Tunukabuni claims that Shah 'Abbas II had wanted to make Muhammad Baqir Sabziwari *qāḍī* of Isfahan but died before he could appoint him; when his son, Shah Sulayman, came to power he chose to appoint Majlisi instead.[62] Tunukabuni's garbled account is clearly flawed for there are no records of Majlisi ever having held the post of *qāḍī*. However, in *Zindigānī-i Majlisī*, Safari writes that Shah Sulayman, who initially patronized non-externalists such as Sabziwari and Aqa Husayn Khwansari, approached Sabziwari with a view to making him *imām jum'a* of Isfahan. Sabziwari is said to have rejected him outright, whereupon a member of the Shah's court proposed that the ruler offer the position to Majlisi.[63] Around the same time, Majlisi had penned a treatise entitled *Raj'a* (The Return), in which he cited a Tradition transmitted from Imam Ja'far al-Sadiq foretelling the rise of the Safavids from Gilan and Azarbaijan as precursors of the return and rule of the Hidden Imam.[64] The Tradition in question was later disputed by Mir Lawhi, a sworn enemy of the Majlisi family, and in all respects it would appear that Majlisi was attempting to ingratiate himself with the new ruler.[65]

Majlisi, who fully accepted the legality of Friday prayer in the absence of the Hidden Imam, was said to have set great store by the weekly congregational assembly. Apart from the Friday prayer, which he conducted in Isfahan's Masjid-i Shah, or royal mosque, he would also conduct communal worship during the month of Ramadan, especially during the three nights known as *iḥyā*, held to commemorate the martyrdom of Ali.[66] Mir Muhammad Husayn Khatunabadi, in *Hadā'iq al-muqarribīn*, states that 'thousands of believers' would flock to pray behind Majlisi and to hear his sermons which followed the Friday prayer ceremony. Khatunabadi bemoans the fact that:

> Now, five years after (Majlisi's) death, no-one gathers in congregational worship as they did during his lifetime. The mosques, which were once filled with the sweet sound of his edifying sermons and fruitful advice, are now empty. When he was alive he would advise people on what they should and should not do, in such a lucid and simple way that everyone could understand. But now no-one

knows what to do...[67]

Majlisi's popularity apparently had a great effect on Shah Sulayman, who, as his reign progressed, grew less and less enamoured of the non-externalists and gravitated increasingly towards the simplistic, uncomplicated externalism of Majlisi and his like. Shah Sulayman allowed himself to be courted by the externalists and was known to treat them with great generosity. Majlisi himself curried favour publicly with the Shah, to the point of reprimanding fellow scholars for impropriety in the Shah's presence.[68] Unsurprisingly, Majlisi openly supported the monarchy and, as Said Arjomand has pointed out, supplied the clear legitimization of kingship that had hitherto been absent from the official Twelver Shi'ite political ethos. In his *'Ayn al-hayāt*, in the section entitled 'On the Rights of Kings, Obedience to them, Praying for their Moral Uprightness, and not questioning their Majesty,' Majlisi writes:

Know that the Kings of the True Religion (*dīn-i haqq*) have many rights on their subjects, since they protect them and repel the enemies of religion from them: their religion, life, property and honour are secure because of the protection of kings. Therefore the subjects must pray for the kings and recognize their rights.[69]

Majlisi opines that even if kings are tyrannical and unjust, one must obey them and pray that they may improve. Disobedience to them, he declares, brings affliction (*balā*), and to attract *balā* is forbidden according to the dictates of *taqiyya*.[70] Majlisi thus sanctioned the principle of legitimacy of the temporal rule of kings, but did not go so far as to endorse the rights of kings to religious rule: this would have undermined drastically the position of the *fuqahā* as the supreme source of religious authority, leaving them in a position of total subservience to the monarchy. The political ethos of the Twelver Shi'ite externalists will be discussed in greater detail in Chapter Five in the section on *intizār*.

Majlisi's unwavering support and loyalty led Shah Sulayman to appoint him as *shaykh al-islām* of Isfahan in 1098/1687. In *Waqāi' al-sinīn* the aforementioned Khatunabadi writes:

On the 4th of Jumada al-awwal 1098, his most High and Exalted Majesty, Shah Sulayman Safawī, out of the insistence that he nurtured in his heart that the holy laws of Islam be spread throughout the land, appointed Mawlana Muhammad Baqir Majlisi to the post of *shaykh al-islām* to the royal court at Isfahan; and, out of respect for the *'ulamā* and in order to gain their pleasure, actually allowed the words 'I beseech thee' to fall from his exalted tongue.[71]

As Khatunabadi points out, the appointment of Majlisi to the office of *shaykh al-islām* at the age of 61 gave him unrivalled power as the chief religious dignitary of the realm. His first task was to endeavour to 'promote the knowledge (*'ilm*) and *hadīth* of the Shi'ites, to protect the *'ulamā* and the defenceless people, to enjoin the good (*amr bi'l ma'rūf*) and prohibit the forbidden (*nahy 'an al-munkar*), to curb the opponents of Islam, and to eradicate the oppression (*zulm*) and despotism (*zūrgū'ī*) of the past, which no-one else had been able to stop'.[72] One of Majlisi's first acts was to destroy the idols of a Hindu temple that had been set up by Indian merchants resident in the capital. The Hindus apparently tried to bribe the Shah with large amounts of money in order to prevent the destruction of their place of worship, but 'the Shah and his courtiers always went out of their way to co-operate with him (i.e. Majlisi) and never tried to prevent him from carrying out his religious duties.'[73] The idols were duly smashed and the heartbroken Hindu keeper of the temple consequently committed suicide.[74]

Majlisi also pursued a vigorous anti-Sunni and anti-Sufi policy, converting minorities wherever and whenever possible to the Twelver Shi'ite creed. The sources indicate that as many as 70,000 non-Twelvers were converted by Majlisi; apparently they accepted Twelver Shi'ism without duress, merely by reading Majlisi's works.[75] Twelver Shi'ite missionaries were sent to areas where non-Twelver minorities still existed, particularly in Afghanistan;[76] the anti-Sunni repression that intensified under Majlisi's spell as *shaykh al-islām* has been seen by some as an important cause of the disaffection of the Sunni populace of Afghanistan, which culminated in the Afghan invasion and the eventual overthrow of the Safavid dynasty.

Majlisi's term as *shaykh al-islām* continued into the reign of Sultan Husayn (1694-1722), whom Majlisi crowned as Shah. Sultan Husayn was a lily-livered, outwardly pious individual over whom Majlisi is said to have exerted great influence. Upon the new Shah's accession, Majlisi asked for three decrees to be passed: wine-drinking was to be abolished; faction-fighting was to be outlawed; and the sport of pigeon-racing was to be made illegal. Only the fate of the *farmān* prohibiting wine is known: thousands of bottles of vintage wine from the royal cellars were smashed. The enforcement of the decree was short-lived, however, since those at court and in the royal family were loathe to abandon their addiction to alcohol.

Measures against the use of tobacco were also taken. More importantly, Majlisi also obtained a decree for the expulsion of Sufis from the capital, which was rigidly enforced.[77]

Majlisi and the post of *mullā-bāshī*

In the *Tadhkirat al-mulūk* (Memorial for Kings), a manual of Safavid administration completed in 1726, the anonymous author begins by describing the office of *mullā-bāshī* as the most important religious office in the realm. The *mullā-bāshī* was:

> ... the head of all the *mullas* ... (he) had a definite place near the throne, none of the scholars and *sayyids* sitting nearer than he is in the King's presence. [The *mulla-bashi*] did not interfere in any affairs except by soliciting pensions for students and men of merit, by removing oppression from the oppressed, by interceding for the guilty, by investigating the problems of the Sacred Law and by giving consultations in law-suits and [other] affairs [ruled by] the *Shari'at*.[78]

As the author points out, the office of *mullā-bāshī* did not exist during the reigns of the previous Safavid rulers, although at any one time there was always one scholar – generally accepted as the most learned – who carried out functions more or less identical to those mentioned above. For example, as *shaykh al-islām* of Isfahan, Majlisi in effect became *mullā-bāshī* before the actual creation of the title.

According to *Tadhkirat al-mulūk*, the post of *mullā-bāshī* was introduced towards the end of the reign of Sultan Husayn; its first incumbent was one Mir Muhammad Baqir who, the author notes, 'fell short of his contemporary Aqa Jamal' in learning.[79] The aforementioned Mir Muhammad Baqir, the text continues, also founded the famous Chahar Baqh *madrasa* in Isfahan and became its first rector. Vladimir Minorsky, the translator and editor of *Tadhkirat al-mulūk* identifies the first holder of the office of *mullā-bāshī* – Mir Muhammad Baqir - as none other than Muhammad Baqir Majlisi, and goes on to note the 'strange dislike of the author for ... Majlisi, the all-powerful restorer of the Shi'a orthodoxy.'[80]

However there are several points which prove that Minorsky was wrong. First and foremost, Majlisi died in 1111/1699-1700, only a few years into the reign of Sultan Husayn, whereas the *Tadhkirat al-mulūk* states that the office of *mullā-bāshī* was conferred on Mir Muhammad Baqir towards the end of Sultan Husayn's reign. Secondly, Khatunabadi states that the Chahar Bagh *madrasa* was inaugurated in 1122/1710-11, over a decade after Majlisi's death, and that its rector for life to whom the *Tadhkirat al-mulūk* refers is not Majlisi but Mir Muhammad Baqir Khatunabadi (d. 1127/1715). The inscription on the tombstone of the latter clearly identifies him as the first rector of the Chahar Bagh *madrasa*, the tutor of Sultan Husayn, and the *mullā-bāshī*.[81] Furthermore, the appellation '*mīr*' was given only to *sayyids* – and nowhere in the sources is Majlisi accredited with this title. The *Waqāi' al-sinīn* establishes 1124/1712-13 as the year in which the office of *mullā-bāshī* was created;[82] the fact that Muhammad Baqir Majlisi could not have been the first incumbent of the new office is further confirmed by Danishpazhuh in his *Fihrist*.[83]

Thus it becomes clear that Majlisi never held the title of *mullā-bāshī*, although he did carry out almost identical functions while serving as *shaykh al-islām* during the reigns of Shah Sulayman and Sultan Husayn.

Majlisi's written works

Muhammad Baqir Majlisi was by far the most prolific author of the Safavid period. *Fayd al-qudsī* lists 13 Arabic titles and 53 Persian works which are undoubtedly from the Majlisi pen, although when one considers that many of these works each runs to several volumes – the modern edition of *Bihār al-anwār* alone covers over a hundred – then it is clear that the size of his output is meaningless in terms of the number of titles. The 66 works listed in *Fayd al-qudsī* contain a total of 1,402,700 *bayt*. Divided by 73, the number of Majlisi's years, this comes to 19,215 lines a year or 53 a day; if we calculate for his period of maturity, say, 58 years, then the annual amount is 24,170 or 67 lines per day.[84] Tunukabuni claims that Majlisi wrote at least 1000 lines a day, a gross exaggeration but typical of externalist hagiography and of the attitude which holds that the vaster the output, the greater the writer.[85]

Majlisi's works – the *Bihār* will be discussed separately later on – are overwhelmingly externalist in content, the vast majority being centred on the lives, miracles and deaths of the Imams and on the myriad rules and regulations that govern the practical, everyday life of the Twelver Shi'ite believer. Works on *ma'rifat al-nafs* or *ma'rifat Allāh* are conspicuous by their absence.

In the writings of Majlisi, the Imams as historical figures and their lives and sayings come to the foreground of religious discussion and practice, while their Traditions serve as the basis for the codification of religious ritual for which Majlisi is responsible. In *Hilyat al-muttaqīn*, for instance, Majlisi brings together various Traditions attributed to the Imams concerning the everyday activities and personal etiquette proper for a believer: how he should dress, eat, take ablutions, cut his nails, urinate, and so on; the prayers he should recite on entering the bathroom, the verses he should repeat when blowing his nose – in short, everything pertinent to the most minute and seemingly trivial of personal acts, and all supposedly on the authority of the Imams.[86]

Zād al-ma'ād is another collection of Traditions which deals at great length with the rites that are to be observed throughout the year: prayers on the occasion of the birth and death dates of the Imams, litanies to be read on certain anniversaries and festivals, and so on.[87]

Tuhfat al-zā'ir is a pilgrimage manual containing information on the etiquette to be observed when visiting the Twelver Shi'ite holy places, namely the tombs of the Imams and their descendants, and the prayers and invocations to be offered there.[88] *A propos* the visiting of Twelver shrines, Said Arjomand has highlighted the fact that in the writings of Majlisi, the importance of pilgrimage to Mecca (*hajj*) has been played down in favour of *zīyāra*, or pilgrimage to the shrines of the Imams.[89] The *hajj* stresses the universality of the Muslim community, and the rites performed there have also been interpreted by certain writers as being emblematic of the carnal soul's repentance from self-worship and of the journey to God.[90] The practice of *zīyāra*, however, tends to foster the cult of the Imam as saviour and intercessor, and by doing so further externalises belief by shifting the emphasis from the theocentrism of the *hajj* to the imamocentrism of *zīyāra*. Pilgrimage to the shrines was given relatively little importance by the early Twelver scholars, yet Majlisi saw to it that *zīyāra* became an important part of Twelver doctrine. Pamphlets containing special prayers to be read at the different shrines (*ziyārat-nāma*) proliferated.

Majlisi wrote several treatises on the correct way of performing the canonical prayer (*salāt*), on the payment of *zakāt* and on the rules of fasting. Such works of jurisprudence were the stock-in-trade of the externalists. Supererogatory prayers (*du'ā*), especially those handed down in connection with the Imams, are also given great importance by Majlisi. Although the original meaning of the word *du'ā* is to call on God through the medium of the Divine names, for the externalist the purpose of *du'ā* would appear to be the granting of personal wishes and the fulfilment of worldly needs, many of which are directed and expressed through the personae of the Imams. In *Zād al-ma'ād*, for instance, there are numerous examples of the benefits to be gained in this world from supererogatory prayers for curing stuttering, aches and pains, avoiding abortion, finding lost objects, and so on.[91] In *Munājātnāma*, Majlisi puts forward the theory that each day is split up into twelve 2-hour sections, each one of which is 'governed' by one of the Imams. Whenever one prays, one is to direct the prayer through the particular Imam responsible for the hour in which the prayer is offered.[92] Many of Majlisi's Persian works comprise translations from Arabic of supererogatory prayers attributed to the Imams, such as *Du'ā-i Kumayl* and *Zīyārat al-jāmi'a*, a prayer to be read when visiting any of the tombs of the Imams.[93]

Majlisi's reliance on the scriptural rather than the rational, on the externalia rather than the fundamentals, is thrown even more sharply into focus when one contrasts his approach with that of the early, pre-Safavid Twelver Shi'ite scholars, who, if not internalists, were at least prepared to give the question of belief the importance which, as the cornerstone of Islam, it presumably warrants. Said Arjomand, although failing to grasp the important implications of the issue, has highlighted Majlisi's blatant over-externalization of the faith by contrasting his *Haqq al-yaqīn* with Kulayni's *al-Kāfī* and 'Allama Hilli's *Bāb al-hādī 'ashara*, a work which represents the climax of the systematisation of Twelver Shi'ite theology two centuries before the Safavids.[94]

Haqq al-yaqīn is dated 1109/1697-98, one year before Majlisi's death, and is thus probably his swansong. It is also undoubtedly one of his most popular pieces of writing. Aqa Muhammad Kirmanshahi, writing in 1219/1804-05, says:

> The writings of (Majlisi) are so popular and so famous that there is no place, be it in the lands of Islam or the lands of the infidels, that is without one of his works. I heard from some trustworthy people that long ago, a ship that was travelling the ocean hit a storm, and the travellers on the ship, after much trouble and despair, reached a far-off island where nothing of Islam had ever been heard. The travellers were taken in as the guests of a man on that island, who, incredibly, turned out to be a Muslim. The travellers asked how it was that he, on an island full of infidels, with no traces of Islam, had come to be Muslim. The man opened a cupboard and brought out a book: it was 'Allama Majlisi's *Haqq al-yaqīn*. The man said: "My tribe and I embraced Islam thanks to the bounty and guidance of this book."[95]

Haqq al-yaqīn is in fact no less than Majlisi's definitive statement in Persian of the Twelver Shi'ite creed. Ostensibly it concerns *usūl al-dīn*, but in actual fact is given over largely to blow-by-blow accounts of the terrors of hellfire, plus the ritual vilification of the first three Caliphs. In *Haqq al-yaqīn* by contrast to *al-Kāfī*, the virtues of knowledge (*fadīlat al-'ilm*) and the difference between reason and ignorance receive no attention whatsoever, while *īmān* and *kufr* (belief and unbelief) are discussed perfunctorily towards the end. The section on God and His attributes, names and acts is extremely brief, this being in sharp contrast with the attention this very pivotal question receives in Hilli's *Bāb al-hādī 'ashara*. In the latter, the question of Divine justice (*'adl*) is central, with Hilli discussing how the will of God functions in the cosmos and how it is compatible with human free-will. It is largely, Hilli points out, upon the idea of Divine justice that the explanation of prophethood, the *imāma* and the Resurrection depends. *Haqq al-yaqīn*, however, includes no mention of the question of Divine justice.

Prophecy, too, is dealt with superficially, and then only in the context of the Prophet's miracles. The bulk of the book is taken up with the denigration of the first three Caliphs (approximately 125 pages) and the resurrection, details of which are described over 170 pages in the most minute detail.[96] Philosophical and rational proofs for the existence and necessity of resurrection are eschewed; one is told simply that one must believe, but not why one must believe or how. The whole question of the significance of the resurrection and the hereafter for the personal life of the individual in this world is passed over: *īmān* is either seen to be lacking or is taken for granted, and any advice on how it may be acquired, sustained or increased is not given, and the whole area of internalism that is germane to the question of resurrection and man's ultimate fate is completely ignored.

The fact that Majlisi wrote much of his work in Persian made it possible for his voluminous output to reach the masses, whose imagination and loyalty he was able to capture. His simplistic and rigidly dogmatic statements of what he saw as the tenets of the Twelver Shi'ite creed were much more digestible for the masses than the teachings of the philosophers. As Browne says in his *Literary History of Persia*:

> The great achievements of the Shi'a doctors of the later Safawi period, such as the Majlisis, was their popularisation of the Shi'a doctrine and the historical *Anschauung* in the vernacular. They realized that to reach the people they must employ the language of the people – in a simple form – and they reaped their reward in the intense and widespread enthusiasm for the Shi'a cause which they

succeeded in creating.[97]

Oceans of light? Majlisi's *Bihār al-anwār*

The teachings of the Twelve Imams – their sayings and practices – were, like those of the Prophet, committed to paper at a very early stage by their companions and contemporaries, who transmitted Traditions from their leaders either directly or through others who claimed to have heard their utterances. The great majority of Twelver Shi'ite Traditions are attributed to the 5th and 6th Imams, Muhammad Baqir and Ja'far al-Sadiq. Groups of Traditions were collected into separate works known individually as *asl* (principle or source), each written by a contemporary of an Imam; in all, some 400 of these works were written and enjoyed steady circulation among Twelver Shi'ite scholars during the lifetime of the later Imams and throughout the so-called 'lesser occultation.' The 400 'sources' were later incorporated - albeit not in their entirety – into more comprehensive and scholarly collections, most notably the four canonical books of the Twelver Shi'ite creed. The narrations taken from the 400 *usūl* appear in a much more orderly fashion in these later works, and most of them are arranged loosely according to subject matter. It is thanks to these works that we are able to gain insight into the political, social and religious ideas and currents prevalent among the early Twelver Shi'ite communities.

Many of the 400 *usūl* – and it is not known how many copies, if any, of each one were in circulation – were gradually lost or hidden away in private libraries. Majlisi deplored the fact these important sources had been forgotten as a result, he says, of 'the dominance of kings and rulers opposed to Shi'ism, and leaders who had gone astray; or because of the propagation of worthless sciences by ignoramuses who feign excellence and intellectual perfection, or because the '*ulamā* had not paid proper attention to them in the past.'[98] The Traditions of the Family of Ali, he argues, are more comprehensive and of greater value than any other science or branch of knowledge. Consequently, Majlisi decided to gather together as many of the *usūl* as he could, searching far and wide and appealing for help to anyone who might have had anything of worth in his possession. Friends and students were despatched to all corners of the realm, and even overseas, to scout for books and manuscripts; material was sought from places as distant as Yemen.[99] In time, Majlisi was able to gather some 200 of the *usūl* and embark upon a project that was to last more than thirty years, yielding, finally, his *magnum opus*: the vast, encyclopaedic collection of Twelver

Shi'ite Traditions entitled *Bihār al-anwār* (Oceans of Light). The *usūl* which Majlisi was able to collect were for the most part in disarray. Majlisi himself complains that the Traditions were not arranged according to subject, and that their general disorder might have been one of the reasons for their falling into disuse. Majlisi says that he made *istikhāra*, asked for God's help and then began to work, endeavouring to record all of the traditions scattered throughout the *usūl* in one place, under proper subject headings. Each chapter was begun with verses from the Koran which correspond to the title of the chapter, and comments of various exegetes relating to those verses were added wherever necessary. Majlisi's own explanations are of two kinds: those concerning language and etymology, which he begins with the heading *mu'allif* (author); and those which actually offer an interpretation of the Traditions themselves.

The compilation of the *Bihār al-anwār*, which was begun in 1077/1666-67 but never completed, was not a task that Majlisi was engaged in alone. Tunukabuni mentions that Mulla 'Abdullah Shushtari, a student of Majlisi who spent much of his time with his teacher in the latter's library in Isfahan, corrected or helped to correct many of the original 26 volumes of the *Bihār*; Shaykh Jaza'iri, another of Majlisi's students, and Amina Bigum, Majlisi's sister, are also known to have contributed to the work.[100] Many of Majlisi's other students were also said to have been directed by their teacher to extract from the *usūl* Traditions concerning a certain subject and then to write them on a piece of paper, leaving enough room for Majlisi to make any comments should he deem it necessary.[101] The fact that many Traditions appear without comment or criticism suggests that Majlisi did not do the lion's share of the work, let alone all of it as his hagiographers would lead us to believe. Ali Dawani, for instance, berates those who claim that Majlisi was helped in the compilation of the *Bihār* and states that it is clearly all his own work, but then goes on to contradict himself by saying, quite justifiably, that help from others in writing such a momentous piece of work should not detract from the greatness of the author.[102]

There is, however, little in the *Bihār* that can be called original, unless it be the scattered comments of Majlisi himself. Tunukabuni, in *Qisas al-'ulamā*, objects to one scholar's calling Majlisi a *muhaddith*, a term which, he says, denotes nothing more than a mere scribe.[103] The *Bihār* is, however, for the most part simply a collection of Traditions, many of them obscure and of doubtful authenticity, the compilation of which Majlisi may be said to have supervised and, on occasions, checked and commented upon. In this light, a more apt term with which to describe Majlisi would be *mudawwin* (compiler), or at best *musahhih* (editor). Even the term *muhaddith*, which

Tunukabuni objects to so vehemently, would be unsuitable given that it implies some kind of rigorous, systematic process of selection of Traditions on the basis of authenticity.

There is no indication, however, of whether any particular Tradition in the *Bihār* is genuine or not: Majlisi himself offers no explanation. In this context Ali Dawani says that the *Bihār* is like an ocean in which both pearls and slime may be found.[104]

This uncritical acceptance of any Traditions which happened to come his way has led to Majlisi's critics accusing him of opportunism and forgery. Indeed it would have been more scholarly of Majlisi to establish the authenticity of the Traditions and then comment upon them rather than include dubious narrations and leave them without comment. In this context the dictum of Ibn al-Jawzi immediately springs to mind:

> Among the ways wherein the devil deludes the Traditionists is the reporting of spurious traditions without stating that they are spurious.[105]

It does not seem unreasonable to suggest that unreliable Traditions from earlier sources could have been systematically weeded out and a collection of sound narrations, based on the scattered *usūl* and perhaps on par with the four canonical works of Kulayni *et al*, produced. As it now stands the *Bihār* is a *mélange* of anything and everything, the sound and the weak all grouped together indiscriminately. What is even more likely to raise suspicions against Majlisi is the fact that certain obvious fabrications are dwelt upon by him at great length and treated as sound; occasionally they are mentioned without comment and the reader is left to make his own interpretation.

Yet despite this, and despite the fact that the work was penned in Arabic, the *Bihār* fired the interest and imagination of the *fuqahā* and, when translated, the people themselves. Most of the volumes of the *Bihār* have been translated into Persian, some more than once, and Urdu versions also exist. Volume XIII, which deals with the Hidden Imam, has been translated by four different people, and a measure of its popularity is reflected in the fact that the most recent of these translations, by Ali Dawani in the early 1960s, has run to over sixteen editions in Iran.[106]

Majlisi vis-à-vis Sufism and other 'innovations'

The rise to prominence of the externalist *fuqahā* in the roles of *mujtahid*, *shaykh al-islām*, scholar and prayer-leader in the latter part of the Safavid era was coupled with, and, for the most part, facilitated by, sustained attacks by the externalists on all other forms of religious orientation which they perceived to be antithetical to their own. The *'aqlī* sciences such as philosophy, theology and *hikma*, together with their respective spokesmen and exponents, invariably came under attack, but it was against Sufism and its adherents that the *fuqahā* conducted their most passionate and vociferous opposition. Such rigor was not characteristic of the Twelver Shi'ite *fuqahā* alone, although their zeal was unquestionably matchless.

Throughout the history of Islam, the denunciation of any practice even remotely suggestive of deviation from the Koran and the *sunna* has been common-place in the writings and preaching of Muslim scholars, not least in the case of Sufism. Because of the flexibility of the term Sufism – the fact that it is used to cover a wide spectrum of outlooks and practices – it often happened that certain Sufis themselves would castigate others for lack of propriety with respect to the dictates of the Koran and *sunna*. Abu Yazid al-Bistami, for example, remonstrated with one of his followers over an act that was not strictly in accord with the *sharī'a*, while Junayd al-Baghdadi asserted that all Sufi knowledge 'is derived strictly from the Book and the *sunna*; so he who has not recited the Koran and written the *hadīth* has no right to talk about our knowledge.'[107] Generally speaking it has been 'popular' Sufism – the cult of the wandering dervishes or Qalandars – that has borne the brunt of the attacks, while 'high' Sufism, or, more correctly, Islamic gnosticism and theocentric internalism, has been more or less tolerated. Mulla Sadra, himself an internalist who was to fall foul of the orthodox *'ulamā*, also condemned popular Sufism in the strongest terms.[108]

The Twelver Shi'ite *fuqahā* of the late Safavid period wasted no time in waging an all-out crusade against Sufis of all types and persuasions, and numerous treatises were written to refute their beliefs. Mulla Muhammad Tahir al-Qummi, Majlisi's teacher and *shaykh al-islām* of Qumm, was particularly vociferous. During the reign of Shah 'Abbas II he had fulminated in this regard against Muhammad Taqi Majlisi and Mulla Khalil Qazwini, both of whom were favoured by the ruler. Qummi stated that the doctrine of the Sufis and philosophers was contrary to the religion of Islam and the teachings of the Koran.[109] Hurr al-'Amili, the *shaykh al-islām* of Mashhad, produced 1000 Traditions that he claimed were transmitted in refutation of the Sufis.[110] And the usually sanguine Ni'matullah Jaza'iri (d. 1112/1700-01) attacked the late Shaykh Baha'i for his association with the 'heretics, Sufis and those who believe in the doctrine of divine love.'[111]

Unlike Qummi, Majlisi never devoted an entire work to the refutation of what he called 'this foul and hellish growth',[112] although his anti-Sufi sentiments run like a leitmotif through his major works. However, the importance that he attached to the refutation of Sufism may be gauged from the fact that a whole section of his treatise entitled *I'tiqādāt* (Beliefs), written in a single night during a trip to Mashhad at the request of an unnamed devotee, is given over to this issue. Effectively, therefore, an explicit refutation of all Sufi-inspired ideas is presented as a fundamental of belief, albeit by implication.

Majlisi's attacks are levelled mainly at what, for the orthodoxy at least, were the obviously questionable practices of popular Sufism prevalent among the dervish orders - but not confined to them - such as singing and dancing (*samā*), group invocation and recitation (*dhikr-i jallī*), abstention from meat (*tark-i haywānī*), laxity in the observance of *sharī'a* regulations, seclusion from society (*gūsha-gīrī*), and so on.

Abstention from meat is not allowed, Majlisi declares, since it leads to bodily and mental weakness; little wonder, he argues, that the Sufis talk such nonsense, given the fact that they shut themselves away in their caves or cloisters for forty days and nights without meat.[113] The Sufis' ritualised withdrawal from the world and everyday occupations, usually for forty days and nights at a time (*chilla-nishīnī*), is condemned since any kind of *gūsha-gīrī* brings about indifference to the essentials (*wājibāt*) of belief, among which Majlisi enumerates: social contact with other Muslims; guiding others and advising them as to their religious duties (*amr wa nahy*); teaching others the rules and regulations of religion (*dīn*); visiting the sick; attending funerals; meeting the material and spiritual needs of others; and enforcing the laws of Islam on the social level. Conveniently enough, Majlisi appears to forget the fact that solitary retreat was a renowned practice of Muhammad, the Imams and most of the prophets mentioned in the Koran.

The practices of *dhikr-i khafī* and *dhikr-i jallī*, says Majlisi, have no scriptural basis whatsoever and thus constitute an innovation (*bid'a*). All innovations, Majlisi asserts, are forms of misguidance, and misguidance leads to hellfire. Not content with such heresies, the Sufis have also contrived to subvert the very fundamentals of belief; Majlisi vehemently attacks the concept of *wahdat al-wujūd* and accuses the Sufis of believing in coercive predetermination (*jabr*) and the abrogation of acts of worship (*suqūt-i 'ibādāt*).

In *I'tiqādāt* Majlisi warns his fellow believers to 'protect your religion and faith from the deceptions of these devils and charlatans, and steer clear of their tricks which are designed to fool the ignorant masses.'[114] Apart from such abominations, how, asks Majlisi, will the followers of these people account for their allegiance to them on the day of reckoning? How can one follow the likes of Hasan al-Basri, who has been cursed in various Traditions? How could one follow Sufyan al-Thawri, who was an enemy of Ja'far al-Sadiq? Or Ghazali, who was clearly a *nāsibī*, claiming *imāma* in the same way that Ali was Imam and declaring that whoever curses Yazid is a sinner? How could one follow Ghazali's accursed brother, Ahmad, who wrote that Satan is one of God's closest and most favoured creatures? Jalal al-din Rumi, whose *Mathnawī* was and still is referred to in Iran as the 'Persian Koran', is singled out by Majlisi on account of his statement that Ibn Muljam, the assassin of Ali, will intercede for that Imam on the day of judgement. Majlisi also attacks Rumi's famous line, 'colourlessness fell prey to colour', and declares that belief in *jabr*, *wahdat al-wujūd* and the abrogation of ritual worship permeates every page of Rumi's writings.[115] Ibn al-'Arabi attracts opprobrium on account of his theory of *wahdat al-wujūd* and also the fact that he claimed to have ascended to heaven (*mi'rāj*) and seen that Imam Ali's place there was lower than that of the first three Caliphs. Finally Majlisi castigates all Sufis for 'claiming to know the secrets of the cosmos but remaining ignorant of what is *halāl* and *harām* or how inheritance is distributed', and so on.[116]

The practices of popular Sufism were clearly suspect in the eyes of both the legalist *fuqahā* and, indeed, the exponents of 'high' Sufism and gnosticism themselves, and Majlisi is able to offer reasonable criticism when refuting them. The question of the 'high Sufis' – the Rumis and the Ghazalis – is a much thornier one, and the ambiguity of many of their concepts made it extremely difficult for the externalist *fuqahā* to find fault on strictly religious grounds. Even an extreme case such as that of Hallaj's ecstatic outburst '*Anā al-haqq*' (I am the Truth) and '*Anā Allāh*' (I am God) were, according to one (Sunni) *faqīh*, open to interpretation: such statements are so ambiguous that they could have been uttered as much in pure sincerity as in associationism (*shirk*) and heresy.[117] Majlisi never goes into detail when outlining his criticisms of the 'high' Sufis with regard to their fundamental beliefs: instead he directs his attacks against the apparent anti-Shi'ite and anti-*sharī'a* remarks of his opponents.

Apart from purely religious considerations it was necessary for the externalists to battle with and uproot Sufism in all its forms. The non-externalists – especially the 'high' Sufis – were dangerous for the simple reason that they placed *īmān* and *ma'rifa* above everything else and saw no special place of honour in the Islamic community for the *faqīh*, whose sole responsibility in theory was to advise on matters of jurisprudence. The contempt that Mulla Sadra held for those *fuqahā* who overstepped this mark has already been noted.

Popular Sufism was even more problematic given the support it obviously had from the illiterate Muslim masses: as already noted, many Sufi adherents were expelled from Isfahan on Majlisi's orders.[118] Majlisi tackled the problem by tarring both popular and orthodox Sufism with the same brush, accusing all of those under the Sufi banner with heterodoxy, innovation (*bid'a*) and unbelief. All Sufis – and thus all who pay what must have seemed to Majlisi to be inordinate attention to the inner realities of belief – were thus held to be *kāfir* and deserving of hellfire. It is this indiscriminate lumping together of all those scholars and thinkers whose particular ideological leanings did not tally with his own that casts serious doubt on Majlisi's motives; for the dismissal and denigration of philosophy, *hikma* and Sufism could only have served to secure the monopoly of the externalist *fuqahā* on the religious allegiance of the masses. So determined was he to eradicate all traces of non-externalist sympathy, and so aware was he of the dangers inherent in being even remotely connected with Sufism that Majlisi took great pains to exonerate his own father of the accusations levelled against him:

> God forbid that you think my father was a Sufi! He was acquainted with the sayings of the Imams, and such a person cannot be a Sufi. He was a man of great piety, and initially he would call his piety Sufism in order to win the trust of the Sufis and thus be able to influence them and prevent them from uttering inanities and committing vile acts. In this way he was able to guide many of them. At the end of his life, when he saw that there was no hope and that (the Sufis) are the enemies of God and in a position of dominance over the masses, he revealed his hatred for them. I know my father's methods and policies better than anyone, and the writings he penned concerning this matter are with me...[119]

Majlisi's unqualified denunciation of all forms of non-externalism becomes even more questionable when one considers that a scholar such as Ibn Taymiyya, who spent most of his life struggling against non-orthodox Islam, displayed remarkable regard for early Sufis such as Junayd and Abu Yazid al-Bistami for the simple reason that they recognised in the strict adherence to the Koran and the *sunna* 'the foundation of all mystical experience.'[120] Essentially an externalist, Ibn Taymiyya admitted that he actually found Sufi ideals very beautiful and viewed them as a source of spiritual and intellectual satisfaction. The problem as he saw it lay in the excesses committed in the name of Sufism. Furthermore, he inveighed against anything that constituted an innovation; Majlisi, on the other hand, condemned the Sufis as heretics and innovators, yet himself turned a blind eye to – and in some cases actively encouraged – many innovations propagated in the name of Twelver Shi'ite orthodoxy. Also, while denigrating the non-externalists on account of their supposed heresies he administered to the spiritual needs of two weak and ineffective rulers and their courtiers whose vice and debauchery knew no bounds, but which were tolerated by Majlisi with hardly a murmur of protest.

Majlisi's interpretation of the terms *'ilm* and *'ulamā*

Majlisi's interpretation of the words *'ilm* and *'ulamā* is of fundamental importance if one is to understand not only his personal position but also the ideological foundations of the group of scholars who rose to prominence at the end of the Safavid era. For Majlisi, the word *'ilm* denotes knowledge of the scriptural sciences, in particular of the transmission and interpretation of Traditions attributed to the Prophet and the Imams:

> And the knowledge implied in (Ali's) words, 'Knowledge is incumbent upon every Muslim' is the knowledge of God's commands, of prayer and *zakāt* and fasting: and the repositories of this knowledge are the Holy Imams and those whom they have designated as successors from among the *muhaddithūn* and the *fuqahā*.[121]

Consequently, an *'ālim* is one who has studied and mastered *fiqh* and *hadīth*. As explained in the previous chapter, externalism – the study of the *furū' al-dīn* – concerns for the most part the rules and rites which pertain to the outward show of submission that is Islam. Knowledge of these rules and rites calls for a detailed understanding of traditions, Koranic commentary, the principles of jurisprudence (*usūl al-fiqh*), and Arabic. Anyone who gains such knowledge is entitled, according to Majlisi, be called an *'ālim*. Since the prerequisites of externalist knowledge do not include *īmān* – the degree of which, being in no way determined by judgement of externals, is impossible to gauge – then it is possible in theory for an individual who has no sound belief in the fundamentals of Islam to become an *'ālim* in the popular sense of the word; indeed it is these pseudo-*'ulamā* whom Ghazali and Mulla Sadra berate in their treatises aimed against the externalist *fuqahā.*

The Koran exalts 'those who know' (*'ulamā*) by saying that it is only they who fear God. It is clear that the knowledge implied in the Koranic verse is not the knowledge of externalia such as is transmitted through *fiqh* and *hadīth*. If, as Majlisi states, the term *'ilm* refers to the knowledge of *hadīth*, then one must conclude that the most fearful of God's slaves are those who are acquainted with the Traditions of the Prophet and the Imams. As a corollary, the externalist *fuqahā* are the most fearful of God's slaves: Majlisi and those who follow his line of thinking are thus elevated to a position of veneration in the Twelver Shi'ite community second only to the Prophet and the Imams themselves. The famous Tradition which states that 'the *'ulamā* are the inheritors of the prophets' conveniently confirms this.

Thus in the eyes of the undiscerning masses, the *'ulamā* – or, more precisely, the *fuqahā* – are seen as standing above all suspicion as far as belief and sincerity are concerned: if they are the inheritors of the Prophet, and the true interpreters of his words, how indeed are they to be doubted? It is thus that the religious base of the *'ulamā* among the people is firmly cemented, for it is inconceivable that a simple believer could ever doubt the credibility of a *faqīh* or a *muhaddith* or *mufassir*, for such a person – at least in the eyes of the undiscerning – *must* be a believer since he is an *'ālim*. The respect and reverence enjoyed by the *'ulamā* in Muslim society must be understood in the context of the assumption – conscious or otherwise – that the possessor of *'ilm* is also the possessor of *īmān*.

The Twelver Shi'ite externalist *fuqahā* have always been seen as charismatic individuals by their followers; the *fuqahā* of the Safavid period, with Majlisi at the helm, re-interpreted *'ilm* in such a way that it became coterminous with *fiqh*, thus enabling their position as charismatic leaders of the community to become enshrined in the tenets of the new orthodoxy. Numerous *karāmat*, or saintly miracles, came to be attributed to the *fuqahā*: the biographies included in books such as *Qisas al-'ulamā* are replete with accounts of their miraculous deeds and dreams.[122] The *fuqahā* were experts in jurisprudence, while the masses, who were for the most part illiterate, were forced to refer to them for guidance on matters of *fiqh*; however, with the renewed emphasis on the charismatic quality of the *fuqahā/'ulamā*, the Twelver masses came to see them not only as a means and point of reference in secondary matters, but also as intermediaries in matters of belief. Thus it is that the *'ulamā* are lauded in Traditions as being the means of clinging to the infallible Imams as the 'Ark of Salvation' (*kishtī-i nijāt*); their pens are superior to the blood of the martyrs; they are the doors to Heaven, and to insult them would bring the wrath of God down upon the offender, and so on. The function of *shafā'a* or intercession was claimed by them, and they also performed *istikhāra* on behalf of the Twelver faithful. The *fuqahā* had posited that the only way to God was though gaining recourse (*tawassul*), through prayer, to the Imams; now, by setting themselves up as the sole interpreters of the teachings of the Prophet and Imams, and as the inheritors of Prophetic knowledge, the *fuqahā* became the intermediaries through which the masses, of which Majlisi was overwhelmingly contemptuous, could reach the Imams and thus gain indirect access to God. Thus the third tier of the ascending hierarchy leading to the Divine throne was established and an unofficial Twelver Shi'ite 'clergy' brought into existence.[123]

The descendants of Muhammad Baqir Majlisi

Although relatively little is known about the lives and works of Majlisi's forefathers, the same can hardly be said of his descendants. Thanks no doubt to the position of Majlisi at the end of the Safavid era and the pivotal role he played as the restorer of the 'orthodoxy', the names and works of his descendants and those of his siblings have been well recorded. By and large, Majlisi's family tree reveals a plethora of *fuqahā*, *muhaddithūn* and personalities of high political and religious standing.

According to the *Mir'at al-ahwāl*, Muhammad Baqir Majlisi had two brothers and four sisters: both of his brothers were scholars and all of his sisters were married to scholars. One brother, Mulla 'Azizullah (d. 1074/1663-64) was a renowned externalist and *belles-lettrist* with a wealth to rival the richest merchants of the day. The other brother, Mulla 'Abdullah (d. 1084/1673-74) emigrated to India. Of Muhammad Baqir's four brothers-in-law, two hailed from Mazanderan, one originated from northern Azarbaijan, and the fourth – about whom the source provides no information – came from the province of Fars.[124]

Mulla Muhammad Salih Mazandarani (d. 1081/1670-71) came to Isfahan from his home province when quite young, apparently to escape poverty. His aptitude for the scriptural sciences so impressed Muhammad Taqi Majlisi that he gave him his daughter, Amina Bigum, in marriage. Amina Bigum was herself well-versed in the scriptural sciences and was said to have attained the status of *mujtahid* in her own right.[125]

Among the second generation of Muhammad Taqi's descendants there are at least nine who became or married scholars, establishing links with prestigious merchant and *sayyid* families. Muhammad Baqir's daughters married scholars, some of them related. One of his sons married into the *sādāt* of Ardistan. Another daughter married one of his students, Muhammad Salih Khatunabadi, who succeeded his father-in-law as *imām jum'a* of Isfahan at the beginning of the 12th/18th century. The post remained hereditary in this line for the next hundred years, with the Majlisi family maintaining its continuity as the scholarly elite of Isfahan throughout the period of tribulation wrought upon the city by the Afghan invasion. Mir Muhammad Husayn Khatunabadi (d. 1151/1738-39), Muhammad Baqir's grandson, became *imām jum'a*, *shaykh al-islām* and *mullā-bāshī*, and continued in his grandfather's footsteps by implementing a vigorous anti-Sufi policy, one in which he himself is reported to have personally had recourse to physical violence.[126]

The third generation intermarried with other clerical families in Isfahan and further afield in Mashhad, Najaf and Karbala. A great-grandson of Muhammad Taqi was the first of several Majlisis to move to Bengal, where they ensured the growth of Twelver Shi'ite institutions and patronage for Twelver Shi'ite scholars.[127]

The fourth generation continued to produce scholars in Isfahan, although in the Mazandarani line there is ample evidence of *fuqahā* tying themselves to the richer classes of the bazaar, seeking new means of economic security when their links to the court were disrupted during the Afsharid *interregnum*. The links between the externalists and the bazaar and the relative political independence this engendered were to prove crucial to the growth of externalist power in the 19th and 20th centuries. This generation did produce scholars, however, one of the most notable being Aqa Muhammad Baqir Bihbihani.[128]

Bihbihani, the first major scholar after Majlisi, established Karbala as the foremost centre of Twelver Shi'ite scholarship in the 12th/18th century. He continued the work of Majlisi in narrowing and defining the scope of orthodoxy in Twelver Shi'ism, but whereas Majlisi had concentrated on the 'purification' of Twelver Shi'ism through purging it of non-externalism, Bihbihani focused his attention on the central question of jurisprudence. He claimed that all who disagreed with the principles of *'aql* (reason) and *ijtihād* as sources of law must be regarded as unbelievers. His attacks were centred on the then prominent Akhbari school, and his subsequent victory over its adherents paved the way for a substantial increase in the power and influence of the Usuli *mujtahidūn*, thus setting the tone and direction of Twelver Shi'ite development up until the present time. If Majlisi is the restorer of Twelver Shi'ite orthodoxy, then Bihbihani can be seen as the founder of a new stage in the jurisprudence of that orthodoxy, a concomitant of which was that the *mujtahid* was henceforth considered to be the vicegerent of the Prophet (*khalīfat al-rasūl*), a designation only one step away from the concept of *wilāyat al-faqīh*, the cornerstone of the present Iranian constitution.[129]

Other important members of the Majlisi clan include Sayyid Muhammad Mahdi Tabataba'i Burujirdi, know as Bahr al-'ulum (d. 1212/1797-98).[130] Arguably the most esteemed externalist scholar of the early Qajar period, he was responsible for the shift of the centre of Twelver Shi'ite scholarship from Karbala to Najaf. Ayatullah Husayn Burujirdi (d. 1961), the last sole *marja'-i taqlīd* in Iran, was also able to trace his lineage back to Majlisi, and thus it is claimed that the Majlisi family has produced no less than five *maraji'-i taqlīd*: Muhammad Taqi Majlisi; Muhammad Baqir Majlisi; Wahid Bihbihani; Bahr al-'ulum; and Ayatullah Burujirdi.[131]

Thus the Majlisi family can be seen to run the whole gamut of religious orientations, from the Sunni/Sufi theocentrism of Hafiz Abu Nu'aym through the ambiguous, middle-ground syncretism of Muhammad Taqi Majlisi, to the staunchly imamocentric externalism of Muhammad Baqir and the increasingly legalistic orthodoxy of his descendants, none of whom, according to the sources, expressed any serious inclination towards non-externalism. Accordingly, the Majlisi family can, in its evolution, be seen as a reflection and microcosm of the gradual rise to predominance of Twelver Shi'ite externalism in Safavid Iran.

Notes

1. The biography of Majlisi, *Fayd al-qudsī*, appears in full in volume 102 of *Bihar II* and will henceforth be referred to simply as *Fayd*.

2. Aqa Ahmad Kirmanshahi Bihbahani, *Mir'āt al-ahwāl-i jahān namā* (British Library, London: Persian Ms. Add. 24,052).

3. Danishpazhuh's *Fihrist* has been used extensively in Chapters Three and Four of the present work.

4. *Fayd*, p. 9.

5. Muhammad b. Ali Ardabili, *Jāmi' al-ruwāt* (Qum. 1403/1982-83), vol. 2, p. 78.

6. Muslih al-din Mahdawi, *Tadhkirat al-qubūr yā dānishmandān wa buzurgān-i Isfahān* (Isfahan, 1348 Sh./1969-70), p. 162.

7. See: E.G. Browne, *A Literary History of Persia* (Cambridge: CUP, 1930), vol. 4, pp. 120, 366, 403-4; Lawrence Lockhart, *The Fall of the Safavi Dynasty and the Afghan Occupation of Persia* (Cambridge: CUP, 1958), pp. 70-2.

8. V. Minorsky (ed.), *Tadhkirat al-Mulūk: A Manual of Safavid Administration* (Cambridge: CUP, 1980)

9. Arjomand, *The Shadow of God*, pp. 158-9 and *passim*.

10. Hafiz Ghulam Halim Shah 'Abd al-Aziz Dihlawi, *Tuhfa ithnā 'asharīyya* (Luckhnow, 1885), p. 166.

11. Mehdi Bazargan, personal interview with the author, February 1979.

12. See, for example, the views of Shah Ni'matullah Wali, who was born and who most probably died a Sunni, in his *Dīwān* (Tehran, 1352 Sh./1973-74), pp. 684-5, 734-5, 746-7.

13. On the misconception surrounding Shaykh Baha'i, see: Andrew Newman, 'Towards a reconsideration of the "Isfahan School of Philosophy": Shaykh Baha'i and the role of the Safawid 'ulama,' in *Studia Iranica*, no. 15/2 (1986), pp. 165-99.

14. Critiques of Majlisi should not, however, be seen as resting on this misidentification alone; to view them as such would be a gross over-simplifcation.

15. Danishpazhuh, *Fihrist*, vol. 3, p. 1134.

16. Pampus, *Die Theologische Enzyklopädie*, p. 55; Danishpazhuh, *Fihrist*, vol. 3, p. 1134; *Fayd*, p. 108.

17. Khwansari, *Rawdāt al-jannāt*, p. 391; *Fayd*, pp. 106-8.

18. Mahdawi, *Tadhkirat al-qubūr*, p. 163.

19. Tunukabuni, *Qisas*, p. 152.

20. Muhammad Taqi Majlisi, *Lawāmi'-i Sāhibqirānī* (Tehran, 1913), vol. 1, p. 903.

21. Ali Dawani, *Mahdī-i maw'ūd, tarjuma-i jild-i sīzdahum-i Bihār al-anwār* (Tehran: Dar al-Kutub al-Islamiyya, 1350 Sh./1971-72), p. 54; *Fayd*, p. 110.

22. Muhammad Taqi Majlisi, *Risāla-i tashwīq al-sālikīn* (Tabriz, 1332 Sh./1953-54).

23. *ibid.*, p. 28.

24. Danishpazhuh, *Fihrist*, vol. 2, p. 609; Tabrizi, *Rayhānat al-adab*, vol. 3, p. 461.

25. Danishpazhuh, *Fihrist*, vol. 2, p. 609.

26. Muhammad Tahir's attack and Muhammad Taqi's defence appeared in a work entitled *Tawdīh al-mashrabayn wa tanqīh al-madhhabayn*, a thousand copies of which were said to have been in circulation in Isfahan. See: Danishpazhuh, *Fihrist*, vol. 3, pp. 1503-4. See also: Aqa Buzurg Tihrani, *al-Dharī'a*, vol. 4, pp. 495-98.

27. Danishpazhuh, *Fihrist*, vol. 3, p. 1134.

28. Tabrizi, *Rayhānat al-adab*, vol. 3, p. 457.

29. Only Aqa Ahmad Kirmanshahi, author of *Mir'āt al-ahwāl*, cites 1038/1628-29 as Majlisi's year of birth.

30. Tunukabuni, *Qisas II*, p. 204.

31. Dawani, *Mahdī-i maw'ūd*, p. 65.

32. *ibid.*, p. 209.

33. Tabrizi, *Rayhānat al-adab*, vol. 3, p. 457.

34. S. Safari, *Zindagāni-i Majlisī* (Mashhad, 1335 Sh./1956-57), p. 67.

35. *ibid.*, p. 12; *Bihār II*, vol. 1, pp. 2-3.

36. Arjomand, *The Shadow of God*, p. 152. Arjomand's contention that Muhammad Baqir Majlisi had made a dramatic change of allegiance from Sufism to externalism is totally unsupported by the sources of the period; furthermore nothing in Majlisi's writings points in that direction.

37. Khwansari, *Rawdāt al-jannāt*, p. 603.

38. *ibid.*, p. 330.

39. *ibid.*, p. 360

40. *ibid.*, p. 150.

41. *ibid.*, p. 395.

42. *ibid.*, p. 397.

43. 'Amili, *Amal al-āmil*, vol. 2, p. 296.

44. Khwansari, *Rawdāt al-jannāt*, p. 615.

45. Afandi, *Rīyād al-'ulamā*, vol. 2, pp. 30-31.

46. Khwansari, *Rawdāt al-jannāt*, p. 398.

47. Afandi, *Rīyād al-'ulamā*, vol. 4, p. 386.

48. 'Amili, *Amal al-āmil*, vol. 2, p. 288.

49. *ibid.*, p. 353.

50. Khwansari, *Rawdāt al-jannāt*, p. 287.

51. Personal correspondence with 'Allama Burqa'i, March 1987. On the contention that Majlisi held views on jurisprudence midway between the Akhbari and Usuli stances, see: Hossein Modaressi Tabataba'i, *An Introduction to Shi'i Law* (London: Ithaca Press, 1984), p. 54.

52. *Bihār II*, vol. 1, p. 2.

53. *ibid.*, pp. 2-3.

54. *ibid.*, p. 3.

55. *ibid.*

56. Tunukabuni, *Qisas*, p. 209.

57. *Fayd*, p. 29.

58. For biographical details of Jaza'iri, see: Tabrizi, *Rayhānat al-adab*, vol. 2, pp. 253-4. On the unfinished *Maqāmāt al-nijāt*, see: Danishpazhuh, *Fihrist*, vol. 3, pp. 1540-5.

59. Yusufi, *Surūr al-'ārifīn*, p. 22.
60. For more insight into the trinity of *haqīqa, tarīqa* and *sharī'a* see: Trimingham, *Sufi Orders*, pp. 135 and 142-3.
61. Pampus, *Die Theologische Enzyklopädie*, p. 32.
62. Tunukabuni, *Qisas II*, p. 249.
63. S. Safari, *Zindagānī-i Majlisī*, p. 53.
64. See the section on *intizār* in Chapter V of the present work.
65. *ibid.*
66. Mir Muhammad Husayn Khatunabadi, *Hadā'iq al-muqarribīn*, quoted in Dawani, *Mahdī-i maw'ūd*, p. 67.
67. *ibid.*
68. Tunukabuni, *Qisas II*, p. 292.
69. Muhammad Baqir Majlisi, *'Ayn al-hayāt* (Tehran, 1333 Sh./1954-55), p. 499.
70. *ibid.*, p. 505.
71. Sayyid 'Abd al-Husayn Khatunabadi, *Waqāi' al-sinīn wa al-a'wām* (Tehran: Chapkhana-i Islamiyya, 1352 Sh./1973-74), p. 540.
72. Dawani, *Mahdī-i maw'ūd*, p. 62.
73. *ibid.*
74. *Fayd*, p. 21.
75. Tunukabuni, *Qisas II*, p. 205.
76. Khatunabadi, *Waqāi'*, pp. 531-2.
77. Momen, *An Introduction to Shi'i Islam*, pp. 114-117; Lockhart, *The Fall of the Safavi Dynasty*, p. 76; Tunukabuni, *Qisas II*, p. 249.
78. Minorsky, *Tadhkirat al-Mulūk*, p. 41.
79. *ibid.*
80. *ibid.*, p. 110.
81. Mahdawi, *Tadhkirat al-qubūr*, p. 158.
82. Khatunabadi, *Waqāi'*, pp. 565-66.
83. Danishpazhuh, *Fihrist*, vol. 3, p. 1136.
84. Muhammad Baqir Majlisi, The Life And Religion of Muhammad [*Hayāt al-qulūb*, vol. 2], transl. by Rev. James L. Merrick (San Antonio: Zahra Trust, 1982), p. 387.
85. Tunukabuni, *Qisas II*, pp. 205-6.
86. Muhammad Baqir Majlisi, *Hilyat al-muttaqīn* [with *Risāla-i Husayniyya*] (Tehran, 1334 Sh./1955-56).
87. Muhammad Baqir Majlisi, *Zād al-ma'ād* (Tehran, 1320/1903-04).
88. Muhammad Baqir Majlisi, *Tuhfat al-zā'ir* (Tabriz, 1312/1894-95).
89. Arjomand, *The Shadow of God*, p. 169.
90. See: Ali Shari'ati, *Hajj*, transl. by Somayyah and Yaser (Bedford, Ohio: FLINC, 1977).
91. Prayers of this kind from *Zād al-ma'ād* and other similar compilations can be found in 'Abbas Qummi, *Kulliyyāt-i mafātīh al-jinān* (Tehran: Intisharat-i Guli, 1389/1969-76), *passim*.
92. Muhammad Baqir Majlisi, *Munājātnāma*, (Mashhad, 1354 Sh./1975-76), pp. 3-4. See also: Qummi, *Mafātīh al-jinān*, pp. 315-43.

93. The Arabic/Persian texts of both prayers can be found in *Mafātīh al-jinān*: *Du'ā-i Kumayl* on pp. 127 to 139 and *Zīyārat al-jāmi'a* on pp. 1085 to 1098.
94. Arjomand, *The Shadow of God*, pp. 168-9.
95. *Fayd*, p. 11.
96. Arjomand, *The Shadow of God*, p. 309, n. 35.
97. Browne, *The Literary History of Persia*, vol. 4, pp. 416-7.
98. *Bihār II*, vol. 1, p. 3.
99. *Fayd*, p. 34.
100. Danishpazhuh, *Fihrist*, vol. 3, pp. 1138-40; Tunukabuni, *Qisas II*, p. 208.
101. Tunukabuni, *Qisas II* p. 151.
102. Dawani, *Mahdī-i maw'ūd*, p. 82.
103. Tunukabuni, *Qisas*, pp. 204 -5.
104. Dawani, *Mahdī-i maw'ūd*, p. 90.
105. Ibn al-Jawzi, 'The Devil's Delusion [Talbis Iblis], trans. by D.S. Margouliath in *Islamic Culture*, vol. 10 (1936), p. 27.
106. Ali Dawani, *Mahdī-i maw'ūd, tarjuma-i jild- sīzdahum-i Bihār al-anwār* (Tehran: Dar al-Kutub al-Islamiyya, 1350 Sh./1971-72).
107. Muhammad Umar Memon, *Ibn Taimiya's Struggle against Popular Religion* (The Hague, 1976), p. 25.
108. Sadr al-din Muhammad b. Ibrahim al-Shirazi, *Kasr al-asnām al-jāhilīyya fī dhamm al-mutasawwifīn* (Tehran, 1340 Sh./1961-62). This is a fairly standard manual depicting the notorious antinomian excesses of certain Sufi followers.
109. Danishpazhuh, *Fihrist*, vol. 3, pp. 1503-5.
110. Ma'sum Ali Shah, *Tarā'iq al-haqā'iq*, vol. 1, pp. 178-80 and 257-58.
111. *ibid.*, vol. 1, p. 285.
112. Muhammad Baqir Majlisi, *Risāla-i su'āl wa jawāb* (Tabriz, 1332 Sh./1953-54), p. 4.
113. Dawani, *Mahdī-i maw'ūd*, p. 129.
114. *ibid.*, p. 128.
115. *ibid.*, p. 135.
116. *ibid.*, p. 136
117. Memon, *Ibn Taimiya's Struggle*, p. 31.
118. Lockhart, *The Fall of the Safavi Dynasty*, p. 76; Tunukabuni, *Qisas*, p.249.
119. Danishpazhuh, *Fihrist*, vol. 3, p. 535.
120. Memon, *Ibn Taimiya's Struggle*, p.25.
121. Safari, *Zindagāni-i Majlisī*, p. 13. See also: *Bihar II*, vol. 1, pp. 1-5 and also vol. 2, *passim*, for Majlisi's comments on the Twelver traditions concerning *'ilm* and *'ulamā*.
122. See: Tunukabuni, *Qisas II*, *passim*. For the *karāmāt* of Muhammad Taqi Majlisi, see pp. 204-14 and 231-33.
123. On the intercession of the Imams, see: Muhammad Baqir Majlisi, *Hayāt al-qulūb* (Tehran, 1374/1954-55), vol. 3, p. 38. See also: Muhammad Baqir Majlisi, *Tuhfat al-zā'irīn* (Tehran, 1334 Sh./1955-56), pp. 360-5.
124. See: Pampus, *Die Theologische Enzyklopädie*, pp. 53-92 for details of the Majlisi family tree.
125. Kirmanshahi, *Mir'āt al-ahwāl*, foll. 33b-34a.

126. Pampus, *Die Theologische Enzyklopädie*, pp. 60-61; Lockhart, *The Fall of the Safavi Dynasty*, p. 117.

127. On the presence of Shi'ism and Iranian-born *'ulamā* in India during this period, see: Juan R. Cole, *Imami Shi'ism from Iran to North India*, 1722-1856 (Ph.D. thesis University of California, Los Angeles, 1984).

128. On the links between the *fuqahā* and the bazaar, see: Nikki R. Keddie, 'The Roots of the Ulama's Power in Modern Iran' in *Scholars, Saints and Sufis*, ed. by N. Keddie (Berkeley and Los Angeles: University of California Press, 1978), pp. 211-229.

129. For biographical details of Bihbihani, see: Ali Dawani, *Ustād-i kull Āqā Muhammad Bāqir b. Muhammad Akmal ma'rūf bi Wahid-i Bihbihānī* (Qum, 1958).

130. Tabrizi, *Rayhānat al-adab*, vol. 1, pp. 144-5.

131. There is controversy over the question of the first *marja'*. Most classical as well as modern scholars of Twelver Shi'ite history tend to simplify the entire process by listing all prominent Shi'ite scholars, from Kulayni to Khumayni, as *marāji'*. See in this context: Michael M.J. Fischer, *Iran: From Religious Dispute to Revolution* (Cambridge, Massachusetts: Harvard University Press, 1980), pp. 252-54.

Chapter 5

Externalism in focus: the Twelver Shi'ite doctrines of *intizār* and *raj'a*

Introduction

Although we have said much about the internalist-externalist dichotomy in general, and about externalism and its exponents in particular, we have yet to discover precisely how the externalist *Weltanschauung* translates in practice, in the exposition of doctrines fundamental to both Islamic and Twelver Shi'ism. To this end we must now acquaint ourselves with Majlisi's highly idiosyncratic approach to Twelver eschatology, and in particular the return of the Mahdi at the end of time. For it is the corpus of Twelver Traditions supporting the doctrine of the return of the Hidden Imam which is especially representative of the spirit of externalism - albeit with an imamocentrically internalist core - championed so vigorously by Majlisi and his fellow jurists.

Messianism in Islam

The belief in an expected saviour, who will appear before the end of time to destroy the forces of evil and establish the rule of justice and equity on earth, is shared by most of the major religions. Christians, Jews and Zoroastrians, who at different times were subjected to the rule of those who did not share their religious culture, cherished their Traditions concerning a future saviour from a divinely chosen line. Such a saviour was expected to come or reappear, by God's will, to end the sufferings of the faithful and terminate the rule of the enemies of God and establish His kingdom on earth. Although the terms 'messiah' and 'messianism' have a particularly Judaeo-Christian colouring and connote a particular set of Judaeo-Christian beliefs, it is nevertheless possible to employ them in an Islamic context. Naturally, the Christian, Jewish and Islamic traditions differ in the way the formula of the expected saviour is presented. The Christians think of a 'second coming', the Jews of one who is yet to appear, while Muslims believe that a person will 'appear' (*zuhūr*) or 'rise' *(qīyām)* near the end of time. The Islamic saviour is the Mahdi, the charismatic eschatological figure who, as the preordained leader, will rise up to launch a massive social transformation in order to restore the rule of God and fill the earth with peace and justice. The Islamic saviour embodies the aspirations of his followers in the restoration of the purity of Islam, which will bring true and uncorrupted guidance to all mankind, creating a just social order and a world free from oppression in which the Islamic revelation will be the norm for all nations.

Although there is indeed a similarity between Islamic messianism and the Judaeo-Christian ideas concerning the Messiah, the doctrine of Mahdism as held by Muslims has distinctly different features. Unlike the Christian doctrine, the Islamic concept of salvation does not see man as an innate sinner who is to be saved through spiritual regeneration; nor does it conceive of its people's salvation in nationalistic terms, as Judaism does, with the assurance of the realization of the kingdom of God in a promised land by a unique, autonomous community. In Islam – at least for the Sunni majority – the emergence of the Mahdi is simply a corollary of the historical responsibility of the religion's followers, namely the establishment of the ideal politico-religious community, the *umma*, with a worldwide membership embracing all those who believe in God and His revelation through the prophet Muhammad. As such, messianism does not play the same pivotal role in Islam that the concept of a divinely chosen saviour plays in other monotheistic religions. For this reason, most Muslims, while expecting the appearance of the Mahdi, do not consider belief in him to be an essential element of the Islamic creed.[1]

The historical responsibility of Muslims to strive for justice in this world also carries within itself the potential for the revolutionary challenge of Islam to any order which might threaten its realization. The seeds of this responsibility, which were to blossom in the form of numerous rebellions throughout the history of Islam, were sown by the Prophet himself.

Muhammad was not only the bringer of a new religion but also the guardian of a new socio-political order. His message, embodied in the Koran, provided both spiritual and socio-political impetus for the creation of a just society based on divinely revealed principles. Consequently, in the years following Muhammad's death, a group of Muslims emerged who, disillusioned with the state of affairs under the Caliphate, looked back to the early period of Islam – the 'Golden Age' which was dominated by the charismatic figure of Muhammad, both prophet and statesman, and which came to be regarded as the only ideal epoch in Islamic history, unsullied by the corruption and worldliness that was to characterize the later Islamic caliphates and sultanates. Taking their cue from the special, divinely-sanctioned status of the Prophet, some of his followers began to look forward to the rule of an individual from among his descendants, 'whose name will also be Muhammad, whose patronym will also be like that of the Apostle of God, and who will fill the earth with equity and justice, as it had been filled with injustice, oppression and tyranny.'[2] Consequently the personal devotion of the faithful to the Prophet led to their awaiting the advent of a divinely-guided saviour from his family (*ahl al-bayt*), even though the Koran does not foretell the appearance of the Mahdi to guide the believers in the last days before the end of time.

It is inevitable that the constant emphasis in the Islamic revelation on the establishment of justice in both personal and societal affairs would fill a group of people who saw themselves as wronged and oppressed with even greater hopes for the appearance of a saviour figure. With the establishment in Islam of various dynasties and regimes which were seen to be lacking in the promotion of the Islamic ideal, the need for a deliverer became crucial. This was especially true in the case of the early Shi'ites, who sympathized with the claims of the descendants of the Prophet as being heirs to the prophetic mission. The most salient factor in the development of Twelver Shi'ism was the concept of a messianic Imam, the Mahdi, whose appearance would herald the end of corruption and wickedness.

The term *al-mahdī* and its early use

The term *al-mahdī* is the passive participle of the Arabic verb *hadā*, 'to guide', and means 'the one who has received correct guidance.' Nowhere in the Koran does the term *al-mahdī* appear, although *al-hādī*, or 'guide', which is the active participle of *hadā*, is used twice as an epithet of God.[3] The eighth form of the same stem, *ihtidā* or 'to accept guidance for oneself' is used in the Koran to describe anyone who embraces the guidance provided by God and acts upon it. The term *al-mahdī* is similar to *muhtadi*, the passive participle of *ihtidā*. However, in no sense is the word *muhtadī* used in the Koran to denote a particular individual: anyone may receive and act upon guidance and thus be described as *muhtadī*.[4] Thus there exists no clear, unambiguous indication in the Koran of any divinely-inspired figure who will come, re-appear or rise at the end of time to deliver the downtrodden from their oppression and restore justice and equity: if such a concept exists in Islam it does not have a direct Koranic basis as far as the surface text of the Koran is concerned.

The term *al-mahdī* was given to certain people during the early years of Islam as an honorific title. The Prophet's favourite poet, Hasan b. Thabit (d. 54/673-74) used the term *al-mahdī* to describe Muhammad himself, while the poet Jarir also used it to describe the prophet Abraham.[5] The Sunnis also gave it to the first four Caliphs, who were known as *al-khulafā al-rāshidūn al-mahdiyyūn*, the divinely-guided caliphs.[6] The third Shi'ite Imam, Husayn b. Ali, was also given the title *al-mahdī b. al-mahdī*.[7]

According to Rajkowski, Abu Ishaq Ka'b al-Himyari (d. 34/654-55) was the first person to use the term *al-mahdī* in the sense of saviour or deliverer.[8] Yet it is interesting to note that the second Caliph, Umar, had toyed with the idea of occultation earlier than this. When Muhammad died in 11/632, Umar claimed that the Prophet had gone into concealment and would soon return; this was swiftly refuted by Abu Bakr, who referred to verses 39:30-1, which state that all human beings die.[9] Al-Mukhtar, who revolted in Kufa in 66/685-86, named Ibn al-Hanafiyya (d. 81/700-01) as a claimant to the title of Imam and also called him *al-mahdī* in what was clearly a messianic context.[10] Later the Kaysaniyya sect denied Ibn al-Hanafiyya's death and proclaimed that he was the promised Mahdi, who had concealed himself and would one day rise, sword in hand, to eliminate injustice. The Kaysanite concept of mahdism played an important role in early Islamic political history, with the Abbasid movement, which finally did away with the Umayyad regime, having its roots in the Kaysanite sect.[11]

The Zaydis also use the term *al-mahdī* in the sense of a deliverer when describing their leaders who rose in arms against the Abbasids: Muhammad al-Nafs al-Zakiyya (d. 145/762-63) and Muhammad b. Ja'far al-Sadiq (d. 203/818-19) are but two examples.[12]

As for the Imami Shi'ites, the majority gave the title in its messianic sense to each of the Imams after his death. For example, after the death of Ja'far al-Sadiq in 148/765-66, some of his followers contended that he had not died but had gone into occultation.[13] Another group, the Waqifiyya, claimed the same for al-Sadiq's son, Musa al-Kazim, saying that he was *al-qā'im al-mahdī* who would one day rise to restore justice and equity.[14] The eleventh Shi'ite Imam, Hasan al-'Askari, was also the focal point of messianic claims, while the most significant use of the term *al-mahdī* was made with reference to al-'Askari's son, Muhammad. After the alleged disappearance of Muhammad b. Hasan in 260/873-74, a small faction of the followers of the house of Ali claimed that Muhammad b. Hasan was the final Imam and

190

the Mahdi, who had gone into concealment and would return one day to restore justice to a world that had been filled with tyranny. From this point onwards both the Twelver Shi'ite sect and the belief in Muhammad b. Hasan al-Askari as the Hidden Imam or the Mahdi came into being.

The Mahdi in the Traditions

The love of justice, peace and harmony and the desire for relief after pain and oppression are innately human traits which have become embodied, *mutatis mutandis*, in the messianic concepts of salvation inherent in the doctrines of the world's major religions. The desire for a better world and a more equitable social order are not solely the products of religious thought. For instance, Marx's idea of a classless society typified by justice, brotherliness and reason - a new world towards which the formation of all previous history has been moving - is a form of secular messianism in which man, as his own saviour, takes the central role; the Marxian vision is inspired by man's innate need for order, stability and well-being. For Marx, however, the realization of the new age will be an historical event and not a supernatural one like the second coming of Christ in modern Christian belief.

In Islam, as in Marxism, man achieves his own salvation – albeit with the notable difference that man is seen as being answerable only to God and not to his fellow comrades. Unlike Christianity, however, the Islamic revelation does not posit the existence of a Christ-like figure of salvation: the concept of the Mahdi is something that can be deduced only from the Traditions. It is for this reason that for the majority of Muslims the appearance of the Mahdi is not a fundamental of belief.

Yet given the fact that man has an innate desire for a better world, and taking into consideration the charismatic nature of the early Islamic leaders and the concomitant tendency of the Muslims to project their aspirations onto individual figures, is it not possible that those narrations which specify the appearance of the Mahdi could be later additions to the corpus of Traditions? Are the claims made by the likes of Ibn al-Hanafiyya, which relate to the eschatological usage of the term *al-mahdī*, based on authentic Prophetic Traditions concerning a future restorer of Islam? Or are these Prophetic Traditions merely a fabricated but totally natural extension and scriptural embodiment of early Muslim desire for a better or ideal society?

Sunni Traditions on the Mahdi

There are a number of Traditions attributed to the Prophet in the *hadīth* collections concerning the Mahdi, his family, his patronym and his general character. The Mahdi, it is claimed, will be a descendant of the sons of the Prophet's daughter, Fatima.[15] His colouring will be that of an Arab, his body will be like that of an Israelite, and his name and patronym will be the name and patronym of the Prophet.[16] The Prophet is claimed to have said that he himself, Hamza, Ja'far, Ali, Hasan, Husayn and the Mahdi will be masters over the inhabitants of paradise.[17] In another Tradition, Muhammad is said to have declared that the Mahdi will be from his progeny, will be similar to him in looks and character, and will have the same name and patronym. The Mahdi will enter a state of occultation and there will be chaos and confusion in the world in which people will be spiritually lost. The Mahdi will then appear, like a shooting star, to fill the earth with justice and equity, as it was filled before with oppression and injustice.[18] According to Ibn 'Abbas, Muhammad is reported to have said, 'How shall God destroy a nation, the beginning of which is myself, the end of which is Jesus, and the very centre of which is the Mahdi, who will be from my family?'[19]

In his work on mahdism, Muhammad Salih Osman concludes that the aforementioned Traditions are weak (*da'īf*) and contradictory (*mutadārib*). 'Therefore,' he says, 'their attribution to the Prophet Muhammad is to be very much doubted.'[20] Whether they are spurious or not, the market for Traditions concerning the Mahdi seems to have been a buoyant one: twenty-six of the Prophet's companions narrated Traditions concerning the Mahdi, and on their authority some thirty-eight scholars recorded these Traditions in *hadīth* collections.[21] It would seem that there is evidence enough to suggest that either Muhammad or one of his closest companions had foretold that one day a man from among his descendants would rise to renovate the house of Islam; yet it is equally clear that the political turmoil of the first and second *hijra* centuries encouraged some people to exploit the Prophet's promise of an expected deliverer in order to use it in their own struggle for power.

The Sunni *hadīth* collections contain only three Prophetic Traditions concerning the twelve Imams who would succeed Muhammad. According to Jabir b. Samura, a companion of Muhammad, the Prophet is said to have foretold the existence of twelve *amīrs*, all of whom would hail from the Quraysh.[22] Umar b. al-Khattab reported that the Prophet said that there would be twelve imams (*a'imma*) after him, all of them from the Quraysh.[23] 'Abdullah b. Mas'ud, when asked about the successors of the Prophet, said that the Prophet had informed him that there would be twelve caliphs, the same number as that of the leaders (*nuqabā*) of the Israelites.[24] These Traditions have been transmitted by the Sunni *muhaddithūn* and are considered authentic. However, they indicate only that the Prophet was to be succeeded by twelve leaders: the word *imām* appears in only one of the Traditions. Furthermore none of the Traditions foretells that the twelfth leader will go into occultation and then reappear as the Mahdi. Likewise, the Traditions concerning the Mahdi himself mention only that he will be from the progeny of Muhammad - not that he will be the twelfth Imam.

The unspecified identity of the Mahdi in the Sunni Traditions – the authenticity of which must remain open to question – explains why, as a salvific figure, he plays such a peripheral role in the Islamic belief system as understood and propagated by the vast majority of Muslims. The comparatively low profile of the Mahdi in the Sunni eschatological schema would also seem to be in keeping with the absence of any clear indications of the Mahdi's existence in the Koran.

The Mahdi in Shi'ite Traditions: Volume XIII of Majlisi's *Bihār*

Volume XIII of *Bihār al-anwār*, which deals exclusively with Twelver Shi'ite Traditions concerning the Mahdi, was completed in 1078/1667-78, although certain narrations used in the work, such as the controversial *chahārdah hadīth*, which were utilised in order to incorporate the Safavid dynasty into the 'last days' scenario, appeared earlier in separate compilations.[25]

Under its alternative title, *Kitāb al-ghayba* (The Book of Occultation), volume XIII of the *Bihār* is divided into 36 sections: 1) the birth of the Mahdi and the biography of his mother; 2) the names and titles of the Mahdi; 3) the decree prohibiting all mention of the Mahdi's 'special' names; 4) the Mahdi's attributes and lineage; 5) Koranic verses which refer to the Mahdi; 6) Shi'ite and Sunni Traditions which were narrated about the Mahdi; 7-15) the Traditions of the individual Imams concerning the Mahdi; 16) the predictions of soothsayers concerning the Mahdi; 17) a discourse by Shaykh Tusi on the occultation; 18) the occultation of the Mahdi compared with that of the prophets; 19) examples of longevity; 20) the miracles performed by the Mahdi; 21) the four special representatives of the Mahdi; 22) accounts of those who have falsely claimed to be representatives of the Mahdi; 23) accounts of those who claim to have seen the Mahdi during the lesser occultation; 24) the Tradition of Sa'd b. 'Abdullah; 25) the reason for the occultation; 26) The test, trials and tribulations of the Shi'ites during the occultation; 27) the excellence of 'waiting for relief' (*intizār al-faraj*); 28) accounts of those who claim to have seen the Mahdi during the greater occultation; 29) accounts of those who claim to have seen the Mahdi in recent years; 30) the signs ('*alāmāt*) preceding the Mahdi's return; 31) the day of the Mahdi's return; 32) the rule of the Mahdi; 33) the Tradition of Mufaddal b. Umar; 34) the *raj'a* or 'return' of the Imams; 35) the Mahdi's successors and descendants; and 36) decrees issued by the Mahdi during his occultation.[26]

Majlisi, while using his usual sources, relies heavily in volume XIII on earlier compilations dealing specifically with the question of the occultation and the reappearance of the Mahdi such as the *Kamāl al-dīn wa tamām al-ni'ma* by Shaykh Saduq and *Kitāb al-ghayba* by Shaykh Tusi. By far Majlisi's most conspicuous source is the work entitled *al-Ghayba* by Muhammad b. Ibrahim b. Ja'far al-Nu'mani (d. 360/970-71). It is interesting in this context to note that in the composition of *al-Ghayba*, Nu'mani relied extensively on the information given by Ibrahim b. Ishaq al-Nahawandi (d. 286/899-900), whose own work on the subject reflected the views of the *ghulat*.[27]

In the author's view, four sections of volume XIII stand out as being of particular relevance to the question of externalism, both as it stood at the time of Majlisi, and as it stands today. These chapters are: the test (*imtihān*) of the Shi'ites during the occultation; the excellence of *intizār*, the Tradition of Mufaddal b. Umar; and the *raj'a* of the Imams. The first two deal with the trials and duties of the Twelver Shi'ites during the greater occultation, and as such lay the foundations upon which the subsequent socio-political and religious attitudes and orientations of the Twelver Shi'ites are structured. The second two focus on what is basically the outcome of *intizār*, namely the return of not only the Mahdi but also the rest of the Imams at the end of time. The *raj'a* is of particular relevance since it is in a sense the final cause or goal of Twelver Shi'ite externalism, the ultimate objective of the *wilāya* of the Imams, and the core concept in the belief system of the Twelver faithful.

The concept of *intizār*

Complementary to the doctrine of *ghaybat-i kubrā* (the greater occultation) is the notion of *intizār* or 'waiting for the return of the Hidden Imam.' By definition, *intizār* is a state of passive expectancy, a doctrine of hope and trust that the Hidden Imam will one day reappear and fill the world with justice and establish the kind of ideal Islamic society that Twelver Shi'ites believe existed only during the short caliphate of Ali b. Abi Talib.

Majlisi's compilation of Traditions on *intizār* comprises two distinct categories: the virtue of *intizār* as a component of belief; and the duties of the Twelver Shi'ites during the absence of the Imam and up until and including the cataclysmic events that are to occur immediately prior to his return.

The doctrine of *intizār* has important connotations for the personal and political lives of the Twelver Shi'ite faithful during the occultation of the Imam. Firstly, given the absence of the Imam as religious leader and source of spiritual inspiration, what are the personal duties of the Twelver Shi'ites as believers *vis-à-vis* their Creator, and upon whom is the duty of religious leadership to be devolved? Secondly, given the absence of the Imam as political leader of the Twelver Shi'ite community, as the inheritor of Ali and the embodiment of the ideal Islamic *khalīfa*, in whom the temporal and the religious are fully integrated, what should be the attitude of the Twelver Shi'ites to the question of earthly government? Before considering these two aspects, we need to familiarise ourselves with the Traditions in question and, more importantly, with Majlisi's interpretation of them.

The Traditions in the *Bihār* which deal with *intizār* are grouped under two main headings: the trials (*imtihān*) of the Twelvers during the occultation; and the 'excellence of waiting' for the return of the Imam (*fadīlat al-intizār*). Other Traditions pertaining to *intizār* in the context of events that are supposed to take place during the occultation and immediately prior to the return of the Imam can be found scattered throughout other sections of Majlisi's work; his identification of certain apocalyptic figures mentioned in Traditions with members of the Safavid dynasty, collected in a separate work entitled *Kitāb al-raj'a* and otherwise known as *Chahārdah hadīth*, appears in volume XIII in the chapter on the signs (*'alāmāt*) of the Imam's reappearance, but since they are germane to the question of *intizār* they will be discussed here also.

The occultation of the Imam: a test for the Twelver Shi'ites

The disappearance of the Mahdi and his subsequent occultation is presented in the Traditions as a severe test for the Shi'ite faithful. A Tradition attributed to Imam Muhammad Baqir describes the Shi'ite faithful as being like collyrium (*surma*): one knows when it is applied to the eyes but one does not know when it will be washed out. A time will come when a Shi'ite will begin the day in the correct religion (*dīn al-haqq*, i.e. Shi'ism) but by nightfall will have left it.[28]

The occultation will bring much hardship and many schisms. The Shi'ites will undergo a process of 'sifting' (*ghirbāl*) in which the unbelievers will be rooted out from the believers.[29] Some of the Shi'ites, according to a Tradition attributed to Imam Ja'far Sadiq, will be like broken glass: through hardship and trials they will have shattered but can be melted down and joined together again. Others will be like smashed earthenware pots which, once having disintegrated, cannot be reassembled.[30]

A substantial number of Traditions prohibits the naming of the Hidden Imam and the fixing of a specific date and time for his return; others freely allude to the number of years which is supposed to elapse before the return of the Imam and the termination of Shi'ite suffering. It is clear from both kinds of Tradition that the adherents of the Imams at that time anticipated the Mahdi's rise in the near future. One Tradition, narrated on the authority of Imam Muhammad Baqir by one Abu Hamza Thamali, has the latter asking the Imam why Ali's prophecy - namely that the Mahdi would appear after 70 years - had remained unfulfilled. Muhammad Baqir replies that since Imam Husayn was martyred, God decided to prolong the trial of the Shi'ites until the year 140/757-58. When this date had passed and nothing had happened it became clear that God had decided to postpone the 'relief (*faraj*) from suffering' indefinitely.[31]

The doctrine used to justify this apparent change of divine will is known as *bada'* or 'divine alteration', a concept formulated by the early Shi'ites to justify their political failures.[32] That the Traditions often run at variance with each other, namely in the sense that some specify a date for the Hidden Imam's reappearance while others expressly prohibit it, reveals clearly that the concept of a Mahdi or hidden saviour was still in the process of modification and was far from unambiguous. One Tradition discourages the fixing of any particular time for the reappearance of the Imam in the near future on the one hand, yet on the other refers to conflict and discord – a true reflection of the political situation at the time of the Imams – and assures the Twelver faithful that the return of the Mahdi is close at hand. No doubt even a vague knowledge of the time of the *zuhūr* would have warmed the hearts of the Twelver faithful during those oppressive early days, but one wonders exactly how many descriptions of the events which are supposed to lead up to the *zuhūr* were narrated simply to provide solace. Given the severe tone of the Imams when warning against fixing a time for the Mahdi's reappearance, one is led to doubt all of the Traditions which describe the events of the last days and which predict the appearance of the Imam.

The applicability of certain Traditions, namely those which deem all governments before the rise of the Mahdi to be illegitimate, must also be called into question. It is obvious that if the Imams believed that their ultimate victory was in the near future they would have given their followers hope by describing the trials and tribulations which would herald the Imam's return, while at the same time securing their loyalty by declaring all non-Imami governments usurpatory and thus illegitimate. How they would have stood politically had they realised the true length of the *ghayba* is another matter; in the light of subsequent developments it is not unreasonable to assume that they would have formulated a specific political ethos, the true significance of the prolonged absence of which has only in recent years been made clear.

Thus in many Traditions, those who predict a specific time for the Mahdi's rise are accused of mendacity on a grand scale: no-one should wish to hasten the Imam's return but should instead resign himself and submit to the will of God.[33] This does not stop Majlisi, however, from interpreting one of the Traditions according to the method of *abjad* and revealing that the most likely date for the Mahdi's return is 1195/1780-81.[34]

According to one Tradition, the *ghayba* will continue for as long as there is unrest among the Shi'ites; the subsequent rise of the Mahdi will be a matter that is completely out of the hands of the people.[35] This Tradition is also pregnant with political implications: the Shi'ites through their own behaviour are, in effect, preventing the return of the Imam. In order that he may return they must forget their troubles and, in the words of many other Traditions, remain calm.[36] Yet there is nothing positive and practical that they can do: the *zuhūr* is at the command of God alone and has nothing to do with the will of the people.[37]

The overall emphasis in this first group of Traditions is on the hardship and test of trials and tribulations that the Shi'ites are to undergo during the *ghayba*. One Tradition states that the Mahdi will appear only when all of the faithful are thoroughly demoralised and in despair;[38] another states that two-thirds of the people will have perished before the return of the Mahdi, although it does not specify whether it refers to all people or simply to the Shi'ite faithful.[39] In short, the *ghayba* is presented as an initially short period – seventy years is one estimation – in which the Shi'ites are to undergo hardship, persecution and discord. The historical sources provide ample evidence that the troubles prophesied by the narrators as a prerequisite of the Mahdi's reappearance were wholly pertinent to the lives and times of the Imams and their followers, and thus one can understand the heart-warming effect that the narrations concerning the Mahdi's imminent rise, with all its attendant signs and portents, would have had on the Shi'ite faithful.

The Traditions do not seem to have been designed to accommodate a period longer than that specified by the Imams, whose calls for *taqiyya* in the context of the question of the Mahdi were made obviously without the foreknowledge that Twelver Shi'ism would one day become the official religion of a whole nation, and that, in theory at least, the practice of dissimulation would become redundant. Yet Majlisi was able to present the Traditions as though they were totally relevant to the times in which he lived, without any apparent concern for the inconsistencies and contradictions which arise as a result of their being applied to the socio-political context of the Safavid era.

It should also be noted that the *imtihān* referred to in the Traditions connotes, in true externalist fashion, the trials and tribulations of Twelver Shi'ites as a minority among Sunnis, and not the hardships which all believers will, according to the Koran, undergo in order that their belief and submission may be strengthened.[40] Self-preservation in the face of oppression from an alien majority, the practice of *taqiyya* in all circumstances, patient submission to the will of God and hope in the imminent return of the Imam – all of this might have been pertinent to the Shi'ite community during the lifetime of the Imams. However, this kind of *imtihān* is difficult to reconcile with the conditions obtaining in Safavid Iran, where the Twelver Shi'ites were no longer a minority, where *taqiyya* had been rendered theoretically unnecessary, and where belief in the return of an Imam who would do away with injustice and tyranny sat uneasily alongside the belief that the Safavid rulers were the shadow of God on earth and a reflection of the divine. The *imtihān* remained, nevertheless, a wholly externalistic one, despite the fact that its preconditions had been drastically altered.

The Traditions on *intizār*

The word *intizār*, the 8th form verbal noun from the root n-z-r, carries the meaning of waiting and anticipation, biding one's time, looking on in passive anticipation, and so on.[41] In the Traditions collected in the *Bihār*, it is the 'expectation of release from suffering' (*intizār al-faraj*) which is enjoined upon the believers, the word *faraj* signifying the freedom from grief or sorrow caused by a particularly trying ordeal or calamity. The patient endurance of all calamities sent by God is enjoined upon Muslims in the Koran.[42] In Majlisi's collection, several Traditions – one narrated on the authority of the Prophet – mention the merit of *intizār al-faraj* without specifying the nature and cause of the suffering. In one Tradition the Prophet is reported to have said: 'The best of all acts carried out by my people is their expectation (*intizār*) of release from suffering, granted to them by God.' To which Majlisi adds: '... God, Who in His benevolence, will make the Lord of the age reappear to save the people from the claws of oppression and wretchedness.'[43] Forbearance in the face of suffering, a virtue enjoined by the Koran and acknowledged by all Muslims, is subject to a narrower interpretation by the Twelver Shi'ites, who see suffering as a particular corollary of the absence of the Imam.

Several of the eighty or so Traditions on the excellence of *intizār* class it as the best (*afdal*) of all actions, and in one narration it is classed as synonymous with worship (*'ibāda*).[44] A Tradition attributed to Ali calls on the people to wait for release from suffering and not to despair of God's mercy, for the best action in the sight of God is to wait patiently for release; the Tradition goes on to say that to move mountains with one's bare hands is easier than waiting for a government (*dawla*) that has been postponed. The people must ask God for help, practise patience and forbearance, and not act rashly or in haste out of their desire for the rule of Truth (*dawlat al-haqq*). Those who rush matters will regret it: they must tell themselves that their period of waiting will not be a long one so as to avoid the 'hardening of hearts' (*qasāwat al-qalb*).[45]

Another Tradition attributed to the Prophet has it that *intizār* is not only the best action but also the very best kind of worship.[46] Belief in the Hidden Imam is the interpretation given to the Koranic verse, "Guidance for the righteous ones who believe in the Unseen," where the righteous ones are the Shi'ites of Ali and the Unseen is God's proof to man, the Hidden Imam.[47]

A Tradition attributed to the fourth Imam, Zayn al-'Abidin, says that whoever remains devoted to the Imams during the *ghayba* will receive from God the reward of a thousand martyrs;[48] whoever dies during the *ghayba* with love for the Imams in his heart will enjoy a status similar to that of the companions of the Prophet.[49] Acts of worship which, given the tyranny of the illegitimate regime, must be carried out clandestinely during the *ghayba*, are more meritorious than those performed openly after the return of the Imam: God will increase the rewards of those who persevere in their religious duties in secret, out of fear of oppressive rulers.[50] Again, this last Tradition infers implicitly the illegitimacy of all regimes and rulers preceding the rise of the Mahdi.

Apart from cultivating hope in the future rise of the Mahdi, the Twelver

Shi'ites are encouraged to stay on their path (*tarīq*), which Majlisi interprets as belief in Shi'ism and the 12 Imams.[51] Other Traditions stress steadfastness in the *dīn*, or in the creed ('*aqīda*), both of which are taken as denoting Twelver Shi'ism.[52] No Tradition emphasizes *īmān*, unless it be *īmān* in Twelver Shi'ism or the occultation of the Imam, and exhortations to self-knowledge and gnosis of God do not figure among the Traditions at all. Belief in God is, as usual, assumed; it is belief in the *ghayba*, the *zuhūr* and the *raj'a* which is posited as a source of strength and comfort for the Twelver Shi'ites during the long oppressive years of the occultation.

A salient feature of the *intizār* Traditions is the call for submission to the will of God not only in the context of the prolonged disappearance of the Imam but also in the face of social and political events and, most notably, the tyranny of the ruling powers. One narration in this context, attributed to Imam Baqir, is worth quoting in full:

> Abu al-Jarud relates that he asked Imam Muhammad Baqir for some edifying advice. The Imam said to him, "I advise you to lead a pious life and, when these people (i.e. the masses) are in tumult and attain power (i.e. through rebellion), to stay in your house and avoid association with those who rise up in revolt; for their rebellion has no basis and has no clear end or aim. Know that the Umayyad reign will be a long one, which no-one will be able to take away from them. But when our rule comes, God will give the leadership to any one of you from the *ahl al-bayt* that he wishes; whichever one of you acknowledges that rule will have an esteemed position in our eyes; and whichever of you dies before our rule is established (and who has the desire for that rule in his heart) will be recompensed in the life to come. Know that no people or tribe has risen or will rise to defeat oppression and tyranny without being obliterated by a calamity, except for those who fought alongside the Prophet at the battle of Badr, and who shall rise once more...[53]

The above narration clearly intends to dissuade the Twelver Shi'ite faithful from attempting to take their own fate into their hands by rising up against oppressors or, indeed, from associating or aligning with anyone who rebels against the ruling powers. The forces of oppression, symbolized in this Tradition by the Umayyads, cannot, it would seem, be challenged by the people, who must abstain from political involvement and adopt a quiet and pious life, practising the rites and rituals of Twelver Shi'ism under the cloak of *taqiyya* while patiently awaiting the return of the Hidden Imam.

Several other Traditions prescribe political quietism and social reclusion. According to Ja'far al-Sadiq, the Shi'ite faithful must sit in their homes and not leave them, for the 'rule of Truth' (*dawlat al-haqq*) which is rightly theirs will take a long time to materialize.[54] A Tradition ascribed to the same Imam has it that those who act in haste concerning the *zuhūr* - presumably those who pre-empt the *zuhūr* by themselves resorting to rebellion - will be annihilated; those who patiently await the return of the Imam will be saved. The people must become like the 'scraps of *kelīm*' in their houses; those who revolt and cause discord will suffer as a result.[55] Another Tradition, attributed to Imam Baqir, says that those from the *ahl-al-bayt* who rise before the return of the Imam will be like defenceless chicks, mere playthings in the hands of children. Just as the earth and sea are calm, the people (i.e. the Twelvers) must also be calm. They must in no circumstance rebel against anyone in the name of the Imams of the *ahl al-bayt*. Only God can bring about the 'rule of Truth' through the return of the Hidden Imam; it is not in the hands of the people. One must obey the Imams and submit to whatever comes to pass.[56]

Elsewhere it is stressed that while one is awaiting the return of the Mahdi, one must strive to know the Imam – although it is never made clear how – for whosoever dies without knowing the Imam will have died a death of ignorance. To know one's Imam has great benefits, even if one dies before the *zuhūr*, and if one does die before the *zuhūr*, his 'waiting (*intizār*) will itself have been a release and a joy.[57] Apart from this, one must strive to carry out all of the obligatory duties laid down in the *sharī'a*, which remain incumbent on the individual despite the absence of the Imam. The Twelver Shi'ites during the occultation are superior to those in the company of the Mahdi for the simple reason that the former must contend with tyrannical regimes, against which they move neither tongue nor hand nor sword in opposition.[58] The best a believer can do during the occultation is to keep a check on his tongue and stay at home.[59]

Finally, the Tradition most pertinent to the apolitical undertones of *intizār* is related by Majlisi from Kulayni and is attributed to Ja'far al-Sadiq:

> Any flag that is raised (by a ruler) before the rise of the Mahdi will have been raised by an idol, and those who obey (this ruler) will have obeyed other than God.[60]

The politico-religious implications of *intizar*

In the light of the revolution of 1979 in Iran and the subsequent implementation of the doctrine of *wilāyat al-faqīh*, one looks back to past developments in Twelver Shi'ism in order to trace the evolution of Twelver Shi'ite political theory and, by locating its antecedents, to view the current trend in the context of its own history.

In one sense, a comparison of the Islamic Republic of Iran with Safavid Iran, at least insofar as general religious orientation is concerned, reveals striking similarities, the most salient being that externalism still predominates, albeit in a different guise and with different socio-political implications. This will be discussed in greater detail in the final section of this chapter.

As for the Twelver Shi'ite political ethos and the attitude of the Twelver *fuqahā* to the question of government and political involvement, the events of the past two decades in Iran signify a radical and dramatic departure from tradition, especially tradition as it is enshrined in the *Bihār* and in the ideas of Muhammad Baqir Majlisi. The notion that the *faqīh* might embrace both temporal and religious power was one that never entered the heads of the Safavid *fuqahā*, and the idea that this could come about through rebellion and revolution would have been anathema to them, however indisposed some of their number might have been towards the rulers of the day. Thus while in content the orientation of the *fuqahā* of the Islamic Republic is for the most part identical to that of their Safavid counterparts, in form it is totally different and wholly without precedent in the history of Twelver Shi'ism.

It has become something of a cliché to assert that Islam does not distinguish between the temporal and the religious, and that there is no concept of giving unto Caesar what is Caesar's and unto God what is God's. To state, as Said Amir Arjomand has done, that the God of Islam neither wields political authority nor acts as the political source of that authority is perhaps to confuse practice with theory.[61] It is true that in the majority of Muslim states and kingdoms throughout history there has been in practice a split between the 'actual' and the 'ideal', which in turn connotes a dichotomy of 'temporal' and 'sacred', or 'secular' and 'religious'. The idea that a human life can be compartmentalized into the 'sacred' and the 'temporal' is at odds with the teachings of the Koran and the majority of Muslim scholars, even if they and their co-religionists have rarely been able to adhere to them. Arjomand's claim also overlooks the fusion of 'sacred' and 'temporal' rule in the practice of Muhammad himself and also in the practice of the rightly-guided Caliphs. For Muslims the best actual realization of the ideal is held to have taken place during the lifetime of Muhammad, and it is to his example that they all look for inspiration; that they have never been able to attain the ideal is another matter, albeit one that does not affect its perceived validity.

In general, the actual historical realization of the Islamic ideal has taken many forms but has never been able to recapture the fusion of 'temporal' and 'sacred' in the charismatic practice of Muhammad. As A.K.S. Lambton points out:

> Later empires, the Umayyad, the 'Abbasid, the Fatimid, the Ottoman, the Safavid and others, represent different compromises between the world and the ultimate authority of truth.[62]

The *sharī'a* had, in theory at least, absolute authority, but the extent to which it was implemented varied in different regions and at different times. There was, however, always a general consensus among Muslims that the only way in which the ideal Islamic society, symbolized by Medina at the time of the Prophet, could come about was though the application of the *sharī'a* and the subjugation of all men to it. It was on the question of how to bring this about that differences later arose, especially between the Shi'ites and the Sunnis.

The tendency among Muslims to see the world in terms of the religious and the secular – a notion alien to the Koran and clearly yet another off-shoot of the confusion arising from misperceptions of the *īmān*/Islam relationship – produced the concept of worldly political authority which grew up alongside the concept of authority based on the *sharī'a*, embodied in the government of Muhammad at Medina, and posited since as the 'ideal Islamic government' or the ideal caliphate to which all men must aspire. As Lambton explains, the vast majority of empires that have existed since the time of Muhammad have been led by dynasts whose main motive was power for its own sake: power as the means of self-aggrandizement and not as a basis for the implementation of the *sharī'a* in its entirety. And, as Lambton points out, the authority of the *sharī'a* cannot be implemented without power, yet power without authority is tantamount to tyranny.[63]

It is this relationship between authority (*hukm*) and power (*sultān*) that has occupied the mind of many a Muslim *faqīh* throughout the centuries. While there has always been a minority of Muslims who have refused to cooperate with the theoretically suspect governments - namely those with *sultān* but without *hukm* - the majority has always tended to cooperate, believing that the best way to preserve the *sharī'a* and to maximize its application was to work with the government. In this way the guardians of the *sharī'a* – the *'ulamā* – could also persevere to make known to the rulers the duties incumbent upon them as leaders of Muslims and theoretical defenders of the faith. The Sunnis tended to recognise the authority of any government so long as it possessed power enough to maintain order in the land. To resist the ruler and bring about a state of rebellion and anarchy was much worse, in the eyes of the *'ulamā*, than having to obey a tyrant. This accommodation by the Sunnis does not mean that they were unaware that power without authority was tantamount to tyranny or *zulm*; on the contrary, the Sunni *fuqahā* and *hukamā* were always at pains to point out that kings had duties too, which, as Muslims and slaves of God, they were bound to fulfil, and of which they needed to be made aware by the *'ulamā*. The interplay between the ruler and the *'ālim* – with the latter acting as counsellor to the former in matters of religious duty – features heavily in the poetry of the Sufis and forms the basis of the whole 'mirror for princes' literary genre.

The realisation that the practical act of government was implemented in most cases through power rather than authority, and that it was the king or sultan rather than the caliph that was calling the tune, led to the integration of the notion of kingship as an 'essential element of the imamate' into the political ethos of Muslim scholars.[64] Ghazali and Nizam al-mulk in particular were responsible for formulating theories of government in which the sultanate, as the symbol of coercive power, would complement the institutional authority of the caliph and would be aided by the *'ulamā* – or, more correctly, the *fuqahā* – whose knowledge was indispensable for the execution of religious and legal duties required by the *sharī'a*. The Tradition which has it that the sultan is the 'shadow of God' on earth, in which the word *al-sultān* (lit. 'power') referred originally to temporal power in general, came now to be interpreted as referring to the person of the sultan himself. The concept of the ruler as *zill Allāh* (shadow of God) was expounded further by Nizām al-mulk in his *Sīyāsat-nāma*, who saw kingship as an imitation of the government of God. These ideas were not new, but they were new to Islam, and it was these ideas which gained currency in the medieval Muslim world, and which were prevalent at the time of Isma'il I's rise to power.

For the Twelver Shi'ites, however, the concept of authority was very different. In the 'authority verse' in the Koran, in which believers are instructed to 'obey God, obey the Prophet and obey those in authority', the phrase 'those in authority' was interpreted as a reference to the 12 Imams, all of whom, it was believed, had been designated as temporal and spiritual leaders of the Muslim community by the Prophet and ultimately by God. The disappearance of the 12th Imam and his subsequent occultation presented the Twelver Shi'ite scholars with a dilemma, as we have already seen. In the absence of the Imam, all governments were considered automatically to be illegitimate. At the same time, however, rebellion had been outlawed on the practical grounds that the resultant disorder and risk of anarchy would be far more detrimental than acquiescence in the face of a tyrannical ruler – all of this despite the fact that in the martyrdom of Husayn, the Twelvers possessed a symbol of resistance and revolution that could have been evoked at any point in time, but which was not actually utilized until relatively recently.

The attitude of the Safavid *fuqahā* to government and kingship must be seen, then, in the light of such considerations. Safavid kingship saw as the source of its authority the theory that the ruler is the shadow of God on earth. This in turn was buttressed by the authority which they no doubt felt came from their alleged connection to the 7th Imam, Musa al-Kazim, a spurious claim which effectively allowed them to parade as heirs to the caliphate of Ali.

In his book *Islamic Messianism*, Abdulaziz Abdulhussein Sachedina criticizes Professor Lambton for saying that in the absence of the Imam, 'all government, even if the holders of actual power were Shi'i, was regarded as unrighteous by the Shi'i divines', and goes on to mention that this is a much later interpretation, dating back only to the Qajar period, for the early Twelver scholars did not mention anything about the unrighteousness of government during the occultation.[65] It is true that any references to the illegitimacy of government were at best indirect, and it is also true that as time passed and practice superseded theory in terms of relevance, the attitude of the Twelver Shi'ites became increasingly ambivalent. However, this should not mask the fact that in the Traditions of the Imams, all governments preceding the rule of the Mahdi are illegitimate, and the supporters of these governments are guilty of *shirk* or associationism: any flags which are raised prior to that of the Mahdi symbolize tyranny; no allegiance can be paid to any ruler except the Mahdi, and so on. These Traditions are explicit; even if, as it may be argued, they refer to circumstances obtaining during the lifetimes of the Imams themselves, when release from suffering was held to be imminent, the fact remains that they were narrated time and time again by Twelver scholars through the ages without any modifying statements from them as to the relevance or irrelevance of the Traditions for the time in question.

Prior to the Safavid period there had been virtually no change at all in the way Twelver Shi'ite scholars viewed the question of government: pressed on the point, all would have clearly upheld the theory that in the absence of the Hidden Imam, any kind of government is the government of usurpers and thus illegitimate. However, practical demands – including the fact that they owed their recently established positions as guardians of Iran's new official creed to the patronage of the Safavid rulers – obviated any overt protest on the part of most of the Twelver *fuqahā* against the theoretical illegitimacy of the Safavid regime. There were certain *fuqahā* – Muqaddas Ardabili and Shaykh Ibrahim Qatifi are two notable examples – who did dissociate themselves from the rule and affairs of state, but the extent of their animosity towards the Safavid kings as usurpers is not clear, and in any case their tacit rejection of kingship did not mean that they harboured any desires for temporal power themselves. Although the Safavid *fuqahā* eventually found themselves with a base strong enough from which to bid for the position of supreme source of authority – religious and temporal – in the Safavid state, and although towards the end of the Safavid era the Twelver *fuqahā* had virtual control over the Shah and were potentially able to press forward their own programme of just, Islamic government as typified by the caliphate of Ali, none of this was to be. Even though the *fuqahā* had manoeuvred themselves into positions of religious power, there was no question of direct or indirect religious rule, no concept of *wilāyat* for the *faqīh*, or, for that matter, for anyone else except the Imam.

The original objective of Twelver Shi'ism - an objective which cannot have been lost on the Safavid *fuqahā* but which they appear to have constantly and conveniently overlooked - is the upholding of justice, itself the *raison d'être* of Ali's claim to the caliphate. For the Twelver Shi'ites, Ali is the epitome of justice and his brief rule as caliph an idealized example of the perfect implementation of the *sharī'a*. Ali's letter to Malik Ashtar, counselling him on the way to govern, shows clearly that political involvement and participation in government were not things that he would have prohibited for his followers.[66] The ambivalence of the Twelver Shi'ite *fuqaha* of the Safavid era can only be a corollary of what Arjomand calls the 'de-politicization' of the *imāma*, which in turn is a concomitant of the occultation of the Hidden Imam.[67]

The occultation of the Mahdi actively disallows the Twelver Shi'ite community from taking the necessary steps to create an Islamically-structured and governed society, the implicit assertion being that all governments – even those ruled by Shi'ites – before the return of the Imam are illegitimate, and that any uprising which takes place in the name of

Shi'ism against tyranny and injustice finds no sanction in Twelver *fiqh* and is thus also illegal. This clearly paves the way for the undermining of the political nature of the *imāma*, which in its embryonic state was an overtly political as well as religious concept. The *fuqahā* continued to stress the historical rights of Ali, thereby implying that justice must be carried out - presumably via Islamic rule - yet they were prevented from doing so on account of the absence of the Imam. In these circumstances the *imāma* loses its political colouring and becomes a purely otherworldly notion: the imamocentric internalism which focuses on the personae of the Imams as semi-divine occupants of the unseen celestial realm who participate in the ongoing creation of the cosmos and intercede on behalf of the Shi'ite faithful.

The Sunni scholar, Bediüzzaman Said Nursi, founder of the contemporary Nurcu movement in Turkey, divides the Twelver Shi'ites conceptually into two groups: those Shi'ites who rejected the first three Caliphs as usurpers of Ali's rights, whom he calls the 'Shi'ites of *khilāfa*'; and those Shi'ites whose support for Ali is not political – and hence not divisive – but spiritual, in the sense that they consider Ali to be, after the Prophet, the best interpreter of the Islamic revelation: these he calls the 'Shi'ites of *wilāya*'. It is the first group, the politically-oriented adherents of Ali, to whom we object, says Nursi, and not the second – so long as the veneration of Ali by this group does not become excessive and idolatrous.[68] By Majlisi's time, a thousand years after the drama of the succession to the Prophet, the concept of *imāma* had lost its political import and all that was left was the hysterical anti-Sunni invective, levelled against the first two Caliphs, Abu Bakr and Umar. The historical rights of Ali were still stressed by the Safavid *fuqahā*, but the socio-political relevance of these rights for the time – namely the Safavid era - were totally overlooked. The Safavid *fuqahā*, then, were 'Shi'ites of *khilāfa*' in only the strictly historical sense, which amounted to little more than vehement sectarian sloganeering. It is also debatable whether the Safavid *fuqahā* could be said to have fitted Nursi's description of 'Shi'ites of *wilāya*', since by this he is referring to those who follow Ali as the supreme communicator of the truths of belief, a role which Nursi admits fitted Ali better than it did the other companions.[69] However, the *wilāya* of Ali as recognized by the Safavid *fuqahā* often overlooks Ali's supposed genius as an interpreter of the Koran, an exponent of *ma'rifa* and as patron-saint of most of the Sufi brotherhoods.

The distinctly otherworldly picture of the Imams as painted in the *Bihār* cannot, then, in this sense be termed religious – at least not in the sense intended by Nursi in his classification. In the author's view, the 'Shi'ism of *wilāya'*, if it exists at all, can be found in the likes of Mulla Sadra and Haydar Amuli, who, incidentally, believed that the main function of the Mahdi would be to preach *īmān* and spread belief in Islam.[70] However, as we have already seen, it is a matter for debate whether this can actually be called Shi'ism at all, at least in the orthodox sense of the word. Therefore when it is stated that the *imāma* was robbed of its political kernel and left with only a religious husk, it must be understood that the religion in question is the imamocentric externalism of Twelver Shi'ism, a religion whose central figures – the Imams – are all-important in terms of the unseen and the hereafter, but whose impact on the dynamics of *īmān* and Islam in this world is negligible.

The occultation of the Imam was in reality a veritable millstone around the necks of the Twelver *fuqahā*, the dilemma it posed them being that although society must be governed in some way, until the arrival of the Mahdi all governments are deemed unlawful. This naturally led to a compromise, and to a stance which is in practice much nearer to the Sunni attitude to authority and government than perhaps most Twelver Sh'ites might have cared to admit. Among the Twelver *fuqahā* of the Safavid era, three basic positions *vis-à-vis* the government can be discerned: total rejection; cautious accommodation; and wholehearted endorsement.

Total rejection was rare and did not in any way constitute a serious intent to challenge Safavid kingship and secular power: dissociation from rulers was in any case considered a virtue, although it should not be construed as an expression of opposition. The dissociation from the government which obtained in Safavid Iran was quietist and not revolutionary: there is no record of any *faqīh* in that period claiming that the *fuqahā* rather than the kings should rule, or that the Safavid regime should be overthrown by violent means.

Cautious accommodation or compromise was, as far as the sources reveal, by far the most common stance – cautious in the sense that although the majority of Twelver Shi'ite *fuqahā* were often more than willing to work in a system that was in theory illegitimate, their accommodative posture was not designed to bestow *shar'ī* legitimacy on the temporal rulers.

Accommodation in the Sunni sphere had taken place at a much earlier stage and by this point in time had evolved into unequivocal legitimization. The Ottoman government, as Norman Calder points out, had embraced and supported a religious tradition which confirmed and promoted the legitimacy of the government. Highly flexible, this tradition had as its major benefit stability; in Calder's opinion, the longevity of the Ottoman dynasty compared with that of the Persian ruling houses of the same period was one of the fruits of the Sunni political ethos.[71] Accommodation for the Twelver Shi'ite *fuqahā*, for whom the government was by definition tyrannical, was naturally riddled with paradox. For example, *fuqahā* may be appointed by tyrants and may impose *shar'ī* penalties, but must believe while doing so that they are acting with the permission of the Hidden Imam and not with that of the secular ruler who appointed them; the process of land tax collection (*kharāj*), pronounced legitimate during the *ghayba*, was entrusted to an agent, namely the ruler or governor, who was clearly illegitimate (*jā'ir*), and so on.[72] The earliest example of compromise in Safavid Iran is that of Shaykh Karaki, whose exploits in early Safavid Iran were discussed earlier. He may be seen as the archetypal compromiser: although his views on the restriction of the possible legitimate agents of the *sharī'a* to only the *faqīh* obviously implied the illegitimacy of the secular government, he was a trusted confidant of Shah Tahmasp and early in his career wrote a treatise on the permissibility of prostration (*sajda*) before rulers. Although one may object, as Shaykh Ibrahim Qatifi did, to the apparent opportunism of Shaykh Karaki, it is quite plain to see that if the Twelver *fuqahā* had not reached such a compromise they would never have been able to secure the positions they did. The benefits accruing to the *fuqahā* from their partial sell-out to the Safavid government are obvious.

Wholehearted acceptance of the Safavid dynasty seems to have been championed by the masses throughout the greater part of the era, this being a legacy of the Tradition that exalts rulers as the 'shadow of God' on earth; this Tradition had enjoyed currency in Iran long before the advent of the Safavids and was re-emphasized after their rise to power, with the added ingredient of descent from the Imams to give greater authority. The devotion and support of the Persians for their kings seem to have been immense if Chardin's remarks are anything to go by, for in the eyes of the masses:

> ...their Kings are Sacred and Sanctified, in a peculiar manner above the Rest of Mankind, and bring along with them wheresoever they come, Happiness and Benediction.[73]

Despite the fact that Shah Tahmasp's *farmān* to Shaykh Karaki had made official the split between the temporal and the sacred, as far as the people were concerned royalty and religion were virtually synonymous, whatever connotations the prolonged occultation of the Hidden Imam might have had. Despotism, as was shown earlier with reference to Shah 'Abbas, was seen as a 'Divine secret': there was no act of corruption, however profane or un-Islamic, that could not be tolerated by the people's belief in the divine right of kings, and in the 'decree and determining' (*qadā wa qadar*) of God. According to Chardin's accounts, the incongruity of the rulers' public face as shadow of God on earth and protector of religion, and his private face as wine drinker and violator of sacred laws, was not lost on certain of the most discerning and forthright scholars, yet the majority view was one in which the image of the ruler as the *walī* of God, whose commands were to be obeyed without question, remained untarnished.[74]

The epitome of what has been termed wholehearted acceptance of the Safavid dynasty is Muhammad Baqir Majlisi, whose views on kings and their rights were treated summarily in the previous chapter. With what appears to be total disregard for the many Traditions he himself collected which outlaw explicitly *all* governments preceding the rise of the Mahdi, Majlisi endorses the right of the Safavid kings to temporal rule with considerable gusto, although he stops short of accrediting them with religious authority, which, after all, was in the possession of externalists such as himself. However, according to Majlisi, it is thanks to the Safavid kings only that Twelver Shi'ism has its place in the people's hearts:

> It is only too clear to all men of wisdom and discernment that it is the exalted Safavid dynasty which must be thanked for the continued existence of the glorious religions of their illustrious forefathers in this land. All believers are beholden to them for this bounty. And it is because of the rays from the sun of this sultanate (i.e. the Safavids) that this insignificant mote (i.e. Majlisi) has been able to bring together the Traditions of the Pure Imams into the twenty-five volumes known as *Bihār al-anwār*. It was while I was engaged in my work that I came across two Traditions in which (the Imams) foretold the appearance of this exalted dynasty (*dawla*) and gave to the Shi'ites the glad tidings that this glorious dynasty would be connected (*ittisāl*) in time to the government of the Hidden Imam of the House of Muhammad.[75]

The above passage is taken from Majlisi's own introduction to his treatise *Chahārdah hadīth*.[76] The Traditions in question concern the rise and reappearance of the Mahdi, and the first two of these purport to foretell the emergence of the Safavids as precursors of the Mahdi's rule. In volume XIII of *Bihār al-anwār*, Majlisi includes them in the section which deals with the signs and portents of the 'last days'. According to the first Tradition:

> Our *qā'im* (the Mahdi) will appear when someone rises in Khurasan

and conquers and Multan and passes through the island of Banu Kawan. A man from our line shall rise in Gilan and the people of Abar (a village near Gurgan) and Gilan will support him. The flags of the Turks will fly for the sake of my son while all about him are scattered. Thousands will be prepared for war and the ram will slaughter his child. Another will rise to avenge the death of that child...only then will the *qā'im* rise.[77]

Majlisi says that the one who rises in Khurasan is either Hulagu or Genghis Khan, while the 'man from our line' is none other than Shah Ism'ail I. The reference to the 'ram' killing his child is an allusion to Shah 'Abbas I, who killed his son, Prince Safi Mirza, while the one who avenges that death is Shah Safi, the son of Safi Mirza, who retaliated by slaying several of Shah 'Abbas's other offspring. It is possible, adds Majlisi, that the rise of the Mahdi will occur soon, given that these incidents have come to pass.[78] The second Tradition is as follows:

I see a people in the East, rising in order to claim their rights (i.e. the caliphate) but failing to do so. They rise up again but fail a second time. They brandish their swords once more; this time they are given that which they have sought, but they do not accept it until they are well established. But still they will not attain (the world government of Al-i Muhammad) – only your master (i.e. the Mahdi) can do that.[79]

According to Majlisi, this Tradition contains a reference to the rise and rule of the Safavid dynasty, which will precede immediately the rise and rule of the Mahdi.[80] The quotations above stand as they appear in *Bihār al-anwār*; in *Chahaārdah hadīth*, however, the 'man from our line' is translated into Persian by Majlisi as 'a king shall rise from among us.'[81] Majlisi's alteration of the Tradition during translation hardly seems necessary considering that he interpreted the original Tradition as referring to Shah Isma'il I and the Safavid dynasty.

Traditions which predict the future and mention events and historical figures who are to play a part in the unfolding of Islamic history are known as *malāhim*. Many appear among the Prophetic Traditions and in works such as the *Nahj al-balāgha*.[82] For the most part, those attributed to Muhammad are specific in nature, naming exact names and locating precise events. The Traditions in *Bihār al-anwār* which foretell the events leading up to the reappearance of the Mahdi are notoriously vague and lend themselves to all kinds of interpretation. As noted previously, *Chahārdah hadīth* made its appearance shortly before the accession of Shah Sulayman and may be seen possibly as a means by which Majlisi was able to curry favour with the new ruler. If this was his ploy then it was clearly most effective. On the other hand, by incorporating the Safavids into the 'last days' scenario and thus giving them a certain charisma and their rule a patina of inevitability, Majlisi might have been trying to countermand objections to the impiety of the Safavid kings, noted by Chardin, that had been raised by some of the *fuqahā* - chiefly, it should be added, as a result of Shah 'Abbas II's non-externalist leanings. In the opinion of Mir Lawhi, a contemporary of Majlisi and arguably his most vehement critic, it was in order to ingratiate himself with the new ruler that Majlisi felt compelled to interpret the Tradition in the way that he did. Majlisi's treatise apparently caused quite a stir among the scholars of the day; Mir Lawhi decided that the brouhaha could be ended only if an answer to Majlisi's treatise were written.

Mir Lawhi's attack on Majlisi's treatise is founded not on any doubt as to the validity of the concept of mahdism or *raj'a per se*, but on his objection to Majlisi's use of free interpretation of a spurious Tradition to prove the legitimacy of the Safavid dynasty. This is not to say that Mir Lawhi was in any way a detractor of the Safavid rulers: what appears to have roused his indignation is the assumption that the Safavid rulers were in need of scriptural support for their rule. Mir Lawhi firmly believed that Majlisi had written the treatise on *raj'a* solely in order to further his own interests and make a name for himself among the people. In his polemical tract *Kifāyat al-muhtadī fī ma'rifat al-Mahdī*, written to counter Majlisi's treatise, Mir Lawhi writes:

> Those who claim to possess knowledge and would write books and treatises in order to become famous in the eyes of the people should refrain from citing contradictory narrations, or should at least try to clear up the contradictions; they should also refrain from quoting weak Traditions with obscure and mysterious contents, which they use merely in order to further own interests.[83]

Mir Lawhi says that the appearance of Majlisi's treatise caused a considerable furore among the scholars of the day, and that he felt obliged to write a treatise in reply in order to 'put Majlisi straight'.[84] He says that:

> Our kings are the sons of lords *(khwāja-zāda)* and masters. There is no need for anyone (to prove this) by resorting to such narrations and interpreting in them in such a manner. If (these Traditions) fall into

the hands of our enemies, the Shi'ite *'ulamā* will become notorious in the eyes of the masses as men of duplicity and unrighteousness.[85]

The Traditions quoted by Majlisi in his treatise are, according to Mir Lawhi, mostly weak (*da'īf*) and without basis.[86] Majlisi comes under fire for attributing narrations to scholars erroneously and for referring Traditions to sources in which no such Traditions appear.[87] He is also taken to task by Mir Lawhi for failing to see the glaring contradictions in the contents of the Traditions. One, for instance, narrated on the authority of Ja'far al-Sadiq, prohibits anyone from determining or stating a time or date for the awaited return of the Imam or, for that matter, any other hidden leader, while another is used by Majlisi to adduce, through the *abjad* system, the coming of the Abbasids as a prelude to the rise of the Hidden Imam.[88] Historically and geographically, too, Majlisi is at fault in Mir Lawhi's opinion: the Safavids rose not from the east or from Gilan but from the west, from Azarbaijan and Tabriz; Genghis Khan did not conquer Multan, and so on.[89]

Mir Lawhi's objections to Majlisi on academic grounds are but the tip of an iceberg of personal animosity felt by him towards both Muhammad Baqir and Muhammad Taqi Majlisi. Mir Lawhi's quite reasonable indignation over the dereliction of scholarly duty on Majlisi's part to eschew the spurious is weakened somewhat by this sub-text of personal ill-will, in much the same way that Qatifi's attacks on Karaki were apparently not so much the protestation of an indignant scholar as the carping of a bitter rival. Thus to Mir Lawhi, Muhammad Baqir Majlisi becomes 'that mentally deranged infidel', while Muhammad Taqi is demonised as 'the satanic shaykh.'[90]

However, to find a detractor of Majlisi is not necessarily to find a detractor of externalism or, more specifically, of the wholehearted endorsement of the Safavid dynasty that permeates Majlisi's writings. The externalists may have attacked each other mercilessly over the means, but as far as the end was concerned they were of one mind: the *fuqahā* were the representatives of the Hidden Imam and their function was to govern not the worldly but the religious life of man. By the time Majlisi compiled the *Bihār*, the position of the *faqīh* as representative of the Imam had been largely worked out, although obviously scholars would go on to proffer further theories and make theoretical modifications as various circumstances dictated.

Majlisi, although not a *faqīh* in the strict sense of the word, did however add a new element to the debate over the position and function of the Twelver Shi'ite *'ulamā* in general and the *faqīh* in particular. In section 36 of volume XIII, he presents a decree (*tawqī'*) that is claimed to have been issued by the Hidden Imam during the 'lesser' occultation:

> As for the events which occur (al-hawādith al-wāqi'a), refer to the
> narrators (ruwāt) of our Traditions (ahādīth) who are my proof to
> you, while I am the proof of God to them.[91]

The Hidden Imam's decree was received by one Ishaq b. Ya'qub in reply to his question concerning matters of jurisprudence, such as whether fermented barley water is permissible (halāl) to drink or not. According to the version of the tawqī' preserved by Shaykh Tusi in his Kitāb al-ghayba, the last part of the sentence reads: '...and I am the proof of God to you all ('alaykum)',[92] whereas Majlisi's reads '...and I am the proof of God to them (i.e. the narrators).' Whether Majlisi tampered with the tawqī' himself is open to question. The important point here is that according to his reading the narrators alone would become directly answerable to the Imam and not all the Twelver Shi'ite faithful as individuals: a hierarchy is thus formulated in which the commonalty follow the rulings of the narrators (i.e. the externalist fuqahā), who in turn are answerable to the Imam, who in turn stands as intercessor between them and God. Ali Dawani, the translator of volume XIII into Persian, comments that the tawqī' shows that during the 'greater' occultation the word 'ruwāt denotes the fuqahā, the mujtahids and the marāji' al-taqlīd of the Twelver Shi'ites'.[93]

A brief summary, then, of the concept of intizār and its socio-political and religious implications according both to the Traditions presented in volume XIII and to their presenter, Muhammad Baqir Majlisi, is as follows:

The period of time from the disappearance of the Mahdi in 329/941 until his reappearance prior to the end of time is known as the 'greater' occultation (al-ghaybat al-kubrā) and is a time of great trial and tribulation for the Twelver Shi'ites. The test (imtihān) which they will undergo will sift out the real believers in the existence of the Hidden Imam from the unbelievers. During this period they are advised to cling steadfastly to their belief in the tenets of Twelve Shi'ism and to endeavour to gain knowledge (ma'rifa) of their Imam. The concept of 'ilm prescribed by the Koran is taken by the Twelver fuqahā to signify knowledge of the commands of God (ahkām) and knowledge of the channels through which those commands are conveyed, i.e. the Imams of the ahl al-bayt. The earthly channel through which this knowledge is conveyed is the faqīh, muhaddith or mujtahid: adherence to these individuals enables the believer to gain spiritual access to the Imam, who in turn provides the means whereby one is able to have recourse to God. Belief consists not in knowledge of self, knowledge of God or in spiritual striving (*jihād al-nafs*) but in attention to the minutiae of the external, secondary acts of religion (*furū' al-dīn*), and in passive expectation (*intizār*) of the Imam's return.

The concept of *intizār* also serves to cushion the blows of tyranny and oppression that rain down on the heads of the Twelver Shi'ites from every leader and government until the return of the Imam, for during his absence all earthly governments are illegitimate, and paying allegiance to them is tantamount to *shirk* or associationism. Whatever abjection a Twelver Shi'ite faces as a result of the tyranny of the usurpers, he must accept with resignation and consider it part of the test. He must withdraw as far as possible from social and political interaction with others; on no account must he oppose the tyrant or try to rise up in rebellion. The tyranny of kings is a divine secret, and it is God and not man who decides when tyranny shall be lifted from the heads of the Shi'ites. The Shi'ites must stay in their homes, adhere to the rites and rituals of their creed, and pray that God may expedite the return of the Imam.

The return of the Twelve Imams: the doctrine of *raj'a*

Just as the martyrdom of Husayn b. Ali at Karbala serves as an emblem of the oppression under which all Twelver Shi'ites, like the 12 Imams before them, are destined to exist, the doctrine of Mahdism and the return of the Imam symbolizes the eventual victory of justice over tyranny, of relief after hardship and sorrow. In its simplest form, the return of the hidden Imam is merely a particular crystallization of the belief, held by adherents of all major religions, in the primacy of good over evil, represented by an earthly persona who will restore the rule of God upon earth. However, the figure of the Mahdi in the Twelver Shi'ite Traditions is paradigmatic in another sense, for the term *al-mahdī* signifies not only a single leader who will return to mete justice to all, but also all of the other Imams, each one of which will make a reappearance on earth at the end of time.

What can be understood from volume XIII of the *Bihār* is that the reappearance or *raj'a* of the other eleven Imams fulfils ostensibly the same purpose as that of the twelfth Imam, namely the implementation of justice and the reintroduction of the Islamic laws or *sharī'a* in their originally intended form. Yet there is a caveat. For it is readily discernible from the wording and tenor of the text that the underlying emphasis of the *raj'a* of the 12 Imams lies not upon the principle of universal justice *per se* but upon the personal fate of the 12 Imams themselves – and, by extension, that of the

Twelver Shi'ite faithful – and their enemies. If the doctrine of Mahdism in general serves to deflect attention from the notion of divine justice and personal salvation that is to obtain following the resurrection (*ma'ād*), then the uniquely Twelver Shi'ite doctrine of *raj'a* shifts the attention even further away from the idea of universal peace and justice that are to accrue from the revival of pristine Islam, and focuses, instead, directly upon the personae of the Imams themselves. While the relief from oppression that will supposedly be enjoyed by all believers as a result of the *raj'a* of the Imams is presented as the most obvious corollary of their return, it is the vengeance which they will seek from their long dead but now apparently resuscitated opponents that overshadows all other considerations and appears to be, in the final analysis, the *raison d'être* of their dramatic reappearance from the grave. In the concept of *raj'a* the tragedy of the Imams reaches full circle, and the imamocentric internalism of the Twelver Shi'ites has its finest hour.

The historical development of the doctrine of *raj'a*

The notion of a return to earth of certain believers prior to the resurrection was one held in connection with Muhammad himself, particularly in the incident in which Umar expressed the belief that the Prophet would return from the grave after forty days.[94]

Belief in *raj'a* seems to have been prevalent in Shi'ite circles from quite early on, with the main element being the return of the Imams and their offspring, who had not died but would reappear on earth to establish the rule of justice and equity. It was believed, for example, that Muhammad b. al-Hanafiyya had not died but would return to earth after a long concealment. It was from this belief that the Kaysanite sect was formed.[95] Later, in different Shi'ite sects, the notion of *raj'a* was to be found in connection with almost every Shi'ite Imam. The Imams were believed to be in concealment and not dead, as in the case of the Waqifiyya, who believed that the 7th Imam, Musa al-Kazim, would one day re-emerge from occultation and assume the office of Imam, and another group who believed the same about the 11th Imam, Hasan al-'Askari.[96]

Traditions on the subject of *raj'a* appear in the very earliest collections and may be seen as having developed hand in hand with the doctrine of the rise of the Mahdi. As such, the concept of *raj'a* – which again, it must be stressed, has no explicit Koranic basis – as the return to earth of a number of believers, headed by the Imams, grew out of the intense personal anguish felt by the followers of the Imāms when they realised that their leaders were, one by one, leaving the world without ever having fulfilled their true roles as leaders of the Islamic *umma*.

As in the case of the Mahdi, the *raj'a* of the Imāms would seem to be an inevitable corollary of the despair that the Shi'ite minorities must have felt during the lifetime of the Imāms as a result of blows such as the 'usurpation' of Ali's rights to the Caliphate, the martyrdom of Husayn at Karbala, and the hardship suffered by the other Imāms, several of whom were imprisoned and all of whom were supposedly murdered. The charisma of these figures, whose right to lead the *umma* was, their followers believed, God-given, was clearly such that it was unthinkable to the ordinary Shi'ite believer that God would allow injustice - injustice to the Imāms, that is - to continue indefinitely, and the world to end without the Imāms ever having attained their rightful position. Umar's unwillingness to believe that Muhammad had actually died has already been noted; given the intense devotion of the early Shi'ites to their Imāms – devotion which often bordered on the heretical, and shades of which are still apparent in the *Bihār* – it is not difficult to see why the idea of *raj'a* was able to gain currency. Like the reappearance of the Mahdi, the *raj'a* of the Imāms undoubtedly helped the Shi'ites to hold up under unbearable situations and to hope for a better future and a just world in which the rights of Ali would finally be fulfilled.

Although they differ on the particulars of the *raj'a*, the leading *muhaddithūn* and *mutakallimūn* of early Twelver Shi'ism are all in agreement on the general concept of the return of the Imāms. Shaykh Saduq in his *I'tiqādāt* cites several Koranic verses to support the notion, one of them being Jesus's ability to raise the dead, who presumably lived on earth once more, just as the Imāms, their followers and opponents will at the end of time.[97] The 'sleepers in the cave' (*ashāb al-kahf*), who slept for some three hundred and nine years before being resuscitated, are also cited. Saduq then quotes the Prophet as saying that whatever befalls his community in the future will mirror past events. If it is true that history repeats itself, asserts Saduq, then *raj'a*, which occurred in the past, must also occur again in the future.[98]

Shaykh Mufid in his hagiography of the Imāms, *al-Irshād*, writes that one of the 'signs of the last days' (*'alāmāt*) will be the return to earth of the dead from their graves. Alive once more, they will meet and talk with one another and pay each other visits. Commenting on Ja'far al-Sadiq's narration which holds that, 'Whosoever disbelieves in temporary marriage (*mut'a*) or the return of the dead (*raj'a*) before the Resurrection is not of us', Mufid asserts that the Imām was affirming belief in these two tenets as peculiar to the followers of the *ahl al-bayt* and the Shi'ites alone. Mufid also quotes Sharif Murtada, who is reported to have said that *raj'a* denotes the return of an unspecified number of Twelver Shi'ite faithful who will aid the Mahdi in his cosmic undertakings.[99]

The doctrine of *raj'a* in the *Bihār al-anwār*

Majlisi's collection of Traditions concerning *raj'a* is divided into two sections: one, under the heading of *raj'a*, which presents approximately 126 Traditions covering general aspects of the doctrine; and another, which consists of a single Tradition, narrated supposedly on the authority of Ja'far al-Sadiq by his companion Mufaddal b. Umar. This latter Tradition extends to almost forty pages, and is easily the longest Tradition in the whole collection.

The general Traditions on *raj'a*

The general Traditions on *raj'a* consist of Koranic verses, interpreted in such a way as to allude to the return of the Hidden Imam and the other Imams; prayers which are to be recited by the Twelver Shi'ite faithful and which call upon God to bring back the petitioner during the *raj'a* as one of the Imams' followers; and straightforward Traditions simply affirming the necessity and certainty of *raj'a* in principle. The overall picture one receives from these Traditions, drawn from various sources, is a somewhat confusing one; as usual, Majlisi does not consider it necessary to explain the many contradictions that exist in the body of the narratives. One Tradition, attributed to the 5th Imam, calls upon the Shi'ite faithful to practice *taqiyya* and to deny belief in *raj'a* if asked about the subject. This is clearly a throwback to the time of the Imams themselves when it was felt no doubt that the return of the Mahdi and the other eleven Imams was not far off.[100]

Several Traditions assert that Husayn b. Ali will be the first to emerge from the grave.[101] This will happen, according to one Tradition, after the appearance of the Mahdi. He will be accompanied by the same 72 people who perished alongside him at Karbala. The Mahdi will give a ring – presumably the signet ring of kingship – to Husayn. The Mahdi will then die and Husayn will wash, enshroud and bury him.[102] Felicity at that time will belong to Husayn and his descendants, and they will take revenge on their murderers and oppressors.[103] Husayn will be aided chiefly by the angels, who arrived in Karbala too late to help him in his first earthly incarnation and who have, since that day, been weeping over his martyrdom.[104] Another Tradition dispenses with the usual figure of 72 as the number of Husayn's helpers and states that during the *raj'a* he will have 75,000 men at arms.[105]

Ali will return at the same time or shortly afterwards. He will carry a flag and be accompanied by 30,000 men from Kufa with the express purpose of seeking revenge from Mu'awiya and all their other enemies. 70,000 other Shi'ites will also rally around Ali. The armies of Ali and Mu'awiya will meet once more in an apparent reconstruction of the battle of Siffin. This time, however, Mu'awiya's army will be slaughtered to the very last man. On the day of judgement, Ali's opponents will be placed alongside Pharaoh and his followers and subjected to the worst possible torture. Then Ali and the Prophet will return to earth and the Prophet will become sultan of the whole world, and the Imams his commanders. The messengership of Muhammad will be open and manifest to all: he will not be forced to hide as he first did in Mecca. God will give the dominion of the whole of the cosmos, from the day of its creation to the day of resurrection, to the Prophet.[106]

Emphasis on revenge, as in the above narrative, stands out in most of Majlisi's Traditions on the *raj'a*. One, attributed to Imam Rida, calls upon people to tolerate patiently the oppressive rulers who govern them and await a day when the Mahdi will come to 'drag the followers of falsehood (*ahl al-bātil*) from their graves' in order to seek revenge.[107] Furthermore, God has promised Ali in the Koran that he will be avenged in this world - presumably during the *raj'a* - as well as in the hereafter.[108] During the *raj'a*, whoever has oppressed the family of Muhammad will be ready to give the whole world, if they only but possessed it, to escape the dire punishments that await them.[109] The *nawāsib* or Sunni extremists will undergo the worst punishments: at the time of the *raj'a* they will be eating filth (*najāsa*).[110]

According to another Tradition, the Imams will come back to life in this world to exact retribution (*qisās*); naturally this means that their enemies will also be returned to life. After taking revenge, the Imams will live for thirty months and then will all die together on the same night. Having avenged themselves their hearts will be at peace and healed. Their enemies will, on the other hand, suffer the most painful torments of hell.[111]

It is unclear whether the above Tradition refers to the Imams or to other Shi'ites, for the period of thirty months is totally at odds with the other narratives. Apart from the narration already mentioned which specifies a long rule by Husayn during the *raj'a*, another Tradition states that while the Mahdi will rule for only 19 years, one member of the Prophet's household will reign for 309 years, the same length of time as that spent by the 'sleepers in the cave' (*ahl al-kahf*).[112] Another Tradition claims that the Prophet will return to earth and reign for 50,000 years, while the reign of Ali will last 44,000 years.[113]

The *raj'a* Traditions are also in disagreement over exactly who will return. One Tradition has it that when the Mahdi rises up, God will revive a group of Shi'ites with their swords and lead them to him.[114] Another claims that anyone who believes (in the *ahl al-bayt*) but who dies before the *raj'a* will reside with the Imams in heaven until the return of the Mahdi, at which point God will revive them and dispatch them to the Mahdi's side.[115] Another narration has it that all of the prophets from the past, together with all of the Imams, will return from the grave to help Ali: he will rule the world and the true meaning of the title *amīr al-mu'minīn* will be realised.

According to another Tradition, any believer who has been slain will return to die a natural death, whilst any believer who has died a natural death will be returned in order to be slain, thus receiving the mantle of martyrdom.[116] Elsewhere it is stated that only the 'pure believers' (*mu'min khālis*) and absolute polytheists (*mushrik mahd*) will reappear.[117] A saying attributed to Ja'far al-Sadiq reveals that the 'path of God (*sabīl Allāh*) mentioned in the Koran refers in fact to 'the way of Ali and his offspring'. Whoever dies in the way of Ali and in devotion to him will, if his death was a natural one, be returned in order to be martyred; if his death was through martyrdom he will be returned to meet a natural end.[118]

Many Koranic verses are adduced to prove the doctrine of *raj'a*; the ability of either the Imams or the later compilers of Traditions to read into almost any verse of the Koran signs which refer directly to the Imams strengthens the tendency of the Twelver Shi'ite *fuqahā* to externalise the fundamentals of belief and reduce them by giving them an overtly imamocentric flavour. The concept of resurrection is no exception, and thus we see verses which are clear references to the resurrection of man in the hereafter, and interpreted as thus by orthodox exegetes, portrayed as portents of the *raj'a* of the Imams:

- 50:41-2 – "And listen for the Day when the Caller will call out from a place quite near, the Day when they will hear a mighty Blast in very truth: that will be the Day of Resurrection." These verses are said by Majlisi to be more in line with *raj'a* than with the resurrection since the revenge of the prophets and the Imams must take place in this world.[119]

- Verse 43:4 – "And verily the hereafter will be better for thee than the present." The 'hereafter' mentioned in this verse is said to refer to the *raj'a* since the *raj'a* will be better for the Prophet than his previous earthly existence.[120]

- Verse 10:45 – "One day He will gather them together: it will be as if they had tarried but an hour of a day: they will recognise each other: assuredly those will be the lost who denied the meeting with God and refused to receive true guidance." Ja'far al-Sadiq is reported to have said that this verse concerns the *raj'a* and not, as the Sunnis claim, the resurrection and the hereafter.[121]

- Verse 79:6 – "One Day everything that can be in commotion will be in violent commotion." The word 'commotion' (*rājifa*) is said to refer to Ali, who will rise from the grave shaking the dust from his hair and hastening to the side of Husayn, who will have assembled 75,000 men.[122]

- Verses 80:17-23 – "Woe to man! What hath made him reject God? From what stuff hath He created him? From a sperm drop He hath created him, and then mouldeth him in due proportions; then doth He make his path smooth for him; then He causeth him to die, and putteth him in his grave, then, when it is His Will, He will raise him up again. By no means hath he fulfilled what God commanded him". These verses, understood by orthodox exegetes to describe man's creation, life, death and resurrection, are interpreted in the *Bihār* as having been revealed concerning Ali, who was unable to carry out his duties during his first life and who will be brought back once more during the *raj'a* to perform them as God instructed him.[123]

- Verse 36:52 – "They will say: 'Ah! Woe unto us! Who hath raised us up from our beds of repose?' a voice will say: 'This is what God Most Gracious had promised, and true was the word of the apostles!'" This too is offered in the *Bihār* as proof of the *raj'a*, when the Mahdi will come and drag the followers of falsehood from their graves in order to exact revenge from them.[124]

Other verses, not concerned specifically with the resurrection or the hereafter, are also adduced as references to the return to earth of the Imams. Thus the 'signs' (*āyāt*) of God, usually held to signify the verses of the

Koran and the cosmos itself, are interpreted as the Imams who will return at the end of time;[125] 'those who may turn back (*yarji'ūn*)', which in verse 43:28 refers to the descendants and followers of Abraham, are interpreted as as the Imams who will return (*yarji'ūn*) to earth;[126] one day in the hereafter, which will be like 50,000 earth years, is said to be the length of time the Prophet will reign during the *raj'a*; the 'certainty of mind' (*'ilm al-yaqīn*) which the unbelievers will wish they had had during this life is said to concern the enmity between the Imams and their enemies, and so on.

A substantial number of verses that deal unambiguously with the question of the resurrection and the hereafter are offered in the *Bihār* as proof of the *raj'a*. The third fundamental of belief, namely belief in the resurrection and the day of judgement, becomes obscured by the doctrine of *raj'a* to such an extent that the reader is left with the impression that it is not the personal and individual fate and outcome of man that is at the core of the Koranic teachings on the afterlife but, rather, the return and victory of the Imams.

This tendency to see the Koran as a vehicle for imamocentric internalism is summed up best by the words of a Tradition narrated on the authority of Ja'far al-Sadiq and reported by Majlisi, who makes no comment on it:

> The Koran is in four parts: one quarter was revealed concerning the Imams; one quarter was revealed concerning their enemies; one quarter was revealed concerning ordinances and commands; and one quarter was revealed concerning that which is forbidden and that which is lawful.[127]

In this Tradition is encapsulated the underlying religious ethos of Twelver Shi'ism as portrayed by the Safavid *fuqahā*: an Islam whose central core of revelation embraces both imamocentric externalism (namely the half of the Koran which deals with *ahkām* as expounded by the Imams), and imamocentric internalism (namely the other half of the Koran which centres on the personae of the Imams themselves).

The rest of the general Traditions on *raj'a* comprise supererogatory prayers (*du'ā*) which are to be recited by those who believe in the *raj'a* and, in the case of certain invocations, who wish to be returned to earth alongside the Mahdi and the other Imams. The most renowned of them, the *Du'ā-i 'ahd*, ends with an entreaty to the Mahdi to hurry back to earth. Whoever recites the prayer for forty mornings in succession will be raised up with the Mahdi and will help him during the *raj'a*.[128]

The curious Tradition of Mufaddal b. Umar

The 'Tradition of Mufaddal,' as it is known, is the longest one in the *Bihār* and arguably the most contentious and controversial. Dealing with the particulars of the *zuhūr* of Mahdi and the subsequent *raj'a* of the Imams, it has a virulently anti-Sunni theme and serves as a stark and chilling symbol of the sense of oppression and thirst for revenge that characterised the early Twelvers and also the majority of the Twelver Shi'ite *fuqahā* of the Safavid era. Mufaddal was known to have held extremist views before his long association with Imams Ja'far al-Sadiq and Musa al-Kazim.[129] That Ja'far al-Sadiq could have held the kind of rabidly anti-Sunni view reflected in this Tradition is open to serious question, especially when one considers that he named two of his own offspring after Abu Bakr and Umar, the two figures whom the Tradition vilifies so blatantly. Furthermore, aspects of the Tradition which run at total odds with the most basic Koranic precepts are unlikely to have come from the mouth of al-Sadiq, whose authority as an interpreter of the Koran and a master of the art of exposition of *tawhīd* or Divine unity is acknowledged by Sunnis and Shi'ites alike. A detailed summary of the Tradition is as follows:

Mufaddal once asked the Imam Ja'far al-Sadiq about the time of the Mahdi's reappearance. The Imam replied by saying that this knowledge is the 'knowledge of the Hour', which only God possesses.[130] Anyone who predicts a time for the Mahdi's rise is committing shirk by associating his knowledge with that of God.[131] No speculation about the birth, disappearance, occultation or return of the Hidden Imam is allowed, all of this being tantamount to distrust in the Decree and Determining (*qadā wa qadar*) of God.

When the Mahdi finally does reappear he will put an end to all schisms and sectarian discord: all religions will become one. That religion will be Islam, just as the religion of Abraham and the other prophets was Islam.[132]

When the Mahdi first appears, no-one will see him. During his occultation, he will have lived in the company of angels and believers from among the *jinn*, but he will rise alone. He will reappear in Mecca, wearing the clothes of the Prophet and a yellow turban and patched sandals. He will be carrying the Prophet's staff and shepherding a thin goat. He will approach the *ka'ba* in this manner and no-one will recognise him. He will enter the *ka'ba* and stay there as night falls. When it is dark, the angels Gabriel and Michael and the other celestial groups will descend to him. Gabriel will put himself at the Mahdi's disposal. The Mahdi will touch Gabriel's cheek with his hand and thank God that the Divine promise concerning his return was

223

true. He will then stand between the *rukn* and *maqām* and shout: "O nobles and those who are close to me! O you who were preserved on earth by God in order to come to my aid! Come forward and obey me!" These helpers will then flock to him from east and west, some from their place of worship and others from their beds, having heard the Mahdi's call. Pillars of light will then appear in the sky so that everyone on earth will see them. This light will send the believers into raptures, although at this point they will still be unaware of the Mahdi's return. By morning, all (of these believers) will be assembled with the Mahdi: there will be 313 of them, the same number as that of the Prophet's soldiers at the battle of Badr. At this point, Husayn b. Ali will also return, along with 12,000 Shi'ites.

Any pledge of allegiance to any ruler before the return of the Mahdi is synonymous with disbelief (*kufr*) and hypocrisy. God will curse anyone who pays such allegiance, which is accepted only by the Mahdi himself. The Mahdi will sit with his back to the wall of the *ka'ba*, light emanating from his hands, and receive allegiance. Gabriel will be the first to kiss his hand, followed by the angels and the *jinn*. The inhabitants of Mecca will ask what is happening but will still not recognise the Mahdi or those who are with him.

Then, when the sun has risen, a voice will be heard calling out from the east. It will be heard by all men on earth. In perfect Arabic it will cry, "O people of earth! This is the Mahdi, from the family of Muhammad," and the voice will call out the names of the Prophet and the other eleven Imams. The caller will invite the people to pay allegiance to the Mahdi so that they may find true salvation should they desist they will perish. All of the angels and *jinn* will kiss his hand and promise to obey him. All of the people on earth will have heard and will discuss the event with one another.

As the sun begins to set, someone will call out from the west, "O people of earth! Your lord, 'Uthman b. al-Anbatha, the Ummayad, has risen in Palestine. Go to him and pledge allegiance, so that you may be saved." All of those who have sworn allegiance to the Mahdi will refute the call and say, "We have heard but will not obey." Those who have doubts about the Mahdi will be led astray. Then the Mahdi will lean against the *ka'ba* and say: "Whoever wishes to see Adam and Seth, know that I am they; whoever wishes to see Noah and Shem, know that I am they; whoever wishes to see Abraham and Ishmael, know that I am they; whoever wishes to see Muhammad and Ali, know that I am they ... I am Hasan and Husayn ... I am all of the Pure Imams. Accept my call and come to me so that I may inform you about anything you wish. Anyone who has read the holy scriptures and divine scrolls will hear them from my lips." He will then read all the divine scriptures in their original form, before they were distorted.

The Mahdi will then appoint a deputy to rule over Mecca, while he himself moves on to Medina. Before he leaves he will demolish the *ka'ba* and rebuild it as it was during the time of Adam. He will also rebuild the sacred mosque (*masjid al-harām*). All traces of former oppression in the form of mosques and palaces will be destroyed.

The Mahdi's deputy in Mecca will be slaughtered by the inhabitants of the city. The Mahdi will despatch an army of *jinn* and instruct them to kill everyone there save for the true believers. Only one out of a thousand people will remain.

The Mahdi will take up residence in Kufa, where all believers will then be assembled. All of the people of the world will wish that they could reside there, so hallowed will be its soil. Kufa will grow so large that its outskirts will envelop Karbala. Karbala at that time will be the gathering place for angels and believers. It will be so elevated in God's esteem that any believer who stands in Karbala and asks God for provisions will be provided with a thousand times more than the whole world. All of the towns and cities once vied with each other for the title of best place on earth; for example, the *ka'ba* used to think that it was better than Karbala, but God sent a revelation telling the *ka'ba* to keep quiet, saying that Karbala, since it housed the shrine of Imam Husayn, was the best place one earth. It was from there that the Prophet made his ascension (*mi'rāj*) and it is there that there will always be blessings and goodness, until the rise of the Imam.

In Medina, the position of the Mahdi will be so exalted that the believers will rejoice and the unbelievers will moan with dismay. The Mahdi will approach the grave of the Prophet. "Is this my ancestor's grave?" he will ask. The people will say that it is. "And who are those who are buried alongside him?" the Mahdi will ask. The people will reply that two of the Prophet's companions (Abu Bakr and Umar) are interred adjoining the Prophet's shrine. "Who are they?" the Mahdi will ask. "And how is it that from among all people these two are buried here?" The people will say, "O Mahdi, they were the Caliphs and fathers-in-law of the Prophet."

The Mahdi will then give orders for the grave to be opened and Abu Bakr and Umar to be exhumed. The people will obey. When the bodies of Abu Bakr and Umar are taken out of the grave it becomes clear that their flesh has remained uncorrupted by centuries of death; they are still as fresh as the day they died. The Mahdi will ask, "Does anyone know these men?", to which the people will reply, "Yes, we know them by their attributes; they were boon companions of the Prophet." The Mahdi will ask, "Do any of you have doubts concerning these two men?" The people will say that they do not. Then the Mahdi will rebury the corpses.

Three days later, the Mahdi will order the bodies of Abu Bakr and Umar to be exhumed once more. Again the corpses are seen to be fresh and untainted by decay. The devotees of Abu Bakr and Umar will rejoice, for they will see this as a sign of the Caliphs' righteousness. "We are proud of our devotion to these two men," they will say. Then one of the Mahdi's followers will call out: "All those who love these two companions, stand to one side!" The people will split into two groups. The Mahdi will then command the group which professes devotion to Abu Bakr and Umar to recant and express their hatred for them. This group will say, "O Mahdi! Before we knew what you felt about these two Caliphs we did not hate them. And now, now that we see (through the miracle of their bodies being preserved) that they have such an exalted position in God's sight, how can we hate them?"

The Mahdi will then, by God's leave, command a swirling black wind to descend on the devotees of Abu Bakr and Umar and destroy them. Then he will command his men to bring the bodies of the two companions down from the tree on which they have been hanging according to his previous orders. By God's leave he will bring Abu Bakr and Umar back to life and then give orders for everyone to assemble.

The Mahdi will then give the people a detailed account of the two companions' lives and deeds. He will give an account of the slaying of Abel by Cain; the trial of Abraham by fire; the incarceration of Joseph in the well; the punishment of Jonah in the belly of the whale; the murder of Yahya; the crucifixion of Jesus; the torture of Jirjis (St. George) and Daniel; the wounds of Salman al-Farsi; the incident in which the door of the house of Ali was burned by an angry mob, injuring Fatima and causing her to miscarry; the poisoning of Imam Hasan; the martyrdom of Husayn and his followers and children. All of these incidents will be blamed by the Mahdi on Abu Bakr and Umar. All of the blood spilled unlawfully from the beginning of time, all rapes of innocent women, all treachery and acts of vice, all sins and oppression and injustice, all acts of wrongdoing from the time of Adam until the rise of the Mahdi – all of these will be blamed on Abu Bakr and Umar. The case against them will be proven, and they will confess to their crimes.

At this point the Mahdi will invite anyone present who has been wronged by Abu Bakr and Umar to come forward and exact retribution. This will take place. The two companions will be strung up once more from the branch of a tree. The Mahdi will then command a fire to rise up out of the ground. The fire will consume the tree and the companions along with it. The Mahdi will command the wind to scatter the ashes of Abu Bakr and Umar over the sea.

But this will not be the end of their torture, for on the day of resurrection all believers will assemble with the 'Fourteen' (Muhammad, Ali, Fatima and the other eleven Imams) to take further revenge from the two companions. They will be put to death and revived a thousand times a day and their tortures will never cease.

The Mahdi will then proceed to Baghdad, which will be the most accursed city on God's earth. Corruption and insurrection will destroy the city and it will be deserted. Woe to Baghdad and its people! All of the tortures visited on men since the day of creation will descend on Baghdad. Woe to anyone living there! The people of Baghdad will be the most corrupt on earth: they will have known such opulence and ease that they will imagine it is heaven on earth. Lies, vice, depravity, drunkenness, adultery and murder will be such that God will destroy the city by the means of its own wrongdoing. He will unleash armies on it from all directions and Baghdad will be flattened without a trace.

At this point a Hasanid *sayyid* will rise in Daylam and invite people to the side of the Mahdi. Men of strong faith will rise from Talighan on swift horses. They will be equipped with weapons and will cut a swathe through (Persia), killing every tyrant that tries to stop them, until they reach Kufa where they will take up residence.

The Hasanid *sayyid* will meet the Mahdi and he and his men will pledge allegiance. Only the Zaydites from among the people will refuse to kiss the Mahdi's hand. The Zaydites will reject the return of the Mahdi as sorcery. The Mahdi will advise them to think again, but they will refuse and finally he will be forced to slay them.

The Mahdi will then prepare to fight the Sufyani in Damascus: the latter will be captured and beheaded on a rock. Husayn b. Ali, with 12,000 trusted companions and 72 of his fellow martyrs from Karbala will then appear. This will be a 'return of light' (*raj'at nūriyya*). Ali will reappear and erect a tent, one pole of which will be in Najaf, one in Medina, one in Mecca and one on the hill of Safa, near Mecca. The heavens and the earth will be illuminated and the secrets of all men revealed. Nursing mothers will flee in terror from their offspring. The Prophet and his companions and all of those who believed in his prophethood will return to earth. Also, all of those who refused to believe in him and who opposed him will be returned so that vengeance may be extracted from them.

Then all of the Imams will reappear and line up in front of the Prophet in order to complain of the oppression they have suffered in their previous earthly existence. "We have been accused, oppressed, cursed, threatened, imprisoned and poisoned," they will say. The Prophet will weep bitterly and say, "O my children! I have indeed suffered more than you."

One by one the Imams will step forward to recount their tragedies. Fatima will be the first to plead for justice. She will vilify Abu Bakr and Umar on account of their wrongful appropriation of her land at Fadak, their usurpation of the Caliphate, and their forced entry into Ali's house. Then Ali will step forward and make similar complaints, and this will continue until all of the Imams have pleaded for justice and asked for revenge for all of the oppression and tortures they received from their opponents during their first lives. Finally, the Mahdi will step forward to complain about all those who disbelieved in his return.

Having heard all of their pleas for justice and revenge, the Prophet will turn to the Imams and say, "I thank God that He kept His promise to us and made us inheritors of the earth. We can live in any part of Heaven that we choose. How good is the reward of those who work righteous deeds! God's help and victory are at hand." He will then read the Koranic verse which describes this victory, a victory which comes to wash away all sins.

At this point Mufaddal asks Ja'far al-Sadiq what sins the Prophet could possibly have had. Ja'far al-Sadiq answers that the Prophet once asked God to make him responsible for all of the sins of the *shī'a* of Ali. God granted this request, placed all of the burdens of the sins of the *shī'a* on his shoulders, and then forgave him. But, said Sadiq, this must not be told to all Shi'ites in case some of them become lax in their actions and thus deprive themselves of the Prophet's intercession and of God's mercy.

The Mahdi will then return to Kufa where golden locusts will rain from the sky. He will then destroy the mosque erected by Yazid after the martyrdom of Husayn at Karbala. He will also destroy all other mosques built by tyrants. [End of Tradition].[133]

To none of the contents of the above Tradition has Majlisi any objection, and the only criticism that he makes is directed at Mufaddal's scrambling of historical facts concerning the identity of the founder of Samarra, the Mahdi's birthplace. The rest he accepts without question.

As for the attribution of all sins to the two companions, Abu Bakr and Umar, Majlisi staunchly defends the Tradition. The reason, he says, is quite clear: Abu Bakr and Umar deprived Ali of his rights (i.e. to the Caliphate) and this resulted in all of the other Imams being deprived of their rightful positions. Consequently, tyrannical caliphs came to power, who will rule until the rise of the Mahdi. This tyranny is the source of, and reason, for the infidelity of all infidels, the vice of all sinners, and the going astray of all who have gone astray. If the Imam (i.e. Ali) had become Caliph he would have been able to prevent unbelief and sin and going astray. The reason he was unable to do so during his own short caliphate was that Abu Bakr and Umar had already laid the foundations of tyranny and oppression, and these had taken root in the hearts of the people. The sins of all men are attributable to Abu Bakr and Umar because these two men did not object to the evil deeds of men like themselves. If they had objected to evil, they themselves would not have committed it. And if anyone does not object to evil deeds it is as though he himself has committed them.[134] Majlisi then goes on to say that it is not unreasonable to suppose that the impure spirits of Abu Bakr and Umar may actually participate in the evil deeds of ordinary men, just as the pure spirits of the Imams are present in the good deeds of the prophets.[135]

It is clear that Majlisi's attribution of all sins to the first two Caliphs in the 'Tradition of Mufaddal' is in total contradiction with the Koranic concept of divine justice as presented in many of its verses. Man's misfortunes – earthly or otherwise – are held by the Koran to be the result of his own misdeeds, and not the works of others.[136] Man will be judged by his own record, and not by the record of his fellow human beings.[137] Most explicit and unambiguous is the Koranic statement on personal responsibility: 'Every soul draws the meed of its acts on none but itself: no bearer of burdens can bear the burden of another.'[138]

As in the case of so many other Traditions narrated in the *Bihar*, Majlisi appears not to notice the glaring contradictions and flagrant violations of Koranic teaching in the narratives; if he does notice them then he conveniently overlooks them. To be fair, it is true that a great number of Traditions, be they authentic or spurious, may have passed into the *Bihar* without his inspection, collected and edited by his students. It is only when he himself actually comments on a particular Tradition that his own view and position come under the spotlight, as in the case of the Tradition in question.

However, in his enthusiasm to confirm the demonisation of Abu Bakr and Umar, Majlisi seems to have genuinely overlooked another highly pertinent comment reputedly made by al-Sadiq, namely that any allegiance paid to a ruler before the advent of the Mahdi is tantamount to *kufr* or unbelief. In his comments on the 'Tradition of Mufaddal', Majlisi himself demurs that because of the 'sins' of the first two Caliphs, all rulers from that day forward until the coming of the Mahdi were bound to be despotic. The notion of unbroken tyranny until the end of time, while dovetailing neatly with the Twelver Shi'ite ethos of suffering and martyrdom, sits uneasily alongside Majlisi's own wholehearted acceptance of the Safavid dynasty and the fulsome praise he showers on its rulers as propagators and defenders of Islam. This stark contradiction, barely touched upon by the Twelver scholars of the time, is possibly one of the reasons why Majlisi attempted to incorporate the Safavid rulers in the 'last days' scenario: by transforming figures such as Shah Isma'il into prophesied precursors of the Hidden Imam, he allowed them to partake of the charisma that such a role would carry with it, thereby deflecting attention from the fact that according to other Traditions, each and every one of the Safavid rulers was by definition an usurper whose claim to power was rejected by the Imams, and whose supporters, through their allegiance, were cursed by God.

The *raj'a*: a major factor in Twelver Shi'ite externalism

Islamic externalism, in the broadest sense of the term, implies an under-emphasis of the core aspects of the religion – most notably the centrality of *īmān* and *ma'rifa* – and an over-emphasis of its secondary concerns, the main pillar of which is action ('*amal*) and whose basic vehicle of expression is *fiqh* and *hadīth*. In the case of Twelver Shi'ism, as we have seen, a new element is added: imamocentric internalism, in which knowledge (*ma'rifa*) is basically knowledge of the Imam (*ma'rifat al-imām*), without which one cannot be a true believer. Imamocentric internalism, in which the figure of the Imam is pivotal, does not overthrow theocentric internalism but overshadows it, to the point where half of the Koran is perceived as pertaining to the Imams and their enemies, and the other half to God's ordinances concerning the allowed and the forbidden, jurisdiction over which is the domain of the Imams themselves. By its very nature, imamocentric internalism goes hand in hand with *fiqh* and *hadīth* in the externalization of religious belief, that is in the sense that it focuses primarily on other-then-God rather than on God, or rather than on those fundamental beliefs the total assimilation of which the Koran deems essential for salvation.

The doctrine of *raj'a* is an externalizing factor *par excellence* in that it effectively plays down the *qīyāma* or resurrection and focuses attention not upon the justice which, according to the Koran, will be meted out to each individual, but upon the very particularized justice that will be the lot of the Imams following their return to earth. If justice is to be for all, then it will be a purely secondary consideration: since the oppression and suffering of the Twelver Shi'ites throughout history is held to be a corollary of the oppression and suffering of the Imams, relief (*faraj*) will obtain only when the Imams take revenge on their oppressors and secure their rights. It is the suffering of the Imams and their eventual victory which form the cornerstone of the twin doctrines of *intizār* and *raj'a*, and as such the fate of the individual appears to be of little consequence, the question of reward or punishment being academic given the fact that thanks to the Prophet's intercession, the sins of all Twelver Shi'ites have already been forgiven.

The period of *intizār*, then, as a precursor to the *zuhūr* and *raj'a* is patient, uncomplaining toleration of the world as it is, together with ardent belief in certain individuals who will return to earth to take revenge on those who were primarily responsible for making the world how it is – namely, the enemies of the Imams - and thus in a somewhat circuitous manner secure justice. Before the advent of the Mahdi, all earthly governments are unlawful and therefore oppressive, yet the Twelver Shi'ite believer can do nothing to alleviate this oppression save by nurturing hope for future relief. The practice of *taqiyya* is enjoined, self-isolation recommended, and total submission to fate prescribed. Although the martyrdom of Husayn is extolled, any attempt to emulate him by rising up in the face of tyranny before the coming of the Mahdi is condemned, and allegiance to anyone except the Mahdi is synonymous with unbelief. The Twelver Shi'ite must patiently bear whatever is heaped upon him and await the return of the Mahdi and the other Imams in order to secure relief from oppression: indeed, *intizār* is posited as its own reward.

The role of the Imams is, of course, all-important in the doctrines of *intizār, zuhūr* and *raj'a*. As the *Bihār* demonstrates, history is *their* story. The usurpation of the rights of Ali to the Caliphate, the martyrdom of Husayn in defence of those rights, the subsequent oppression of all Twelver Shi'ites on account of their belief in those rights, and the eventual return of the Imams to earth in order to secure those rights – these are the major recurring themes in Twelver Shi'ite devotional life as portrayed by the *Bihar*.

In short, the *zuhūr* and the *raj'a* provide a panoramic backdrop against which the tragedy of the Imams is brought to a climax. One by one the leading characters return to the stage, heralded by the Mahdi, to perform the triumphant final act in full view of revived and reassembled spectators. The Prophet will conquer the world with his revelation; Ali will begin a rule lasting thousands of years; the martyrs of Karbala will be avenged; and evil – in the form of the enemies of the Imams – will be expunged from the face of the earth. The wheel turns full circle and the promise of God, namely that the Imams should become heirs to the earth, is finally and irrefragably fulfilled.

Safavid Shi'ism and Alid Shi'ism: a contemporary critique

The most vehement attack in recent years on the particular face of Islam presented by the Twelver Shi'ite *fuqahā* of the Safavid era was conducted by the late Iranian sociologist and self-styled Islamologist, Ali Shari'ati. His highly polemical tract, *Tashayyu'-i 'Alawī, tashayyu'-i Safawī*, echoes of which resound through his whole corpus of writings, may be seen as one of the central pillars supporting the revitalization of Twelver Shi'ite Islam among the younger generation of Iranian Muslims in the past forty years.

Shari'ati's views on the Twelver Shi'ism embodied in works such as the *Bihār* are crystallized in the final passages of the aforementioned work, in which he looks at the basis of Twelver Shi'ism from two standpoints: one which he calls 'Safavid Shi'ism', a rubric which encompasses all that Shari'ati sees as a gross distortion and misrepresentation of Shi'ite Islam; and one which he terms Alid Shi'ism' - for him the true, original and ideal Islam.

According to Shari'ati, the concept of *imāma* as preached by the Safavid *fuqahā* consists of belief in twelve holy, infallible, supernatural and suprahuman names (*ism*) that are the only means through which one may approach God, namely through intercession. They are twelve angels to be worshipped, twelve minor gods arranged around the 'great God'. In Alid Shi'ism, however, the *imāma* is pure and revolutionary leadership designed to guide the people and construct the ideal society; the Imams are the embodiment of religion who must be known and followed, and from whom awareness and knowledge is to be acquired.[140]

According to Shari'ati, the concept of *'isma* or infallibility in Safavid Shi'ism consists of belief in the special essence and exceptional qualities of beings in the unseen realm who are unlike other men and who cannot err or sin, namely the 'fourteen pure ones' (*chahārdah ma'sūm*). This belief implies that the rule of traitors and the religious authority of corrupt and impure clerics (*ruhānī*) are only natural since all men save for the Imams are fallible. In Alid Shi'ism, however, *'isma* means belief in the purity and righteousness of the intellectuals, socially-aware leaders and the responsible guardians of the faith, and of science and government. This means a negation of the rule of traitors and a negation of the authority of corrupt clerics attached to the ruling power.[141]

The concept of *wilāya* in Safavid Shi'ism, says Shari'ati, means loving only Ali and abandoning all responsibilities, since it is through this love that one attains Paradise or avoids Hell. In Safavid Shi'ism, the *wilāya* of the house of Ali has nothing to do with how society should be ruled; rather, it is an aid to God in His supervision of the cosmos. In Alid Shi'ism, however, *wilāya* means loving only the leadership and government of Ali, and of governments similar to that of Ali, whose leadership is like a light which guides mankind, and of which all men, for the sake of justice, are in need.[142]

As for justice itself, Shari'ati says that in Safavid Shi'ism it becomes a subject for theological debate: justice is relevant only to the hereafter, and man's interest in the question is limited to speculation on how God will judge men and mete out justice in the world to come. The question of justice is irrelevant to this world: justice in this world is the domain of Shah Abbas. In Safavid Shi'ism, that which belongs to Caesar is rendered unto Caesar, and that which belongs to God is rendered unto Him. This world is the realm of Shah Abbas; the world of the hereafter is the realm of God. In Alid Shi'ism, justice means believing that since God is just and the cosmos founded on justice, society too must run according to the dictates of justice; injustice and inequality are unnatural states and, as such, are anti-God. Justice is the supreme aim of prophethood.[143]

In Safavid Shi'ism, says Shari'ati, *intizār* entails spiritual and practical submission to the *status quo*; it justifies corruption and looks upon everything with the eye of predestination. It is the antithesis of responsibility, for it brings despair to the heart and engenders the belief that all action is doomed to failure. In Alid Shi'ism, however, *intizār* is spiritual and practical readiness, coupled with belief in an eventual and inevitable change for the better. In Alid Shi'ism, *intizār* is revolution; it is the belief that the world must be changed and that oppression will end and justice prevail; it is the belief that the downtrodden classes will rise up and inherit the earth.[144]

According to Shari'ati, in Safavid Shi'ism the doctrine of *ghayba* or occultation absolves the individual of all personal responsibility; *ghayba* renders redundant all of Islam's social rules. The *ghayba* posited by the Safavid *fuqahā* obviates social responsibility on the part of the individual since it is the Hidden Imam alone who can lead the community. It is only the Imam to whom allegiance can be paid and to whom men must answer; since he is absent, however, man can do nothing. In Alid Shi'ism, *ghayba* makes man responsible for choosing his own fate, belief, leadership and social and spiritual way of life. It makes him responsible for choosing an aware and responsible leader from among the people who can act as successor to the Imam.[145]

In short, in Shari'ati's analysis, Safavid Shi'ism is the Shi'ism of ignorance (*jahl*) and blind devotion; it is the Shi'ism of innovation (*bid'a*), discord (*tafraqa*), otherworldly justice, irresponsibility, associationism (*shirk*), intellectual stagnation (*jumūd*) and death. Alid Shi'ism, by contrast, is the Shi'ism of awareness and conscious devotion; it is the Shi'ism of sanctioned custom (*sunna*), concord, earthly justice, responsibility, Divine unity, independent judgement (*ijtihād*) and martyrdom. Safavid Shi'ism cries over the death of Husayn; Alid Shi'ism follows in Husayn's path and views Karbala not as a tragedy but as a blueprint for revolution. Safavid Shi'ism enslaves; Alid Shi'ism liberates.[146]

From *Tashayyu'-i 'Alawī* and his other writings it is clear that Shari'ati's criticism of the Safavid *fuqahā* is markedly different from Ghazali's attack on the corruptors of the terms '*ilm* and '*ulamā* or Mulla Sadra's invective against the hide-bound externalists of his day. Shari'ati does not take the Safavid *fuqahā* to task on the grounds that they have neglected the question of *ma'rifat Allāh* or *ma'rifat al-nafs* for the sake of *fiqh* and *hadīth*, although he is at times quite scathing in his rejection of their overemphasis on jurisprudence. It was not the question of belief which bothered Shari'ati but rather the question of action – revolutionary action – that he saw as the aim and *raison d'être* of Shi'ism. In this respect, Shari'ati's attack on the externalism of the Safavid *fuqahā* should not be seen as that of a concerned internalist wishing to redress the balance between the two aspects of the revelation - internalism and externalism - but rather as that of someone who wishes to redefine externalism on his own terms, without anchoring his thesis in an internalist ethos.

Shari'ati's development of the concept of Alid Shi'ism, a system identified with the authoritative figure of Imam Ali, was appraised by Nikkie Keddie as follows:

> By systematizing the concept of Alid Shi'ism, Shari'ati attained a double result: he detached himself from the petrified official Islam rejected by idealistic youth, and he brought a new and combative meaning to Shi'a concepts. Even prayer in this renovated Islam took on a political meaning, tied to action. This insurrectional meaning of common prayer was particularly developed in the 1978-1979 revolution.[147]

Only a full and detailed study of all of Shari'ati's writings would enable one to confirm or refute the implication made by one writer that Shari'ati's allegiance to Shi'ism was almost purely utilitarian in nature, and that the key concepts of Shi'ism were remolded as vehicles for his own political aims.[148] What is important from the point of view of the present work is that Shari'ati was able to identify the problems of externalism yet, instead of advocating a return to fundamentals in the manner adumbrated by Ghazali and Mulla Sadra, set about prescribing a whole new set of values which, although appearing to be totally divorced from what he calls the 'stagnation' of Safavid Shi'ite externalism, in practice amount to little more than a variation on the same theme.

Undoubtedly it was the stultifying effect that the externalism of the Safavid *fuqahā* had on the masses - especially with respect to questions such as the *ghayba* and *intizār* in which patience, resignation and submission were enjoined - that prompted Shari'ati, whatever his inner motives, to interpret Twelver Shi'ism in a new and revolutionary way. Although it may be argued that certain features such as the martyrdom of Husayn at Karbala and the rise of the Mahdi are pregnant with revolutionary meaning, it was the negative aspects of these features that had traditionally been stressed by Twelver scholars; although Islam as a political vehicle was obviously not unknown before the writings of Shari'ati gained popularity, he was possibly the first contemporary Iranian thinker to interpret Islam as a total 'ideology': an ideology of emancipation and liberation with an overwhelmingly political flavour.

In rejecting the *fuqahā* of the Safavid period, whom he used as a symbol of religious stagnation, he also tended to reject all figures of authority operating in the traditional Islamic world; he wrote, he says, not as a philosopher or an historian or a *faqīh* or a theologian but as one who is above or divorced from all of these. In doing so he overlooked the fact that not all Muslim scholars are Safavid externalists, and that all knowledge does not necessarily concern the minutiae of rules on ablution or detailed information about the events of *raj'a*. Thus he writes:

> Others advise us saying: first you must think, gain knowledge, do scientific (*'ilmī*) research, read books, attend religious classes, study under learned teachers, learn philosophy, Sufism, *fiqh* and *usūl* (jurisprudence), theology, logic, languages, literature, history, theosophy and ethics from the experts so that you become versed in the scriptural and rational sciences, so that you know all there is to know about the world and God and His attributes and necessary being and contingency and the philosophy of existence, the world of the unseen, substance and accident – all the secrets of creation – only then can you pass to the next stage, the stage of action: the correction of the self.[149]

That which really matters for Shari'ati, namely societal action, does not come until much later in his parody of the Koranic process of 'knowledge – belief – action' as set out in his book *Shī'a, hizb-i tamām*. God-knowledge and belief are not for Shari'ati the purpose of Koranic teaching:

> Of course, 'belief in God' must be the basis of enjoining good deeds upon others and prohibiting evil ... but in my opinion, God's main purpose in creating man was not that man should believe in God – since God is not in need of man's belief – but rather that man should struggle in the name of his fellow men to being about that which is good and do away with that which is evil.[150]

In Shari'ati's interpretation of Shi'ism, and indeed of Islam in general, action always speaks louder than words. Belief, if not played down completely, is overshadowed by the urgent need for revolutionary awareness and social responsibility. Awareness of the truth cannot come through intellectual striving or the acquisition of knowledge, declares Shari'ati: it is only in 'becoming' that we can really 'be' and discover the truth. It is only in action that the truth manifests itself.[151]

Shari'ati's Islam is not the Islam of individual man gaining knowledge of God, believing in Him, correcting himself and acting as an example for others in order to gain salvation; rather, his Islam is a vehicle for collective, political expression in which belief is merely assumed to be there as a basis, in which action is all important, and in which the key tenets of the faith are reduced to little more than political formulae. When one considers the concepts of *intizār* and *raj'a* as expressed in the *Bihar*, in which Islam is reduced to waiting to avenge the Imams while patiently enduring oppression, it is easy to see why Shari'ati placed so much emphasis on social responsibility and societal action, or why the ultimate goal that he preached as the most external expression of his beliefs was nothing but permanent revolution. Yet in his rejection of the figures of authority in the world of Islamic scholarship – the *faqīh*, the *hakīm*, the *mutakallim* and the *adīb* – and his assumption that the *fuqahā* of the Safavid era were emblematic and representative of 'traditional' Islam as a whole, and which he opposed, it may be argued that Shari'ati threw out the baby along with the bathwater. Rejection of 'traditional' Islam also meant rejection of those scholars who were just as much at odds with externalism as he was.

In short, Shari'ati's attack on what he calls Safavid Shi'ism is concentrated fundamentally on the failure of the latter to provide the masses with a theology of protest. The externalism of the Safavid *fuqahā* – their obsessive preoccupation with rite and ritual – comes under heavy fire, but it is not the predominance of imamocentrism to the detriment of theocentrism that concerns Shari'ati. For him it is the obfuscation of what he perceives to be the fundamental message of Shi'ism, namely justice through revolution, to which he objects.

If Shari'ati is to be given credit as the thinker who revivified the Twelver Shi'ite message, then his stance can be seen largely as a response and reaction to the externalism of the Safavid *fuqahā*, for whom the question of revolt, rebellion or revolution was as far from their minds as the concepts of self-knowledge and divine gnosis. Shari'ati does not inveigh against the tendency of the Safavid *fuqahā* to overlook completely the question of *ma'rifa* and *īmān* precisely because he does not hold that knowledge and belief have primacy over action, unless, of course, that knowledge and belief pertain to the revolutionary 'ideology' of what he terms 'red Shi'ism' - red as opposed the 'black Shi'ism' of the Safavids.[152] It is the opinion of the writer that if the Safavid *fuqahā* were guilty of taking for granted the belief of the people and stressing action in the form of individual rite and ritual, Shari'ati is equally at fault for taking for granted belief and stressing action in the form of rebellion and revolt. What concerns Majlisi and Shari'ati alike is action: for Majlisi, action consists of religious ritual, while for Shari'ati it consists of revolution. Like Majlisi, Shari'ati did not invite the people to rethink their belief and reconsider their own individual position *vis-à-vis* the Creator; rather he called upon them to re-evaluate the 'revolutionary' nature of Twelver Shi'ism as exemplified by the Imams.

By definition, then, Shari'ati was also an externalist. If Safavid Shi'ism can be summed up as the religion of *fiqh*, Shari'ati's Shi'ism can be summed up as the religion of politics. In either case, the central core of Islamic teaching, namely theocentric internalism, is either banished to the periphery or totally overlooked.

Finally, Shari'ati, whose teachings are at the core of the Islamic 'revival' in Iran during the 60s and 70s, outlines his vision of the Islam of the future:

> The Islam of tomorrow will not be the Islam of the *mullā*; the Islam of Qum and Mashhad will also change. The (religious) students have shown that they do not believe what these 'signs' (*āyāt*) dictate to them; the decline of this whole class (*sinf*) which, with all its weapons and experience, has taken on the defenceless Husayniyya, shows that the power of religion lies no longer in the hands of these official, hereditary guardians (*mutawalliyyūn*)...The Islam of tomorrow will be the Shi'ism not of Sultan Husayn but of Imam Husayn. The religion of tomorrow will not be the religion of

ignorance and oppression, blind zeal and fanaticism, outmoded ideas and superstition, indiscriminate acceptance and imitation, repetition, tears, abjection and weakness...No! the religion of tomorrow will be the religion of conscious choice and justice, awareness and freedom, revolution and revolutionary movement, construction and science, culture, art and literature, society and responsibility, innovation and advancement ... it will be forward-looking and in charge of its own destiny.[153]

To determine which parts of Shari'ati's vision have been realized and which remain unfulfilled is left to the reader. The fact remains that even though the guardians of the Islamic revolution may have failed to live up to Shari'ati's expectations, the course they are charting is, like his and like that of their Safavid counterparts and predecessors, unequivocally externalist in nature. With its emphasis on action, on continuous revolution, on an Islam that must be seen to be done, the present Islamic regime may on the surface appear worlds apart from its Safavid ancestor, and with respect to method it most certainly is. Yet it may be argued that as far as the obfuscation of the central message of *īmān* is concerned, the present regime has, by substituting politics for *fiqh*, simply taken over where the Safavid *fuqahā* left off.

Notes

1. The relative insignificance of Mahdism for the Sunnis and their attacks on the doctrine as espoused and promulgated by the Shi'ites are dealt with summarily in: Hamid Enayat, *Modern Islamic Political Thought* (London: The Macmillan Press, 1982), pp. 44-6.
2. A.J. Wensinck, *A Handbook of Early Muhammadan Tradition* (Leiden, 1927), p. 139.
3. Verse 22:54 – '...for verily God is the Guide of those who believe, to the straight Way.' Verse 25:33 – '...but enough is thy Lord to guide and help.
4. For example, see verse 7:178 – "Whom God doth guide, -he is on the right path: whom He rejects from His guidance, - such are the persons who perish."
5. I. Goldziher, *al-'Aqīda wa al-sharī'a fī al-Islām*, transl. by Muhammad Yusuf (Cairo, 1378/1958-59), pp. 327-8, 376-8.
6. Ibn A'tham al-Kufi, *Kitāb al-futūh* (Hyderabad, 1972), vol. 5, pp. 31 and 34.
7. Muhammad b. Jarir al-Tabari, *Tārīkh al-rusul wa al-muluk*, ed. by de Goeje (Leyden, 1879-1901) vol. 2, p. 546.
8. W.W. Rajkowski, *Early Shi'ism in Iraq* (Ph.D. Thesis, SOAS, University of London, 1955), pp. 166-7.
9. Verses 39:30-31 – "Truly wilt thou die (one day), and truly they (too) will die (one day). In the end will ye (all), on the Day of Judgement, settle your disputes in the presence of your Lord."
10. Hasan b. Musa al-Nawbakhti, *Firaq al-shī'a*, ed. by Ritter (Leipzig, 1931), pp. 33-4.
11. See: Sachedina, *Islamic Messianism*, pp. 10-11. For a fuller account of the Kaysanite roots of the Abbasid movement, see: Ansari, *Madhāhib ibtidā'ātha al-sīyāsa fī al-Islām* (Beirut, 1973), pp. 152-8, 199-214.
12. Ibn Tawus, *al-Iqbāl* (Tehran, n.d.), p. 53.
13. Muhammad b. Ali al-Saduq, *Kamāl al-dīn wa tamām al-ni'ma* (Tehran, 1378/1958-59), p. 37.
14. Hashim Ma'ruf al-Hasani, *Sirat al-a'imma al-ithnā 'ashar* (Beirut, 1397/1976-77), vol. 1, p. 370.
15. Ibn Maja, *Sunan*, vol. 2, p. 1368.
16. Muhammad b. 'Isa al-Tirmidhi, *Sunan al-Tirmidhī* (Cairo, 1356/1937-38), vol. 4, pp. 505-6.
17. Ibn Maja, *Sunan*, vol. 2, p. 1368.
18. *Kamāl al-dīn*, pp. 286-7; *Tirmidhī*, vol. 4, pp. 505-6.
19. Ahmad b. Muhammad al-Tha'labi, *'Arā'is al-majālis* (Cairo, n.d.), p. 363.
20. Muhammad Salih Osman, *Mahdism in Islam up to 260 A.H./874 and its relation to Zoroastrian, Jewish and Christian Messianism* (Ph.D. Thesis, University of Edinburgh, 1976), p. 204.
21. See: 'Abd al-Muhsin al-'Abbad, *'Aqīdat ahl al-sunna wa al-athar fī al-mahdī al-muntazar* (Qumm, 1971), vol. 1, pp. 33-5.
22. Ibn Hanbal, *al-Musnad* (Cairo, 1313/1895-96.
23. Lutfullah al-Safi Gulpayigani, *Muntakhab al-athar fī al-imām al-thāni 'ashar* (Tehran, n.d.), p. 40.
24. Ibn Hanbal, *al-Musnad*, vol 1, p. 398.

25. Danishpazhuh, *Fihrist*, vol. 3, pp. 1203-13.
26. These topics span volumes 51-53 of the new edition of *Bihār al-anwār* (*Bihar II*).
27. Nu'mani, also known as Ibn Abi Zaynab, studied *hadīth* transmission under Kulayni in Baghdad. He endeavoured to prove the necessity of the occultation by relating Traditions on the authority of the Prophet and the Imams predicting its occurrence. He took most of his Traditions from early authors who wrote on the subject, regardless of their doctrinal views. He was the first scholar to posit two occultations. He died in Syria around the year 360/970-71.
28. *Bihār II*, vol. 52, p. 101.
29. *ibid.*, vol. 52, p. 114.
30. *ibid.*, vol. 52, p. 105.
31. *ibid.*, vol. 52, p. 105.
32. On the doctrine of *badā* and its relationship with Mahdism, see: Sachedina, *Islamic Messianism*, pp. 153-6.
33. *Bihār II*, vol. 52, p. 104; vol. 53, p. 97.
34. For Majlisi's *abjad* calculations, see: *Bihār II*, vol. 52, pp. 107-9.
35. *ibid.*, vol. 52 pp. 110-11.
36. *ibid.*, vol. 52, p. 135.
37. *ibid.*, vol. 52, pp. 110-11.
38. *ibid.*, vol. 52, p. 111.
39. *ibid.*, vol. 52, p. 113.
40. Verses 2:155-7 – "Be sure we shall test you with something of fear and hunger, some loss of goods or lives or the fruits (of your toil), but give good tidings to those who patiently persevere, - who say, when afflicted with calamity: 'To God we belong, and to Him is our return': - they are those on whom (descend) blessings from God, and Mercy, and they are the ones that receive guidance."
41. Hans Wehr, *Arabic Dictionary*, pp. 975-77.
42. For example verses 3:186, 3:200, 10:109 and 40:155.
43. *Bihār II*, vol. 52, p. 122.
44. *ibid.*, vol 52 p. 122.
45. *ibid.*, vol 52 p. 123.
46. *ibid.*, vol. 52, p. 125.
47. *ibid.*, vol. 52, p. 124.
48. *ibid.*, vol. 52, p. 125.
49. *ibid.*
50. *ibid.*, vol. 52, pp. 127-8.
51. *ibid.*, vol. 52, p. 133.
52. *ibid.*
53. *ibid.*, vol. 52, p. 136.
54. *ibid.*, vol. 52, p. 139.
55. *ibid.*, vol. 52, p. 138.
56. *ibid.*, vol. 52, pp. 139-40.
57. *ibid.*, vol. 52, pp. 141-2.
58. *ibid.*, vol. 52, p. 142.
59. *ibid.*, vol. 52, p. 139.

60. *ibid.*, vol. 52, p. 143.
61. Arjomand, *The Shadow of God*, pp. 32-34.
62. A.K.S. Lambton, 'Concepts of Authority in Persia: Eleventh to Nineteenth Centuries A.D.' in *IRAN*, vol. 26 (1988), p. 96.
63. *ibid.*
64. *ibid.*, p. 97.
65. Sachedina, *Islamic Messianism*, p. 212, n. 73.
66. For an English translation of Ali's letter, see: Chittick (ed.), *A Shi'ite Anthology*, pp. 67-89.
67. Arjomand, *The Shadow of God*, pp. 179-80.
68. Said Nursi, *Lema'lar* (Istanbul: Sinan Matbaasi, 1959), pp. 20-21.
69. Bediüzzaman Said Nursi, *The Miracles of Muhammad* (Istanbul, 1985), pp. 31-33.
70. E. Kohlberg, 'Amoli', *Encyclopaedia Iranica*, vol. 1, p. 985.
71. Norman Calder, 'Legitimacy and Accommodation in Safavid Iran' in *IRAN*, vol. 25 (1987), p. 103.
72. *ibid.*, pp. 97-99.
73. Sir John Chardin, *The Travels of Sir John Chardin into Persia and the East Indies* (London, 1691), p. 11.
74. Sir John Chardin, *Voyages du Chevalier Chardin en Perse et autre lieux de l'Orient*, ed. by L. Langlès (Paris: Le Normant, 1811), vol. 5, pp. 215-16.
75. Danishpazhuh, *Fihrist*, vol. 3, pp. 1212-3.
76. For details of *Chahārdah hadīth*, see: Danishpazhuh, *Fihrist*, vol. 3, pp. 1203-12.
77. *Bihār II*, vol. 52, pp. 236-7.
78. *ibid.*, vol. 52, p. 237.
79. *ibid.*, vol. 52, p. 243.
80. *ibid.*
81. Sachedina, *Islamic Messianism*, p. 73.
82. Danishpazhuh, *Fihrist*, vol. 3, pp. 1206.
83. *ibid.*, vol. 3, p. 1211.
84. *ibid.*, vol. 3, p. 1498.
85. *ibid.*, vol. 3, p. 1212.
86. *ibid.*, vol. 3, p. 1211.
87. Danishpazhuh, *Fihrist*, vol. 3, p. 502.
88. *ibid.*, vol. 3, p. 1501.
89. *ibid.*, p. 1500.
90. *ibid.*, vol. 3, p. 1499.
91. *Bihār II*, vol. 53, p. 181.
92. Muhammad b. Hasan al-Tusi, *Kitāb al-ghayba* (Najaf, 1965), p. 231.
93. Dawani, *Mahdī-i maw'ūd*, p. 1251.
94. Jassim M. Hussain, *The Occultation of the Twelfth Imam* (London: The Muhammadi Trust, 1982), p. 13.
95. On the Kaysaniyya, see: Sacheddina, *Islamic Messianism*, pp. 10-11.
96. *ibid.*, pp. 39-54.
97. Dawani, *Mahdī-i maw'ūd*, pp. 1228-9.

98. *ibid.*, p. 1229.
99. *ibid.*, pp. 1231-2.
100. *Bihār II*, vol. 53, pp. 39-40.
101. *ibid.*, vol. 53, p. 39.
102. *ibid.*, vol. 53, pp. 103-4.
103. *ibid.*
104. *ibid.*, p. 106.
105. *ibid.*, vol. 53, pp. 106-7.
106. *ibid.*, pp. 74-5.
107. *ibid.*, vol. 53, p. 89.
108. *ibid.*, vol. 53, p. 76.
109. *ibid.*, vol. 53, p. 51.
110. *ibid.*
111. *ibid.*, vol. 53, p. 44.
112. *ibid.*, vol. 54, p. 103.
113. *ibid.*, vol. 53, p. 104.
114. *ibid.*, vol. 53, p. 93.
115. *ibid.*, vol. 53, p. 97.
116. *ibid.*, vol. 53, p. 71.
117. *ibid.*, vol. 53, p. 39.
118. *ibid.*, vol. 53, pp. 40-41.
119. *ibid.*, vol. 53, p. 65.
120. *ibid.*, vol. 53, p. 59.
121. *ibid.*, vol. 53, p. 51.
122. *ibid.*, vol. 53, pp. 106-7.
123. *ibid.*, vol. 53, p. 99.
124. *ibid.*, vol. 53, p. 89.
125. *ibid.*, vol. 53, pp. 53-4.
126. *ibid.*, vol. 53, p. 56.
127. *ibid.*, vol. 24, p. 305.
128. Danishpazhuh, *Fihrist*, vol. 3, p. 1213.
129. Mufaddal was a former follower of Abu al-Khattab, the founder of the extremist Khattabiyya sect. His early views are discussed in: Muhammad b. Umar b. 'Abd al-'Aziz al-Kashi, *Kitāb al-rijāl* (Mashhad, 1348 Sh./1969-70), pp. 321-29.
130. The 'knowledge of the Hour' (*'ilm al-sā'a*) is presented in the Koran as knowledge of the day of reckoning and not the rise of the Mahdi as posited in the Tradition. For example, see verses 31:34 and 34:3.
131. Astonishingly, Majlisi seems to be unaware of the fact that he himself was open to charges of shirk by dint of his *abjad* predictions of the time of the Mahdi's rise and re-appearance.
132. See verse 22:78.
133. *Bihār II*, vol. 53, pp. 1-38.
134. *ibid.*, vol. 53, p. 37.
135. *ibid.*

136. Verse 42:30 – 'Whatever misfortune happens to you, is because of the things your hands have wrought, and for many (of them) He grants forgiveness.'
137. Verse 17:71 – 'One day We shall call together all human beings with their (respective) Imams: those who are given their record in their right hand will read it (with pleasure), and they will not be dealt with unjustly in the least.'
138. Verse 6:164.
140. *ibid.*, pp. 320-1.
141. *ibid.*, p. 321.
142. *ibid.*, pp. 321-2.
143. *ibid.*, p. 323.
144. *ibid.*, pp. 323-4.
145. *ibid.*, p. 324.
146. *ibid.*, pp. 324-5.
147. Nikkie R. Keddie, *Roots of Revolution: an Interpretative History of Modern Iran* (Newhaven: Yale University Press, 1981), p. 220.
148. See: Hamid Dabashi, 'Ali Shari'ati's Islam: Revolutionary Uses of Faith in a Post-Traditional Society,' in *The Islamic Quarterly*, vol. 27, no. 4 (1983), pp. 203-22.
149. Ali Shari'ati, *Shī'a* (Tehran: Husayniyya-i Irshad, 1357 Sh.1978-79), pp. 23-4.
150. *ibid.*, p. 81.
151. *ibid.*, p. 19.
152. Ali Shari'ati, *Bā mukhātab-hā-i āshinā* (Tehran: Husayniyya-i Irshad, 1397/1976-77), p. 142.
153. *ibid.*, p.14.

Chapter 6

Conclusions

The rise to predominance of the jurist (*faqīh*) in the Islamic world of learning in general, and in the Twelver Shi'ite sphere in particular, has at its roots two major factors: ambiguity and confusion over the precise meaning and practical implications of the terms *īmān* and *islām*; and the changes in meaning undergone by key Koranic terms such as '*ilm*, '*ulamā* and *fiqh*.

The Koran posits a clear, albeit highly idealistic, process through which a man must go in order to be able to call himself a Muslim: deliberation (*tafakkur*) on the cosmos; knowledge ('*ilm*) of the nature and meaning of creation, and of the existence of a Creator to which all created beings as 'signs' (*āyāt*) point; belief (*īmān*) in God; submission (*islām*) of the heart to all of the truths that belief implies; and adherence to the rites, rules and regulations of the communal religion known as Islam. However, this schema rarely corresponds with reality, for as the Koran itself asserts, most men neither ponder, nor truly believe, nor truly submit – and of those who do come to believe, most do so deficiently, while many of those who claim to have submitted have, in actual fact, submitted only through their practice of the external acts of Islam, and not in the internal, spiritual sense of *islām*, which is the domain of the heart and the acme of belief.

That *īmān* and *islām* are conceptually different is quite clear from several Koranic verses; both Shi'ite and Sunni Traditions also reflect this. The fact that *īmān* is the cornerstone of *islām*/Islam and thus totally fundamental is also a matter for agreement between various Sunni and Shi'ite scholars, past and present.

However, ambiguity in the use of the word *islām*, which in Arabic cannot be differentiated from the word 'Islam' by the use of capitals as it can in English, tended from the outset to blur the distinction between the internal, personal submission of the individual (*islām*) and the formal profession of adherence to the religious community (Islam). This was compounded by the inability - or unwillingness - of certain early exegetes to clarify the distinction. This may have been the result of a desire to preserve unity, a reflection of the belief that in the very earliest Islamic community, all Muslims were also *muslims*. The idea that *islām* is a question of birthright, or that belief is possible only through *islām* – ideas which are alien to the Koran – began to appear in Koranic commentaries of both Sunni and Shi'ite exegetes; in this light it is not difficult to understand why individuals born into an Islamic environment may consider themselves to be believers purely by dint of their affiliation to the Muslim community, and thus, by equating *īmān* with Islam, shift the emphasis that should, according to the Koran, be on the internal truths of belief onto the external display of submission.

Parallel to the developments in the interpretation of the terms *īmān* and *islām* came the changes which occurred in the meaning of key Koranic terms such as *'ilm*, *'ulamā* and *fiqh*. Given the fact that most Muslims were oriented to the externals of Islam - the *furū' al-dīn* - it was only natural, thanks to the simple question of supply and demand, that from among the ranks of Muslim scholars it was the jurists, the *fuqahā*, who would predominate. By the end of the 6th/12th century, scholars such as Ghazali were in a position to bemoan the fact that the true knowledge - the knowledge of self, of God and of the Hereafter - had been overshadowed by the knowledge of externals, of the minutiae of the myriad rules and regulations which had evolved to constitute Islamic orthopraxy. The terms *'ilm* and *fiqh*, which originally denoted knowledge of God, came now to mean knowledge of God's commands, while the term *'ulamā* - which in the Koran denotes those who know, and thus fear, the Creator - was now applied to anyone versed in the 'subsidiary principles of Islam', the *furū' al-dīn*.

Consequently there emerged two groups of scholars: the 'externalists', whose scholarly endeavours were concerned with knowledge of God's commands, the *sharī'a* and thus with Islam; and the 'internalists', whose teachings focused largely on self-knowledge (*ma'rifat al-nafs*), divine gnosis (*ma'rifat Allāh*) and the cultivation of *īmān*. Internalism was traditionally the preserve of the Sufi brotherhoods, although there were exceptions. There were also individuals who endeavoured to preserve the harmony that is supposed to exist between the internal and external expressions of Islam, according primacy to *iman* but not forsaking the practical demands of Islamic law. Tension between the internalist and externalist discourses existed in all Muslim scholarly communities, but nowhere was it as marked – or, with hindsight, as significant for future developments in the interpretation of the Islam – as it was in Safavid Iran.

Pre-Safavid Iran was dominated by two main religious currents: mainstream or 'high' Sufism; and *ghuluww* or extremist folk-Sufism with a markedly pro-Alid flavour. The spirit of internalism lived on during this period in the form of orthodox Sunni Sufi orders, of which the Safavids were, in their early stage, a prime example. From Anatolia through Iran and into Transoxania, 'high' Sufi orders such as the Mawliyya, the Ni'matullahiyya and the Naqshbandiyya were the main channels of internalist expression. Devotion to the family of Ali was clearly evident in these orders, but this should not be construed as constituting the 'moderate Shi'ism' (*tashayyu'-i hasan*) that has often been posited as one of the reasons Twelver Shi'ism was able later to impose itself so rapidly on the Iranian populace. Extremism, or *ghuluww*, came in the form of popular movements and quasi-Sufi orders with highly unorthodox and often heretical beliefs concerning in particular the Shi'ite Imams. Unlike the 'high' Sufis, the *ghulāt* seemed largely to have considered the *sharī'a* defunct, and its laws and ordinances went unheeded. Undisciplined religiosity – strictly speaking, neither internalist nor externalist – allowed political and military ambition to run riot, and it is largely from the *ghulāt* that the various popular anti-establishment revolts which took place in the area during this period found their inspiration.

On the level of rite and ritual, the majority of the Iranian populace was Sunni, adhering to the Shafi'ite and Hanafite schools of jurisprudence. The rise of Sufism in general, and *ghuluww* in particular, had gone hand-in-hand with a temporary decline in orthodox religious externalism, although the adherents of the 'high' Sufi orders and groups such as the *ahl-i futuwwa* and the *ahl-i ukhuwwa* endeavoured to remain faithful to their Sunni doctrines and combine the introspective spirituality of Sufi internalism with obedience to the dictates of the *sharī'a*.

One such group was the Safawiyya, an orthodox Sunni-Sufi Order which, under its first four leaders, commanded the respect and reverence of rulers and masses alike. Totally in keeping with its mainstream religious internalism, the Safawiyya was politically quietistic and harboured no aspirations to temporal power. With the advent of Junayd as its head, however, the Order was transformed into a military organization with a decidedly extremist, pro-Shi'ite religious orientation: contemplative, internalist Sufism was replaced with openly heterodox *ghuluww*, a transformation that was little more than a pretext for Junayd's political ambitions. Under Junayd's son, Haydar, the Safawiyya increased its military activity until it was able, with the support of the fanatical Qizilbash, to place Shah Isma'il I on the throne at Tabriz. With this dramatic politico-religious metamorphosis, the Safawiyya were to change the face of Iran completely.

Given Isma'il I's spiritual allegiance to the Twelve Imams, it was only logical that he and his advisers would adopt a form of externalism that was not only in keeping with their own pro-Alid beliefs but which would also serve to stabilize the state. Orthodox Twelver Shi'ism, with its recognised legal framework and highly elaborate system of dogma, was the natural choice, this despite the fact that Isma'il and his advisers were, like the vast majority of the Iranian populace, ignorant of the finer points of Twelver doctrine: the only manual of Twelver Shi'ite jurisprudence that could be found was one that had long since gathered dust in the corner of an obscure private library, and a celebrated historian of the time had trouble remembering when Twelver Shi'ism had last made an appearance on the Iranian religious scene. That the Order's sudden conversion to the Twelver cause was politically motivated thus seems certain. Twelver Shi'ite orthodoxy would have the desired stabilizing effect, and its immediate propagation was vital if the doctrinal uniformity that was so crucial to the Safavid retention of power was to come about. The adoption of Twelver Shi'ism would, moreover, effectively isolate Iran from its Sunni neighbours and thus foster a stronger awareness of national identity for the Safavids to exploit.

For three hundred years prior to the advent of the Safavids, orthodox Twelver Shi'ism had developed mainly outside Iran, administering to the spiritual and jurisprudential needs of small enclaves of Twelver Shi'ite faithful in areas such as Jabal 'Amil in southern Lebanon, al-Ahsa and Bahrain. The first Twelver *fuqahā* imported by Isma'il hailed mainly from these areas, and from the outset it became clear that the doctrines they espoused were considerably different from those of the people upon whom the new state religion was to be imposed. The position of the Twelver *fuqahā* as the representatives of the Hidden Imam, and as the repositories of the teachings of the Imams, meant that they were markedly more oriented towards the secondary disciplines of *fiqh* and *hadīth*, and the source of scholars upon which Isma'il drew was almost exclusively externalist in outlook. Superficially, then, it is easy to draw parallels on this count between them and their Sunni counterparts.

The radical difference between the Twelver *fuqahā* and the majority of the Iranian population lay not, however, in matters of *fiqh* but in the fundamentals of belief, the concept of *imāma* being crucial to Twelver dogma. So central was the notion of *imāma* to the Twelver Shi'ites that the relationship of most Twelvers with the spiritual life had developed on radically different lines from that of the Sunnis: whereas the latter had found a channel for internalist expression mainly in Sufism, the Twelver Shi'ites had their own form of compensation for the spiritual deficiencies of legalistic religion, namely devotion to the Imam. In the words of one Imami Tradition, half of the Koran concerns the things that God has allowed or prohibited, i.e. the rules and regulations of the *sharī'a*, while the other half concerns the Imams and their enemies. In this light it may be concluded that although from the point of view of externalism there is little difference between Twelver Shi'ism and the four schools of Sunni jurisprudence, on the level of internalism they are sharply divided. While the Twelver Shi'ites of the Safavid era would not have ignored the fundamental notion of belief in God, it was belief in God *through* the channel of the Imams which was of paramount importance, so much so in fact that Traditions were circulated to the effect that belief in God is not possible without belief in the Imam, or that it is only through the channel of the Imams, and accordingly through the Twelver *fuqahā* as the representatives of the Imams, that any kind of religious knowledge, be it internalistic or externalistic, can be obtained.

The nomocentric legalism of the Twelver *fuqahā*, coupled with the imamocentrism that underpinned it, clashed immediately with the non-externalistic religious ideals of the vast majority of the Iranian population. All forms of religious expression other than their own were suppressed by the Twelver *fuqahā* and their followers. This was, of course, totally in line with the objectives of the nascent regime, for the consolidation of Safavid power depended on the ability of the new ruler to eradicate all potential centres of opposition. Sufism, Sunnism and Qizilbash extremism were all targets for the opprobrium of the incoming Twelver *fuqahā*; vilification of the first three Caliphs was institutionalized and all those objecting to the new ruling were brutally silenced. Twelver *fuqahā* found convenient niches for themselves in the posts of *shaykh al-islām, imām jum'a, mudarris* and *pīshnamāz*, from which they were able to spread the Traditions of the Imams and successfully impose their doctrines on the masses.

Yet although the initial suppression of non-externalism was savage, and the verbal attacks in the form of anti-Sufi and anti-Sunni treatises sustained, the Safavid era was not quite the 'struggle for supremacy' that some writers have claimed it to be. From the point of view of religious authority, the non-externalists - most of whom had adopted Twelver Shi'ism only nominally - could not compete with the immigrant Twelver *fuqahā*, whose expertise in Twelver *fiqh* and *hadīth* guaranteed them supremacy in that particular area. From the point of view of temporal authority, the Twelver *fuqahā* lacked a coherent political ethos. While in theory all governments save for that of the Hidden Imam were illegitimate, in practice there had to be a ruler; given the absence of any clear directive on the part of the Imams for their successors, the *fuqahā*, to take the reigns of temporal power into their own hands, the Twelver jurists were for the most part content to leave temporal authority to their benefactors, the Safavid rulers, while appropriating the religious allegiance of the masses for themselves.

The struggle between the Twelver externalists and their non-externalist rivals was for the most part an ideological one, a 'war of the pen' that was to continue throughout the Safavid era. As they strengthened their foothold in Iran, the *fuqahā* flooded the mosques and religious seminaries with countless tracts and treatises on all aspects of Twelver doctrine. The vast majority of Safavid scholarly writing was, as Afandi has shown, externalist through and through. The classical works of Twelver Shi'ism were commented upon, translated and reworked. The issues which most concerned the externalists centred upon points of law, upon questions such as the permissibility or impermissibility of the Friday prayer in the absence of the Imam, or upon the validity of *ijtihād* and *taqlīd* – issues which were to have vital importance for the future of the Twelver *fuqahā*, and which served, as did most of their pursuits, to marginalize internalism and its representatives even further. It goes without saying that fundamental questions such as belief, self-knowledge and knowledge of God were conspicuous by their absence from the works of the vast majority of Twelver *fuqahā*.

Internalist thought lived on, however, if not in the teachings of the Sufi brotherhoods then in the writings of philosophers and theosophers such as Mulla Sadra, Mir Damad, Mir Findiriski, Rajab Ali Tabrizi – all of them Shi'ite in name but deeply theocentric in outlook. The waxing and waning of the fortunes of these non-externalist scholars depended largely on the whims and caprices of the ruler of the day, and for the most part - at least until the reign of Shah Sulayman and the advent of Muhammad Baqir Majlisi - although refutations and counter refutations of each other's respective outlooks continued to be written, the externalist *fuqahā* and the non-externalist/internalist philosophers, theosophers and mystics were able to co-exist relatively peacefully. Indeed, a *modus vivendi* was at times reached which allowed for the emergence of a form of Twelver Shi'ite syncretism, an overlapping of interests reflected in the writings of philosophers who were also versed in *fiqh*, or scholars who were *fuqahā* first and foremost but who endeavoured to integrate into their writings elements of theocentric internalism.

Towering over the final decades of the Safavid era stands 'Allama Muhammad Baqir Majlisi, hailed by his peers as the *mujaddid* of the age, the 'seal' of the *mujtahids* and as a scholar unique in his own time. If output is any indicator of scholarly status, then it must be conceded that he is *the* outstanding figure in the Safavid Twelver Shi'ite world of learning. No other Safavid *faqīh* has been able to match Majlisi in popularity or readership: the works which bear his name are by far the most widely read of all popular Twelver Shi'ite writings. Yet a closer look at his work reveals the fact that he contributed virtually nothing to the development of *fiqh* and *hadīth* as scholarly disciplines.

The move from theocentrism to imamocentrism took its greatest strides during the closing decades of the Safavid era, and it was mainly under the auspices of Majlisi, whose crowning achievement was to codify the scattered sayings of the Imams into a more or less coherent whole, that the externalisation of the fundamentals of Islamic belief in terms that were suitable to one particular branch of Islamic knowledge, namely *fiqh* and *hadīth*, reached its zenith. The key, quite obviously, lay in the accessibility of the basic doctrines of Twelver Shi'ite doctrine to the people at large. Writing mostly in Persian, Majlisi was able to reach the widest possible audience. Conveying simple, uncluttered dogma in the language of the common people - whom he was said to despise - he was able to draw on the general tendency of the Muslim masses towards the superficial and, at the same time, fill the spiritual vacuum that had appeared as a result of the decline of the Sufi brotherhoods with treatise after treatise on the lives, sayings, trials, tribulations, miracles and powers of the Imams.

Concerned primarily with the exoteric rather than the esoteric; with the practicalities of Islamic orthopraxy rather than the introspection and deliberation of emergent *īmān*; and with the personae of the Imams rather than the truths of revelation, Twelver Shi'ism under the auspices of Majlisi became truly orthodox, and all other views were rejected and often forcibly repressed. True to his externalist ideals, Majlisi preached that *īmān* was incomplete without belief in the Imam, and that *'ilm* was confined to knowledge of the sayings of the Imams, and of the myriad ordinances narrated from them which were meant to regulate every facet of the Twelver Shi'ite believer's life.

If, for Majlisi, *'ilm* consists primarily in the knowledge of *hadīth*, then the Koranic verse which states that the *'ulamā* are the most fearful of God's slaves must refer, in his schema, to the *fuqahā*; as a corollary, Majlisi and his co-jurists are elevated to a position of veneration in the Twelver Shi'ite community second only to the Prophet and the Imams. The famous Tradition which states that 'the *'ulamā* are the inheritors of the prophets' most conveniently confirms this. It is largely thanks to Majlisi and his teachings on *'ilm* that the fuqaha were able to consolidate their popular base and win the virtually unconditional respect of the simple Twelver faithful. Indeed, how could the credibility of a faqih ever again be doubted, given that he and his colleagues were the representatives of the Imam? Furthermore, since he is an *'ālim*, and thus, according to Majlisi's creative interpretation, truly fearful of God, how can the jurist not remain forever beyond reproach?

If externalism and non-externalism/internalism had been able to co-exist relatively peacefully before, this was hardly the case during the lifetime of Majlisi. He chose to tackle the problem of internalist opposition by tarring both popular, antinomian folk-Sufism and orthodox, 'high' Sufism with the same brush, accusing all of those under the Sufi banner of heterodoxy, innovation and unbelief. All Sufis - and thus all who pay what must have seemed to Majlisi to be an inordinate amount of attention to the inner realities of belief - were declared unbelievers and deserving of hellfire. The vices of the Shah, however, despite being equally as objectionable in theory as the antinomian exploits of the Sufis, did not seem to concern the 'Allama; indeed he more than any other Safavid *faqīh* championed the monarchy and hailed the Safavid kings as precursors of the rule of the Hidden Imam.

It is in the context of the occultation of the Hidden Imam, the Mahdi, that the externalism of Majlisi and the Twelver *fuqahā* comes into sharp focus. According to the Traditions presented by Majlisi in his *magnum opus*, the *Bihār al-anwār*, the absence of the Hidden Imam is a period of great trial for the Twelver Shi'ites, the pain of which will be alleviated only with the return of the Mahdi and the reappearance of the other eleven Imams. During the occultation, all rulers are technically usurpers and thus their governments are illegitimate. The Twelver Shi'ites, however, must endure tyranny and oppression with patience and steadfastness. They must neither revolt nor support rebellion, for any who rise to claim power before the return of the Mahdi will be classed as infidels. The Twelver faithful must keep calm and cling to the teachings of the Imams as conveyed to them by their representatives and inheritors, the *fuqahā*. Justice will come only with the return of the Mahdi and the dramatic reappearance of the rest of the *ahl al-bayt*.

What is apparent, however, from Majlisi's presentation of the doctrine is that justice will be limited to the vengeance that the Imams will seek from their long dead but now miraculously resuscitated opponents. If the doctrine of Mahdism in general serves to deflect attention from the notion of divine justice and personal salvation that is to obtain following the Resurrection, then the uniquely Twelver Shi'ite doctrine of *raj'a* - the return of the Imams - shifts the attention even further away from the idea of universal peace and justice that is to accrue from the revival of pristine Islam and focuses, directly, on the personae of the Imams themselves. While the relief from tyranny that will supposedly be enjoyed by all believers as a result of the *raj'a* of the Imams is presented as the most obvious corollary of their return, it is the revenge that will be wrought on their old opponents - on Abu Bakr and Umar in particular - that overshadows all other considerations and appears to be, in the final analysis, the sole reason for their return from the grave. In the concept of the occultation, the rise of the Mahdi and the appearance of the Imams with their new book and their new, revitalized Islam, the tragedy of the Imams reaches its climax, and the imamocentric internalism of the Twelver Shi'ite *fuqahā* has its finest hour.

Finally, it must be said that while Majlisi's writings still command respect in certain Twelver circles even today, many of the more contentious and controversial narrations presented by him in his vast corpus of writings have been dismissed as spurious. Majlisi himself has been discredited by certain modern Twelver writers as a bigot and a charlatan who forged Traditions in order to curry favour with the rulers of the day, and who championed political quietism in favour of the status quo in order to maintain the high profile of the *faqīh* in Twelver Shi'ite social and religious life. Reaction against the political quietism of Majlisi and his fellow *fuqahā* can be seen as a major factor in the acquisition by twentieth-century Twelver Shi'ism of a new and revolutionary face: a Shi'ism that does not advocate the teaching of endless tracts on the minutiae of ablution, or upon the need to take revenge on the oppressors of Ali or Husayn, but rather a Shi'ism that stresses social awareness and constant revolution; a Shi'ism that, by stressing politics rather than *fiqh*, and revolution rather than weeping over the death of Husayn, continues, deliberately or unwittingly as the case may be, to champion the externalist discourse and obfuscate the eternal truths and realities of *īmān*.

Select Bibliography

Abbād, 'Abd al-Muhsin. *'Aqīdat ahl al-sunna wa al-athar fī al-mahdī al-muntazar*. Qum, 1971.

'Abd al-Bāqī, Muhammad Fu'ād. *Mu'jam al mufahris lī alfāz al-Qurān al-karīm*. Beirut, 1363/1943-44.

Ahsā'ī, Ibn Abī Jumhūr. *al-Mujlī*. Tehran, 1329/1911.

Al-Attas, Syed Muhammad Naquib. *Islam, Secularism and the Philosophy of the Future*. London: Mansell Publishing, 1985.

Albasānī, Shaykh Muhammad Sa'īd b. Muhammad Kāzim. *Tārīkhcha-i hayāt*. Mashhad, 1372/1952-53.

_____*Darūngarī wa burūngarī*. Mashhad, n.d.

Algar, Hamid. 'Shi'ism and Iran in the eighteenth century' in T. Naff and R. Owen (eds.), *Studies in Eighteenth Century Islamic History*. London, 1977

_____'The Naqshbandī Order: A Preliminary Survey of its History and Significance' in *Studia Islamica*, vol. 44 (1976), pp. 123-152.

_____'Some Observations on Religion in Safavid Persia' in *Iranian Studies*, vol. 7 (1974), pp. 286-293.

Allouche, Adel. *The Origins and Development of the Ottoman-Safavid Conflict*. Berlin: Klaus Schwarz Verlag, 1983.

'Āmilī, Muhammad b. Hasan al-Hurr. *Wasā'il al-shī'a*. Beirut, 1391/1971.

_____*Amal al-āmil* (ed. by A. Husaynī). Najaf, 1385/1965-66.

'Āmilī, Muhsin al-Amīn. *Khitat Jabal 'Āmil*. Beirut, 1983.

'Āmilī, Zayn al-dīn. *al-Rawdat al-bahiyya fī sharh al-lum'at al-dimashqiyya*. Tabriz, 1275-76/1955-56.

Āmulī, Hasan Hasanzāda. *Ma'rifat al-nafs*. Tehran: Markaz-i Intishārāt-i 'Ilmī wa Farhangī, 1362 Sh./1983-84. 3 vols.

Āmulī, Haydar. *Jāmi' al-asrār wa manba' al-anwār*. India Office Library, MS Arberry 1349.

Ardabīlī, Ahmad b. Muhammad. *Majma' al-fā'ida wa al-burhān*. Tehran, 1272/1855-56.

Ardabīlī, Muhammad b. 'Alī. *Jāmi' al-ruwāt*. Qum, 1403/1982-83. 2 vols.

Arjomand, Said Amir. 'Religious Extremism (Ghuluww), Sufism and Sunnism in Safavid Iran: 1501-1722' in *Journal of Asian History*, vol. 15, no. 1 (1981), pp. 1-35.

_____*The Shadow of God and the Hidden Imam*. Chicago: The University of Chicago Press, 1984.

'Asar, Sayyid Muhammad Kāzim. *'Ilm al- hadīth.* Tehran, 1354 Sh./1975-76.

'Āshūr, Mustafā Zakī. *Badī' al-zamān Sa'īd Nūrsī.* Köln: Mihrab, n.d.

'Askari, Seyyed Hasan. 'Religion and Development' in *The Islamic Quarterly*, vol. 30. no. 2 (1986), pp. 75-81.

Aubin, Jean. 'Les Sunnites du Larestan et la chute des Safavides' in *Revue des etudes islamiques*, vol. 33 (1965), pp. 151-171.

_____ 'La politique religieuse des Safavides' in *Le Shi'isme Imamite.* Paris: Colloque de Strasbourg. 1970.

_____ 'Tamerlan à Bagdad' in *Arabica*, vol. 9 (1962), pp. 303-309

_____ *Materiaux pour la Biographie de Shah Ni'matullāh Wali Kermani: Jāmi'-i Mufīd.* Tehran, 1956

_____ Shah Ismā'īl et les notables de l'Iraq persan' in *Journal of the Economic and Social History of the Orient*, vol. 2, no. 1 (1959), pp. 35-81.

'Azzawī, Abbās. *Tārīkh al-'irāq bayna ihtilālayn.* Baghdad, 1935-50. 4 vols.

Bahrānī, Yūsuf. *Lu'lu'at al-Bahrayn.* (Ed. by M.S. Bahr al-'Ulūm). Najaf, 1386/1966-67.

Baljon, J.M.S. *Religion and Thought of Shah Wali allah Dihlawi 1703-1762.* Leiden: E. J. Brill, 1986.

Banani, Amir. 'Reflections on the social and economic structure of Safavid Persia at its zenith'in *Iranian Studies*, vol. 2 (1978), pp. 83-116.

Bāzargān, Mihdī. *Gumrāhān.* Tehran, 1362 Sh./1983-84.

Bellan, L.L. *Chah 'Abbās I.* Paris, 1932.

Browne, E.G. *A Literary History of Persia.* Cambridge: CUP, 1930, 4 vols.

Bucaille, Maurice. *La Bible, le Coran et le Science.* Paris: Seghers, 1976.

Bukhārī, Abū 'Abdullāh Muhammad b. Ismā'īl. *Sahīh al-Bukhārī.* Istanbul: Hilal Yayinlari, 1298/1977-8.

Burckhardt, Titus. *Introduction to Sufi Doctrine.* London, 1975.

Burqa'ī, Sayyid Abū al-fadl 'Allāma. *Muqaddima bar tābishī az Qur'ān.* Tehran, 1985.

Calder, Norman. *The Structure of Authority in Imami Shi'i Jurisprudence.* University of London, Ph.D. thesis, London, 1980.

_____ 'Legitimacy and Accommodation in Safavid Iran' in *IRAN*, vol. 25 (1987), pp. 91-105.

Carmelites. *A chronicle of the Carmelites in Persia and the papal Mission of the XVIIth and XVIIIth Centuries.* London, 1939. 2 vols.

Chardin, J. *Les voyages du Chevalier Chardin en Perse et autre lieux de l'Orient*, (ed. by L. Langlès). Paris: Le Normant, 1811. 10 vols.

Chittick, William C. (ed.), *A Shi'ite Anthology.* London: The Muhammadi Trust, 1980.

Cole, Juan R. *Imami Shi'ism from Iran to North India, 1722-1856.* University of California, Ph.D. thesis, Los Angeles, 1984.

Corbin, H. 'Confessions extatiques de Mīr Dāmād' in *Mélange Louis Massignon.* Damascus, 1956.

_____ *La Philosophe Shi'ite.* Tehran, 1969.

Cragg, Kenneth. *The House of Islam.* Belmont: Dickenson, 1969.

Dabashi, Hamid. 'Ali Shari'ati's Islam: Revolutionary Uses of Faith in a Post-Traditional Society' in *The Islamic Quarterly*, vol. 27, no. 4 (1983), pp. 203-22.

Dānishpazhūh, Muhammad Taqī (ed.) *Fihrist-i kitābkhāna-i ihdā'ī-i āqā-i Mishkāt bi kitābkhāna-i dānishgāh-i Tihrān.* Tehran: Intishārāt- Dānishgāh-i Tihrān, 1330-1338 Sh/1951-60. 3 vols.

_____ 'Dāwarī miyān-i pārsā wa dānishmand' in *Nashriyya-i Dānishkada-i Adabiyyāt-i Tabriz*, vol. 9, 1336 Sh./1957-58.

Danner, Victor. (with W.M. Thackston). *Ibn 'Ata'illah: The Book of Wisdom – Khwaja Abdullah Ansari: Intimate Conversations*, London: SPCK, 1979.

Dawānī, 'Alī. *Mahdī-i maw'ūd, tarjuma-i jild- sīzdahum-i Bihār al-anwār.* Tehran: Dār al-Kutub al-Islāmiyya, 1350 Sh./1971-72.

_____ *Ustād-i kull Āqā Muhammad Bāqir b. Muhammad Akmal ma'rūf bi Wahīd-i Bihbihānī.* Qum, 1958.

Dhahabī, Muhammad b. 'Uthmān. *al-Muntaqā min minhaj al-i'tidāl.* Cairo, 1374/1954-55.

Dickson, M.B. *Shāh Tahmasp and the Uzbeks*, Princeton University Ph.D. thesis, Princeton, 1958.

_____ 'Lockhart's The Fall of the Safawi Dynasty' in *JAOS*, vol. 82 (1962), pp. 503-517.

Dihlawī, Hāfiz Ghulām Halīm Shāh 'Abd al-Azīz. *Tuhfa ithnā 'ashariyya.* Lucknow, 1885.

Du Mans, Rafael. *Estat de la Perse en 1660.* (Edited by C. Schefer). Paris, 1890.

Eberhard, E. *Osmanische Polemik gegen die Safaviden im 16. Jahrhundert nach arabischen Handschriften.* Freiburg. 1970.

Elgood, Cyril. *Safavid Medical Practice.* London, 1970.

Eliash, Joseph. 'Misconceptions regarding the judicial status of the Iranian ulama'in *International Journal of the Middle East*, vol. 10 (1979), pp. 9-25.

Enayat, Hamid. *Modern Islamic Political Thought.* London: The Macmillan Press, 1982

Falsafī, Nasrullāh. *Zindagānī-i Shāh 'Abbās-i Awwal .* Tehran, 1332 Sh./1953-54. 3 vols.

_____ 'Jang-i Chaldirān' in *Majalla-i Dānishkada-i Adabiyyāt-i Tihrān*, vol. 1 (1953-4), pp. 50-127.

Farāhānī, 'Ali Tughā'ī. *Himam al-thawāqib*, Tehran: Library of Madrasa-i Siphahsālār, MS. 1845.

Fischer, Michael M.J. *Iran: From Religious Dispute to Revolution.* Cambridge, Massachussets: Harvard University Press, 1980.

Gardet, L. 'ISLĀM' in *EI²*.

Gaudefroy-Demombynes, M. *La Syrie a l'epoque des Mamelouks.* Paris, 1923.

Gemelli-Careri, J.F. 'A Voyage Round the World' in Churchill, J. (ed.). *A Collection of Voyages* (Vol. 4). London, 1704.

Ghaffārī, Qādī Ahmad. *Tarikh-i jahān-ārā.* Tehran, n.d.

Ghazālī, Abū Hamīd Muhammad. *Kitāb al-'ilm.* Translated into English as *The Book of Knowledge* by N.A. Faris. Lahore: Ashraf Press 1962.

Gibb, H.A.R. *Islam.* Oxford: OUP, 1975.

Glassen, Erika 'Schah Ismā'īl I und die Theologen seiner Zeit' in *Der Islam*, vol. 48 (1971/2), pp. 254-268.

_____ 'Schah Ismā'īl, ein Mahdi der Anatolischen Turkmenen?' in *ZDMG* 121 (1971), pp. 61-9.

Gobineau, Count. *Les religions et les philosophies dans l'Asie centrale*. Paris, 1865.

Goldziher, I. *al-'Aqīda wa al-sharī'a fī al-Islām*. (Translated by M.Yusūf). Cairo, 1378/1958-59.

Gulpāyigānī, Lutfullāh al-Sāfī. *Muntakhab al-athar fī al-imām al-thānī 'ashar*. Tehran, n.d.

Hakluyt Society. *Travels of Venetians in Persia*. London, 1873.

Hanbal, Ahmad b. *al-Musnad*. Cairo, 1313/1895-6. 6 vols.

Hanīfa, Abū. *al-Ibāna*. Cairo, 1348/1929-30.

Hasanī, Hāshim Ma'rūf. *Sīrat al-a'imma al-ithnā 'ashar*. Beirut, 1397/1976-77. 2 vols.

Hidāyat, Ridā Qulī Khān. *Mulhaqāt-i Rawdat al-safā*. Tehran, 1275/1858-59. 10 vols.

Hijazi, 'Abd al-Ridā. *Qur'ān dar 'asr-i fadā* Tehran: Kānun – Intishārat, 1354 Sh.1975-76.

Hinz, Walther. *Irans Aufstieg zum Nationalstaat im fünfzehnten Jahrhundert*. Berlin/Leipzig, 1936.

Hodgson Marshall G. 'How did the early Shi'a become sectarian' in *JAOS*, vol. 75 (1955), pp. 1-13.

_____ 'The Safavī Empire: Triumph of the Shī'ah, 1503-1722' in *The Venture of Islam*, vol. 3. Chicago, 1974.

Hollister, J.N. *The Shi'a of India*. London 1953.

Hussein, Jassim M. *The Occultation of the Twelfth Imam*. London: The Muhammadi Trust, 1982.

Ibn 'Abbās, Abdullāh. *Tanwīr al-miqbās*. Tehran: al-Maktabat al-Islāmiyya, d. 1377/1957-8. 6 vols.

Ibn Battūta, Muhhamad b. 'Abdullāh. *Rihla*. Beirut, 1960.

Ibn Bazzāz, Tawakkul b. Ismā'īl. *Safwat al-safā*. India Office, MS. 1842.

Ibn al-Jawzī. 'The Devil's Delusion [Talbīs Iblīs] (translated by D.S. Margouliath) in *Islamic Culture*, vol. 10 (1936), pp. 20-39.

Ibn Māja Muhammad b. Yazīd. *al-Sunan*. Cairo: Dār Ihyā al-Kutub al-'Arabiyya, 1372/1952-53. 2 vols.

Ibn Rūzbihān. *Tarīkh-i ālam-ārā-i Amīnī* (transl. by V. Minorsky as *Persia in A.D. 1478-1490*). London, 1957

Ibn Tāwūs,'Alī. *al-Iqbāl*. Tehran, n.d.

Ibn Taymiyya, Taqī al-din. *Minhāj al-sunnat al-nabawiyya fī naqd kalām al-shi'at al-qadariyya*. Cairo, 1962. 2 vols.

Iqbāl, 'Abbās. *Tārīkh-i mufassal-i Irān*. Tehran, 1312 Sh./1938.

Isbahānī, Mīrzā 'Abdullāh Afandī. *Riyād al-'ulamā wa hiyād al-fudalā*. Qum, 1401/1980-81. 6 vols.

Izutsu, Toshihiko. *The Concept of Belief in Islamic Theology*. Tokyo, 1965.

_____ *Ethico-Religious Concepts in the Qur'ān*. Montreal, 1966.

Jabre, Farid. *La Notion de Certitude selon Ghazali*. Paris, 1958.

Jackson, A.V.W. *From Constantinople to the Home of Omar Khayyam.* New York, 1911.

Jawāhirī, G. (ed.) *Kulliyāt-i Shaykh Bahā'ī.* Tehran, n.d.

Kaempfer, E. *Dar darbārī-i shāhanshāh-i Īrān.* (Translated by K. Jahāndārī). Tehran, 1350/1971.

Kāshānī, Muhsin Fayd. *Ā'ina-i shāhī.* Shiraz, 1320 Sh./1941.

——*Raf' al-fitna.* Tehran: Kitābkhāna-i Markazī Dānishgāh-i Tehran, MS. 3303.

Kashī, Muhammad b. 'Umar b. 'Abd al-'Azīz. *Kitāb al-rijāl.* Mashhad, 1348 Sh./1969-70.

Kasrawī Tabrīzī, Ahmad. *Shaykh Safī wa tabārish.* Tehran. 1342 Sh./1963.

——*al-Tashayyu' wa al-shī'a.* Tehran, n.d.

——'Bāz ham Safawīyya' in *Āyanda,* vol. 2 (1927-8).

Keddie, Nikkie R. *Roots of Revolution: an Interpretative History of Modern Iran.* Newhaven: Yale University Press, 1981.

——'The Roots of the Ulama's Power in Modern Iran' in *Scholars, Saints and Sufis.* (Edited by N.R. Keddie). Berkeley and Los Angeles: University of California Press, 1978.

Khāmini'ī, Sayyid 'Alī. *Tarh-i kullī-i andīsha-i islāmī dar Qur'ān.* Tehran, 1354 Sh./1975-76.

Khātūnābādī, Sayyid 'Abd al-Husayn. *Waqāi' al-sinīn wa al-a'wām.* Tehran: Chāpkhāna-i Islāmiyya, 1352 Sh./1973-74.

Khumaynī, Rūhullāh. *Tawdīh al-masā'il.* Tehran, 1979.

Khwāndamīr, Ghīyāth al-dīn. *Habib al-siyyar fī akhbār afrād al-bashar.* Tehran, 1333 Sh./1954-55. 4 vols.

Khwānsārī. Muhammad Bāqir. *Rawdāt al-jannāt.* Tehran, 1304/1887.

Kirmānshāhī, Āqā Ahmad. *Mir'āt al-ahwāl-i jahān-namā.* London: British Library, Persian MS. Add. 24,052.

Kishāwarz, Karīm. 'Nahdat-i sarbidārān dar Khurāsān' in *Farhang-i Irān zamīn,* vol. 10 (1962), pp. 124-224.

Kissling, H.J. 'Badr al-din b. Kadi Samawna' in *EI²*.

Köprülüzade, Mehmet Fuat. 'Türk edebiyatinda mutasavviflar', summarised by L. Bouvat as 'Les premiers mystiques dans la literature turque' in *Revue du Monde Musulman,* vol. 43 (1921), pp. 236-82.

Krusinski, T.J. *The History of the Late Revolutions in Persia.* London, 1740.

Kūfī, Ibn A'tham. *Kitāb al-futūh.* Hyderabad, 1972.

Kulaynī, Muhammad b. Ya'qūb. *Usūl al-kāfī.* (Abridged edition translated and edited by A.A. Shabistari). Tehran: Kitāb furūshi-i Amīrī, 1351 Sh./1972-73.

——*Kitāb fadl al-'ilm.* (Translated by S.M. Rizvi). Tehran: WOFIS, 1398/1977-78.

Lāhījī, Shaykh Muhammad. *Sharh-i gulshān-i rāz.* (Edited by K. Samī'ī). Tehran, 1337 Sh./1958-59.

Lambton, A.K.S. 'Quis Custodiet Custodes' in *Studia Islamica,* vol. 5 (1956), pp. 125-46.

——'Concepts of Authority in Persia: Eleventh to Nineteenth Centuries A.D.' in *IRAN,* vol. 26 (1988), pp. 95-103.

Lewis, B. 'Some observations on the significance of heresy in the history of Islam' in *Studia Islamica*, vol. 1 (1953), pp. 43-63.

Lockhart,L. *The Fall of the Safavi Dynasty and the Afghan Occupation of Persia.* Cambridge: CUP, 1958.

Mahdawī, Muslih al-dīn. *Tadhkirat al-qubūr yā dānishmandān wa buzurgān- i Isfahān.* Isfahan, 1348 Sh./1969-70.

Mahjūb, Muhammad Ja'far. 'As fadā'il wa manāqib-khwānī tā rawda-khwānī' in *Iran Nameh* vol. 3, no. 3 (Spring, 1984.

Majlisī, Muhammad Bāqir *Bihār al-anwār.* Beirut, 1403/1982-83. 110 vols. New printed edition.

_____ *Tuhfat al-zā'ir.* Tabriz, 1334/1955-56.

_____ *The Life and Religion of Muhammad* [*Hayāt al-qulūb*, vol. 2]. (Translated by Rev. James L. Merick). San Antonio: The Zahra Trust, 1982.

_____ *Risāla-i su'āl wa jawāb.* Tabriz, 1332 Sh./1953-54.

_____ *Zād al-ma'ād.* Tehran, 1320/1903-04.

_____ *Hilyat al-muttaqīn.* Tehran, 1334 Sh./1955-56.

_____ *Munājātnāma.* Mashhad, 1354 Sh./1975-76.

_____ *'Ayn al-hayāt.* Tehran, 1333 Sh./1954-55, p. 499.

Majlisī, Muhammad Taqī. *Lawāmi'-i Sāhibqirānī.* Tehran, 1913.

_____ *Risāla-i tashwīq al-sālikīn.* Tabriz, 1332 Sh./1953-54.

Malcolm, Sir John. *History of Persia.* London, 1815. 2 vols.

Maqdīsī, Shams al-dīn Abū 'Abdullāh. *Ahsan al-taqāsīm.* (Edited by M.J. de Goeje). Leiden, 1906.

Maqrīzī, Taqī al-dīn. *al-Khitat.* Cairo, 1326/1908-09.

Mazzaoui, Michael M. *The Origins of the Safavids: Shi'ism, Sufism and the Ghulāt.* Wiesbaden, 1972.

_____ 'The Ghazi backgrounds of the Safawid State' in *Iqbāl Review*, vol. 12, no. 3 (1971), pp. 79-90.

Memon, Muhammad Umar. *Ibn Taimīya's Struggle against Popular Religion.* The Hague, 1976.

Minorsky, Vladimir. *La Perse au XVe Siecle entre la Turquie et Venise.* Paris: E. Leroux, 1933.

_____ (ed.), *Tadhkirat al-Mulūk.* Cambridge: CUP, 1980.

_____ 'Jihan Shah Qaraqoyunlu and his Poetry' in *BSOAS*, vol. 16 (1954) pp. 271-297.

_____ 'The Poetry of Shah Ismā'īl I' in *BSOAS*, VOL. 10 (1942), pp. 1006a-1053a.

_____ 'Kizilbāsh' in *EI².*

Molé, M. 'Les Kubrawīya entre Sunnism et Shiisme' in *Revue des Etudes Islamiques*, vol. 29, no. 1 (1961), pp. 61-142.

Momen, Moojan. *An Introduction to Shi'i Islam: The History and Doctrines of Twelver Shi'ism.* New Haven: Yale University Press, 1985.

Moreh, V.B. 'The status of religious minorities in Safavid Iran' in *Journal of Near Eastern Studies*, vol. 40 (1981), pp. 119-134.

Morris, James Winston. *The Wisdom of the Throne: an Introduction to the Philosophy of Mulla Sadra.* Princeton: Princeton University Press, 1981.

Morton, A.H. 'The Ardabīl shrine in the reign of Shāh Tahmāsp I' in *Iran*, vol. 12 (1974), pp. 31-64 and vol. 13 (1975), pp. 39-58.

Munshī, Iskandar. *Tārīkh-i ālamārā-i Abbāsī*. (Edited by E. Yarshater, translated by R. Savory). Boulder, Colorado, 1978.

Mustawfī, Hamdullah. *Tārīkh-i guzīda*. (Edited by A.H. Nawā'ī). Tehran, 1336-39 Sh./1957-61.

_____*Nuzhat al-qulūb*. (Translated by G. Le Strange). London: Luzac and Co., 1919.

Mutahharī, Murtadā. *'Adl-i ilāhī*. Tehran: Intishārāt-i Islāmī, 1397/1976-77.

_____*Huqūq-i zan dar islām*. Tehran, 1357 Sh./1978-79.

_____*Insān wa islām*. Tehran, 1357 Sh.1978-79.

Nadvi, Muzaffar al-din. 'Pirism – Corrupted Sufism' in *Islamic Culture*, vol. 9 (1935), pp. 475-84.

Nasr, Seyyed Hossein. *Sufi Essays*. London, 1972.

_____*Sadr al-dīn Shīrāzī and his Transcendent Theosophy*. Tehran, 1978.

_____ 'Religion in Safavid Persia' in *Iranian Studies*, vol. 7 (1974), pp. 271-286.

Nasrābādī, Mīrzā Muhammad Tāhir. *Tadhkira-i Nasrābādī*. Tehran: Furughi, 1352 Sh./1973.

Natanzī, Mahmūd. *Nuqāwāt al-āthār fī dhikr al-akhyār*. (Edited by I. Ishrāqī). Tehran, 1350 Sh./1971-72.

Nawā'ī A.H. *Asnād wa mukātabāt-i tārīkhī; Shāh 'Abbās-i Awwal*. Tehran, 1352 Sh./1973-74.

Nawbakhti, Hasan b. Mūsā. *Firaq al-shi'a*. (Edited by Ritter). Leipzig, 1931.

Nazīrī, Yahya. *Qur'ān wa padīdahā-i tabī'at az dīd-i dānish-i imrūz*. Tehran, 1358 Sh.1979-80.

Newman, Andrew. 'Towards a reconsideration of the "Isfahan School of Philosophy": Shaykh Baha'i and the role of the Safawid 'ulama,' in *Studia Iranica*, no. 15/2 (1986), pp. 165-99.

Nikitine, Basil. 'Essai d'analyse du safvat al-safa' in *Journal Asiatique*, vol. 245 (1957), pp. 385-394.

Nūrī, Shaykh Yahyā. *Huqūq wa hudūd-i zan dar islām*. Tehran, 1340 Sh./1961-62.

Nursi, Said. *Emirdag Lahikasi*. Istanbul: Sinan Matbassi, 1959.

_____ *Lema'lar*. Istanbul: Sinan Matbaasi, 1959.

_____ *Şua'lar*. Istanbul: Sinan Matbaasi, 1959.

_____ *Mektubat*. Istanbul: Sinan Matbaasi, 1959.

_____ *The Miracles of Muhammad*. Istanbul, 1985.

Osman, Muhammad Salih. *Mahdism in Islam up to 260 A.H./874 and its relation to Zoroastrian, Jewish and Christian Messianism..* University of Edinburgh, Ph.D. Thesis, 1976.

Pampus, Karl-Heinz. *Die Theologische Enzyklopädie Bihar al-Anwar des Muhammad Baqir Al-Maglisi*. Bonn, 1970.

Perry, R.J. 'The Last Safavids 1722-1773' in *Iran*, vol. 9 (1971), pp. 59-69.

Pourjavady, Nasrollah (with Wilson, Peter Lamborn). *Kings of Love: The Poetry and History of the Ni'matullahiyya Sufi Order*. Tehran, 1978.

Qazwīnī, Muhammad Tāhir Wahid. *'Abbāsnāma*. Arak, 1329 Sh./1950-51.

Qumī, 'Abbās. *Mafātīh al-jinān*. Tehran: Intishārāt-i Gulī, 1389/1975-76.

Qumī, Qādī Ahmad. *Khulāsāt al-tawārīkh*. Berlin: Deutsche Staatsbibliothek, MS Or. 2202.

Rahbar, Daud. *God of Justice: A study in the Ethical Doctrine of the Quran*. Leiden, 1960.

Rahman, Fazlur. *The Philosophy of Mulla Sadra*. Albany: State University of New York Press, 1975.

Rāzī, Fakhr al-dīn. *Mafātīh al-ghayb*. Istanbul, 1307/1891. 8 vols.

Rāzī, Najm al-din. *Mirsād al-'ibād min al-mabda' ilā al-ma'ād*. (Edited by M. Riyahi). Tehran, 1352 Sh.1973-74.

Ridā, Rashīd. *Tafsīr al-Qur'ān al-karīm, tafsīr al-manār*. Cairo: Matba'at al-Kubrā al-Amīrīyya, 1367-1375/1948-1956

Ringgren, Helmer. *Islam, 'aslama and Muslim*. Uppsala, 1949.

———'The conception of faith in the Koran' in *Oriens*, vol. 4 (1951), pp. 1-20.

Röhrborn, K. *Provinzen und Zentralgewalt Persiens im 16. und 17. Jahrundert*. Berlin, 1966.

Rosenthal, Franz. *Knowledge Triumphant*. Leiden: Brill, 1970.

Ross, Sir E.D. 'The Early Years of Shah Isma'il, Founder of the Safavi dynasty' in *JRAS* (April, 1896), pp. 249-340.

Rūmlū, Hasan. *Ahsan al-tawārīkh: A Chronicle of the early Safavids*. (Edited and translated by C.N. Sedon). Baroda, 1931-4. 2 vols.

Sachedina, A.A. *Islamic Messianism*. Albany: State University of New York Press, 1981.

Sadr, Sayyid Muhammad Bāqir. *Inqilāb-i mahdī wa pindārhā*. (Translated by S.A. 'Alam al-hudā). Tehran, 1363 Sh./1984-85.

Sadūq, Muhammad b. 'Alī. *Kamāl al-din wa tamām al-ni'ma*. Tehran, 1378/ 1958-59 and 1395/1975-76).

Safarī, S. *Armaghān al-awliyā'*. Mashhad, 1344 Sh./1965-66.

———*Zindagānī-i Majlisī*. Mashhad, 1335 Sh./1956-57.

Safawī, R. *Zindagānī-i Shah Ismā'īl Safawī*. Tehran, 1341 Sh./1962.

Sanson, Nicholas. *The Present State of Persia*. London, 1695.

Sarwar, Ghulam. *History of Shah Isma'il Safawi*. Aligarh, 1939.

Savory, R.M. *Iran Under the Safavids*. Cambridge: CUP, 1980.

———'The Principal Offices of the Safawid State during the Reign of Tahmasp I' in *BSOAS*, vol. 24, no. 1 (1961), pp. 65-85.

———'The Office of Khalīfat al-Khulafā Under the Safavids' in *JAOS*, vol. 85 (1965), pp. 497-502.

———'The Safavid State and Polity' in *Iranian Studies*, vol. 7 (1974), pp. 179-212.

———'Some reflections on totalitarian tendencies in the Safawid State' in *Der Islam*, vol. 53 (1976), pp. 226-241.

———'A 15th Century Propagandist at Harāt' in *American Oriental Society, Middle West Branch, Semi-centennial volume*. London, 1969.

Schimmel, Annemarie. 'The Ornament of the Saints' in *Iranian Studies*, vol. 7 (1974), pp. 88-111.

Schuon, Frithjof. *Islam and the Perennial Philosophy*. London, 1976.

Shāh, Ma'sūm 'Ali. *Arā'iq al-haqā'iq*. Tehran, 1339 Sh./1960-61. 3 vols.

Shaltūt, 'Allāma. *Sayrī dar ta'ālim-i islām.* (Translated by S.K. Khalīlīyān). Tehran, 1344 Sh./1965-66.

Sharī'atī, 'Alī. *Bā mukhātab-hā-i āshinā.* Tehran: Husayniyya-i Irshād, 1397/1976-77.

_____ *Fātima Fātima ast.* Tehran, 1336 Sh./1957-58.

_____ *Islāmshināsī.* Mashhad, 1347 Sh./1968-69.

_____ *Pidar, mādar, mā muttahamim.* Tehran, 1976 Sh./1967-68.

_____ *Hajj.* (Translated by Somayyah and Yaser). Bedford, Ohio: FLINC, 1977.

_____ *Mas'ūliyyat-i shi'ī būdan.* Tehran, 1352 Sh./1973-74.

_____ *Shī'a.* Tehran: Husayniyya-i Irshād, 1357 Sh./ 1978-79.

_____ *Tashayyu'-i alawī wa tashayyu'-i safawī.* Tehran, 1352 Sh/1973-74.

Shaybānī, N.M. *Tashkīl-i shāhanshāhī-i Safawī: ihyā-i wahdat-i millī.* Tehran, 1345 Sh./1966-67.

Shīrāzī, Mīrzā Makhdūm. *al-Nawāqid li-bunyān al-rawāfid.* London: British Museum MS. Or. 7991.

Shīrāzī, Mullā Sadrā. *al-Asfār al-arba'a.* (Edited by M.R. al-Muzaffar). Tehran, 1378/1958-59. 4 vols.

_____ *al-Shawāhid al-rubūbiyya.* (Edited by J. Āshtīyānī). Mashhad, 1346 Sh./1967-68.

_____ *Sih Asl.* Tehran: Intishārāt-i Mawlā.1365 Sh./1986-87.

_____ *Tafsīr sūrat al-wāqi'a.* Tehran: Intishārāt-i Mawlā. 1404/1983-84.

_____ *Kasr al-asnām al-jahilīyya fī dhamm al-mutasawwifīn.* Tehran, 1340 Sh./1961-62.

Shūshtarī, Nūrullāh. *Ihqāq al-haqq.* Tehran, 1376/1956-57. 2 vols.

_____ *Majālis al-mu'minīn.*Tehran: Kitābfurūshi-Islāmīyya. 1375-6/1955-57. 2 vols.

Sirhindī, Shaykh Ahmad. *Maktūbāt.* Lucknow, 1307/1889.

Smith, Jane I. 'Continuity and Change in the Understanding of "islām"' in *Islamic Quarterly,* vol. 16, no 3 (1972), pp. 121-39.

Smith, W. Cantwell. 'The Special Case of Islam' in *The Meaning and End of Religion.* New York, 1964. pp 75-108.

Sohrweide, Hanna. 'Der Sieg der Safaviden in Persien und seine Rückwirkungen auf die Shīiten anatoliens im 16. Jahrhundert' in *Der Islam,* vol. 41 (1965), pp. 95-223.

Sourdel-Thomine, J. 'Inscriptions arabes de Karak Nuh' in *Bulletin d'Études Orientales,* vol. 13 (1949-51), pp. 71-84.

Spicehandler, E. 'The persecution of the Jews of Isfahan under Shāh 'Abbās II (1642-1666)' in *Hebrew Union College Annual,* vol. 46 (1975), pp. 331-356.

Strothman, R. 'Ghālī' in *Shorter Encyclopaedia of Islam.*

Sümer, Faruk. *Safavi Devletinin Kuruluşu ve Gelişmesinde Anadolu Türklerinin Rolü.* Ankara, 1976.

Tabarī, Abū Ja'far Muhammad b. Jarīr. *Jāmi' al-bayān fī tafsīr al-Qur'ān.* Cairo, 1323-29/1900-11. 30 vols. in 9.

_____ *Tārīkh al-rusul wa al-mulūk.* (Edited by de Goeje). Leyden, 1879-1901. 10 vols.

Tabātabā' ī, Hossein Modaressī. *An Introduction to Shī'i Law.* London: Ithaca Press, 1984.

Tabātabā'ī, Sayyid Muhammad Husayn. *Tafsīr al-mīzān.* Tehran, 1364 Sh./1985-86.

Tabrīzī, Husayn Karbalā'ī. *Rawdat al-jinān wa jannāt al-janān.* Tehran, 1344 Sh./1965-66. 2 vols.

Tabrīzī, M.A. *Rayhānat al-adab.* Tehran, 1367/1947-48. 4 vols.

Tahmāsp, Shah. *Memoirs of Shāh Tahmāsp.* Calcutta, 1912.

Tavernier, J.B. *Voyages de M.J.B. Tavernier en Turquie, en Perse et aux Indes.* Paris, 1713. 6 vols.

Tha'labī, Ahmad b. Muhammad. *'Arā'is al-majālis.* Cairo, n.d.

Tihrānī, 'Alī. *Akhlāq-i islamī.* Mashhad, 1977. 2 vols.

Tihrānī, Āqā Buzurg. *al-Dharī'a ilā tasānīf al-Shī'a.* Beirut: Dār al-Adwā', 1988. 26 vols.

Tirmidhī, Muhammad b. Īsā. *Sunan al-Tirmidhī.* Cairo, 1356/1937-38. 5 vols.

Togan Zeki Velidi, 'Sur l'origine des Safavides' in *Melanges Louis Massignon.* Damascus, 1957.

Trimingham, J. Spencer. *The Sufi Orders in Islam.* Oxford: Clarendon Press, 1971.

Tschudi, 'Bektashiyya' in *EI².*

Tunukābunī, Muhammad. *Qisas al-'ulamā.* Tehran, 1304/1886 [Lithograph]. Also, Tehran, n.d. [Printed].

Tūsī, Muhammad b. Hasan. *al-Fihrist.* Mashhad, 1972.

———— *Kitāb al-ghayba .* Najaf, 1965.

Walī, Shāh Ni'matullāh. *Diwān.* Tehran, 1352 Sh./1973-74.

———— *Kulliyāt-i ash'ār-i Shāh Ni'matullāh Walī.* (Edited by J. Nūrbaksh). Tehran, 1352/1973-74.

Walsh, J.R. 'The Historiography of Ottoman-Safavid Relations in the sixteenth and seventeenth centuries' in Lewis, B. and Holt, P.M. (ed.). *Historians of the Middle East.* London, 1962.

———— 'Yunus Emre: a 14th century Turkish hymnodist' in *Numen,* vol. 7 (1960), pp. 172-188.

Watt, W. Montgomery. *Islamic Philosophy and Theology.* Edinburgh: UEP, 1979.

Wehr, Hans. *Arabic-English Dictionary.* (Edited by J.M. Cowan). New York: SLS, 1976.

Wensinck, A.J. *A Handbook of Early Muhammadan Jurisprudence.* Leiden, 1927 and 1960.

———— *The Muslim Creed.* Cambridge: CUP, 1932.

Yūsufī, M.K. *Surūr al-'ārifīn.* Tehran, 1984.

Zamīnī, Sa'īd Kāzim. *Sayr wa safar.* Konya, 1987.

Index

'Abbas I, Shah, 95, 97-104, 113, 129,
131, 136, 137, 138, 210, 211, 212
'Abbas II, Shah, 103, 104, 135, 136,
137, 138, 153, 162, 174
Abbasids, 191, 213
Abraham, 7, 18
Abu Bakr, 83, 190, 207, 223, 226,
227, 228, 229, 230
Abu Nu'aym, Hafiz, 113, 152, 181
'adl, 157, 169
Afandi, Shaykh 'Abdallah, 104, 105,
107-13, 116, 117, 120
Afghanistan, 165
ahl al-bātin, 45
ahl al-bayt, 56, 189, 200, 201, 215,
218, 220
ahl al-kitāb, 7
ahl al-zāhir, 45
ahl-i futuwwa, 55, 65
ahl-i ukhuwwa, 55, 65
Akhbarism, 109, 114, 115, 137, 138,
158-60, 181
'Alam al-Huda, 49
Algar, Hamid, 117
Ali b. Abi Talib, Imam, 21, 22, 48,
50, 52, 56-62, 64, 65, 85, 191,
192, 195, 196, 199, 200, 205, 206,
207, 217, 219, 220, 221, 222, 224,
225, 227, 228, 229, 231-34
'ālim, 22, 24, 26, 32, 33, 36, 44, 105,
123, 134, 151, 156, 178, 179, 204
al-mahdī, 190, 191, 192, 216. See
also Mahdi
Alwand, 64
'Amili, Muhammad Hurr al-, 80
'Amili, Muhsin al-Amin, 80

'Amili, Zayn al-din, 81
Amina Bigum, 172, 180
Amuli, Sayyid Haydar, 118, 119,
153, 208
Anatolia, 55, 56, 57, 58, 60, 62, 63,
64, 65
Ansari, 'Abdullah al-, 119
'aqīda, 16, 32
'aql, 5, 30, 46, 156, 157, 162, 181
'aqlī sciences 75, 77, 91, 96, 109,
111, 127, 156
Aq-Qoyunlu, 61, 62, 63, 64
a'māl sāliha, 11, 17
Ardabil, 59, 60, 61-64, 95
Ardabili, Muqaddas, 115, 206
Aristotle, 119
Arjomand, Said Amir, 90, 91, 92, 94,
95, 96, 115, 150, 158, 162, 163,
168, 182, 203, 207
Arjuwan, 64
Ash'ari, Abu al-Hasan al-, 9
Ash'arites, 9
Ashtar, Malik, 207
Askari, Sayid Hasan, 7
Astarabadi, Muhammad Mu'min,
159
Astarabadi, Muhammad Amin, 114
Astarabadi, Sayyid Amir
Muhammad, 102
Attas, S. Naquib al-, 3, 4, 28, 30, 36,
46, 47
Aubin, Jean, 90, 101
āyāt, 2, 5, 17, 34, 36
'Ayn al-hayāt, 163
Azarbaijan, 56, 59, 60, 61, 64, 86,
95, 163, 180, 213

Bāb al-hādī 'ashara, 169
Baba Rasulallah Ishaq, 62
Baba'i sect 58, 62
bada', 196
Baghdad, 49, 52, 65, 79, 80, 227
Baghdadi, Junayd al-, 173
Baha'i, Shaykh, 151, 153, 158, 160, 174
Bahr al-'ulum, 181
Banu Asad, 8, 10, 12, 15-17, 19
Baqir, Imam Muhammad al-, 15, 25, 33, 170, 196, 200
Basri, Hasan al-, 59
Bayqara, Sultan Husayn, 94
Baysunqur, 64
Bazargan, Mihdi, 33, 150
Bazzaz, Ibn al-, 59
Bektashiyya, 55, 58
Bengal, 180
Bihār al-anwār, 150, 158, 160, 167, 170-73, 193, 194, 195, 199, 202, 208, 211, 214, 216-18, 222, 223, 229, 231, 232
Bihbihani, Wahid, 180-81
Bistami, Abu Yazid (Bayazid), 119, 173, 177
Browne, Edward, 170, 182
Bukhari, Imam al-, 24
Burqa'i, 'Allama, 21, 159
Burujirdi, Ayatullah Husayn, 181

Calder, Norman, 208
Chardin, Jean, 209, 210, 212
Christianity, 191
Chubanids, 51
Cragg, Kenneth, 10
da'wa, 3
Damascus, 52
Danishpazhuh, Muhammad Taqi, 85, 113, 149, 154, 166, 182

dār al-'adl, 9
dār al-Islām, 9
Darband, 64
Darwish, Shaykh Kamal al-din, 110, 152, 153
Dawani, Ali, 172, 173, 214
Daya, Najm al-din, 56
Dhahabiyya, 153, 157
dīn, 11-14, 17, 23, 31
Diyarbakir, 62
du'ā, 168

Enayat, Hamid, 117
Erzincan, 64
externalism, 72, 73, 74, 75, 76, 81, 82, 86, 87, 88, 89, 91, 96, 99, 101-07, 110, 111, 114, 116, 117, 120, 121, 131, 133, 135, 136, 138, 150, 151, 153, 154, 162, 163, 177, 178, 181, 190, 194, 202, 208, 214, 223, 230, 234, 235, 237
externalists, 79, 94, 96, 101, 102, 103, 105, 107, 109-13, 115, 118, 119, 123, 124, 131, 134, 135, 136, 137
extremism, 77, 74, 82, 87, 89, 97, 99, 100, 112

Falsafi, Nasrullah, 63
faqīh, 3, 4, 26, 28, 36, 45, 47, 51, 78, 81, 87, 89, 92, 93, 94, 96, 102, 104, 105, 109, 112, 113, 116-19, 123, 124, 128, 136, 137, 154, 158, 161, 176, 179, 181, 202, 204, 206, 209, 214, 215, 235, 237
Farahani, Shaykh 'Ali al-, 109, 135
fard al-'ayn, 3, 36, 47
fard al-kifāya, 4, 27, 28, 36, 47
farmān of Shah Tahmasp, 88, 89

Fars, 64
Farsi, Salman al-, 227
Fatima, 192, 227, 228
Fayd al-qudsī, 151, 149, 158, 167, 182
fiqh, 3, 9, 23, 25-27, 29, 31, 32, 36, 46, 49, 53, 76, 79, 80, 81, 91, 92, 95, 96, 101, 105-08, 109, 111, 112, 116, 120, 121, 122, 123, 125, 128, 130-38, 150, 151, 156, 158, 159, 161, 178, 179, 207, 230, 234, 236, 237, 238
Fiqh al-akbar, 9
Fiqh-i Akbar II, 9
fisq, 9
Friday prayer, 78, 88, 114, 115, 137
fundamentals of belief, 25, 27, 30
fuqahā, 23, 26, 29, 47, 48, 49, 58, 66, 73-79, 82-92, 94-99, 100, 101, 103, 109-20, 122, 124, 150, 151, 154-57, 162, 164, 173, 174, 176, 178, 179, 180, 181, 202-09, 212, 214, 215, 221, 223, 232, 234, 235, 237, 238
furū' al-dīn, 3, 46, 47, 82, 107, 117, 156, 178, 215

Geertz, Clifford, 115
Genghis Khan, 211, 213
ghayba, 194, 197, 198, 200, 209, 214, 234, 235
Ghazali, Imam, 19, 23, 26-35, 45, 75, 82, 96, 118, 120, 122, 127, 129, 131, 135, 204, 234, 235
ghulāt, 52, 57, 58, 60, 65
ghuluww, 49, 52, 53, 57, 58, 60, 61, 62, 65
ghuzāt, 62
Gilan, 163, 211, 213
gnosis, 43, 44, 51, 56, 153

greater occultation, 194, 195

hadīth, 20, 23, 24, 25, 29, 31, 32, 36, 46, 49, 79, 91, 95, 96, 101, 106, 107-12, 116, 120, 121, 122, 123, 125, 150, 151, 156, 158, 160, 161, 164, 174, 178, 192, 193, 196, 211, 212, 230, 234. *See also* Traditions
Hajj Bektash, 62
Hallaj, Mansur, 119
Hanafite, 9, 50, 56, 65, 74, 110, 190, 127
hanīf, 7
Haqq al-yaqīn, 169
Hasan al-'Askari, Imam, 191, 217
Haydar, 60, 63, 64, 65
Hidden Imam, 79, 88, 95, 109, 122, 138, 152-57, 163, 173, 190, 191, 195, 196, 197, 200, 201, 206-15, 218, 223, 230, 234. *See also* Mahdi
hijra, 11
hikma, 20, 26, 173, 176
Hilla, 50, 79
Hilli, Ibn al-Mutahhar 'Allama, 51, 52, 53, 78, 86, 169
Hilli, Mir Ni'matullah, 92
Hilyat al-muttaqīn, 167
Himyari, Abu Ishaq al-, 190
Hindi, Sadr al-din Ali al-, 159
Hurr al-'Amili, Shaykh Muhammad, 115, 158, 159, 174
Hurufiyya, 55, 62
Husayn b. Ali, Imam, 110, 190, 192, 196, 205, 215, 217, 219, 220, 221, 224-29, 231, 234, 235, 238
Husayn, Shah Sultan, 162, 165, 166
Husayni al-'Amili, Nur al-din, 157, 158

'ilm, 2, 3, 4, 12, 20-26, 29, 30-35, 43,
   54, 75, 97, 127, 128, 131, 132,
   133, 134, 137, 155, 164, 169, 177,
   178, 179
'irfān, 20, 56, 95, 102, 117, 129,
   130
I'tiqādāt, 174, 175
Ibāna, 9
Ibn 'Abbas, 12, 14, 19, 21, 192
Ibn al-'Arabi, 118, 119, 126, 129,
   130
Ibn al-Hanafiyya, 190, 192
Ibn Babuya, 49, 77, 111, 136
Ibn Hanbal, Ahmad, 8
Ibn Muljam, 175
Ibn Sina, 119
Ibn Taymiyya, Taqi al-din, 9, 116,
   120, 177
ijāza, 158, 159
ijmā', 52
ijtihād, 78, 109, 114, 115, 123, 137,
   138, 181
Ilkhanid, 51, 52, 53, 55, 57, 59
imām jum'a, 162, 180
imāma, 51, 76, 78, 106, 107, 110-12,
   117, 120, 122, 130, 136, 157, 169,
   175, 207, 208, 232
imamocentrism, 106, 124, 150, 151,
   168
Imams, 56-58, 62, 65, 150, 154, 155,
   157, 160, 167, 168, 170, 175, 177,
   178, 179
īmān, 1-12, 14-20, 29, 30, 33, 43, 44,
   45, 47, 51, 54, 58, 73, 75, 76, 82,
   87, 92, 107, 121, 126, 130, 132,
   133, 134, 150, 156, 169, 170, 176,
   178, 179, 200, 203, 208, 230, 237,
   238
imtihān, 194, 195, 198, 215
internalism, 43, 45, 54, 58, 59, 62,
   63, 65, 75, 76, 91, 96, 101, 102,

   103, 107, 116, 117, 120-24, 127,
   130, 207, 216, 222, 223, 230, 234,
   238
intizār, 187, 194, 195, 199, 200, 201,
   202, 214, 215, 231, 233, 235, 236
Iqbal, 'Abbas, 55
Iran, 4, 24, 30; in pre-Safavid era, 43,
   45, 47-53, 55, 56, 57, 59, 60, 61,
   64, 65, 66
Irshād, 218
Isfahan, 79, 82, 85, 101, 102, 104,
   108, 113, 129, 136, 137, 152, 153,
   154, 155, 162-66, 171, 176, 180,
   182
Isfahani, Mir Mu'izz al-din
   Muhammad, 94, 95
Isfahani, Muhammad Qawam al-din,
   113
Isfahani, Shah 'Inayatullah, 99
islām, 1-4, 6-20, 28, 43
Islam, 43, 44, 46, 47, 48, 51, 54, 56,
   57, 73, 74, 75, 82, 86, 87, 92, 95,
   105, 107, 109, 119, 121, 124, 126,
   132, 133, 135, 149, 150, 155, 157,
   164, 168, 169, 173, 174, 175, 177,
   178, 188, 189, 190-93, 203, 205,
   208, 216, 223, 224, 230, 232, 234,
   235, 236, 238
Isma'il I, Shah, 48, 50, 61, 64, 65,
   66, 74, 77, 81, 83, 84, 86, 87, 88,
   89, 91, 95, 97, 98, 99, 211, 212
Isma'il II, Shah, 97, 98, 99
Ispand, 52

Ja'far al-Sadiq, Imam, 107, 130, 163,
   170, 175, 191, 201, 202, 213, 218,
   220-23, 228
Jabal 'Amil, 50, 79, 81, 87, 88, 94
Jahan Shah, 52, 61, 63
Jalayirids, 52, 59, 60

Jami, 'Abd al-Rahman al-, 113
Jaza'iri, Mirza, 158, 161, 172, 174
Jesus, 7
jihād, 78
Jilani, 'Abd al-Wahid Wa'iz, 127, 128
Jilani, Hasan al-Daylamani, 113
Jilani, Mawla Muhammad al-, 115
jinsiyya, 13
Joseph, 7
Jumhur, Ibn Abi, 118, 119
Junayd (Safavid leader), 60, 61, 62, 63, 65
jurisprudence, 2, 3, 4, 20, 22, 25, 26, 27-32, 46, 48, 49, 50, 51, 56, 59, 65, 66, 73, 74, 76, 77, 80, 81, 86, 96, 107, 108, 109, 114, 116, 121, 126, 157, 159, 168, 176, 178, 179, 181. See also fiqh
Jurjani, Amir Nizam al-din, 94

Kāfī, Usūl al-, 158, 159, 169
kalām, 22, 23, 49, 157
Karaki, Sayyid Husayn al-, 159
Karaki, Shaykh 'Ali Muhaqqiq al-, 79, 80, 81-89, 92-97, 101, 109, 112, 115, 120, 129, 138, 209, 210, 213
Karbala, 180, 181, 215, 217, 219, 225, 228, 229, 232, 234, 235
Kashan, 50, 51
Kashani, Mulla Muhsin Fayd al-, 25, 136, 158, 159
Kashi, Mawla Hasan al-, 86
Kashifi, Husayn Wa'iz, 110
Kaysanites, 190, 217, 239
Kazimi, Shaykh Jawad, 102
Khamini'i, Ali, 5, 36
Khatunabadi, Mir Muhammad Husayn, 161, 163, 164, 166, 180

Khudabanda, Shah Muhammad, 97
khulafā, 63, 64, 190
khums, 78, 108
Khunji, Ibn Ruzbihan, 60, 61, 63, 85, 89
Khurasan, 52, 60, 86, 88, 119, 211
Khwansari, Aqa Husayn, 129, 162
kingship, 204, 205, 206, 208, 219
Kirmanshahi, Aqa Ahmad, 148, 153, 169, 182
Konya, 62
Koran, 1-11, 14, 15, 19-21, 23-26, 29, 31-36, 43, 44, 45, 46, 66, 76, 93, 101, 108, 112, 118, 121, 126, 130, 133, 134, 153, 157, 160, 161, 171-78, 189, 190, 193, 198, 199, 203, 205, 208, 215, 219, 220-23, 229, 230, 231
Kubrawiyya, 55, 56
Kuchak, Hakim, 136
Kufa, 190, 219, 225, 227, 228
Kulayni, Muhammad b. Ya'qub al-, 24, 49, 77, 78, 110, 137, 158, 169, 173, 202

la'n, 84, 98
Lahijan, 64
Lahiji, 'Abd al-Razzaq al-, 136
Lambton, A.K.S., 82, 203, 204, 205
Lawāmi'-i Sāhibqirānī, 154
Literary History of Persia, 170, 182
Lu'lu'at al-Bahrayn, 149

madhhab, 51, 52, 56, 59
madrasa, 155, 158, 166
Mahdi, 52, 57, 77, 79, 86, 87, 190, 188, **189-235**
Mahdism, 106, 188, 215, 216, 239
Majlisi, Maqsud Ali, 152, 153

Majlisi, Muhammad Baqir 'Allama, 106, 110, 136, **148-82**, 190, 193, 194, 195, 196, 197, 198, 199, 200, 202, 207, 210-22, 229, 230, 237
Majlisi, Muhammad Taqi, 136, 213, 148, 149, 152, 153, 154, 155, 156, 157, 159, 174, 180, 181
Majlisi, Mulla 'Abdullah, 171, 180
Majlisi, Mulla 'Azizullah, 180
Malcolm, Sir John, 102
Man lā yahduruhu al-faqīh, 153
manqūl, 156, 159, 161
Maqdisi, Shams al-din Abu 'Abdallah, 55
ma'qūl, 156, 157, 159, 160, 161
ma'rifa, 25, 43, 45, 54, 176, 208, 215, 230, 237
ma'rifat al-imām, 110, 118
ma'rifat Allāh, 75, 118, 129
ma'rifat al-nafs, 54, 75, 121, 132, 133
Marxism, 191
Mas'ud, 'Abdullah b., 192
Mashhad, 159, 174, 180
Mathnawī, 175
Maturidites, 9
Mawlawiyya, 55, 58, 62, 65
Maysi, Shaykh Lutfullah, 129
Mazandarani, Mulla Muhammad Salih, 158, 180, 181
Mazzaoui, Michael, 48, 52, 53
Mecca, 46, 73, 80, 84, 93, 112, 137, 219, 224, 225, 228
Medina, 7, 21, 44, 73, 74, 80, 84, 203, 204, 225, 228
messianism, 188, 191
Minorsky, Vladimir, 60, 63, 149, 151, 166, 182
Mir Damad, 24, 102, 105, 129, 130, 137

Mir Lawhi, 154, 163, 212, 213
Mir 'at al-ahwāl, 149, 180
Mirza Rafi'a, 158
Mongols, 51, 53, 55, 57, 60
Mu'awiya, 112, 219
mu'min, 12, 15
Mu'tazilites, 20, 49
Mufaddal b. Umar, 194, 218, 223, 228, 229, 230
Mufid, Shaykh, 49, 78, 104, 119, 218
muhaddithūn, 77, 81, 91, 134, 157, 178, 180
Muhammad Baqir, 151, 152, 153, 155, 156, 158, 159, 162, 164, 166, 167, 179, 180, 181. *See* Majlisi
Muhammad, Prophet, 6- 8, 10, 11, 13, 15, 21, 22-24, 30, 32-34, 36, 46, 48, 49, 50, 52, 56, 60, 62, 66, 73, 82, 149, 188, 189, 190, 192, 193, 196, 203, 204, 211, 212, 216, 217, 219, 220, 224, 225, 227, 239
mujaddid, 149
mujtahid, 78, 82, 86, 89, 92, 94, 98, 109, 115, 124, 152, 160, 173, 180, 181, 215
mullā-bāshī, 149, 151, 165, 166, 180
munāfiqūn, 9
Munshi, Iskandar, 96
Murji'ites, 1
Musa al-Kazim, Imam, 83, 191, 205, 217, 223
Musha'sha'iyya, 52, 53, 58
Muslim, 44, 45, 46, 47, 48, 51, 55, 57, 58
muslim, 7, 8, 10, 12, 16
Musnad, 8
Mustawfi, Hamdullah, 50, 59
Mutahhari, Murtada, 33

Nafs al-Zakiyya, Muhammad, 190

Nahawandi, Ibrahim b. Ishaq al-, 19
Nahj al-balāgha, 212
Najaf, 49, 79, 100, 154, 180, 181
Najafi, Sayyid Sharaf al-din al-
  Astarabadi, al-, 112
namāz, 63
naql, 45, 46
naqlī sciences, 75, 91, 96, 109, 127,
  156
Naqshbandiyya, 55, 56, 65, 86, 87,
  110, 158
Nasr, Seyyed Hossein, 48, 49, 57
Ni'matullah, Shah, 124, 125, 126
Ni'matullahiyya, 57, 65, 84, 86, 126,
Nizam al-mulk, 204
Nu'mani, Muhammad b. Ibrahim,
  194
Nuqtawiyya, 99
Nurbakhshiyya, 55, 57, 86
Nurcu movement, 124
Nuri, Yahya, 31
Nursi, Said, 124, 207, 208
Nuzhat al-qulūb, 50

Osman, Muhammad Salih, 192
Ottomans, 73

Pampus, Karl-Heinz, 162
pīshnamāz, 82, 92, 94, 96
Plato, 119
Prophet, 189, 190, 192, 193, 199,
  200, 201, 203, 205, 207, 216, 218,
  219, 220, 221, 222, 224, 225, 226,
  228, 231, 232. See also
  Muhammad, Prophet

qadā wa qadar, 5, 18, 161, 210, 224
qādī, 162

Qadi Amir Husayn, 159
Qadi Jahan, 87, 98
qalandariyya, 125, 174
Qara-Qoyunlu, 52, 61, 63
Qatifi, Shaykh Ibrahim, 206, 209,
  213
Qazvin, 87, 88, 98, 101, 108, 137
Qazwini, Muhammad Mahdi al-, 112
Qazwini, Shaykh Khalil, 115
Qisas al-'ulamā, 113, 161, 172, 179
Qizilbash, 58, 63, 64, 65, 73, 82, 86,
  98, 99
Qum, 49, 50, 79
Qummi, Muhammad b. Hasan al-,
  110
Qummi, Muhammad Tahir al-, 115,
  154, 156, 158, 159, 174
Quraysh, 193

raj'a, 187, 194, 196, 200, 212, 215-
  223, 230, 231, 232, 236
Rawdat al-jannāt, 149
Rayy, 50
Razi, Fakhr al-din, 119
Reza Shah, 24
Rida, Rashid, 11, 13, 14, 20, 21, 36
Rīyād al-'ulamā, 81, 86, 118, 104,
  106, 109, 124, 127
Rumi, Jalal al-din, 50, 60, 62, 122,
  175
Rumlu, Hasan, 48

Sabziwar, 50
Sabziwari, Muhammad Baqir, 136
Sachedina, Abdulaziz, 205
Sadr al-din, 59
sadr, 90, 92, 93, 94, 95, 96, 98, 99
Sadra, Mulla, 45, 47, 66, 92, 96, 113,
  114, 118, 122, 127, 129, 130, 135,

136, 137, 208, 234, 235
Saduq, Shaykh 153, 154, 158, 194,
    217
Safavids, 43, 53, 57, 58, 59, 60, 61,
    62, 64, 65, 163, 169 and *passim*
Safawiyya, 55, 57, 59
Safi Mirza, 211
Safi, Shah, 103, 104, 135, 136, 211
Sahīfa-i Sajjādiyya, 154
salām, 6, 10, 27
salāt, 168
Saljuqs, 50, 56, 57, 62
Samawna, Badr al-din, 62
Sarbidarids, 52
Sawaji, Muhammad Yunus al-, 125
Schimmel, 45
scriptural sciences, 45
Shafi'i, 28
Shafi'ites, 9, 50, 56, 59, 65, 74, 124
shahāda, 9
Shahid al-Awwal, 80, 109
Shahid al-Thani, 79
Shahrashub, Ibn, 152
Shahrukh, 61
Shaltut, 'Allama Mahmud, 34
Shami, Shaykh Ali al-'Amili al-, 112
sharī'a, 2, 20, 25, 44, 46, 54, 58, 59,
    61, 65, 78, 87, 90, 97, 106, 117,
    118, 119, 121, 122, 137, 154, 155,
    157, 162, 174, 176, 201, 203, 204,
    205, 207, 209, 216, 239
Shari'ati, Ali, 32, 36, 232, 233, 234,
    235, 236, 237, 238
Sharif Murtada, 218
shaykh, 55, 56, 63
shaykh al-islām, 88, 90, 92, 94, 96,
    102, 136, 162, 164, 165, 166, 173,
    174, 180
Shaykh Baha'i, 88, 101, 102, 103,
    105, 110, 127, 136, 137. See also

Baha'i
Shi'ism, 48, 49, 50, 51, 52, 56, 57,
    58, 59, 61, 65, 66; eschatology of,
    196, 200, 207, 208, 215, 232, 233,
    234, 235, 236, 237, 238, 239 and
    passim
Shi'ites, 12, 15, 20, 23, 24, 46, 50,
    56; and 'last days' scenario, 189,
    191, 194, 195, 196, 197, 198, 200,
    203, 207, 211, 215-20, 223, 224,
    228, 231, 239
Shiraz, 55
Shirazi, Mir Ghiyath al-din Mansur
    al-Dashtaki, 92
Shirazi, Mir Jamal al-din Dashtaki,
    85
Shirazi, Mirza Baba, 112
Shirazi, Mirza Makhdum, 98
Shirazi, Sadr al-din Muhammad
    Dashtaki, 95
Shirazi, Shams al-din Muhammad
    Khafri, 95
Shirvan, 64
Shirvanshah, 64
Shushtari, 'Abdullah b. Husayn, 152,
    158, 159, 171
Shushtari, Qadi Nurullah, 50, 66
Shushtari, Mir Asadullah, 94
Sih Asl, 131-35
Sīyāsat-nāma, 205
Smith, Jane, 11,
Sufis, 9, 20, 23, 156, 165, 173, 174,
    175, 176, 177, 204
Sufism, 23, 45, 48, 49, 52, 53, 54, 55,
    56, 58, 59, 60, 65, 75, 82, 86, 99,
    105, 113, 115, 116-19, 121, 122,
    125, 126, 127, 138, 151, 153, 154,
    173, 174, 176, 177
Suhrawardi, Shihab al-din, 125
Sulayman, Shah, 103, 162, 163, 164,

166, 212
sultān, 204, 205
Sultan al-'ulama, Sayyid Husayn, 136
sunna, 20, 24, 173, 177
Sunnism, 56, 59, 74, 76, 82, 83, 84, 85, 87, 97, 98, 99, 100, 107, 112, 116, 117, 120, 121, 124, 135
Surūr al-'ārifīn, 117

ta'aqqul, 34
Tabari, 12
Tabarra'iyyun, 112
Tabarsi, Husayn b. Muhammad, 148
Tabataba'i, 'Allama, 17, 27, 29, 30, 31, 35
Tabriz, 48, 50, 61, 65, 213
Tabrizi, Mawla Rajab 'Ali, 113
Tadhkirat al-mulūk, 150, 165, 166
Tadhkirat al-qubūr, 152, 182
tafakkur, 2, 6, 20, 30, 34
tafaqquh, 26
tafsīr, 3, 13, 22, 23, 26, 29, 111, 117, 120, 126
Tahmasp, Shah 83, 87, 88, 89, 90, 92, 93, 94, 95, 97, 98, 136, 209, 210
Ta'ifa, Shaykh, 49, 78
taqiyya, 50, 81, 84, 85, 87, 90, 95, 99, 153, 198, 201, 219, 231
taqlīd, 5, 16, 27, 86, 114, 115, 123, 132, 133, 137, 138
Tarīkh-i 'ālamārā-i 'Abbāsi, 94
tarīqa, 54, 59, 60, 65
tasdīq, 9, 11, 12, 17
tashayyu'-i hasan, 65
tawhīd, 4, 11, 12, 26, 30, 45, 107, 118, 119, 120, 121, 122, 126, 132, 133, 157
ta'wīl, 13
Taymurids, 59, 60, 61

Thawri, Sufyan al-, 175
theocentrism, 150, 151, 168, 181
theology, 156, 157, 161, 169, 173
Tihrani, Ali, 30
Trabzon, 62
Traditions, 3, 14, 19, 20, 21, 23, 24, 29, 31, 49, 59, 76, 77, 78, 79, 81, 91, 106, 107, 108, 110, 111, 115, 119, 122, 126, 128, 130, 133-37, 149, 151-59, 161, 167, 170-75, 178, 179, 190, 188, 191-201, 206, 210-20, 223, 229, 230. See also hadīth
Transoxania, 55, 61, 65
Trimingham, J. Spencer, 54, 57
Tuhfat al-zā'ir, 167
Tunukabuni, 113, 161, 162, 167, 171, 172
Turcomans, 62
Tusi, Nasir al-din, 119
Tusi, Shaykh, 49, 158, 194, 214
Tustari, 152
Twelve Imams, 77, 88, 120, 122, 123, 124, 136
Twelver Shi'ism, 48, 49, 50, 51, 52, 53, 57, 58, 59, 60, 61, 66, 77, 73, 74, 75, 76, 81, 82, 84, 86, 87, 88, 89, 91, 92, 94, 95, 101, 104, 106, 107, 110, 117, 118-24, 130, 135, 149, 150-53, 165, 181,189, 198, 200, 201, 202, 203, 206, 208, 210, 217, 223, 230, 232, 235, 237. See also Shi'ism
'ulamā, 20, 23, 24, 26, 27, 29, 30, 32, 34, 35, 43-47, 57, 62, 75, 89, 91, 97, 105, 125, 127, 128, 129, 133, 134, 135, 137, 152, 153, 161, 164, 171, 174, 177, 178, 204, 213, 214, 234
'ulūm, 20, 21, 23, 31

Uljaytu, 51
Umar, 190, 193, 207, 216, 217, 223, 226, 227, 228, 229, 230
Umayyads, 201
usūl al-dīn, 3, 45, 49
Usuli, 109, 114, 115, 158, 159, 160, 181
Uthman, 83
Uzbeks, 73
Uzun Hasan Aq-Qoyunlun, 60, 62, 63, 64

wahdat al-wujūd, 175
Wali Allah, Shah, 123
Waqāi' al-sinīn, 164, 166
Waqifiyya, 191, 217
Wasiyyat Abī Hanīfa, 9

wilāya, 15, 19, 195, 207, 208, 233

Ya'qub, Sultan, 60, 64
Yasawiyya, 58
Yusufi, Muhammad, 47, 161, 162

Zād al-ma'ād, 167, 168
Zahidi, Shaykh Taj al-din, 59
zakāt, 6, 15, 78, 108, 161, 168, 178
Zayn al-'Abidin, Imam, 154, 200
zīyāra, 168
zuhūr, 188, 197, 198, 200, 201, 223, 231, 232.